Herman M. Weisman:
INFORMATION SYSTEMS, SERVICES, AND CENTERS

Jesse H. Shera:
THE FOUNDATIONS OF EDUCATION FOR LIBRARIANSHIP

Charles T. Meadow:
THE ANALYSIS OF INFORMATION SYSTEMS, Second Edition

Stanley J. Swihart and Beryl F. Hefley:
COMPUTER SYSTEMS IN THE LIBRARY

F. W. Lancaster and E. G. Fayen:
INFORMATION RETRIEVAL ON-LINE

Richard A. Kaimann:
STRUCTURED INFORMATION FILES

Thelma Freides:
LITERATURE AND BIBLIOGRAPHY OF THE SOCIAL SCIENCES

Manfred Kochen:
PRINCIPLES OF INFORMATION RETRIEVAL

Dagobert Soergel:
INDEXING LANGUAGES AND THESAURI: CONSTRUCTION AND MAINTENANCE

Robert M. Hayes and Joseph Becker:
HANDBOOK OF DATA PROCESSING FOR LIBRARIES, Second Edition

Andrew E. Wessel:
COMPUTER-AIDED INFORMATION RETRIEVAL

Lauren Doyle
INFORMATION RETRIEVAL AND PROCESSING

Charles T. Meadow:
APPLIED DATA MANAGEMENT

Andrew E. Wessel
THE SOCIAL USE OF INFORMATION—OWNERSHIP AND ACCESS

Hans H. Wellisch:
THE CONVERSION OF SCRIPTS: ITS NATURE, HISTORY, AND UTILIZATION

Eugene Garfield
CITATION INDEXING: ITS THEORY AND APPLICATION IN SCIENCE, TECHNOLOGY, AND HUMANITIES

Citation Indexing

Citation Indexing—Its Theory and Application in Science, Technology, and Humanities

Eugene Garfield
Institute for Scientific Information

A WILEY-INTERSCIENCE PUBLICATION
JOHN WILEY & SONS
NEW YORK • CHICHESTER • BRISBANE • TORONTO

Copyright © 1979 by John Wiley & Sons, Inc.

All rights reserved. Published simultaneously in Canada.

Reproduction or translation of any part of this work beyond that permitted by Sections 107 or 108 of the 1976 United States Copyright Act without the permission of the copyright owner is unlawful. Requests for permission or further information should be addressed to the Permissions Department, John Wiley & Sons, Inc.

Library of Congress Cataloging in Publication Data

Garfield, Eugene.
   Citation indexing.

   (Information sciences series)
   "A Wiley-Interscience publication."
   Includes index.
   1. Science—Abstracting and indexing. 2. Technology—Abstracting and indexing. 3. Humanities—Abstracting and indexing. 4. Citation indexes.
I. Title.
Z697.S5G37   029.5   78-9713
ISBN 0-471-02559-3

Printed in the United States of America
10 9 8 7 6 5 4 3 2 1

Information Sciences Series

Information is the essential ingredient in decision making. The need for improved information systems in recent years has been made critical by the steady growth in size and complexity of organizations and data.

This series is designed to include books that are concerned with various aspects of communicating, utilizing, and storing digital and graphic information. It will embrace a broad spectrum of topics, such as information system theory and design, man-machine relationships, language data processing, artificial intelligence, mechanization of library processes, non-numerical applications of digital computers, storage and retrieval, automatic publishing, command and control, information display, and so on.

Information science may someday be a profession in its own right. The aim of this series is to bring together the interdisciplinary core of knowledge that is apt to form its foundation. Through this consolidation, it is expected that the series will grow to become the focal point for professional education in this field.

Foreword

I like to read some general significance into Eugene Garfield's having offered me the privilege of introducing the reader to this book, which sets out the history, method, and implications of his distinctive contribution to the advancement of science: the first multidisciplinary citation index to the scientific literature. My being a close friend cannot account for his having done so. Gene has many good friends more knowing than I about information science and the methodology of citation analysis. I suspect that the significance of his choice lies precisely there: in his having reached out for a sociologist of science rather than an information scientist. For one of the remarkable things about Eugene Garfield is that along with the imagination, pragmatic judgment, and immense energy required to invent, produce, and develop a useful tool for a seemingly routine but fundamental task in science—searching the literature— he has a deep intuitive sense of the social, cultural, and cognitive structures latent in the practice of science. This found expression in his seeing, from the very start, that his invention of the *Science Citation Index* would develop into a powerful tool for the historical and sociological study of science. I imagine that he wanted to have the subject of the book set squarely within this broader framework rather than the primary but narrower one of information science alone. I accept the inferred assignment with pleasure—and understandable misgivings.

This book is long overdue. Its most immediate didactic value resides in helping the reader to understand the concept and workings of the citation index as a device for making the search of the literature much more comprehensive and far less arduous than was previously possible. The book thus fills an obvious need for a systematic account of the concept and uses of a major bibliographical tool designed to facilitate the practice of science. And it does so with the clarity and informed assurance that one would expect of the man who invented the tool.

Important as it is to fill that need for practical information about citation indexes as a bibliographical tool, for me the chief interest of the book lies elsewhere. That judgment is formed of course,—some would say, biased—by the perspective of a sociologist primarily interested in trying to understand how interacting cognitive and social structures of science affect the thought and behavior of scientists. Indeed, from that standpoint, the citation index itself provides a case study in the process of invention and discovery. Even in bare outline, the case holds its own sociological interest.

We can begin with one aspect of the latent social and cultural structure of science presupposed by the historically evolving systematic use of references and citations in the scientific paper and book. That aspect is the seemingly paradoxical character of property in the scientific enterprise: the circumstance that the more widely scientists make their intellectual property freely available to others, the more securely it becomes identified as their property. For science is public not private knowledge. Only by publishing their work can scientists make their *contribution* (as the telling word has it) and only when it thus becomes part of the public domain of science can they truly lay claim to it as theirs. For that claim resides only in the recognition of the source of the contribution by peers. The greatest ambition of a productive scientist is to do the kind of work that will be much used and much esteemed by fellow scientists best qualified to assess its worth. And, in general, scientific work is esteemed in the measure that others can draw upon it to advance their own future inquiry.

All this is reinforced by the reward system of science. Since recognition by qualified peers is the basic form of extrinsic reward (all other extrinsic rewards deriving from it) and since that reward can be accorded only when the work is made known, this historically evolving reward system provides institutionalized incentive for open publication without direct financial reward. Such peer recognition is usually accorded the first published contribution of its kind, later ones presumably being redundant. But since the cognitive structure of science makes for independent multiple discoveries—functionally equivalent if not identical discoveries—this social and cognitive complex evokes a concern among scientists to get there first and to establish, through prompt publication, their self-validating claims to priority of discovery.

The anomalous character of intellectual property in science becoming fully established only by being openly given away (i.e., published) links up with the correlative moral as well as cognitive requirement for scientists to acknowledge their having made use of it. Citations and references thus operate within a jointly cognitive and moral framework. In their cognitive aspect, they are designed to provide the historical lineage of knowledge and to guide readers of new work to sources they may want to check or draw upon for themselves. In their moral aspect, they are designed to repay intellectual debts in the only form in which this can be done: through open acknowledgment of them. Such repayment is no minor normative requirement. That is plain from the moral and sometimes legal sanctions visited upon those judged to have violated the norm through the kinds of grand and petty intellectual larceny which we know as plagiarism. (Karl Marx testifies to the possible depth of commitment to the norm: for him, plagiarism was the one altogether detestable crime against private property, as witness his preface to the first edition of *Capital* and his further thunderings on the subject throughout that revolutionary book.)

It was of course unnecessary for Eugene Garfield to identify this composite communications-intellectual-property-and-reward system in order to arrive at his concept of the citation index. He only needed the sense that the system provided the ingredients for systematically identifying, through citation indexing, links between the work of scientists that could be put to use both for searching the literature and for exploring cognitive and social relationships in science. It is symptomatic of the direction and pace of development that about half the book is given over to modes of citation analysis designed for the latter kind of development.

Eugene Garfield's account of the birth, adolescence, and early maturity of citation indexing reports other patterns typically found in the evolution of an invention. Detailed procedural research, sometimes in the form of mini-experiments, is designed to test the feasibility of successively expanded and differentiated uses. Self-engendered criticism and external criticism give rise to error-detecting and error-correcting research. The exercise of such organized skepticism exerts pressure for a deeper sociological understanding of the interaction between the communication-and-reward system in science and its cognitive development. As the sociologist Norman Kaplan (1) was perhaps the first to note a dozen years ago and as varied sociological applications of citation analysis (2) since then have made abundantly plain, we need to know more than is yet known about what references and citations do and do not represent if citation analysis is to provide further understanding of how science is socially and cognitively organized and practiced.

Certain patterns of referencing behavior would seem to set limits on the use of citation counts for tracing the long-term genealogy of ideas. One of these patterns has been described as "obliteration by incorporation": the obliteration of the source of ideas, methods, or findings by their incorporation in currently accepted knowledge (3). In the course of this hypothesized process, the number of explicit references to the original work declines in the papers and books making use of it. Users and consequently transmitters of that knowledge are so thoroughly familiar with its origins that they assume this to be true of their readers as well. Preferring not to insult their readers' knowledgeability, they no longer refer to the original source. And since many of us tend to attribute a significant idea or formulation to the author who introduced us to it, the altogether innocent transmitter sometimes becomes identified as the originator. In the successive transmission of ideas, repeated use may erase all but the immediately antecedent versions, thus producing an historical palimpsest in which the source of those ideas is obliterated.

To the extent that such obliteration does occur—itself an empirical question that is only beginning to be examined—explicit citations may not adequately reflect the lineage of scientific work. As intellectual influence becomes deeper, it becomes less readily visible. That influence may operate through acceptance of a theoretical framework, with its basic assumptions, or through standardized procedures of inquiry. In short, it may be canonical knowledge that is most subject to obliteration of source. As Joshua Lederberg noted in the foreword to another of Eugene Garfield's books: "The work that *everybody* knows... is hardly cited at all!" (4). Specialized historical and sociological studies can supplement explicit citations with tacit ones, the kind that can be reconstructed from textual evidence such as eponymous allusions, terminology bearing the stamp of the source of an idea, and the like. But it remains to be seen whether some modes of significant cognitive influence find no expression in references and citations, explicit or tacit.

In the evolution of citation analysis, questions such as these have begun to receive the systematic attention they require. Cole, Cole, and Dietrich, for example, and Garfield, Malin, and Small (5) have addressed themselves to the problem, the latter suggesting that even when obliteration has occurred, "scientific ideas that have been regarded as important or influential can be associated with one or more scientific works that are *at some time* highly cited." It is thus argued that citation counts do not favor mediocrity, since obliteration of this kind takes place only after substantial visibility through citations has occured, a requirement which a large fraction of published work fails to satisfy. All this raises interesting question about the time frames within which citation analysis can effectively trace the genealogy of scientific knowledge.

The reader will find in this book a plentiful variety of other uses to which the data base of the *Science Citation Index* has been put. A good deal is said about one of the most disputed of these: the use—some of us would say, the abuse—of citation counts as the principal or determining basis for assessing the research performance and further potentialites of individual scientists. This was not unforeseen. As early as 1963, just as the first *Science Citation Index* was being published, a cautionary note was sounded about the possible "promiscuous and careless use of quantitative citation data for . . . evaluation, including personnel and fellowship selection." That forewarning came, properly enough, from Gene Garfield (6). He went on to say, "It is preposterous to conclude blindly that the most cited author deserves a Nobel prize."

The closing chapter of this book reexamines the subject in light of the intervening 15 years of research. That chapter can be read less as a newly developed defense of the use of citation analysis for assessing individual scientific performance than as a methodological manual for those who venture into those dangerous waters. A recurring theme in the chapter is the strong reminder that citation counts cannot be responsibly taken as the controlling basis for appraisals of individual performance. At best, they are ancillary to detailed judgments by informed peers. The forensic use of citation counts to compare the impact of scientific contributions by individuals only provides an extreme type of occasion for subjecting such practices to the organized skepticism that is one of the fundamental characteristics of science.

No one reading this book can fail to note its pervading sense of exuberant promise. Citation indexing has been a standard of scientific bibliography for more than a decade but its sociological and historical research potentials presumably have not yet been fully realized. One of its notable contributions to this time has been the emerging specialty of bibliometrics, which builds on the early work of such scholars as Bradford and Gross to define and quantify parts of the multiple structures of science. The growing numbers at work in this field have in their turn begun to ask fundamental questions about citation behavior.

I can report that most of these questions are critically examined in this book. The scientific curiosity coupled with skepticism that led Eugene Garfield first to conceptualize and then to develop a new way of indexing the scientific literature are still at work. Applied to his invention of the *Science Citation Index,* this attitude of mind has led Eugene Garfield and his colleagues—both his colleagues-at-a-distance and his colleagues in the Institute for Scientific Information which he founded—to collaborate on what amounts to an evolving grammar of citation analysis.

ROBERT K. MERTON

Columbia University

References

Forewords ordinarily do not have references appended to them. In the case of this book, however, one simply dares not substitute allusions for explicit references.

1. **Kaplan, N.** "The Norms of Citation Behavior: Prolegomena to the footnote." *American Documentation,* **16**: 179-184, 1965.
2. **Cole, J.R. and Cole, S.** "Measuring the Quality of Sociological Research: Problems in the Use of the Science Citation Index." *American Sociologist,* **6**: 23-29, 1973; **Moravcsik, M.J. and Murugesan, P.** "Some Results on the Function and Quality of Citations." *Social Studies of Science,* **5**: 86-92, 1975; **Chubin, D. E. and Moitra, S. D.** "Content Analysis of References: Adjunct or Alternative to Citation Counting?" *Social Studies of Science,* **5**: 423-441, 1975.
3. **Merton, R. K.** *Social Theory and Social Structure* (New York: The Free Press, 1968) pp. 27-29, 35-38; **Garfield, E.** "The Obliteration Phenomenon." *Current Contents,* No. 51/52: 5-7,(22 Dec. 1975); **Messeri, P.** "Obliteration by Incorporation: Toward a Problematics, Theory and Metric of the Use of Scientific Literature." Columbia University, unpublished ms., 1978.
4. **Lederberg, J.** Foreword to Garfield, E. *Essays of an Information Scientist* (Philadelphia: ISI Press, 1977), p. xiii.
5. **Cole, S., Cole, J. R. and Dietrich, L.** "Measuring the Cognitive State of Scientific Disciplines." Pp. 221-229 and **Garfield, E., Malin, M.V., and Small, H.** "Citation Data as Science Indicators." Pp. 181-182 In Elkana, Y., Lederberg, J., Thackray, A., Merton, R.K., and Zuckerman, H. (eds.) *Toward a Metric of Science: The Advent of Science Indicators* (New York: John Wiley & Sons, 1978).
6. **Garfield, E.** "Citation Indexes in Sociological and Historical Research." *American Documentation* 14:289-291, 1963.

Preface

This book is, in a sense, the biography of an idea. The idea is the one of indexing the literature of science by the material cited by that literature. The idea was turned into reality in 1963 by the first annual edition of the *Science Citation Index*® . As with most new ideas that embody a sharp break with traditional thinking or procedures, the first *SCI*® generated as much emotional controversy as it did reasoned interest. Even today, more than a decade later, there are many scientists whose bibliographic inertia has kept them unfamiliar, or at least uncomfortable, with the logic of a citation search. Yet, despite sizable measures of initial hostility and lingering inertia, the acceptance and use of citation indexes have become widespread in little more than one decade. Any novel idea that becomes established so quickly deserves, it seems to me, to be the subject of a book.

I have been writing about citation indexes to the scientific literature since 1955 (1), almost a full decade before the first annual edition of *SCI*. In that time, I have written a series of papers that would easily fill a volume of several hundred pages. This book is a byproduct of those papers, many of which were digested, reprinted, or cited in my *Essays of an Information Scientist* (2). It originated in a plan to publish reprints of all the papers. Robert M. Hayes, one of the editors of Wiley's Information Sciences Series, maintained however that there is too much redundancy inherent in a long series of individual papers on the same subject for effective communication. He convinced me that the interests of information-science students and practitioners, and scientists with an interest in bibliographic techniques, would be served better by a fresh, clear, concise book on citation indexing. Having accepted that position, I decided to compromise by using the collection of papers as the source material for the book.

I am not completely happy with the compromise. This volume does not serve the need for a historical record nearly so well as a collection of reprints of the original papers. It is, in fact, not a history at all, though there is one chapter that deals with the history of citation indexing. Nor is this volume marked by the discursive style I prefer and used in most of my original papers. On the other hand, this account is undeniably a more tightly organized, concisely written, and lucid exposition of citation indexing and its uses than is the collection of original papers. For that reason, I expect that Hayes is right in his prediction that this book will turn out to be considerably more useful than the collection of papers for the majority of scientists interested in citation indexing. The minority who are interested in working with the historical record will find the primary elements of that record identified in the bibliographies at the end of the chapters.

I refer those readers particularly interested in how I arrived at the idea of a citation index to the scientific literature to Chapter Two, "A Historical View of Citation Indexing." There I try to explain how the idea grew out of a particular set of intellectual interests, professional problems, and serendipitous events. To the extent that the chapter identifies those conceptual elements and explains their interactions, it does a reasonably complete job of describing how the idea of a citation index to the science literature was conceived and how that conception led to the production of the *Science Citation Index*. Yet, after rereading that chapter I am struck by the total omission of an element very critical to the act of accomplishment. That element is personal obsession.

Between the lines of Chapter Two, some readers may perceive an implied tale of frustration—frustration with the shortcomings of traditional techniques, frustration with the general acceptance of the shortcomings, and frustration with the general conceptual and economic resistance to ideas that are novel. My response to these frustrations was a steadily increasing personal obsession, first with the subject of machine indexing, then with the concept of a citation index to the scientific literature, and finally with the reality of the *SCI*. This obsession kept me from being distracted by 10 years of academic, professional, and business demands; led me to run the financial risk of launching a novel type of index in the face of knowledgeable prophecies that no market existed for it; and drove me to gamble the financial success of the Institute for Scientific Information® (ISI®) in an attempt to build a market for *SCI* through education.

I make this point about obsession not to reflect any credit on myself (in fact, I doubt that any psychologist would find much commendatory about obsessive behavior), but to provide a personal insight that might be helpful to the sociologists studying and theorizing about the process of scientific discovery. I am sometimes asked to comment on the question of whether the development of the functional equivalent of *SCI* was inevitable, whether someone else wouldn't have developed such an index if I had not. The general form of that question is, of course, one of the classic questions in the sociology of science. Robert Merton has explored the question with more subtlety and answered it in greater depth than I am able to bring to the subject (3). In fact, he has used the development of *SCI* in particular to illustrate the difficulty of deriving a specific discovery from a general conceptual model (4). He identifies a number of gaps in that model that had to be filled in to arrive at the concept of *SCI*. To his comments I would add just one observation: when the discovery is a novel one, the task of going from a general to a specific conceptual model and then from the concept to reality can be done only by someone obsessed with an idea.

One other point that needs to be made in this preface is that the book does not provide a comprehensive review of all the work in which citation analysis has been used. This is due, partially, to the decision to base the book primarily on my own papers and, partially, to the very rapid growth in the use of citation analysis as a research tool for studying the history and sociology of science. While I think I have covered all the areas in which citation analysis is being used, I am certain that I have not described the work of all the investigators who are using it. I apologize to those who were missed by the broad net of references that I intentionally constructed. If a new edition of the book is required in the future, I will attempt to be more comprehensive.

EUGENE GARFIELD

Philadelphia, Pennsylvania
August 1978

References

1. **Garfield, E.** "Citation Indexes for Science." *Science,* **122**:108-111, 1955.
2. **Garfield, E.** *Essays of an Information Scientist* (Philadelphia: ISI Press, 1977). 2 Vols., 1314pp.
3. **Merton, R. K.** *The Sociology of Science.* Storer, N. W. (ed.) (Chicago: The University of Chicago Press, 1973). Pp. 343-370.
4. **Merton, R. K. and Gaston, J., (eds.).** *The Sociology of Science in Europe* (Carbondale, Illinois: Southeran Illinois University Press and London: Feffer & Simons, Inc., 1977). Pp.47-54.

Contents

Chapter 1
A Conceptual View of Citation Indexing — 1

Chapter 2
A Historical View of Citation Indexing — 6

Chapter 3
The Design and Production of a Citation Index — 19

Chapter 4
The Application of Citation Indexing to the Patent Literature — 37

Chapter 5
The Citation Index as a Search Tool — 41

Chapter 6
A Science-Management Tool — 62

Chapter 7
Citation Analysis as a Method of Historical Research into Science — 81

Chapter 8
Mapping the Structure of Science — 98

Chapter 9
Citation Analysis of Scientific Journals — 148

Chapter 10
Perspective on Citation Analysis of Scientists — 240

Epilogue: The Future of Citation Indexing — 253

Cited Author Index — 257

Subject Index — 259

Illustrations

2.1	Procedure for extracting genetics subset from multidisciplinary data base.	14
2.2	Growth of *Science Citation Index* over the years.	17
3.1	Distribution of citations among journals cited in *SCI*.	22
3.2	Distribution of published items among source journals covered by *SCI*.	22
3.3	Distribution of references among source journals covered by *SCI*.	23
3.4	Computer-processing operations in the production of *Science Citation Index*.	28
3.5	Typical entry from the *Citation Index* of *SCI*.	33
3.6	Typical entry from the *Source Index* of *SCI*.	34
3.7	Typical entry from the *Patent Index* of *SCI*.	34
3.8	Typical entry from the *Permuterm Subject Index* of *SCI*.	35
3.9	Typical entry from the *Corporate Index* of *SCI*.	36
5.1	Eponymic search.	44
5.2	Methodology search.	47
5.3	Reaction followup search.	47
5.4	Compound followup search.	48
5.5	Concept search.	50
5.6	Specific-question search	52
5.7	Overt multidisciplinary search.	53
5.8	Covert multidisciplinary search.	54
5.9	Quick state-of-the-art search.	57
5.10	Development-of-bibliography search.	59
6.1	Nobel Prize winners since 1950	65
6.2	Nobel Prizes and memberships in national academies of science among the 250 most-cited primary authors from 1961 to 1975.	67
6.3	Historiograph of DNA development.	74
6.4	1972 biomedical clusters.	76
6.5	*FSH and LH releasing hormone* cluster in 1972.	77
6.6	Major biomedical clusters in 1972 and 1973.	78
7.1	Citation network of the development of nucleic-acid staining.	82
7.2	Flowchart of major tasks in DNA-history study.	83
7.3	Network diagram of DNA-theory development as defined by I Asimov.	84
7.4	Excerpt of *Nodal Citation Index* from DNA-history study.	87
7.5	Network diagram of DNA-theory development as defined by citation analysis.	88
7.6	Historiograph of the major advances in genetics between 1958 and 1967.	94
7.7	Bibliography of nodal papers in genetics 1958-1967 historiograph.	95
8.1	Functional diagram of co-citation clustering method.	101
8.2	Co-citation pairs that qualified for clustering.	103
8.3	Distribution of clusters by number of cited documents.	103

xx   Illustrations

8.4	Ten largest clusters at level 3.	104
8.5	Block diagram of *nuclear physics* cluster.	106
8.6	Block diagram of *particle physics* cluster.	107
8.7	Word profiles of *nuclear physics* cluster.	108
8.8	Word profiles of *particle physics* cluster.	109
8.9	Methodology of mapping specialties.	112
8.10	Network diagram of level 3 clusters.	113
8.11	Description of level 3 clusters.	114
8.12	Spatial display of *bio-medicine* methods papers.	116
8.13	Network diagram of major *biomedicine* specialty clusters.	117
8.14	Description of *biomedicine* specialty clusters.	117
8.15	Spatial diagram of *cancer research, reverse transcription* macrocluster.	119
8.16	Map of 1972 biomedical clusters	120
8.17	Map of 1973 biomedical clusters.	121
8.18	Map of major natural science disciplinary clusters.	122
8.19	Contour map of 1970 *collagen* cluster.	124
8.20	Contour map of 1971 *collagen* cluster.	125
8.21	Contour map of 1972 *collagen* cluster.	126
8.22	Contour map of 1973 *collagen* cluster.	127
8.23	Contour map of 1974 *collagen* cluster.	128
8.24	Bibliography of documents in *collagen* clusters.	128
8.25	Stability index for *collagen* cluster.	131
8.26	Responses to question about important advances in collagen research.	132
8.27	Responses to question about important papers in collagen research.	133
8.28	Responses to question about leading investigators in collagen research.	133
8.29	Responses to question about conceptual shifts in collagen research.	134
8.30	Map of social science clusters.	138
8.31	Two-dimensional plot of largest social science clusters.	140
8.32	Block diagram of *free recall* cluster.	141
8.33	Spatial diagram of *memory and learning* macrocluster.	142
8.34	List of social science documents cited at least 200 times between 1972-1974.	143
9.1	*Journal Citation Reports* (*JCR*) Journal Ranking Package, Section 1.	151
9.2	*Journal Citation Reports* (*JCR*) Journal Ranking Package, Section 2.	152
9.3	*Journal Citation Reports* (*JCR*) Journal Ranking Package, Section 3.	152
9.4	*Journal Citation Reports* (*JCR*) Journal Ranking Package, Section 4.	152
9.5	*Journal Citation Reports* (*JCR*) Journal Ranking Package, Section 5.	153
9.6	*Journal Citation Reports* (*JCR*) Journal Ranking Package, Section 6.	153
9.7	*Journal Citation Reports* (*JCR*) Citing Journal Package.	155
9.8	*Journal Citation Reports* (*JCR*) Cited Journal Package.	157
9.9	Distribution of citations among cited journals.	158
9.10	The 152 most frequently cited journals.	159
9.11	Journals most highly cited in 1974.	161
9.12	Journals cited most frequently by *Journal of the American Chemical Society*.	164
9.13	Journals cited most frequently by *Biochemistry*.	165
9.14	Journals cited most frequently by *Journal of Chemical Physics*.	166
9.15	Journals cited most frequently by *Journal of Experimental Medicine*.	168
9.16	Major sources of references to *Journal of Experimental Medicine*.	168
9.17	Journals cited most frequently by *Journal of Immunology*.	169

9.18	Major sources of references to *Journal of Immunology*.	169
9.19	Journals cited most frequently by *Annals of Rheumatic Diseases* and *Arthritis & Rheumatism*.	171
9.20	Major sources of references to *Annals of Rheumatic Diseases* and *Arthritis & Rheumatism*.	172
9.21	Journals cited most frequently by *Phytopathology*.	173
9.22	Major sources of references to *Phytopathology*.	173
9.23	Journals cited most frequently by *Acta Pathologica et Microbiologica Scandinavica*.	174
9.24	Journals cited most frequently by *Pathologie Biologie*.	174
9.25	Journals cited most frequently by *Journal of Clinical Investigation*.	176
9.26	Major sources of references to *Journal of Clinical Investigation*.	177
9.27	Journals cited most frequently by *Journal of the American Medical Association*.	179
9.28	Journals cited most frequently by *New England Journal of Medicine*.	180
9.29	Pediatric journals among the 1000 most highly cited journals.	181
9.30	Journals cited most frequently by the highly cited pediatric journals.	182
9.31	Highly cited journals in geology and geophysics.	184
9.32	Major sources of references to *Journal of Geophysical Research*.	185
9.33	Journals cited most frequently by *Journal of Geophysical Research*.	186
9.34	Journals cited most frequently by *Acta Crystallographica*.	187
9.35	Major sources of references to *Acta Crystallographica*.	188
9.36	Fifty journals cited most frequently by 188 physics journals.	189
9.37	Fifty journals ranked by ratio of "physics" citations received to total citations received.	191
9.38	Journals cited most frequently by 16 cancer journals.	193
9.39	Major sources of references to 16 cancer journals.	194
9.40	Major sources of references to botany journals.	195
9.41	Journals cited most frequently by botany journals.	196
9.42	Journals ranked by "botanical impact."	197
9.43	Major sources of references to psychology journals.	199
9.44	Journals cited most frequently by psychology journals.	200
9.45	Journals cited most frequently by psychology journals ranked by "psychology impact."	201
9.46	Journals cited most frequently by agricultural journals.	203
9.47	Major sources of references to agricultural journals.	204
9.48	Journals cited most frequently by engineering journals.	206
9.49	Major sources of references to engineering journals.	207
9.50	Major sources of references to Russian journals in 1972.	209
9.51	Journals cited most frequently by Russian journals in 1972.	211
9.52	Major sources of references to Russian journals in 1974.	214
9.53	Journals cited most frequently by Russian journals in 1974.	216
9.54	Major sources of references to Russian journals in 1969.	218
9.55	Journals cited most frequently by Russian journals in 1969.	220
9.56	Journals cited most frequently by French journals.	225
9.57	Major sources of references to French journals.	226
9.58	Journals cited most frequently by Japanese journals.	228
9.59	Major sources of references to Japanese journals.	229
9.60	Journals cited most frequently by German journals.	231
9.61	Major sources of references to German journals.	232

Chapter One

A Conceptual View of Citation Indexing

The concept of citation indexing is simple. Almost all the papers, notes, reviews, corrections, and correspondence published in scientific journals contain citations. These cite—generally by title, author, and where and when published—documents that support, provide precedent for, illustrate, or elaborate on what the author has to say. Citations are the formal, explicit linkages between papers that have particular points in common. A citation index is built around these linkages. It lists publications that have been cited and identifies the sources of the citations. Anyone conducting a literature search can find from one to dozens of additional papers on a subject just by knowing one that has been cited. And every paper that is found provides a list of new citations with which to continue the search.

The simplicity of citation indexing is one of its main strengths. In compiling a traditional subject index, someone, usually with specialized knowledge of the subject covered, must read, or at least scan, each document and make a series of intellectual judgments. These involve the selection of subject terms that describe the contents of the document. The greater the depth of the indexing (the more terms used to describe the document), the more judgments the indexer must make. These judgments take time, which quickly runs up the cost of the indexing operation and may reduce the timeliness of the finished product. It is not unusual for subject indexes to be a year or more behind the literature, a situation that limits their effectiveness as search tools.

The cost of indexing depth is even more critical. Though most of the major subject indexes are either financed completely or subsidized by the federal government and, therefore, do not pass on full production costs to their subscribers, they all must make a tradeoff between indexing depth and cost.

As a way of getting around this tradeoff, some organizations have adopted in recent years a method called "title word indexing." In this approach to subject indexing, a document is indexed by the terms used by the author in the title of the document. There is no need for an intellectual judgment by an indexer; all terms that appear in the title are considered acceptable indexing terms. A title-word index, therefore, can be compiled much faster, and sometimes cheaper, than a traditional subject index.

There are, however, some penalties associated with the speed and economy of title-word indexing. For one thing, titles tend to be limited in length, which limits the number of terms available for indexing. This produces a rather shallow index, which tends to focus only on the main subjects of the papers and overlooks all the material they contain that is ancillary to those subjects, but may be important to the user of the index. Another penalty is that the ability, and even inclination, of authors to compose titles that accurately describe what they are writing about is very uneven. Consequently, the quality of the terms used in a title-word index also is very uneven.

There are some ways of mitigating these shortcomings. In some title-word indexes, depth is increased by adding subject terms assigned by indexers. In others, the quality of the index is improved by showing each title term in the context of all the other terms with which it has been used.

Citation indexing solves the depth versus cost problem by substituting the authors' citations for the indexer's judgments. This approach has the advantage of eliminating the need for intellectual indexing without compromising either the depth of the index or the quality of its "terms." Since there normally are no limits imposed on the length of bibliographies, there are no artificial limits on the depth of a citation index. And though the quality of bibliographies is variable from author to author and from one type of paper to another (review papers, for example, generally have more comprehensive bibliographies than any other type), the standards of good science exposition and the practice of viewing a good bibliography as a sign of scholarship tend to make citation quality considerably and consistently higher for indexing purposes than title quality.

Another important strength of citation indexing is its search effectiveness. This quality has two components. One is search productivity, which is concerned with finding the largest possible number of relevant papers. The other is search efficiency, which is concerned with minimizing the number of irrelevant papers the searcher must check out to identify the relevant ones.

Indexing depth is the primary quantitative measure of search effectiveness. The more indexing statements used, the more detailed the description of the document. As indexing depth increases, so does the probability that the searcher will satisfy his or her needs. Since the average scientific article contains approximately 15 citations, a citation index has an average depth of 15 "terms." Most traditional subject indexes can't afford to match this depth.

There also is a qualitative side to search effectiveness that revolves around how precisely and comprehensively an individual indexing statement describes the pertinent literature.

The precision of the description is a matter of semantics, which poses a series of problems in a subject index. The basic problem is that word usage varies from person to person. It is patently impossible for an indexer, no matter how competent, to reconcile these personal differences well enough to choose a series of subject terms that will unfailingly communicate the complicated concepts in a scientific document to anyone who is searching for it.

The job is made more difficult by the dynamic nature of language. New terms are introduced, old ones disappear, and new meanings are attached to old words.

Another part of the problem is the need to standardize on the terms used in a subject index in order to exercise some degree of control over the consistency and quality of the indexing. This reduces the richness and variety of language available to the indexer for dealing with the first two problems.

The result of all this is to make the search process more complicated, less productive, and less efficient than it can be.

Citations, used as indexing statements, provide these lost measures of search simplicity, productivity, and efficiency by avoiding the semantics problems. For example, suppose you want information on the physics of simple fluids. The simple citation "Fisher, M.E., *Math. Phys.*, **5**, 944, 1964" would lead the searcher directly to a list of papers that have cited this important paper on the subject. Experience has shown that a significant percentage of the citing papers are likely to be relevant. There is no need for the searcher to decide which subject terms an indexer would be most likely to use to describe the relevant papers. The language habits of the searcher would not affect the search results, nor would any changes in scientific terminology that took place since the Fisher paper was published.

In other words, the citation is a precise, unambiguous representation of a subject that requires no interpretation and is immune to changes in terminology. In addition, the citation will retain its precision over time. It also can be used in documents written in different languages. The importance of this semantic stability and precision to the search process is best demonstrated by a series of examples.

The precision directly affects search efficiency. If, for example, someone is searching the 1971 *Index Medicus* subject index for information on the effect of aspirin on prostaglandin production, a reasonable starting point would be the term "prostaglandins." That term would lead to a list of hundreds of papers organized under a variety of subheadings. The subheadigs most pertinent to the subject of the search would be ANTAGONISTS and INHIBITORS, and BIOSYNTHESIS. The first lists 10 articles, the second, nine. Two articles under each of the subheadings appear to deal with the aspirin–prostaglandin relationship. But the seacher would have to read the titles of all 19 to identify the four relevant ones. In contrast, a search of a 1971 citation index on "Vane, J.R., *Nature New Biology,* **231**, 232, 1971" would lead, in a single step, to a list of 15 papers. Because they had all cited a paper on "Inhibition of Prostaglandin Synthesis as a Mechanism of Action for Aspirin-like Drugs," the precise subject of the search, this list of papers is likely to contain a high percentage of relevant material.

Precision also can affect search productivity. In 1963 an important paper was published on the topic of "seasonal variations in birth." Anyone searching the 1965 edition of *Index Medicus* for information on the subject would be unable to find the key paper unless he or she looked under the unlikely heading of "periodicity."

The importance of semantic stability to search productivity is demonstrated by a search on the subject of "euphenics." This word was first coined by Professor J. Lederberg in a paper published in *Nature* in 1963. Until then, the subject was described by the term "engineering human development," a term that is still used. A search of a subject index on the term "euphenics," while it was still a new word, probably would have identified papers that used that term, but not ones that used "engineering human development." Conversely, a subject-index search on the term "engineering human development" would have been likely to miss papers that used "euphenics." In a citation index, however, all papers that cited the key Lederberg paper would be listed together, regardless of the terms the authors used in describing the subject. Even if the subject index were searched on both terms, there would be a significant difference between its search effectiveness and that of a citation index. A complete search of the subject index would require two lookups, whereas a complete search of the citation index would require only one. As the terminology of the subject has continued to evolve to include "genetic engineering," "plasmid engineering," and "recombinant DNA," the semantic stability of key papers in the field (1) has made the effectiveness of citation searching even more pronounced.

How comprehensively an individual indexing statement describes the pertinent literature is a matter of the disciplinary and time constraints built into it. A subject index covers the literature of a specific discipline or group of disciplines, such as chemistry, medicine, or biology, within a specified time frame, and it imposes these limits on the scope of its indexing terms. This is not the case with a citation index.

Even if a citation index were compiled from the literature of a limited number of disciplines published within a given time frame, the citations it would use as indexing statements would not be bound by these limits at all. Authors consistently cite papers outside their discipline, and the citations range over the entire time spectrum of twentieth-century science. The use of these citations as indexing statements enables a citation index to provide a trail of information that follows the convoluted process of scientific development as it crosses disciplinary lines and moves back and forth in time. This characteristic greatly increases the search productivity of a citation index.

One example demonstrates, rather spectacularly, the cross-disciplinary reach of a citation index. From 1961 to 1969 a citation for one of the classic papers published by Albert Einstein in *Annallen der Physik* in 1906 is linked in a citation index, called *Science Citation Index*, to papers from the *Journal of Dairy Sciences, Journal of the Chemical Society, Journal of Polymer Science, Journal of Pharmacy and Pharmacology, Comparative Biochemistry and Physiology, Journal of General Physiology, International Journal of Engineering Science, Journal of Materials, Journal of the Water Pollution Control Federation, American Ceramic Society Bulletin, Journal of the Acoustical Society of America, Chemical Engineering Science, Industrial and Engineering Chemistry Process Design and Development, Journal of Colloid and Interface Science, Journal of Fluid Mechanics, Journal of Lubrication Technology, Journal of Molecular Biology, Journal of Food Science, Journal of Biological Chemistry, Journal of Sedimentary Petrology, Review of Scientific Instruments,* and the *Journal of the Electrochemical Society.*

Equally as important to search productivity is the time reach of a citation index. As the example of the 1906 Einstein paper showed, a citation-index search can start at any point in time at which a pertinent paper on the subject was published. If that paper was cited during the year covered by the index, the searcher will be brought back to the most recent information. Then the recent papers can be used to cycle back in time to the publication dates of their citations, which again will bring the searcher back to the current literature. In this way a searcher can often use a single edition of a citation index to obtain a view of the historical development of a subject that would require a methodical search of many editions of a subject index.

The ability to search back and forth in time from the past literature to the current literature, to identify cross-disciplinary developments, to eliminate the search restrictions and complexity imposed by semantic problems, and to provide an in-depth index to the literature within a practical time and cost framework have all proved to be as significant in practice as they appear to be in theory. Within 10 years, citation indexing had gained acceptance, despite its newness and departure from traditional indexing methods, as an important method of conducting retrospective searches of the scientific literature.

And its impact has gone beyond even that. Citation indexing has come to play an important role in current-awareness services, library management, and studies of the policies, history, and literature of science.

REFERENCE

1. **Garfield, E.** "Genetic Engineering—Too Dangerous to Continue or Too Important to Discontinue?" In *Essays of an Information Scientist,* Vol. 2 (Philadelphia, ISI Press, 1977). Pp. 335–341.

Chapter Two

A Historical View of Citation Indexing

As with so many other developments, the concept of indexing the scientific literature by citations grew out of an effort to achieve something else. Soon after World War II, federal expenditures in research and development turned sharply upward, beginning a trend that was to continue for two decades. Responding to the stimulus of government spending, the pace of scientific research accelerated and the scientific literature, which reported the activity, increased at an explosive rate. The government, concerned that the systems for information exchange among scientists would be unable to handle the growing volume of literature, sponsored a variety of projects aimed at expanding and improving the facilities and methods for distributing and managing scientific information. One such project, sponsored by the Armed Forces Medical Library (now the National Library of Medicine), was a study at the Johns Hopkins Welch Medical Library on the role machines might play in generating and compiling indexes to the medical literature (1). As a member of the study team, I became interested in whether and how machines could be used to generate indexing terms that effectively described the contents of a document, without the need for the intellectual judgments of human indexers. The concept of a citation index, which eliminates this need, was a product of this interest. As it turned out, machines, per se, were not required.

BITS AND PIECES

The concept of a citation index to the scientific literature was synthesized from bits and pieces of experience and insight accumulated over a period of a few years. The accumulation started with two years of work on the Welch Medical Library project. The study of indexes produced insights into the nature of the intellectual judgments made in the indexing process and the functional relationship between the index and the person using it. There were additional insights into the structure and functional characteristics of both alphabetic and classified subject indexes. While I was doing voluntary abstracting work for *Chemical Abstracts* I recognized that the utility of abstracts was increased by including in them references to abstracts of key papers cited by the authors. This recognition was followed by a recommendation that *Chemical Abstracts* develop an index from their "C.F." ("see also") statements. More importantly, at the suggestion of Chauncey D. Leake, I made a special study of review articles. They play a special role in providing scientists with guideposts to the literature. I soon came to the realization that nearly every sentence in such review articles was supported by a reference. And the sentence itself was an unusually definitive indexing statement of the cited work. And in 1953 I learned, through William C. Adair, a former vice president of *Shepard's Citations*, that there was an index to the case literature of the law that used citations.

Shepard's Citations is the oldest major citation index in existence; it was started in 1873 to provide the legal profession with a tool for searching legal decisions. It does this by listing the citations to precedents used in the cases decided by federal and state courts and various federal administrative agencies. The legal "citator" system provided a model of how a citation index could be organized to function as an effective search tool. It should be noted that at that time it was not an index to legal periodical literature as it is today.

Other bits and pieces came, over the next few years, from the formal study of library sciences and structural linguistics. At first, it seemed that the basic problems to be solved in machine indexing were the ones of identifying the key words in a paper and stringing them together to form useful indexing terms or phrases. Studies of various parts of the literature, primarily in the disciplines of chemistry and medicine, and the indexes to them showed that the problem was more complicated than that.

It is not particularly difficult to identify key words. Theoretically, the simplest approach to generating index headings by machine would be to match the words of a text against a dictionary of indexing terms. This procedure would produce a large number of useful indexing entries; unfortunately, however, it also would produce an even larger number of entries whose relevance to the subject matter of the document was superficial at best. The "noise" created by the large number of irrelevant entries would be so great as to make the index just about useless—all of which means that selectivity is an important characteristic of the indexing process.

Limiting the vocabulary analysis to titles or abstracts would seem to be a way of achieving the degree of selectivity desired. Presumably titles and abstracts deal with only the essence of their documents; and, in fact, studies performed as part of the Welch Library project produced statistical evidence to support the theory that the nature of their selectivity is quite close to the selectivity practiced in the process of indexing by subject headings. Using detailed indexing records of *Chemical Abstracts* and the *Current List of Medical Literature* (predecessor to *Index Medicus*), we found that a significant number (60 to 90%) of the terms used in a given index appear in, or are implied by, the titles and abstracts of the documents covered.

But there is another side to that coin. Titles, by themselves, do not provide all the terms used in an index. Abstracts supply some of the terms missed by the titles but still do not match the full power of the indexing vocabulary, and what they contribute in added detail is gained at the expense of losing some of the selectivity so important to an index (2). Not all key words appearing in the titles and abstracts are useful indexing terms for those particular documents. Elaborate indexing entries are not always paraphrases of sentences in the abstract, and not all significant points covered by an abstract necessarily end up being indexed.

These findings led the research back to the full, original text as the best starting point for an automated indexing process. Since earlier work had shown that simple vocabulary analysis was not selective enough to extract only the important material, obviously, more powerful analytical techniques were needed. Structural linguistics seemed to offer some (3, 4).

The analytical methods of structural linguistics are based on syntax, the grammatical relationships between the words of the sentence. Used mostly in research on mechanical translation and other types of text-analysis problems (5), some of them appeared to offer capabilities close to what is needed for automated indexing. For example, they seemed to be capable, in theory at least, of emulating the classification judgments made in cataloging material for a library, and they provided a way of reducing the text of a document to a statistical summary of classifications that could conceivably be useful in making human indexers more consistent and thorough.

Nevertheless, though syntactic analysis went farther than vocabulary analysis, it did not go far enough. Unable to make qualitative distinctions, it was insensitive to the differences between old and new information and important and trivial information—the qualities on which an indexer's intellectual judgments are largely based.

In addition, even the limited potential of syntactic analysis in an automated indexing process was more theoretical than real. Before the techniques could be automated, someone had to figure out some way for the machine to determine whether the word "paid" in the sentence "They have paid witnesses" is being used as part of the verb phrase "have paid" or the noun phrase "paid witnesses." At the time, this unsolved problem was the main obstacle in the way of automated translation, and it was just as important to the use of syntactic-analysis techniques in automated indexing. Whether the machine was supposed to translate or index, it had to first understand, unambiguously, what it was reading. Since that time, considerable progress has been made in solving these kinds of problems. For one thing, it has been found that when a machine is dealing with a collection of documents, it can make these judgments with a reasonable degree of accuracy by looking at the frequency with which a given phrase occurs.

A SHIFT IN OBJECTIVES

During the accumulation of these bits and pieces, it became obvious that a human indexer does considerably more than identify and string together key words. In assigning terms, a good indexer makes subtle judgments about the relative quality of information and identifies relationships between concepts that go beyond the explicit content of the document being indexed. If it were to succeed, automated indexing would have to match that capability.

There was a question, however, about whether the capability was worth matching. It was difficult, if not impossible, to study the indexing process thoroughly without recognizing that it had a number of shortcomings that drastically limited its utility. One of the major ones was the practice of building indexes around the viewpoints and terminology of individual disciplines, when research was growing increasingly multidisciplinary, and the need for bibliographic tools that stretched across disciplinary lines was growing apace. How could a subject index produced by specialists in a particular discipline from the specialized vocabulary of that discipline be made to interpret material from the viewpoints of all other disciplines?

The question was not original. It was implied by those who advocated more comprehensive indexes (ones that covered more disciplines), more classified indexes, and standardization of terminology and nomenclature—all measures aimed at improving the conventional subject index. Unfortunately, however, as useful as all these measures may be, none of them solve the basic problem of interpreting the work in one subject from the viewpoint of all other subjects.

More comprehensive subject indexes can be nothing more than collections of a number of individual subject indexes, tied together by some central cross-referencing mechanism (6). Classified indexes are nothing more than subject indexes that are arranged hierarchically rather than alphabetically; though they may provide more logical insights than alphabetic indexes, they do not offer any broader interpretation of the material. And terminology and nomenclature reflect, for the most part, the specialization of disciplines. The most that standardization in this area can achieve is to ease communication at the points where disciplines meet; it cannot eliminate the differences in viewpoints, which are inherent and real.

The greatest need, apparently, was for some new type of index that would do a better job of spanning the gap that often existed between the viewpoints of those reporting a particular bit of information and those searching for it. Within this context, a citation index, produced by any means, began looking more useful than a subject index that could be produced by machine.

What looked best about a citation index was the diversity of the insights it provided about the literature of a particular subject and the efficiency and stability with which they could be stated. By using author references to index documents, the limited ability of a subject indexer to make connections between ideas, concepts, and subjects was replaced by the far superior ability of the entire scientific community to do the same thing. This meant that a citation index would interpret each of the documents it covered from as many viewpoints as existed in the scientific community. If an index is looked at as an attempt to represent as much detail of the real world as possible, a citation index would be to a conventional subject index what a full-color photograph would be to a black-and-white line drawing.

The other attraction of using reference citations in place of subject headings was their efficiency and semantic stability. A single reference citation represents as many subject headings as scientists have reasons for citing it. For example, the reference citation KNOWLES W.S., *CHEM TECH*, 2, 590, 1972 represents the subject heading ASYMMETRIC HYDROGENATION because some author cited it for the material it had on that subject. Another author cited it for material on the use of phosphine catalysts, so it also represents the subject heading PHOSPHINE CATALYSTS for anyone using it to find material on that subject. It also has been cited for material on alpha-amino acids, olefin hydrogenation, and ligands, which means that it functions as a heading for all those subjects. And if more people cite it for material on other subjects, the Knowles citation will take on those meanings too. In other words, each reference citation is associated with as many subject meanings as other scientists attribute to it (7, 8).

The semantic stability of citations comes from the fact that KNOWLES W.S., *CHEM TECH*, 2, 590, 1972 identifies a complex set of ideas with a relatively stable meaning, regardless of any changes that may take place in the terminology used later on to describe that subject.

A LOOK AT PRACTICALITY

Despite these kinds of advantages, there were questions to be answered about citation indexing too. Most of them had to do with the practicality of a citation index to the scientific literature. What form should it take? How should it be produced? How big should it be? Should it be selective or comprehensive in terms of disciplines covered?

Most of these questions were answered at a theoretical level in a paper published in *Science* in 1955 (8) in which a citation index to the literature of science was visualized as following the model of *Shepard's Citations*. A numerical coding system would be used to identify all citations, both reference (cited) and source (citing). At the front of the index would be an alphabetic listing of all journals covered, along with their code numbers. The main portion of the index would consist of a coded listing of reference citations, arranged in numerical order, and the source citations for each. Next to each source citation would be some designation showing the nature of the source: original article, review article, abstract, patent, translation, note, etc.

Such an index was visualized as being 50 to 100 times bigger than *Shepard's Citations* if it were to cover all of the journal literature of science. At the time *Shepard's* contained some 1.1 million citations from 30,000 cases a year. It was suggested, however, that not all journals had to be covered, and that by being selective in the coverage, the number of source citations listed each year could be brought down to about 1 million, which was well within the realm of practicality.

Production did not seem to pose any particular problem. The biggest job would be the coding of all the journals and articles covered. Then, following the *Shepard's Citations* model again, a separate index card would be prepared for each reference made in each source article. The cards would show, in code, the article being cited, the source article, and the nature of the source article. The rest of the process could be automated, using tabulating equipment, first, to put the cards into the numerical order of the reference citations and, then, to sort the cards associated with each reference citation into the numerical order of the source citations. After that, the cards would be run through a printer to prepare a master copy from which reproduction-quality page proofs could be prepared. No special subject expertise would be required, and, except for the supervisory level, neither would any special bibliographic expertise.

The utility of a citation index to the scientific literature was explored in a very tentative way by compiling all the references made in the *Journal of Clinical Endocrinology* during a five-year period to the notable paper by Hans Selye on the "General Adaptation Syndrome." Twenty-three references to the paper were found by scanning 500 articles published in the journal during that time.

An analysis of the articles that cited the Selye paper showed a number of interesting things. Although all of the articles were indexed in the *Quarterly Cumulative Index Medicus,* none of them was listed under the subject heading ADAPTATION; no indexer had made the connection or, at least, no one thought that the connection was worth identifying. The subject matter of the citing articles was extremely varied. And a number of the articles confirmed some of Selye's claims.

All of these findings said something positive about the utility of a citation index. It led to papers that would have been missed searching under the most obvious subject heading in a conventional subject index. The range of papers found provided an objective measure of the impact of the Selye paper, and the papers found provided documentation of the confirmation of some of Selye's claims.

In all, this tiny citation index showed that the technique was capable of identifying useful aspects of a paper that were missed by the conventional indexing services. If the book is considered the macro unit of scientific thought, and the journal article regarded as the micro unit, as had been suggested by Ranganathan, the citation index seemed to reach down to the molecular level, which certainly was a useful degree of specificity that was beyond the economic, if not conceptual, capabilities of the subject indexes.

PILOT TESTS

During the late 1950s and early 1960s a series of more elaborate citation indexes were developed that tested the feasibility and utility of the idea more thoroughly. In 1959, the *Journal of the American Statistical Association* published a cumulative citation index to its volumes 35 through 50. The *Annals of Mathematical Statistics* did the same thing in 1962 for its first 31 volumes. Also published in 1962 was a citation index to the *Bibliography of Non-parametric Statistics.* All three of these indexes were one-time efforts that were selective in the references listed. The indexes to the two journals listed only references to the journals; the one to the bibliography listed only references to other items in the bibliography.

What turned out to be the mainstream of development, because it eventually led to the only continuing, comprehensive citation index to the full spectrum of the scientific literature, were two pilot tests conducted by Eugene Garfield Associates, the consulting firm that later became the Institute for Scientific Information® (ISI®)*. The first, conducted in the mid-1950s, involved the development of a citation index to 5000 chemical patents held by two pharmaceutical companies (9). The reference citations were the prior patents cited by examiners to support their decisions (mostly involving rejection or restriction) on applicant claims. In all, some 30,000 source citations to approximately 20,000 patents were compiled.

The connections made by the index were analyzed and compared with the classification decisions made by the Patent Office and the indexing decisions made by *Chemical Abstracts* on the same patents. The analysis showed that the citation index consistently identified subject matter in the source patents that did not show up in either the patent classifications (which, it should be recognized, are based solely on claims that have been granted) or *Chemical Abstracts.*

This test too, then, confirmed the potential utility of a citation index, based on its ability to identify details missed by other systems. The capability was particularly intriguing as it applied to patents, because the information identified by the citation index had to do mostly with the reasons for making negative decisions. It would seem that the ability of a citation index to reach across the lines of patent classifications to identify reasons for rejecting or limiting a particular claim could improve considerably both the effectiveness and the efficiency of the examination process. And if the index included the file of patents that had been completely rejected, which are not classifed, it would be even more useful.

The 1960s test of the value and practicality of a citation index to the scientific literature was on a considerably larger scale, and of broader significance. Working under a grant from the National Institutes of Health, the Institute for Scientific Information produced a series of three pilot citation indexes to the genetics literature (10).

The program started out to test the feasibility and utility of a narrow, discipline-oriented citation index. Genetics was chosen to be the test discipline because it interacted with many other disciplines and, presumably, would gain the most from a bibliographic tool with the multidisciplinary reach expected of citation indexing. The initial plan was to index all the articles published in a list of hard-core genetics journals—ones whose titles included the words "genetics," "heredity," or comparable terms—that had been compiled by an advisory committee of geneticists working with the study group. This strategy made the first point in favor of a comprehensive citation index over a selective one by demonstrating the difficulty of defining a discipline by the primary journals that served it.

The year was 1961. Molecular biology was just beginning to be recognized as a new and important field of study, one that was having a particularly strong impact on genetics. The *Journal of Molecular Biology,* which had been in existence only since 1959, was not included on the list of hard-core genetics journals, but had published genetics papers. Other journals not included on the list also were publishing genetics papers: *Nature,* for example, had published the landmark paper by Watson and Crick on DNA. Obviously, some way had to be found to define the

---

*Registered trademark of the Institute for Scientific Information.

genetics literature that would pick up these papers. The question was how to do it without opening the index to a lot of material that plainly did not qualify as genetics.

The answer took the form of a decision to compile a comprehensive, multidisciplinary data base of citations and to develop a set of criteria that would permit a computer to extract all the material that could be considered relevant to genetics. The rationale behind this approach was that by compiling a comprehensive, multidisciplinary data base, we would pick up all the material relevant to genetics, regardless of where it had been published, and then we could separate it from the rest by applying more elaborate criteria than would be practical in defining initial coverage.

Though it was neat, this resolution of the problem was still unsatisfactory in one sense: it left unanswered the original study questions about the practicality and utility of a selective citation index compiled in a more direct way. Consequently, it was decided to produce two more indexes based on the more limited material available in the list of hard-core genetics journals provided by the advisory committee of geneticists. One would cover the output of 38 journals for a period of five years, from 1958 through 1962. The other, to determine the effect of time span on the utility of a citation index, would cover the output of three hard-core journals over a period of 14 years, from 1949 through 1963.

The revised strategy broadened the scope of the study considerably—and with it, the number of things that could be tested. Besides testing the concept of a citation index, we also would be able to test the relative merits of selective versus comprehensive indexes, and the feasibility of using machine methods to define the literature of a given discipline.

Work started with the compilation of the multidisciplinary data base, which consisted of citations of all the material published in 1961 by the 600 journals covered by *Current Contents*® * and of all the references in that material. The source journals included general ones, such as *Science* and *Nature,* plus those specializing in a broad range of disciplines that included clinical medicine, experimental biology, instrumentation, physics, virology, and, of course, genetics. In all, the data base contained 1.3 million references to 890,000 unique authored items. The 890,000 items cited stretched back in time a full 100 years, though most of them were no more than 10 years old. The average number of references to each cited item was 1.52.

From this comprehensive data base, the computer extracted the citations that applied to genetics for the compilation of the *1961 Genetics Citation Index.* This subset amounted to 19% of the full data base, and consisted of 246,000 references to 146,000 items. The size of the subset was not left to chance. Economic considerations made it necessary to limit the subset to 20% of the data base, and the selection criteria were tailored to accomplish this. The procedure for extracting the subset is shown in flowchart form in Figure 2.1.

Three dictionaries were developed for the extraction process. One was a dictionary of geneticists compiled from a number of sources: the membership lists of the American Society of Human Genetics and the Genetics Society of America;

---

*Registered trademark of the Institute for Scientific Information.

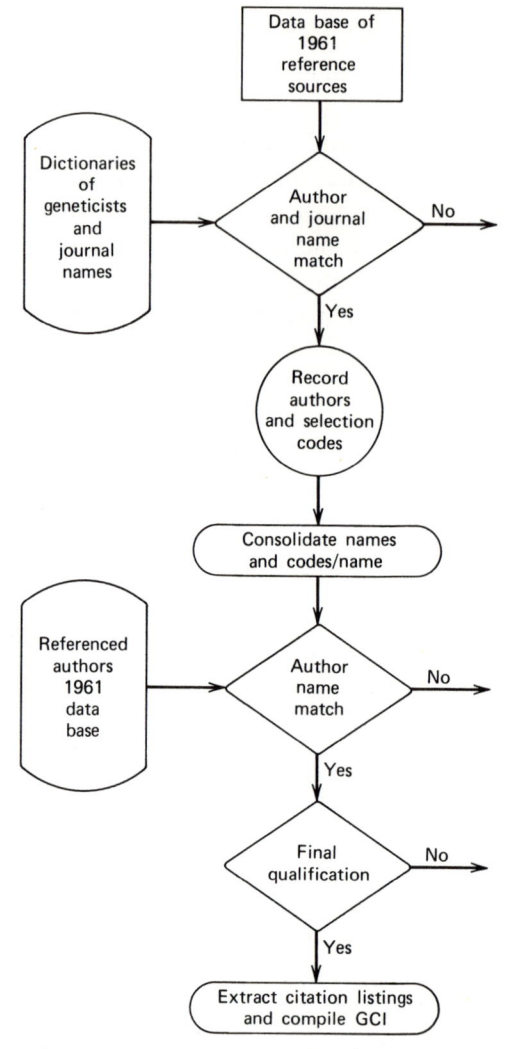

Figure 2.1 Procedure for extracting genetics subset from multidisciplinary data base.

the mailing list of the *Microbial Genetics Bulletin*; the "Bibliography of Human Genetics" from the *American Journal of Human Genetics*; bibliographies on "Mankind Evolving" by T. Dobzhansky, "Human Genetics" by R. R. Gates, and "Medical Genetics" by V. A. McKusick; and an unofficial list of geneticists supplied by NIH. These sources provided a total of 26,000 names.

The other two dictionaries were of hard-core genetics journals. One contained the 43 journals originally selected by the advisory committee of geneticists; the other contained an additional 28 genetics journals included in the source journals covered by the multidisciplinary data base.

The extraction process started with an analysis of the data base citations to determine which source and reference authors and journals were listed in the dictionaries. Every time a match was found, both the source and reference authors involved were recorded on magnetic tape, along with a code that showed the reason for selection.

All the codes listed for each author were then consolidated to produce a list of authors who met at least one of the following criteria:

- Were recognized geneticists.
- Had published in a recognized genetics journal.
- Had cited a recognized geneticist.
- Had cited a recognized genetics journal.
- Had been cited by a recognized geneticist.
- Had been cited by a recognized genetics journal.

This list of authors was run against the list of reference authors in the data base. The codes of those who were represented as cited authors were then checked to see who met the final selection criteria that had been set up to limit the genetics subset to 20% of the full data base. The basis for qualification was being a recognized geneticist, having published in a hard-core genetics journal, or meeting two of the other criteria concerning citing or being cited by a recognized geneticist or genetics journal. All the material pertaining to those cited authors who met at least one of those qualifications was then extracted from the data base and compiled to create a *1961 Genetics Citation Index.*

As was expected, this index provided a much more comprehensive view of the genetics literature than either of the other two. Though it was an index to only the material published in 1961, over 50% of the items cited were more than six years old.

Nevertheless, each of the other two indexes was interesting in its own right. Their relatively narrow scope of coverage was compensated for by the depth provided by their 5- and 14-year time spans. The 14-year span, which covered 1949–1963, provided a remarkable historical view of the field, even though it was based on the work published in only three journals.

CONCLUSIVE ANSWERS

The pilot study that produced the genetics indexes conclusively answered all the questions that had been surrounding the practicality of indexing the scientific literature by citations. It showed, for one thing, that the technique was economically practical. The major manual effort required to code all the entries, as *Shepard's Citations* did, turned out to be unnecessary. On the other hand, a great deal of attention had to be given to the problem of standardizing the author and journal names used in references and unifying all the variations of those names. Fortunately, it was possible to develop special computer programs that accomplished this unification with adequate, though not perfect, consistency. When all the pluses and minuses of citation indexing were added up and compared to conventional subject indexing, citation indexing turned out to be less expensive.

The study also showed that a citation index was eminently useful. A thousand copies of the three citation indexes to the genetics literature were published and distributed to scientists in the field for evaluation. Their responses, and an analysis of the genetics indexes and the multidisciplinary data base from which the 1961 index was derived, showed that a citation index produced a view of the literature that was deeper, more specific, and considerably broader in scope than conventional subject indexes. These qualities made it a more efficient and productive search tool.

The comparison between the genetics indexes and the multidisciplinary data base was particularly enlightening. Though the advantages of a citation index held up whether the index was narrow and selective or broad and comprehensive, they grew considerably more pronounced as the coverage of the index increased. In fact, a comprehensive, multidisciplinary index possessed a dimension of utility that went beyond its role as a search tool. It also provided a view of the literature that threw much light on such murky and important subjects as the bounds of particular disciplines, the interaction between disciplines, the structure of the journal network that is the primary mechanism for exchanging information in the scientific world, the historical development of scientific thought, and the implications and impact of individual pieces of scientific work.

These findings were compelling enough for ISI to decide to publish, on its own, after the government rejected the recommendation, the multidisciplinary data base as the first broad, comprehensive citation index to the scientific literature, and to produce it on a continuing, annual basis. Named the *Science Citation Index*® (*SCI*®)*(11), the index has steadily increased its coverage (see Figure 2.2) to the point where the 1977 edition contained 7.4 million references to 3.8 million items, reflecting the total literature published by 2655 journals and 1400 other sources reporting on all the disciplines of science in all the major scientific languages. In 1973, ISI brought out a companion *Social Sciences Citation Index* ™(*SSCI* ™)†(12). In 1978, it further expanded the application scope of citation indexing as a tool of scholarship by bringing out the *Arts & Humanities Citation Index* (A&HCI) ™†(13).

Probably because *SCI* is so broad and comprehensive, few additional citation indexes to the scientific literature have been published. One that has been is the *Citation Index for Statistics and Probability,* a cumulative one-time effort that covers the journal literature of the field from its inception, early in the twentieth century, through 1966. In addition, the *Journal of Histochemistry and Cytochemistry* published monthly, from October 1966 through September 1973, a citation index to articles published in some 2300 journals that had cited its material. In a sense, this index is a demonstration of the broad range of utility of the *Science Citation Index,* since it is based on information supplied from the *SCI* data base as part of an alerting service offered by ISI under the name *Automatic Subject Citation Alert*® (*ASCA*®)*(14).

The *Citation Index for Statistics and Probability,* compiled by Dr. J. W. Tukey of Princeton University, and published in 1973 as part of the "Information Access Series" of the R & D Press, provides comprehensive coverage (all published articles) of some 40 hard-core journals in the field of statistics and selective coverage of an

---

*Registered trademark of the Institute for Scientific Information.
†Trademark of the Institute for Scientific Information.

	1970	1971	1972	1973	1974	1975	1976	1977
Source Journals	2,192	2,277	2,425	2,364	2,443	2,540	2,717	2,655
Source Journal Issues	17,992	18,976	19,384	20,493	20,719	21,390	22,697	22,480
Source Non-Journals								1,393
Journal Source Items								455,977
Non-Journal Source Items								38,884
Anonymous Source Items	11,320	9,639	10,191	9,806	8,096	7,284	6,405	6,578
Authored Source Items	350,555	354,851	367,423	397,137	392,875	411,617	438,146	488,283
Total Source Items	361,875	364,490	377,614	406,943	400,971	418,903	450,956	494,861
Citations to Authored Items*	4,041,165	4,302,885	4,579,183	4,938,132	5,148,630	5,446,889	6,080,275	7,271,526
Citations to Anonymous Items	55,357	61,037	62,884	61,989	65,265	70,332	74,208	95,065
Citations to Patents	11,425	15,783	17,048	17,299	17,815	18,747	22,070	31,435
Total Citations from Source Items	4,107,947	4,379,705	4,659,115	5,017,420	5,231,710	5,535,968	6,176,553	7,398,026
Unique Cited Authors*	619,872	645,505	688,320	710,992	730,001	772,500	812,974	907,517
Average Number of Citations To Cited Authors	6.52	6.67	6.65	6.95	7.05	7.05	7.48	8.01
Unique Authored Items Cited*	2,340,128	2,449,573	2,596,663	2,729,968	2,817,833	3,005,712	3,245,632	3,776,247
Average Number of Citations To Authored Cited Items	1.73	1.76	1.76	1.81	1.83	1.81	1.87	1.92

Figure 2.2 Growth of *Science Citation Index* over the years.

additional 100 journals through the first 66 years of this century. It contains some 300,000 references from approximately 35,000 articles and reviews.

A third citation index, this one outside of the scientific area, completed the cycle of interaction that led to the development of citation indexing as an established method of managing the scientific literature. In 1968, *Shepard's Citations* introduced the *Shepard's Law Review Citations*. This is a continuing index to more than 100 law reviews and journals that shows references to any legal article written since 1947. As the *Science Citation Index* was inspired in part by the model of *Shepard's Citations,* so was *Shepard's Law Review Citations* inspired in part by the model of *Science Citation Index*.

REFERENCES

1. **Field, H.G., Himwich, W.A., Garfield, E., Whittock, J.M., and Larkey, S.V.** "Final Report on Subject Headings and on Subject Indexing" (Baltimore: Welch Medical Library Indexing Project, Johns Hopkins University, 1955). 47 pp.
2. **Resnick, A.** "Relative Effectiveness of Document Titles and Abstracts for Determining Relevance of Documents."*Science,* **134**:1004–1006, 1961.
3. **Harris, Z.S,** *Structural Linguistics* (Chicago: The University of Chicago Press, 1951; 4th impression, 1960). 384 pp.
4. **Chomsky, N.** *Syntactic Structures* (The Hague; Mouton and Company, 1957).
5. **Sager, N.** "Syntactic Formatting of Science Information." *Proceedings of the Fall Joint Computer Conference, 1972,* **41**:491-800, 1973.
6. **Garfield, E.** "A Unified Index to Science." In *Proceedings of the International Conference on Scientific Information, Washington, D.C., November 16-21, 1958.* 2 Vols., 1637 pp. (Washington, D.C.: National Academy of Sciences—National Research Council, 1959). Vol. 1, pp. 461–474.
7. **Garfield, E.** "Citation Indexes—New Paths to Scientific Knowledge." *The Chemical Bulletin* **43**:11, 1956.
8. **Garfield, E.** "Citation Indexes for Science."*Science,* **122**:108–111, 1955.
9. **Garfield, E.** "Breaking the Subject Index Barrier: A Citation Index for Chemical Patents." *Journal of the Patent Office Society,* **39**:583–595, 1957.
10. **Garfield, E. and Sher, I.H.** *Genetics Citation Index; Experimental Citation Indexes to Genetics with Special Emphasis on Human Genetics* (Philadelphia: Institute for Scientific Information, 1963). 854 pp. Cf. introductory material, pp. i-xviii.
11. **Garfield, E.** "Science Citation Index—A New Dimension in Indexing." *Science,* **144**:649–654, 1964.
12. **Weinstock, M.** "ISI's *Social Sciences Citation Index*: A New, Comprehensive, Multidisciplinary Information Retrieval System." Paper presented at the National Convention of the American Society for Information Science, Washington, D.C., October 23-26, 1972.
13. **Garfield E.** "Will ISI's *Arts & Humanities Citation Index* Revolutionize Scholarship?" *Current Contents.* No. 32, 5–9, August 8, 1977.
14. **Garfield E.** *"ASCA (Automatic Subject Citation Alert).* A New Personalized Current-Awareness Service for Scientists." *The American Behavioral Scientist* **10**:29–32, January 1967.

Chapter Three

The Design and Production of a Citation Index

There is little, if anything, that is simple at all levels of reality. Citation indexing is no exception. At the conceptual level, it provides a simple way around the semantic, intellectual, and economic problems of traditional subject-term indexing (see Chapter One: "A Conceptual View of Citation Indexing"). At the implementation level, however, citation indexing loses much of that simplicity, particularly when it is being implemented on a large scale.

The basic implementation complexities lie in the areas of coverage and production, which are related in a direct way by economics: the more efficient the production process, the more literature one can afford to cover. Though the nature and magnitude of the complexities vary somewhat according to the scope of the index (see Chapter Two: "An Historical View of Citation Indexing"), the best illustration of them, and of their relationship, is the *Science Citation Index.* Because its scope is so much broader than any other citation index to scientific literature, it demonstrates better than any other what is involved in realizing the single most important attribute of the citation-indexing concept—the ability to provide an integrated view of the scientific literature that is unrestricted by disciplinary boundaries.

THE COMPLEXITIES OF COVERAGE

There are three measures of the coverage of a citation index. One is the number and variety of journals from which references are obtained for indexing. Another is the number, variety, and time frame of the references.

In terms of the first measure, *Science Citation Index* (*SCI*) covers several thousand journals from literally every scientific discipline. As for the second measure, all references listed in all original articles, editorials, letters, meeting reports, and notes are indexed without restriction. This means that the cited material listed in *SCI* is not limited by either journal, publisher, or publication type: everything an author references is listed, regardless of where it was published or whether it took the form of a journal article, book, thesis, letter, or report. Nor are the reference citations limited by time period. If references are made to works by da Vinci or Copernicus, they will be included.

By combining these two measures, the annual coverage of *SCI* can be defined as consisting of approximately 500,000 source articles and some 7 million references from 3000 to 4000 journals and multiauthored books of all scientific disciplines. The references identify over 3 million unique cited items, which consist of both journal and nonjournal material, deal with all the subjects of science, and stretch as far back in time as the authors' work took them.

The third measure of coverage is qualitative. Ideally, a comprehensive citation index to the journal literature of science might be expected to cover all the scientific journals published. For a number of reasons, however, this is impractical—and may even be impossible. One reason is that no one knows how many journals are published, because there is no agreement on what constitutes a journal. Some serials appear only once a year—a frequency that throws considerable doubt on any claims that they are journals. Many so-called scientific journals that appear more frequently publish little, if any, material that is a serious attempt to help solve research problems. And many more journals do not last long enough to earn serious consideration.

Another thing that makes the ideal impractical is economics. After eliminating all the serials that suffer from the shortcomings just described, there probably are something on the order of 10,000 left whose intent, frequency, and endurance qualify them as scientific journals. If each of these journals publishes an average of 100 articles a year, the total universe to be covered by a comprehensive citation index would be 1 million source articles a year. Considering that the average article covered in *SCI* requires the creation, entry, storage, and manipulation of a computer record some 1000 characters long, just the data entry and computer costs would make the economic feasibility of complete coverage rather shaky under most real-world circumstances. Economics, therefore, dictates that even a comprehensive citation index must be selective.

Because the problem of coverage is one of practical economics, the criterion for what is covered is cost effectiveness. The cost-effective objective of an index is to minimize the cost per useful item identified and to maximize the probability of finding any useful item that has been published. One factor in achieving this objective is the efficiency with which the index is produced. Another factor, since it costs as much to index a useless item as a useful one, is the utility of the items covered. A cost-effective index must restrict its coverage, as nearly as possible, to only those items that people are likely to find useful.

This is not as impossible as it sounds. The trick is to identify the journals that publish the highest quality material. Expert practitioners in a field can do this easily enough. The difficult part of the job lies in trying to make the coverage as complete as possible by expanding it beyond the core of journals whose importance to a given field is obvious.

In 1953 S.C. Bradford described the difficulty when he wrote in *Documentation* (1), "Articles of interest to a specialist must occur not only in the periodicals specializing in his subject, but also, from time to time, in other periodicals, which grow in number as the relation of their fields to that of the subject lessens, and the number of articles on his subject in each periodical diminishes." In simpler terms, the pursuit of complete coverage of the literature pertinent to a given field takes one farther and farther afield; and the farther away you go, the more journals must be added to the collection to improve coverage. A physical analogy of the situation described by Bradford would be a comet, with the nucleus representing the core journals of a literature and the debris and gas molecules of the tail representing the additional journals that sometimes publish material relevant to the subject. The tail becomes wider in some proportion to the distance from the nucleus.

Bradford first demonstrated this law in a study of the literature of electrical engineering. Others showed that it held true for other segments of the literature as well. On the strength of Bradford's insight and other subsequent findings, information scientists developed a rule of thumb that said that somewhere between 500 to 1000 different journals are required to obtain 95% of the significant literature published in a given field. In other words, an index attempting to identify 95% of the significant journal literature in a single, given field would have to cover 500 to 1000 different journals.

On the surface, Bradford's law would seem to imply that it is economically impossible to provide anywhere near complete coverage of all the literature of science in a single index. Too many journals—500 to 1000, multiplied by the number of disciplines involved—would have to be covered. But that is not the way it works.

All that Bradford talked about was the number of journals involved in publishing the literature of a single field. He did not say that each group of journals was unique to its field, and he did not say anything about how much the journals in one field might overlap other fields.

It turns out that there is a very significant degree of overlap. The evidence of it takes the form of numerous studies showing that relatively few journals are involved in the publishing of an overwhelming majority of the material important enough to be referenced or abstracted. One study of the *SCI* data base (2) shows that 75% of the references identify fewer than 1000 journals, and that 84% of them are to just 2000 journals (see Figure 3.1). The same study also showed (see Figure 3.2) that 500 journals accounted for 70% of the material indexed in *SCI* in 1969 and that almost half of the 3.85 million references published in *SCI* that year came from ony 250 journals (see Figure 3.3).

The same kind of concentration has been shown in studies of the two major services abstracting the chemical literature. A study of the 1974 edition of *Current Abstracts of Chemistry and Index Chemicus*™† (3) shows that 20 journals accounted for 68% of the new compounds announced, that 40 accounted for 88%, and that only 43 journals accounted for 90% of the compounds. A study of *Chemical Abstracts* (4) showed that only 8% of the journals it covers were responsi-

---

†A trademark of the Institute for Scientific Information.

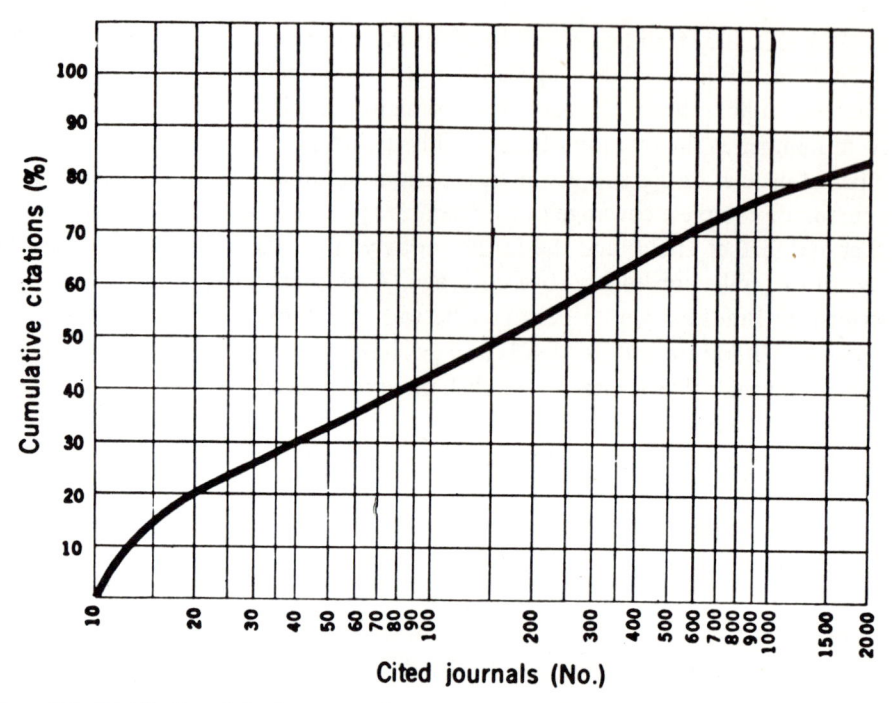

Figure 3.1 Distribution of citations among journals cited in *SCI* shows that 75% of the references identify fewer than 1000 journals and that 84% of them are to just 2000 journals.

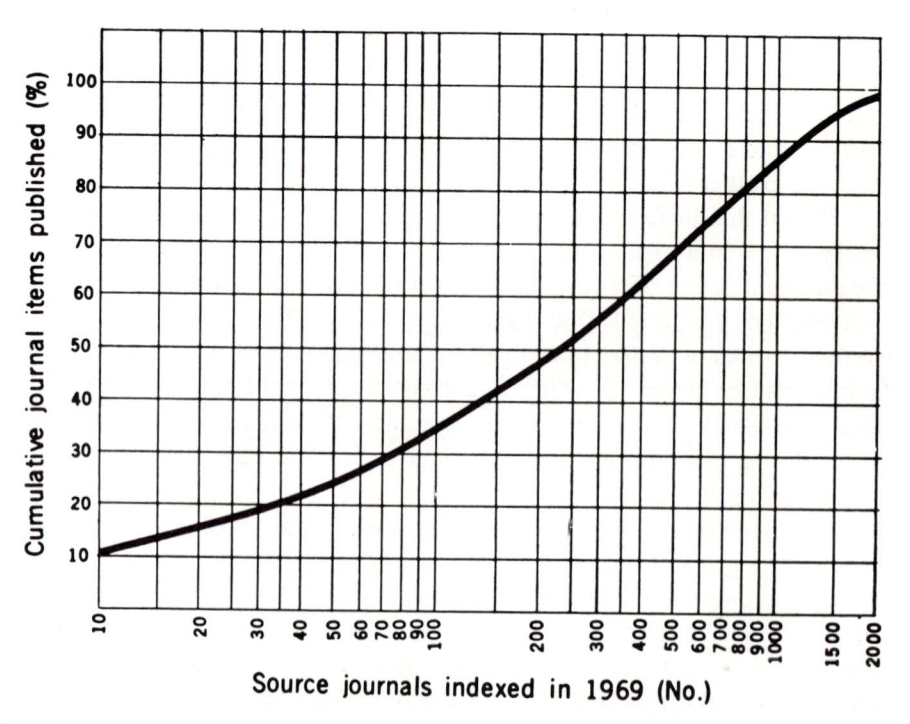

Figure 3.2 Distribution of published items among source journals covered by *SCI* in 1969 shows that 70% of the material indexed was published by only 500 journals.

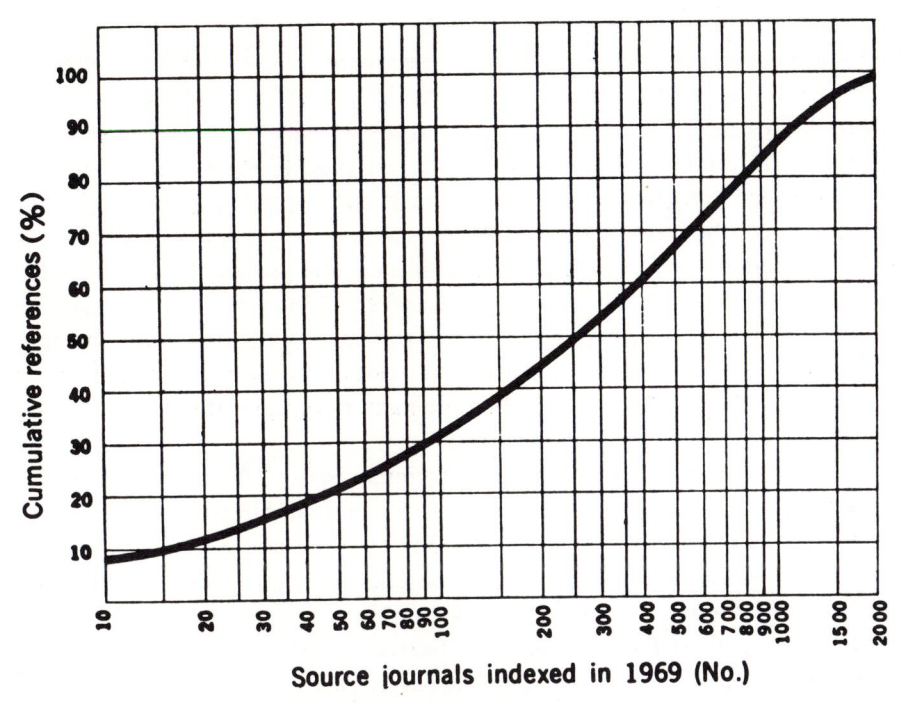

Figure 3.3 Distribution of references among source journals covered by *SCI* in 1969 shows that almost half of the 3.85 million references came from only 250 journals.

ble for the publication of 75% of the items it considered important enough to abstract.

This type of evidence makes it possible to move from Bradford's Law of dispersion to Garfield's law of concentration (5), which states that the tail of the literature of one discipline consists, in a large part, of the cores of the literature of other disciplines. So large is the overlap between disciplines, in fact, that the core literature for all scientific disciplines involves a group of no more than 1000 journals, and may involve as few as 500. In less abstract terms, this means that a good general-science library that covers the core literature of all disciplines need not have any more journals than a good special library that covers all the literature of a single discipline.

Consisting of the total output of some 3000 journals, the coverage of *SCI* is well past the core of all scientific journal literature, and into the area where cost effectiveness becomes critical. For that reason, the judgments that must be made about the quality of the journals being covered, and being considered for coverage, are taken very seriously and are based on the best information available.

Interestingly enough, the best information available consists of the statistics on how frequently journals are cited that can be generated from the *SCI* data base (the collection of computer records from which each edition of *SCI* has been compiled). Since authors refer to previous material to support, illustrate, or elaborate on a particular point, the act of citing is an expression of the importance of the material. The total number of such expressions is about the most objective measure there is of the material's importance to current research. The number of times all the material in a given journal has been cited is an equally objective and enlightening measure of the quality of the journal as a medium for communicating research results.

Two kinds of citation data are used to measure journals. One is a straight citation count: the total number of times a journal has been cited in a given year. The other is something called "impact factor." When a journal, as opposed to a single article, is being measured, the total number of items published by the journal influences the number of times it is cited; the more it publishes, the greater the number of opportunities it has to be cited. Given a large and small journal of equal quality, the large one will be cited more frequently than the small one. The impact factor discounts this advantage of large journals by showing the average citation rate per published item. This is done by dividing the number of times the journal has been cited by the number of items it has published.

Both of these measures are used in a continuing series of studies to keep *SCI*'s coverage cost effective. They are used to monitor journals already being covered; to spot journals not now covered that merit consideration; and, when cost considerations make it necessary, to decide between competing journals that have equal editorial board support for inclusion. One notable example of the value of these measures in keeping *SCI*'s coverage cost effective took place in 1968. An analysis of journal citation rates showed that the Russian journal *Teploenergetica,* which was not covered by *SCI,* was among the 500 most frequently cited journals in the world. It was added the next year.

New journals sometimes impose particularly difficult coverage decisions. It is desirable to cover the worthwhile ones as quickly as possible. Since it usually takes two to three years for the citation rate of a published item to peak, unless it is in a particularly "hot" field, citation counts are not usually relevant to the evaluation of a new journal. In this situation, the people who worry about *SCI* coverage look at such factors as the reputation of the publisher; the geographic representation of the journal's editorial board; its reliability in meeting scheduled publication dates; and its format and bibliographic standards as reflected in article titles, references, authors' addresses, and abstracts. If it is published in a language other than English, the inclusion of English abstracts or summaries is vital. While the journal may translate article titles into English on its contents pages, it may omit this information in the abstract. New journals that score well on these counts are submitted to the editorial advisory board. Those that are added are then monitored annually by citation analyses reported in the *SCI* volume called *Journal Citation Reports.*® *

The purpose of all these activities is to make sure that no significant new or old journal is omitted from coverage. If a journal is picked up in a few years, we will go back to process earlier volumes for the five-year cumulations.

Once we are certain that the best are included, it is extremely difficult to decide which of the hundreds of remaining journals to add. Fundamentally, the decisions are economic ones, since the continued existence of a research journal is an obvious indicator that it is important to someone. In 1978, ISI made the basic decision that

---

*Registered trademark of the Institute for Scientific Information.

any journal suitable for coverage in any *Current Contents* edition should eventually be included in the *SCI* or *SSCI,* since this would ensure uniform processing of over 5000 journals in the system.

The key step to ensuring complete coverage within specialties is to do a field-by-field citation analysis. In this way all significant journals within the field are ranked by impact and citations. It is difficult to imagine an important journal escaping this citation net. But as the coverage of the system is increased to the point where even large numbers of mediocre journals are processed as source journals, then one must evaluate many journals that have purely regional or local value. The failure to include a particular journal may often be interpreted as having political significance, since coverage in *Current Contents* and the *SCI* is often a matter of prestige.

PRODUCTION EFFICIENCY

The other side of the cost-effectiveness coin, production efficiency, is more critical than is generally recognized. The production of citation indexes is more involved than is generally appreciated. Although citation indexing eliminates the expensive intellectual effort associated with traditional subject-term indexing (see Chapter One), producing a citation index of appreciable size is a massive materials-handling and information-processing job.

The job of producing the *Science Citation Index,* as well as the *Social Sciences Citation Index,* begins with "editing" or screening the individual journals that are covered. Every article or editorial item must be examined to determine whether it should be covered. Every item other than minor news notices and advertisements must be marked in some way to simplify the huge job of converting the information into machine language. This so called "pre-edit" process also helps standardize the information that enters the system. Pre-editing involves coding each item as to type, that is, an article or a technical note or editorial. The first and last page of each article must be identified and labeled. In many journals, especially in the social sciences and humanities, extensive marking of cited references is required. Reference formats may differ not only from journal to journal but even from article to article. Pre-editors also identify titles that must be translated into English. In addition, considerable editing must be done of titles, author names, organizational names and addresses, and references.

Titles must be marked and edited to show where they begin and end; eliminate unnecessary words; add pertinent footnote annotations; and standardize punctuation, numerical expressions, and proper names. Scientific notation must be edited to meet rules of standardization and computer processing requirements.

Author names and addresses must be underlined, and each name must be coded to distinguish between primary and secondary authors. Author names must be standardized, too; this includes non-English names, for which the rules of standardization are quite involved. The organizational names in author addresses also must be standardized.

References interspersed throughout the text or split between the text and footnotes, as well as footnotes that contain multiple references, can be the toughest part of the editing job. Most often found in social sciences journals, these types of references require extensive editing notation to identify, integrate, and complete them, and may require the help of a professional translator if they involve non-English citations.

Editing time per journal issue varies anywhere from half an hour to three days. Journals dealing with the social sciences are generally the most time consuming because their bibliographic standards tend to be archaic and their references are frequently complex, often citing exotic types of nonjournal material, such as rare documents, legislation, and laws. It is not unusual to find references scattered throughout the text of a social sciences journal, which means the editor must scan the entire article. Footnotes containing multiple references are common; and the format of references, regardless of where they are found, is eclectic enough to make reformatting the rule rather than the exception. The impact of these problems on productivity is great enough to justify a continuing and sizeable effort to educate editors about the reader and the economic advantages to be gained from adopting simpler, more standardized format rules.

The next production step is putting the edited material into the computer. With *SCI* and *SSCI* this job is done by over 100 data entry operators working two shifts, five days a week. These specially trained "indexers" use keyboard-display terminals connected directly to a central magnetic disk memory. The journals move through this process in large batches. Of course, recording formats have been specified in advance and job control numbers have been assigned to each batch. As part of the job control procedure, individual journals are logged into the system, when assigned to a batch, by name, volume, issue, month, year, accession date and number, and a status-and-date statement. After that, the status-and-date statement in the system log is updated every time the journal moves from one operation to another.

Once a journal has been assigned and logged, it goes to a data entry operator, who verifies and updates the log to let the system know what journal is being worked on and where it is. The operator then works through the journal article by article, keying the pertinent information from each into the system in a three-part sequence.

First comes the basic information that identifies the article: its type, title, page numbers, and primary author. The middle part of the data entry sequence involves additional author information: the address of the primary author and the names and addresses of any secondary authors. The last part of the sequence deals with the references cited in the article.

When all the information about all the articles in the journal have been entered into the system, the operator lets the system know the journal is finished by updating its log. Another operator then goes through the entire data entry sequence again, character by character, to verify the work of the first operator.

Periodically, the verified records created for batches of journals are automatically transferred, under the control of someone working at a supervisory terminal, from the magnetic disk to a magnetic tape. As the records are transferred, they also are reformatted for computer processing.

The data entry workload for *SCI* and *SSCI* can be defined by a variety of numbers, all of them large. Over 2000 source articles, involving some 25,000 cited references, are processed each day. With the record length per source article averaging 1000 characters, the total number of characters entered each day exceeds 2 million. And, if the verification operation is included, the total number of keystrokes per day is something on the order of 4 million.

At this point in the production cycle, the computer takes over, and the information goes through the sequence of processing operations shown in Figure 3.4.

The first step in this sequence illustrates the primary difficulty of preparing scientific information for computer processing. Despite the pains taken in the editing operation to identify, clarify, and standardize everything, and the character-by-character verification performed in data entry to assure keying accuracy, the first thing the computer must do to the tapes from data entry is edit them to make sure that all the records are complete and properly formatted. Some 1% are not and must be recycled through editing and data entry a second time.

Besides checking the content and format of the individual records, which are organized by journal, the computer also checks the journals against a year-to-date file of all the journal issues that have already been processed. Duplicates are recycled back through the journal control people to work out the problems. Those that are not duplicates are copied onto the year-to-date file.

The tapes from data entry are edited this way on a daily basis and accumulated into a weekly data base, which is edited again to verify the daily checks of content and format.

The edited weekly data base is then coded to show what journal records go into what index. Working from information in a master journal file, the computer codes each journal for one of three categories: *SCI* only, *SSCI* only, or both *SCI* and *SSCI*. It then looks at all the articles in the *SCI*-only journals and determines, on the basis of their title words and references, which ones qualify for inclusion in *SSCI* in addition to *SCI*. In 1977, this procedure was expanded to deal with the production of the *Arts & Humanities Citation Index*.

The records on the coded weekly data base are then sorted into four data categories: source data (bibliographic descriptions of the published articles from which the references are taken), citation data (the references made in the source articles), corporate data (names and addresses of the organizations with which the authors of the source articles are affiliated), and patent data (bibliographic descriptions of patents that have been cited in source items). All these categories, except for the one of patent data, correspond to major sections in both *SCI* and *SSCI*; the patent data is included only in *SCI*.

The rest of the weekly processing cycle consists of one refining operation and the creation of separate data bases for each of the two indexes. The refining operation involves the "post-editing" of the source-data file to assure the accuracy of the title information. Post-editing is also concerned with maintaining the currency of a title-word index included in *SCI* and *SSCI* to help users who do not have the name of an author with which to start a search. This is done by checking every key word in every

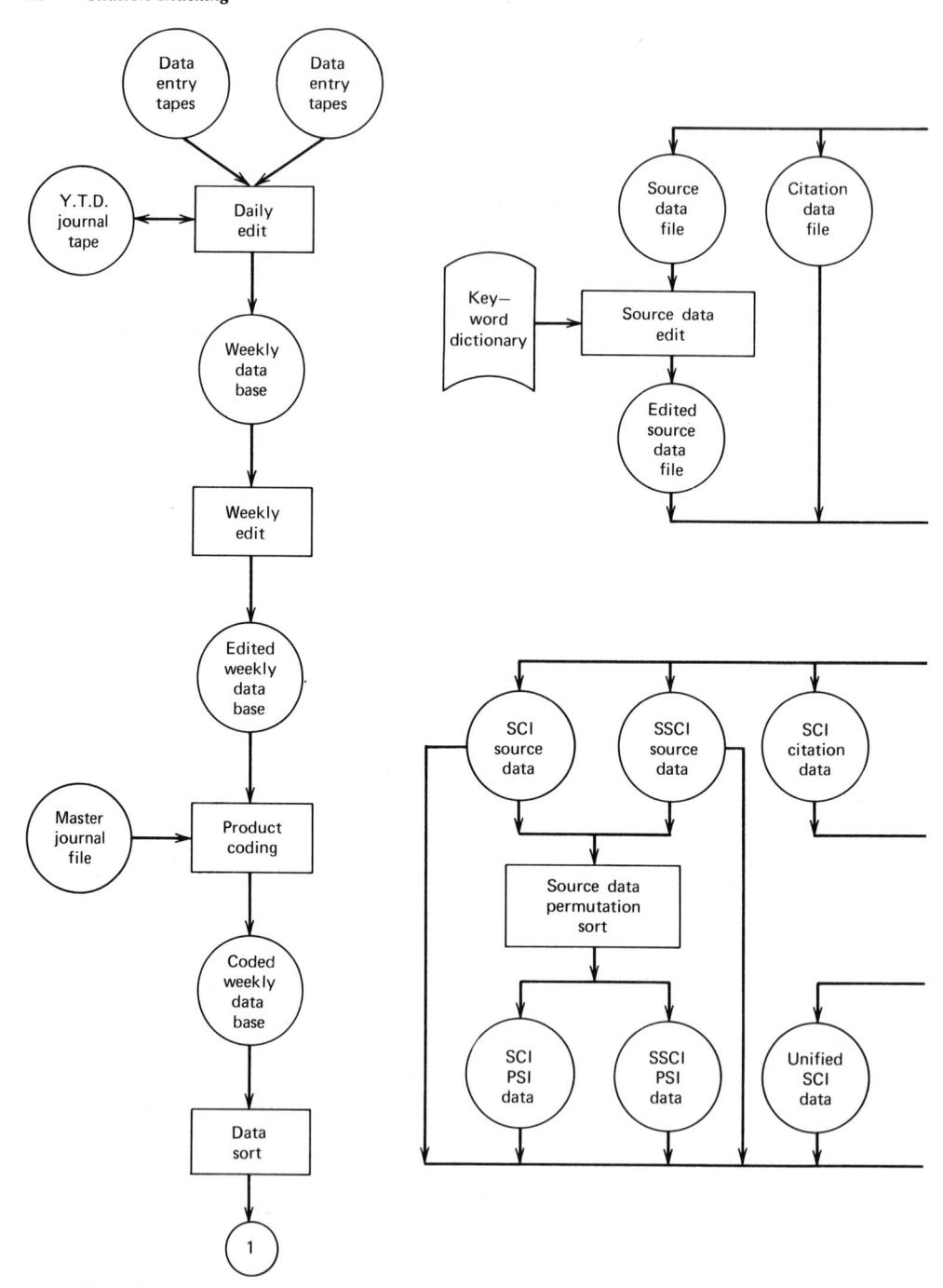

Figure 3.4 Computer processing operations in the production of *Science Citation Index*.

title on the file against a key-word dictionary. Words not found in the dictionary are passed on to editors, who determine whether the words are misspellings of valid words or are words not yet included in the dictionary. Misspelled words are corrected; new ones that are judged to be important are validated and added to the dictionary.

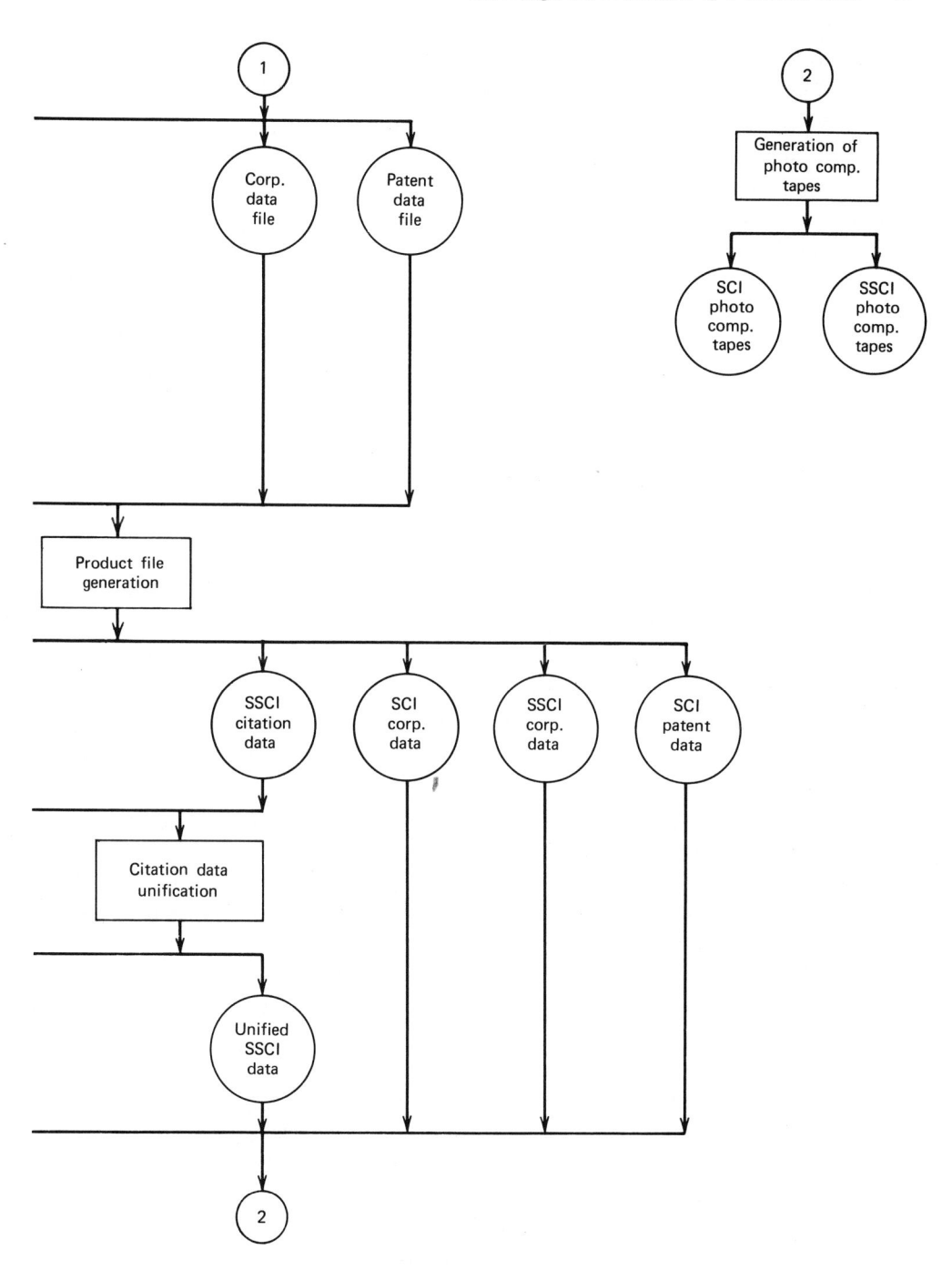

The final operation in the weekly processing cycle is generating separate *SCI* and *SSCI* counterparts of the four files of source, citation, corporate, and patent data. This is done on the basis of the product coding performed earlier.

The rest of the computer processing is done on quarterly, triannual, and five-year cycles. The quarterly cycle is concerned with integrating a three-month cumulation of weekly, *SCI* data files and preparing them for publication. It starts with two operations: the unification of the citation data file and the production of a file for the *Permuterm® Subject Index,* or *PSI,* which is the only component of *SCI/SSCI* for which no file is created during the weekly processing cycle. ("Permuterm" is a registered trademark of the Institute for Scientific Information constructed from the phrase "permuted terms.")

The unification of the citation-data file is concerned, again, with accuracy—this time, with the accuracy of the authors and journals cited in the references. To maximize this point of accuracy, the records on the citation files are sorted by author name, journal, volume, year, and page numbers, so that multiple references to the same citation are batched together. The computer then looks for inconsistencies in the names of the authors and journals cited by each batch of references. Any that are identified are resolved according to rules built into the computer program. The result of this operation is citation data in which the variations that inevitably creep into the spelling of author and journal names have been minimized, if not eliminated.

The *Permuterm Subject Index* is the title-word index mentioned earlier in connection with the editing of the source-data file. Producing a file from which the *PSI* can be published involves permuting all the key words in the source article titles and sorting the word pairs into alphabetical order.

All the *SCI* data files are then consolidated and reformatted by a routine that organizes the material into pages and specifies formats and type fonts. The tapes produced by this routine are used to drive an automatic photocomposition machine, which turns out reproduction-quality page proofs from which offset negatives and plates can be made for printing.

At the time the last quarterly index is prepared, the material for that quarter is consolidated with what had been published in the preceding three quarters to produce a cumulative annual index. Every fifth year, the material for the annual index goes through an extra processing operation in which it is consolidated with the material published in the four preceding annual editions to produce a five-year cumulative edition. This involves considerable changes in the *PSI,* which is refined and made more specific by looking at the frequency with which subject terms occur.

The same thing is done with the *SSCI* files on a four-month cycle.

There are a number of additional accuracy checks in this final stage of production. The first is a detailed check of the first statistically significant batch of pages produced by the photocomposer. The accuracy of the weekly data bases and the effectiveness of the computer routine that merges them are checked by matching a random sample of articles that should be covered in the initial pages against the page proofs. The effectiveness of other key computer programs also is checked in this initial sample by looking for discrepancies and omissions in names, cross references, formats, special signs, and features new to the index. If everything is all right, the rest of the pages are produced. These too are checked, but for such things as print quality, the number of columns per page, and the sequence of columns—all things that can go wrong in the photocomposition stage of production. Only then is the job released to the printer; the printer's work, too, is spot checked, but for all the things that can go wrong in the printing process.

Even at computer speeds, the amount of information processing required to produce a ciation index the size of *SCI* is staggering. Nearly 200 computer hours are required to go from the raw material that comes in daily from data entry to the weekly *SCI* files that are ready for quarterly processing. Another 25 hours of computer time is needed every quarter to go from the consolidated weekly files to the photocomposition tapes. In the last quarter, when the material for the entire year is being consolidated, more than 230 hours is needed to produce the photocomposition tapes, and the five-year cumulative edition takes some 2800 more hours of computer time.

SSCI, which is one quarter the size of *SCI,* uses an additional 60 hours or so of computer time to get to each of the first two sets of triannual photocomposition tapes and approximately another 60 hours for the last, annual cumulative set.

ROLE OF TECHNOLOGY

Theoretically, it is possible to produce a citation index without the aid of computers, though one of the advantages of the concept is the very neat match between its production demands and computer capabilities. From a practical viewpoint, however, computer technology (or, more accurately, information-processing technology) is critical to the cost effectiveness of a comprehensive citation index of the *SCI* type. In keeping with the coverage-production relationship mentioned earlier in the chapter, it improves the scope and depth of coverage that is economically practical by reducing the cost per item indexed.

Exploiting the potential of computer technology for this purpose is a matter of continually searching for production efficiencies among the technological advances. Some of the efficiencies are built into the lower cost per unit of processing offered by succeeding generations of equipment and can be realized merely by upgrading the equipment periodically. Other, more significant efficiencies call for the ability to innovate from the improved functional base provided by the new equipment. The impact that key-to-disk data entry equipment has had on *SCI* production is a case in point.

For a data entry operation as big as the one involved in *SCI,* key-to-disk systems are more efficient than the older keypunch. Job control procedures are easier to implement; keying is done at electronic, rather than mechanical, speeds; and a lot of punched-card handling is eliminated. In addition, each terminal operator has access to a central disk memory, around which ISI has built a production innovation that increases efficiency far beyond the level made possible by the superior speed of key-to-disk systems.

The innovation, called Keysave (6), consists of using the shared disk memory to store an historical file of reference citations from the *SCI* data base. The increase in efficiency comes from reducing the amount of keying necessary to enter and verify reference citations. Instead of keying the full citation, the operator keys in a 14-

character code abstracted from the full citation. Each of the citations on the historical file has attached to it the same sort of coded identifier. If the code the operator enters matches one in the file, the full citation is brought up on the terminal display, where it is verified visually and entered on the disk with a single keystroke.

Every time an operator matches a reference citation against one in the historical file, the number of keystrokes required to enter the citation is reduced from an average of 70 to 14, and the keystrokes normally required for verification are eliminated completely.

The match rate achieved depends on the number of citations in the historical file, which is limited by the size of the central disk memory available with the system. Initially, the file contained enough citations to produce a match rate of 75% on the references that cited journal material. Some changes in the design of the file increased the utilization efficiency of the central memory enough to push the match rate to 85%. Whether the rate can be raised still higher is uncertain, depending upon available memory capacity and how efficiently it is used. Match rates vary considerably from journal to journal. A journal in molecular biology will have rates in excess of 90%, while a rate less than 20% is common for journals in the social sciences and humanities.

Another example of how technology can be used to reduce costs is provided by a system improvement recently implemented in the editing operation. This involves the coding of organizational names and addresses, which pose accuracy and standardization problems in any index.

The entire editing operation associated with making sure that organizational names and addresses are accurate and consistent has been reduced to looking up and writing down two alphanumeric codes. One identifies the name of the organization; the other, the specific department or other organizational unit. The computer uses these codes to pick up full names and addresses from its own file of organizational data.

The productivity impact of this way of handling organizational names and addresses will not be limited to the editing operation. It also will be felt in data entry, where the use of the codes will significantly reduce the number of keystrokes needed to enter organizational names and addresses.

The role of technology in the production of a citation index goes beyond cost cutting into quality improvement. In some cases, the two can be combined, such as with the system for organizational names and addresses, which will enhance the quality of *SCI* by raising its level of standardization. Such an improvement is not an abstract achievement. More consistency and accuracy in organizational names and addresses make it easier for users of the index to contact the authors of source items for reprints of useful papers or for additional information.

More often than not, however, such quality improvements do not go hand in hand with cost reductions; they must be important enough to justify an increase in production costs. A computer-based system that automatically monitors the arrival of journals and tracks them through the processing mill according to a planned schedule, for example, is more expensive than doing the same thing manually. But it does a better job, which produces the important qualitative benefit of increasing the timeliness and comprehensiveness with which *SCI* covers its defined journal base.

FRUITS OF THE LABOR

The object of all this attention to the niceties of coverage and productivity is a multivolume, five-part index to that portion of the scientific journal literature published each year that is most likely to be useful—no matter what particular discipline or speciality is being researched.

The two key parts are the *Citation Index* and the *Source Index.* The *Citation Index* (see Figure 3.5) connects items published during the year with past items they have cited in references. It is organized alphabetically by cited author, using the last name of the first author. Under each cited author are listed, chronologically, the items that have been cited in references. Under each cited item are listed the sources of the references.

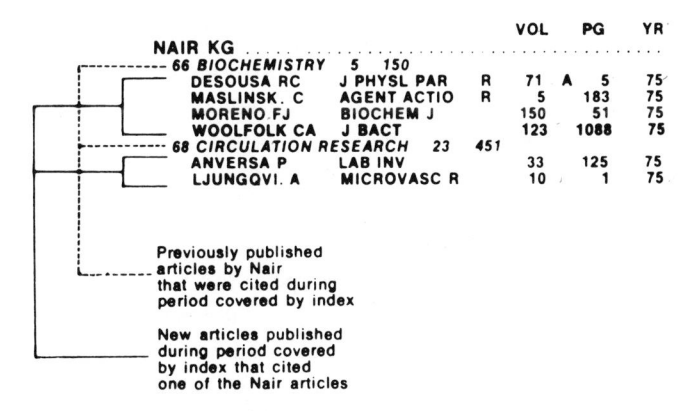

```
                                       VOL    PG     YR
       NAIR KG .........................
       ------ 66 BIOCHEMISTRY  5   150
              DESOUSA RC    J PHYSL PAR   R   71  A   5     75
              MASLINSK. C   AGENT ACTIO   R    5     183    75
              MORENO FJ     BIOCHEM J         150    51     75
              WOOLFOLK CA   J BACT            123    1088   75
       ------ 68 CIRCULATION RESEARCH  23   451
              ANVERSA P     LAB INV            33    125    75
              LJUNGQVI. A   MICROVASC R        10    1      75


       Previously published
       articles by Nair
       that were cited during
       period covered by index

       New articles published
       during period covered
       by index that cited
       one of the Nair articles
```

Figure 3.5 Typical entry from the *Citation Index* section of *SCI*.

Even anonymous items that have been referenced are included. Listed in a separate section, they are organized by journal, organization, and title.

Both the cited and source items are described in the same way (with minor exceptions for anonymous items): by the last name and initials of the first author and the name, year, volume, and page number of the publishing journal. The only thing missing that might be pertinent is the title of the item. In the case of a cited item, the title is unnecessary since it is reasonable to assume that the user must know what it is if he is searching for items that cited it. That, of course, is not the case for the source items, and that is the reason for the *Source Index*.

A straightforward author index to the items published during the year, the *Source Index* (see Figure 3.6) also is organized alphabetically by the last name of the first author. For each source item listed, there is a full bibliographic description: full title; last names and initials of all authors; address of the first author; name, year, volume, and page numbers of the publishing journal; language in which the item was published; and number of references made in the item.

In the *Source Index* for *SSCI*, and the *Arts & Humanities Citation Index,* this description is supplemented by one additional piece of bibliographic intelligence: a list of the reference citations that appeared in each item. Again, as in the *Citation Index,* the reference citations do not include the title. But they do provide a type of abstract

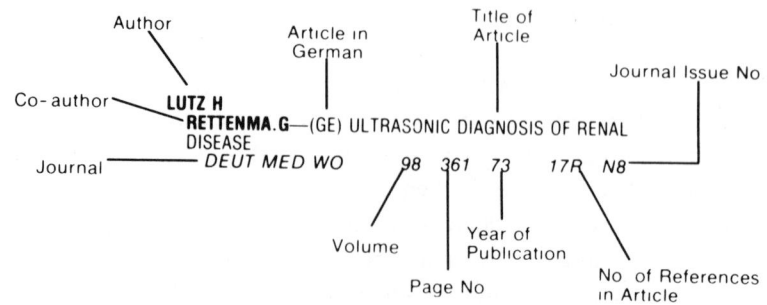

Figure 3.6 Typical entry from the *Source Index* section of *SCI*.

of the item that is useful in making preliminary judgments about its quality, pertinence, and subject orientation; and that is useful, too, in finding other citations with which to continue and refine a search (7).

The inclusion of reference citations in the *Source Index* entries is an expensive feature, which significantly increases both the size of the index and the cost of printing it. But, if the feature's effectiveness, as measured by subscriber utility, turns out to balance the cost, it will be added to the *Source Index* of *SCI* as well.

The other three parts of the *SCI* are the *Patent Index,* the *Permuterm Subject Index,* and the *Corporate Index*—all of which have the same functional relationship to the *Source Index* as does the *Citation Index.*

The *Patent Index* is conceptually the same type of index as the *Citation Index,* except that it deals with patents rather than journal items. Organized by patent numbers that have been referenced, rather than by authors, it provides the same partial description of source articles as the *Citation Index* and must be used in conjunction with the *Source Index* if a more definitive bibliographic description of them is required. Figure 3.7 shows a typical entry in the *Patent Index.* Besides the patent number, the reference citation shows the name of the patent holder, the country that issued the patent, and the year in which it was issued.

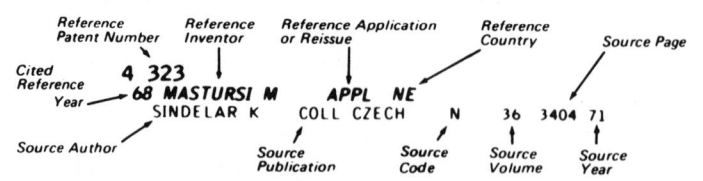

Figure 3.7 Typical entry from the *Patent Index* section of *SCI*.

The *Permuterm Subject Index* (*PSI*) is a title-word index, but one that permits more than the usual amount of search precision by enabling the user to search on a combination of two or more terms. This is done by going one step beyond the usual practice, in simple title-word indexes, of making every significant word in every title an indexing entry. Under each of these entries in the *PSI* are listed all the words with which the entry word has appeared in some title or other (see Figure 3.8). Next to each word in the list is the name of the author of the article whose title contains that particular pair of words. The author's name and the title words permit the searcher to find a complete bibliographic description of the article in the *Source Index.*

The reason for including a subject-word index in a citation index in the first place is to give people a way of taking advantage of the multidisciplinary coverage of *SCI* even when they do not have enough information about a field to perform a citation search. The *PSI* gives them the option of bypassing the *Citation Index* completely, or they can use it to identify an article that will provide them with a starting point for a citation search. If several annual editions or five-year cumulations of *SCI* are available, an article identified by *PSI* three or four years back can function as the

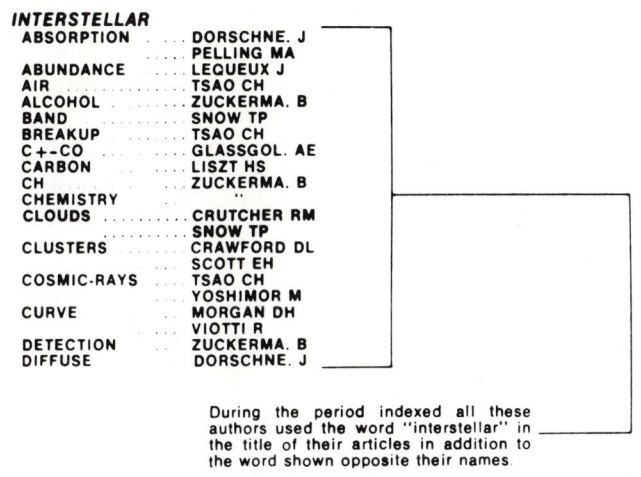

```
INTERSTELLAR
  ABSORPTION    .... DORSCHNE. J
                .... PELLING MA
  ABUNDANCE     .... LEQUEUX J
  AIR           .... TSAO CH
  ALCOHOL       .... ZUCKERMA. B
  BAND          .... SNOW TP
  BREAKUP       .... TSAO CH
  C+-CO         .... GLASSGOL. AE
  CARBON        .... LISZT HS
  CH            .... ZUCKERMA. B
  CHEMISTRY         ''
  CLOUDS        .... CRUTCHER RM
                .... SNOW TP
  CLUSTERS      .... CRAWFORD DL
                .... SCOTT EH
  COSMIC-RAYS   .... TSAO CH
                .... YOSHIMOR M
  CURVE         .... MORGAN DH
                .... VIOTTI R
  DETECTION     .... ZUCKERMA. B
  DIFFUSE       .... DORSCHNE. J
```

During the period indexed all these authors used the word "interstellar" in the title of their articles in addition to the word shown opposite their names.

Figure 3.8 Typical entry from the *Permuterm Subject Index* section of *SCI*.

starting point for the citation search; the bibliographic description of it in the *Source Index* will give all the information needed, saving the time and trouble of obtaining useful reference citations from the full text of a paper.

PSI also serves the secondary purpose of easing people into citation searches, which are unfamiliar to many, by letting them start out with the more traditional search technique. In many cases, they begin conducting citation searches in an attempt to improve the productivity and efficiency of their subject searches.

The *Corporate Index* looks at the journal articles published during the year from the viewpoint of the organizations with which the authors are affiliated. Each organizational entry (see Figure 3.9) shows the articles that the staff has had published during the year. They are identified in the same way as entries in the *Citation Index:* by author and by the name, volume, year, and page number of the publishing journal. Again, the author's name permits the searcher to find a complete bibliographic description of the item in the *Source Index*.

After years of arranging the *Corporate Index* alphabetically by name of organization, it was decided in 1978 to provide a geographical arrangement comparable to *ISI's Who is Publishing in Science*®*. While retaining an alphabetic cross-reference system, the geographic arrangement eliminates the ambiguity of similar names located in different countries. The geographic arrangement permits one to obtain a picture of scientific publication by country or city without sacrificing the ability to

---

*Registered trademark of the Institute for Scientific Information.

		VOL	PG	YR
MAX PLANCK INST BIOL,TUBINGEN,WEST GERMANY			
BISSWANG H	BIOC BIOP A	321	143	73
BRAUN V	J BACT	114	1264	73
ENGELRAE M	BIOC BIOP R	53	812	73
HENNING U	FOL MICROB	18	268	73
	P NAS US	70	2033	73
SORSA V	NATURE-BIOL	245	34	73
TICHY H	GENETICS	74	S276	73
ZARYBNIC V	VIROLOGY	54	318	73

Figure 3.9 Typical entry from the *Corporate Index* section of *SCI*.

observe the patterns of individual institutions. The cross-reference file is especially useful for multinational or multiregional organizations.

The five *SCI* indexes open up the journal literature to exploration from a variety of viewpoints for a multiplicity of purposes. The combination of search flexibility and comprehensive, multidisciplinary coverage produces a powerful tool for literature research.

REFERENCES

1. **Bradford, S.C.** *Documentation,* 2nd ed. (London: Lockwood, 1953).
2. **Garfield, E.** "Citation Analysis as a Tool in Journal Evaluation." *Science* **178**:471–479, 1972.
3. **Garfield, E., Revesz, G.S., and Batzig, J.H.** "The Synthetic Chemical Literature From 1960–1969." *Nature,* **242**:307–309, 1973.
4. **Wood, J.L.** "The Parameters of Document Acquisition at Chemical Abstracts Service." Paper presented at the American University 8th Annual Institute of Information Storage and Retrieval, Washington, D.C., February 14–17, 1966.
5. **Garfield, E.** "The Mystery of the Transposed Journal Lists—Wherein Bradford's Law of Scattering is Generalized According to Garfield's Law of Concentration." In *Essays of an Information Scientist,* Vol. 1 (Philadelphia: ISI Press, 1977). Pp. 222–223.
6. **Garfield, E.** "Project *Keysave*—ISI's New On-Line System for Keying Citations Corrects Errors." *Current Contents,* No. 7: 5–7, February 14, 1977.
7. **Garfield, E.** "Bibliographies, Citations, and Citation Abstracts." In *Essays of an Information Scientist,* Vol. 2 (Philadelphia: ISI Press, 1977). Pp. 190–191.

Chapter Four

The Application of Citation Indexing to the Patent Literature

The *Patent Citation Index* section of *SCI* deserves a few separate words because it realizes only a part of what citation indexing can do to make the patent literature more useful.

The idea of producing a citation index of the patent literature dates back, as far as formal documentation is concerned, to 1949, when Arthur H. Seidel suggested, in the *Journal of the Patent Office Society,* establishing a card file of citation records (1). The file would contain a card for each issued patent, and the card would identify each subsequent issued patent that had cited the prior patent for one reason or another. Seidel's suggestion drew a formal endorsement from Harry C. Hart in a later issue of the *Journal of the Patent Office Society* (2). Besides endorsing the idea of a patent citation index, Hart revealed that he had suggested such a system two years earlier to the Patent Office, which had forwarded the suggestion, with expressed interest, to the publisher of *Shepard's Citations.* Not surprisingly, in view of the role *Shepard's Citations* has played in the law literature, Hart and Seidel were both patent attorneys. Unfortunately nothing came of either of their suggestions.

The first citation index to the patent literature was published in the 1964 edition of *SCI* (3). It was different from the current version of the *Patent Citation Index* in terms of its source-document coverage. It listed not only the references to patents that appeared in the journal literature (which is the extent of the source literature covered by the current *Patent Citation Index*), but also the references that appeared in patents that were issued during the indexed year. Source patents were identified in the *Patent Citation Index* by number and the name of the inventor. A complete bibliographic description, including all inventors, assignees, patent title, classification number, date of issue, and number of references in the patent, was available in the *Source Index* under the name of the principal inventor. This information gave the searcher a sound basis for deciding whether the search should be continued by examining the abstract of the patent's principal claim in the *Official Gazette,* looking up its abstract in *Chemical Abstracts,* or obtaining a copy of the patent itself.

This index came close to exploiting the full power of citation indexing for conducting searches of the patent literature. Its primary shortcoming was that its coverage of the references in the source patents was a bit less than complete. There are two kinds of references in patents: those occasionally provided by the inventor in the text of the application and disclosure and those provided by the patent examiner at the end of the patent. Those provided by the examiner constitute a large majority of the references, and they were the ones picked up by the early *SCI Patent Citation Index.* It was economically impractical to pick up the inventor's references because of the cost of extracting them from the text of the specification.

NATURE OF THE REFERENCES

The nature of the examiner's references makes an important contribution to the effectiveness of a citation index of the patent literature (4). They are generated as part of the search for prior-art that can be grounds for disallowing a claim, restricting the scope of the application, or supporting a legal point. The examiner's prior-art search is conducted within both legal and technological frameworks and is based not only on what is literally stated in the disclosure but also on what is implied. In other words, judgments of what constitutes anticipatory prior-art often are highly interpretive. For all these reasons, the scope of the prior-art search is, more often than not, quite broad, delving into a variety of subclasses, plus the examiner's own files and personal knowledge. Such a search produces references that index the patent in a way that an indexer could not and permit the citation index to reach across subclasses of the patent literature in the same way that it reaches across disciplines and specialties in the journal literature. In other words, a patent citation index can bring together patents that are unrelated in terms of their principal subject matter.

One example makes the point clear: a patent granted to Schoeller in 1934 on "Wetting and Dispersing Agents for Use in the Textile Industries" was classified under 260-458, carbocyclic or acyclic-carbon compounds, which are acyclic sulfuric acid esters. It was subsequently cross-referenced to a multitude of subclasses. The *CA* abstract for the patent was indexed under "dispersing agents" and "wetting agents." There was no organic compound indexing.

The first granted patent that cited Schoeller's work was issued to Lerner in 1948 on "condensation products of cholesteryl esters with polyethylene glycol & process for producing same." The principal class to which this patent was assigned was 260-397.2, which covers sterols (including vitamin D). Neither of these classes, nor any of the numerous subclasses to which the patent also was assigned, corresponded to any of the classifications in which the Schoeller patent was placed. Though it was not possible to determine all the categories under which the Lerner patent was indexed by *CA,* it was found to be indexed under "cholesterol esters" and "glycols, polyethylen." It was not indexed under "sterols."

The next patent to cite the Schoeller patent was issued, also in 1948, to Brown.

The Brown patent was on "waxy polyol ether-esters." Its principal class is 260-234, carbohydrate esters. It was cross-referenced to 260-210 and 260-410.6. Subclass 210 is glycosides, which is not applicable to either the Schoeller or the Lerner patent. Subclass 410.6 covers "synthetically produced higher fatty esters with acyclic polyoxy alcohols" and is applicable to the Schoeller patent, but not the one issued to Lerner. The Brown patent was extensively indexed in *CA* under "waxes," "ethers," "esters," "polyol," "hydroxy compounds," "palmitic acid," "stearic acid," "glycerol," "sorbitol," "mannitol," "D-glucose," "ethylene oxide," "propylene oxide," "lubricants," "cosmetics," "yarns," "sizes," "polishing materials," "coatings," and a number of organic compound headings.

The purpose of the example is not to criticize the Patent Office classification assignments or *CA* indexing, but merely to demonstrate how the scope of the prior-art searches performed by the patent examiners enables a citation index to bring together patents that are apparently unrelated by identifying relationships at a deeper level than the principal subject matter. By examining the wrappers of the patents in the example, we were able to identify the nature of the relationship in that particular case. The records of the Lerner patent show that the examiner did not find the Schoeller patent in the search of the patent file because he did not search any of the classes to which it was assigned. He found it in his own files or his memory or elsewhere. But he found it, and wrote, as a result, "Schoeller describes condensation of various acids, including stearic acid and its ester, with polyethylene glycols."

The examiner of the Brown patent stated in the wrapper, "Schoeller discloses the reaction of a carboxylic acid and diethylene glycol and ethylene oxide. There is no invention in substituting a trihydric alcohol, or a similar polyol, in place of the dihydric alcohol."

These comments show that the relationship between the three patents, then, is the condensation of acids with polyethelene glycols.

RELEVANCY AND UTILITY

The key question, of course, is whether the relationships identified by the citation index make the citing patent, which is the one retrieved, relevant to the interests of the searcher. There are no categorical answers to this question. There is not even an objective measure of relevancy. What one person considers relevant is dismissed by another as being irrelevant. Certainly, inventors and patent examiners have a difficult time agreeing on what is relevant.

The question is best answered by saying simply that a citation index of the patent literature identifies relationships between patents that are not identified any other way, and that these relationships permit the rapid retrieval of information that is relevant to the search a significant percentage of the time. Certainly there is no more useful tool for determining whether the technology disclosed in a particular patent has been modified, improved, or utilized in any way.

It is unfortunate that the Patent Office management has not followed up on any of the citation-index proposals that have been made to them. A citation index for the exclusive use of their examiners probably could be justified on a strict cost-benefit basis just by including all the references from the abandoned applications, which are never classified. The references to the patents that led to the decisions of abandonment represent an important store of information that probably would greatly reduce the number and the length of searches that the examiners must conduct.

As with most innovations, the initiative for developing a comprehensive citation index to the patent literature probably will come from private industry. ISI was forced to drop patents from its source coverage in 1966 because of the economic pressures involved in making *SCI* a comprehensive index to the journal literature. But that does not necessarily mean that we will not try again. In the meantime, a service called Search Check began offering, in 1976, citation searches of a patent file structured around the examiner references on all patents issued since 1947. So the idea of a comprehensive citation index to the patent literature, after lying dormant for a number of years, is once again showing signs of life. Maybe this time the circumstances will be more favorable to its evolution into the type of useful role such an index is capable of playing in managing the patent literature.

REFERENCES

1. **Seidel, A.H.** "Citation System for Patent Office." *Journal of the Patent Office Society,* **31**:554, 1949.
2. **Hart, H.C.** "Re: 'Citation System for Patent Office.' " *Journal of the Patent Office Society,* **31**:714, 1949.
3. **Garfield, E.** "Patent Citation Indexing and the Notions of Novelty, Similarity, and Relevance." *Journal of Chemical Documentation,* **6**:63–65, May 1966.
4. **Garfield, E.** "Breaking the Subject Index Barrier—A Citation Index for Chemical Patents." *Journal of the Patent Office Society,* **39**:583–95, August 1957.

Chapter Five

The Citation Index as a Search Tool

The introduction of *SCI* in 1964 was the first large-scale attempt to apply the citation-indexing concept to the problem of searching the scientific literature. Unfamiliar and unconventional as *SCI* was in terms of its organization and search methodology, it established itself rather quickly as an important literature-retrieval tool: librarians and scientists found that it identified a high percentage of the material published on a given subject and that a high percentage of what it identified was pertinent.

While many factors account for the rapid adoption of *SCI,* the most significant is the *Citation Index* and its use of reference citations as indexing terms. That single feature gives a citation index three unique functional characteristics that have a significant impact on search productivity and efficiency (see Chapter One). The first is a subject categorization of published material that is, semantically, both more precise and detailed. It is also semantically more stable and flexible than conventional subject indexing.

The other two characteristics are a matter of perspective. Citation indexing goes beyond the function of categorizing the literature. It explicitly reveals the intellectual relationships that exist between old and new literature. Each article is a published record of a particular event in the process of scientific development. The citation index shows the relationships between individual events at different points in time. That makes a citation index particularly effective in telling us what has happened to some idea or experiment—whether it has been confirmed, extended, improved, tried, or corrected.

The third characteristic stems from the second. The citation index focuses our attention on the relationships between scientific events. These relationships can, and frequently do identify the otherwise hidden linkages between events that make up what we call disciplines and specialties. Thus citation indexing inherently classifies the literature it covers.

The two characteristics of perspective, plus the semantically different and often superior method of categorizing material make the literature covered by a citation index highly accessible. Indeed, as the literature coverage becomes more comprehensive and multidisciplinary, the citation index becomes increasingly useful.

SAMPLE SEARCHES

In the absence of any truly definitive test of the search performance of a citation index, the best way of demonstrating its utility is by showing what some typical searches require in effort and produce in results (1-3). The following discussion does that, with a series of 10 sample searches conducted in *SCI*. Where appropriate, diagrams are used to show the search graphically (4). Each of the numbers in the diagrams represents a single paper, which may be either a reference citation (used as an indexing term to identify relevant papers), a source citation (identified as having cited a particular paper), or both (once a paper has been identified and judged, by the user, to be relevant, it can be used as a reference citation to extend the search). The arrows indicate the direction of the search from citation to citation. The dots represent a connection between the horizontal and vertical lines linking two citations. The year shown to the right of each citation is the year of publication; in the case of source citations, that year usually corresponds to the *SCI* edition in which the paper was identified, except for those instances when the journal issue involved was published too late to include in the proper edition. The citations listed beside the diagram are the *Source Index* descriptions of papers initially identified in the *Citation Index* lookup.

Bibliographic-Verification Search

Probably the most common type of search is the one concerned with citation verification. It may be a document that is cited in a manuscript being prepared for publication. Or it may be a paper that has been requested on an interlibrary loan. Verification is a major function in every scientific library. This type of search is limited when compared to the scope of the usual literature search. The objective is simply to find a known document. All that is required is to make sure that the document actually exists and to get an accurate, complete bibliographic description of it.

To see how a citation index performs on this kind of search, consider a librarian who has been asked to fill in a reference for a researcher writing a review paper on radioimmunoassays of estradiols, a class of hormonal steroids. The only information supplied is that the reference is to an article by G. E. Abraham in the *Journal of Clinical Endocrinology*. The researcher remembers neither the article title nor the year it was published.

The librarian's first job is to make sure the researcher's memory is accurate—that such a paper actually does exist. This is done by looking in the *Citation Index* of the 1975 edition of *SCI* under the name of Abraham, G. E. It identifies a sizable number of papers published by G. E. Abraham that were cited during 1975. Seven of them were published in the *Journal of Clinical Endocrinology*.

The next step in the search is to obtain the full citations of the seven from the

Source Index of the *SCI* editions involved (1969, 1971, 1972, and 1973). As shown in the sample that follows, those citations explicitly tell the librarian, by their titles, that the first six papers deal with radioimmunoassay work. The seventh may or may not, since the measurement technique is not identified in the title. Two of the six (#1 and #2) also specifically identify estradiol compounds in their titles, so one of them is likely to be the paper that the researcher wants to verify. Paper #7 also is a possibility, because estradiol may be one of the classes of steroids measured. The librarian probably would send the researcher all three citations. One almost certainly would be the missing reference; either, or both, of the other two might be useful additional references that the researcher will want to include.

1. ABRAHAM GE
   Solid-Phase Radioimmunoassay of Estradiol-17Beta
   J CLIN END   29   866   69   N   23R

2. ABRAHAM GE
   ODELL WD SWERDLOF RS HOPPER K—Simultaneous Radioimmunoassay of Plasma FSH, LH, Progesterone, 17-Hydroxyprogesterone, and Estradiol-17 Beta During Menstrual Cycle
   J CLIN END   34   312   72   49R   N2

3. ABRAHAM GE
   SWERDLOF R TULCHINS D ODELL W—Radioimmunoassay of Plasma Progesterone
   J CLIN END   32   619   71   12R   N5

4. ABRAHAM GE
   SWERDLOF RS TULCHINS D HOPPER K ODELL W— Radioimmunoassay of Plasma 17-Hydroxyprogesterone
   J CLIN END   33   42   71   8R   N1

5. ABRAHAM GE
   BUSTER JE KYLE FW CORRALES PC TELLER RC— Radioimmunoassay of Plasma Pregnenolone, 17-Hydroxypregnenolone and Dehydroepiandrosterone Under Various Physiological Conditions
   J CLIN END   37   140   73   N   15R   N1

6. ABRAHAM GE
   BUSTER JE KYLE FW CORRALES PC TELLER RC— Radioimmunoassay of Plasma Pregnenolone
   J CLIN END   37   40   73   13R   N1

7. ABRAHAM GE
   CHAKMAKJ ZH—Serum Steroid Levels During Menstrual-Cycle in a Bilaterally Adrenalectomized Woman
   J CLIN ENDOCR   37   581   73   26R   N4

44 *Citation Indexing*

1. DONNAN FG
   (GE) A THEORY OF MEMBRANE EQUILIBRIUM AND MEMBRANE POTENTIAL IN THE PRESENCE OF NON-DIALYZED ELECTROLYTES. A CONTRIBUTION TO PHYSICAL-CHEMICAL PHYSIOLOGY
   Z ELEKTROCHEM   17:572   11

2. ALEKSEEV OL
   (RS) STUDIES IN ELECTROOSMOSIS - CONDITIONS OF APPLICABILITY OF DONNAN EQUILIBRIUM FOR DETERMINATION OF EXCESS IONS CONCENTRATION IN ELECTRIC DOUBLE-LAYER
   KOLL ZH   35(4):726   73   N   9R

3. BARKER SA
   BURNS RF - REACTOR SEPARATORS INCORPORATING MEMBRANE-BOUND ENZYMES
   CHEM IND L   1973(16):801   73   N 11R

4. DOBOZY OK
   EXPLANATION OF MORDANT DYEING USING ELECTRONIC THEORY
   AM DYE REP   62(3):36   73   58R

5. GHOSH BN
   COLLOIDAL ELECTROLYTES - ATTEMPT TO ACCOUNT FOR OSMOTIC PRESSURE OF SOLS OF GUM ARABIC WHEN CONCENTRATION OF GUM AND THAT OF DIFFUSIBLE ELECTROLYTES ADDED VARY
   J IND CH S   50(2):114   73   9R

6. HOORNAER. P
   LEFEBVRE C   VANHAUTE A - HYPERFILTRATION BY DYNAMICALLY FORMED HYDROUS ZIRCONIUM OXIDE AND ALUMINUM-OXIDE MEMBRANES
   DESALINATN   11(3):315   72   12R

7. JANOSOVA J
   SENKYR J   BARTUSEK M - (CZ) ANALYTICAL USE OF SILVER-IODIDE MEMBRANE ELECTRODE
   CHEM LISTY   67(8):836   73   10R

8. TAMAMUSH. R
   EXPERIMENTAL STUDY OF GIBBS-DONNAN MEMBRANE EQUILIBRIA ACROSS PERMSELECTIVE MEMBRANES WHICH INVOLVE IONS OF STRONG INORGANIC ELECTROLYTES
   B CHEM S J   46(9):2701   73   44R

9. MCNICHOL. B
   IRISH BLOOD - AND ELECTROLYTES
   J IRISH MED   66(14):388   73   26R

10. WEISS RL
    MORRIS DR - CATIONS AND RIBOSOME STRUCTURE .1. EFFECTS ON 30S SUBUNIT OF SUBSTITUTING POLYAMINES FOR MAGNESIUM ION
    BIOCHEM   12(3):435   73   44R

11. WUHRMANN HR
    MORF WE   SIMON W - (GE) MODEL CALCULATION OF EMF AND ION SELECTIVITY OF MEMBRANE ELECTRODE MEASURING CHAINS
    HELV CHIM A   56(3):1011   73   60R

Figure 5.1 Eponymic search using *Citation Index.*

This search illustrates an important characteristic of *SCI.* Any annual edition contains, in the *Source Index,* a sizeable percentage of the significant papers published that year. But the *Citation Index* will contain a large percentage of the significant papers published in previous years. If one accepts the premise that a paper of even minor significance is cited at least once in 10 years, a 10-year span of *SCI,* two five-year cumulations, contains the citations of literally all the significant scientific literature that is known to exist. A single five-year cumulative edition of *SCI,* covering 1965–1969, contains approximately 6.4 million reference citations. A study conducted by Williams and Ping (5) showed that this was a large-enough percentage of the significant literature to include every one of almost 300 biomedical papers that were chosen at random for verification.

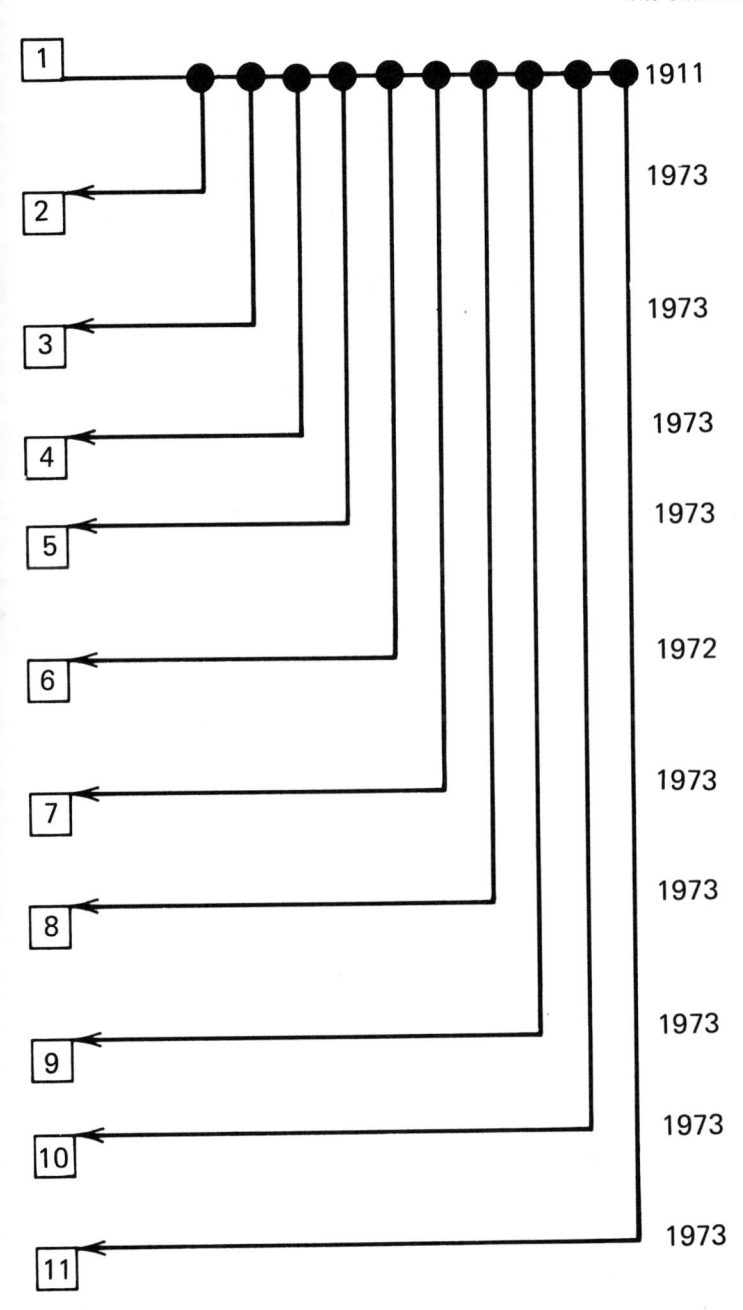

Eponymic Search

An eponymic search is one that involves information on a subject that is named for a person. The practice is quite common in physics, astronomy, chemistry, and, of course, in medicine. Diseases are frequently named for the people who initially discovered or defined them. Hodgkins disease and Bell's palsy are two examples. The problem with searching a subject given an eponymic name is that the name may not be accepted universally as an indexing term. In that case, material on the subject would be identified by generic terminology. Exactly what that terminology may be is something the researcher must determine, usually by trial and error. A citation index frequently enables a researcher to avoid this type of guessing exercise. All he does is use the citation of the primordial paper associated with the eponymic name as a search term. If the paper is not so fundamental that the practice of formal citation has been obliterated, the search generally identifies one or more relevant papers in a single lookup.

For example, consider a researcher doing studies on electro-osmosis. He wants to find out if, and what, work relevant to his own has been done with the Donnan equilibrium theory. The theory predicts the speed and rate at which ions migrate through a permeable membrane. Figure 5.1 shows what is involved in a citation search to answer that question. Using the original paper in which Donnan describes his theory (#1 in Figure 5.1) for a search of the *Citation Index* of the 1973 *SCI*, the researcher finds the 10 citing papers listed in Figure 5.1 (#2 through #11). Two of them, the papers by Alekseev (#2) and Tamamush (#8) are of obvious interest, just on the strength of their titles. The other eight may or may not be useful; the researcher would have to read them to fine out. If there was any need to continue the search, 53 references cited in the two relevant papers could be used as starting points for additional citation searches.

Methodology Search

Searches for information on methodological techniques have always been difficult in conventional subject indexes. Conventional indexing is based on the "main" theme of an article. The methods used are considered secondary to the "main" theme. On the other hand, authors frequently cite the original papers for the methods they use. This practice, saves authors the trouble of writing detailed explanations of their methods. Consequently a citation index is particularly effective for methodology searches.

Figure 5.2 shows a typical citation search for methodological information. A hypothetical example involves a researcher who is having trouble with the Barland method for isolating surface membranes from tissue-cultured cells. He turns to the literature to find out if his unsatisfactory results are typical or are the result of his applying the technique incorrectly. He looks up the Barland paper (#1 in Figure 5.2) in the *Citation Index* of the 1974 *SCI*. This identifies two papers whose titles are found in the *Source Index*. They describe the use of the method in two different applications. Presumably, they will give the researcher some useful information about what results to expect from the method, details about its application, or modifications that can make the method more effective.

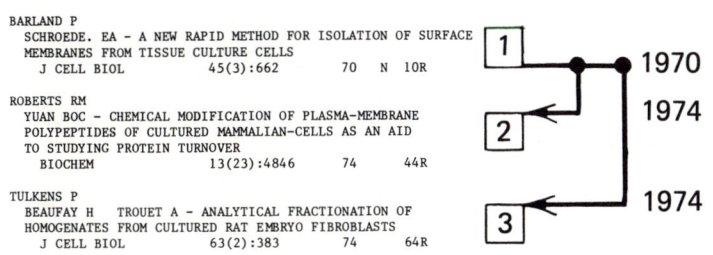

```
BARLAND P
   SCHROEDE. EA - A NEW RAPID METHOD FOR ISOLATION OF SURFACE
   MEMBRANES FROM TISSUE CULTURE CELLS
      J CELL BIOL         45(3):662        70    N   10R
ROBERTS RM
   YUAN BOC - CHEMICAL MODIFICATION OF PLASMA-MEMBRANE
   POLYPEPTIDES OF CULTURED MAMMALIAN-CELLS AS AN AID
   TO STUDYING PROTEIN TURNOVER
      BIOCHEM             13(23):4846      74        44R
TULKENS P
   BEAUFAY H   TROUET A - ANALYTICAL FRACTIONATION OF
   HOMOGENATES FROM CULTURED RAT EMBRYO FIBROBLASTS
      J CELL BIOL         63(2):383        74        64R
```

1 → 1970
2 ← 1974
3 ← 1974

Figure 5.2 Methodology search.

Follow-up Searches

The objective of many literature searches, particularly in the chemical and chemical-processing areas is to follow up an earlier development. Figure 5.3 shows a typical citation search to find out what has been learned about a reaction that involves the metal-hydride reduction of endodicyclopentadienone since it was initially described. The starting point in the search is the citation for the original paper, published in 1970, by W. L. Dilling (#1 in Figure 5.3). The *Citation Index* of the 1974 *SCI* identifies four papers under the reference citation. Their titles show that two of them (#3 and #5) describe the metal reduction of the same, or similar, compound as in the Dilling paper, so it can be assumed that they will be relevant. The other two papers (#2 and #4) would have to be read to determine their relevance.

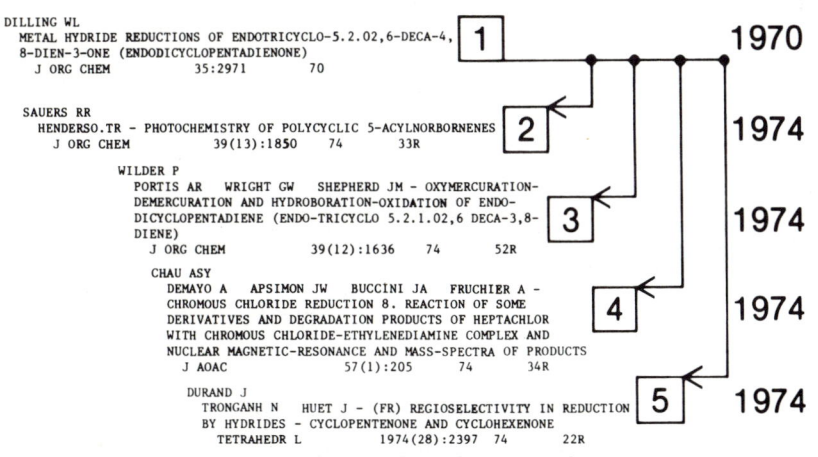

```
DILLING WL
   METAL HYDRIDE REDUCTIONS OF ENDOTRICYCLO-5.2.02,6-DECA-4,
   8-DIEN-3-ONE (ENDODICYCLOPENTADIENONE)
      J ORG CHEM          35:2971          70

   SAUERS RR
      HENDERSO.TR - PHOTOCHEMISTRY OF POLYCYCLIC 5-ACYLNORBORNENES
         J ORG CHEM       39(13):1850      74        33R

      WILDER P
         PORTIS AR   WRIGHT GW   SHEPHERD JM - OXYMERCURATION-
         DEMERCURATION AND HYDROBORATION-OXIDATION OF ENDO-
         DICYCLOPENTADIENE (ENDO-TRICYCLO 5.2.1.02,6 DECA-3,8-
         DIENE)
            J ORG CHEM    39(12):1636      74        52R

         CHAU ASY
            DEMAYO A    APSIMON JW   BUCCINI JA   FRUCHIER A -
            CHROMOUS CHLORIDE REDUCTION 8. REACTION OF SOME
            DERIVATIVES AND DEGRADATION PRODUCTS OF HEPTACHLOR
            WITH CHROMOUS CHLORIDE-ETHYLENEDIAMINE COMPLEX AND
            NUCLEAR MAGNETIC-RESONANCE AND MASS-SPECTRA OF PRODUCTS
               J AOAC     57(1):205        74        34R

            DURAND J
               TRONGANH N   HUET J - (FR) REGIOSELECTIVITY IN REDUCTION
               BY HYDRIDES - CYCLOPENTENONE AND CYCLOHEXENONE
                  TETRAHEDR L  1974(28):2397  74     22R
```

1 → 1970
2 ← 1974
3 ← 1974
4 ← 1974
5 ← 1974

Figure 5.3 Reaction follow-up search.

More extensive and complex is the example, shown in Figure 5.4, of a search to see what follow-up work has been done on a compound, trimethoprim, since it was announced. The search starts in the 1965 *SCI* on the citation for the 1962 announcement paper (#1 in Figure 5.4) and covers a span of nine years. Paper #1 identifies papers #2, #3, #4, #7, #8, #9, #12, #13, #14, and #16 in the 1965–1974 editions of

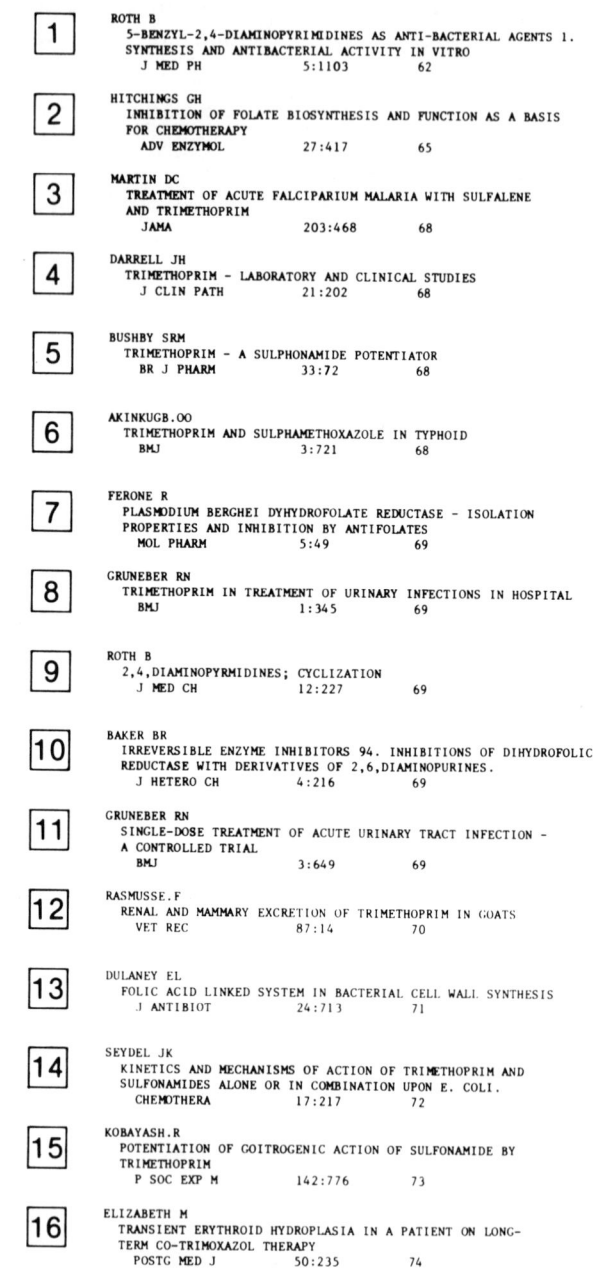

1 ROTH B
 5-BENZYL-2,4-DIAMINOPYRIMIDINES AS ANTI-BACTERIAL AGENTS 1.
 SYNTHESIS AND ANTIBACTERIAL ACTIVITY IN VITRO
   J MED PH   5:1103   62

2 HITCHINGS GH
 INHIBITION OF FOLATE BIOSYNTHESIS AND FUNCTION AS A BASIS
 FOR CHEMOTHERAPY
   ADV ENZYMOL   27:417   65

3 MARTIN DC
 TREATMENT OF ACUTE FALCIPARIUM MALARIA WITH SULFALENE
 AND TRIMETHOPRIM
   JAMA   203:468   68

4 DARRELL JH
 TRIMETHOPRIM - LABORATORY AND CLINICAL STUDIES
   J CLIN PATH   21:202   68

5 BUSHBY SRM
 TRIMETHOPRIM - A SULPHONAMIDE POTENTIATOR
   BR J PHARM   33:72   68

6 AKINKUGB.OO
 TRIMETHOPRIM AND SULPHAMETHOXAZOLE IN TYPHOID
   BMJ   3:721   68

7 FERONE R
 PLASMODIUM BERGHEI DYHYDROFOLATE REDUCTASE - ISOLATION
 PROPERTIES AND INHIBITION BY ANTIFOLATES
   MOL PHARM   5:49   69

8 GRUNEBER RN
 TRIMETHOPRIM IN TREATMENT OF URINARY INFECTIONS IN HOSPITAL
   BMJ   1:345   69

9 ROTH B
 2,4,DIAMINOPYRMIDINES; CYCLIZATION
   J MED CH   12:227   69

10 BAKER BR
 IRREVERSIBLE ENZYME INHIBITORS 94. INHIBITIONS OF DIHYDROFOLIC
 REDUCTASE WITH DERIVATIVES OF 2,6,DIAMINOPURINES.
   J HETERO CH   4:216   69

11 GRUNEBER RN
 SINGLE-DOSE TREATMENT OF ACUTE URINARY TRACT INFECTION -
 A CONTROLLED TRIAL
   BMJ   3:649   69

12 RASMUSSE.F
 RENAL AND MAMMARY EXCRETION OF TRIMETHOPRIM IN GOATS
   VET REC   87:14   70

13 DULANEY EL
 FOLIC ACID LINKED SYSTEM IN BACTERIAL CELL WALL SYNTHESIS
   J ANTIBIOT   24:713   71

14 SEYDEL JK
 KINETICS AND MECHANISMS OF ACTION OF TRIMETHOPRIM AND
 SULFONAMIDES ALONE OR IN COMBINATION UPON E. COLI.
   CHEMOTHERA   17:217   72

15 KOBAYASH.R
 POTENTIATION OF GOITROGENIC ACTION OF SULFONAMIDE BY
 TRIMETHOPRIM
   P SOC EXP M   142:776   73

16 ELIZABETH M
 TRANSIENT ERYTHROID HYDROPLASIA IN A PATIENT ON LONG-
 TERM CO-TRIMOXAZOL THERAPY
   POSTG MED J   50:235   74

Figure 5.4 Compound follow-up search.

SCI. When the search is continued on paper #2 in the 1966–1974 editions of *SCI,* papers #7, #9, and #13 are identified a second time, and three new papers (#5, #10, and #15) are discovered. Searches on papers #3 and #4 during the years 1969 through 1974 produce nothing of interest. A search on paper #5 during the years 1969 through 1974 identifies papers #8, #9, #12, #13, #14, #15, and #16 again and uncovers paper #6 for the first time. Papers #6 and #7 lead to nothing in a search of the

The Citation Index as a Search Tool 49

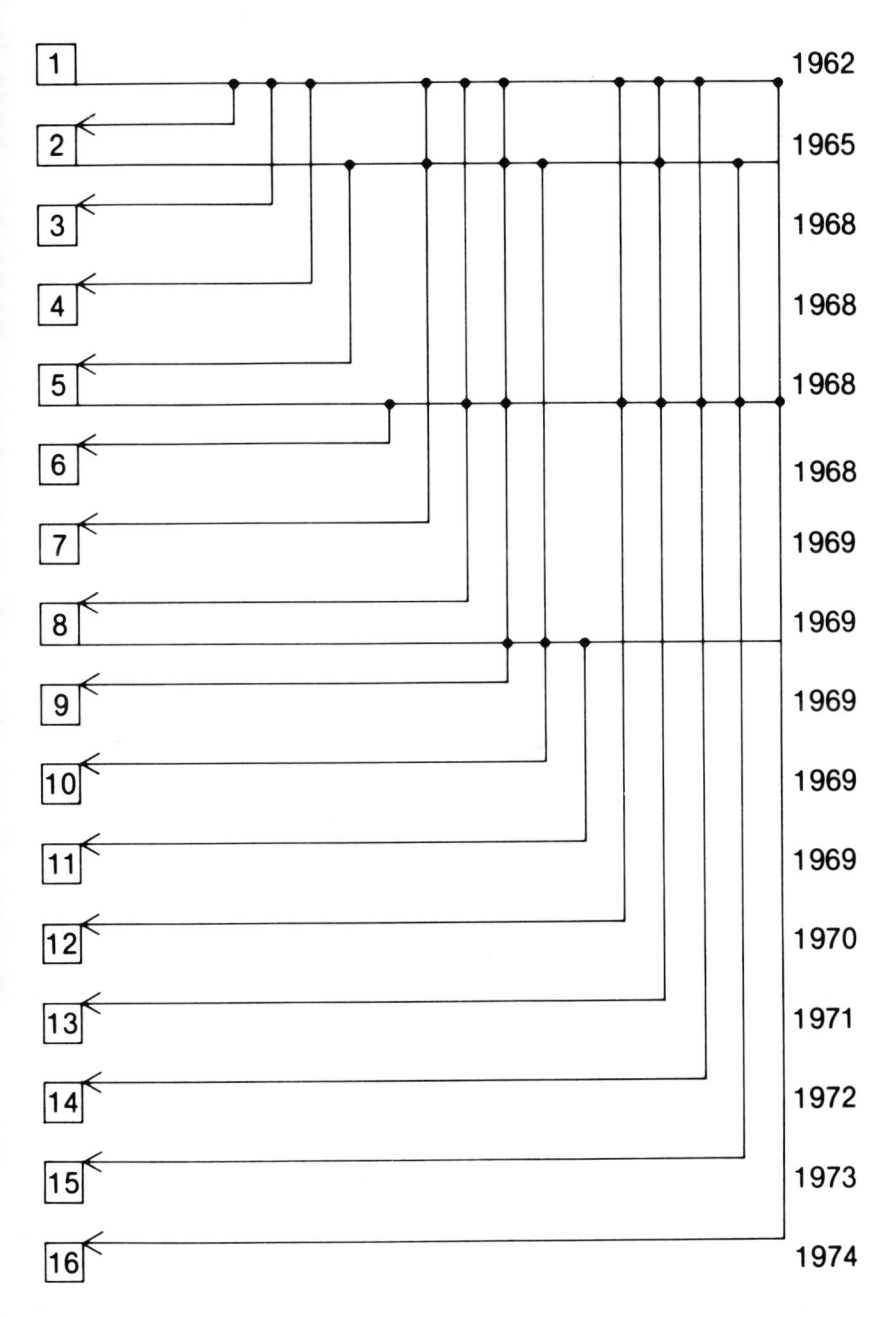

1	1962
2	1965
3	1968
4	1968
5	1968
6	1968
7	1969
8	1969
9	1969
10	1969
11	1969
12	1970
13	1971
14	1972
15	1973
16	1974

years 1970 through 1974. A search on paper #8 during the years 1969 through 1974 identifies #9 and #10 again and #11 for the first time. Papers #9 through #15 produce no new additions to the bibliography when they are used as search points for the years 1969 through 1974. So the search trail ends, though new ones could be started with likely references selected from any of the papers obtained.

The search results consist of a bibliography of 15 papers. They trace the development of trimethoprim through the typical pharmaceutical stages of defining the

```
1. BARDEEN JM
     KERR METRIC BLACK HOLES
        NATURE                  226(5240):64      70         9R

2. CHANDRAS. S
     DEVELOPMENT OF GENERAL RELATIVITY
        NATURE                  252(5478):15      74         17R

3. CHRZANOW. PL
     MISNER CW - GEODESIC SYNCHROTRON RADIATION IN KERR
     GEOMETRY BY METHOD OF ASYMPTOTICALLY FACTORIZED GREENS
     FUNCTIONS
        PHYS REV D              10(6):1701        74         46R

4. DEFELICE F
     NOBILI L    CALVANI M - BLACK-HOLE PHYSICS - SOME EFFECTS
     OF GRAVITY ON RADIATION EMISSION
        ASTRON ASTR             30(1):111         74         28R

5. PRESS WH
     BLACK HOLE PERTURBATIONS - OVERVIEW
        ANN NY ACAD             224(DEC14):272    73         38R

6. PAPINI G
     GRAVITATIONAL RADIATION AND ITS DETECTION
        CAN J PHYS              52(10):880        74         157R

7. SHAPIRO SL
     ACCRETION ONTO BLACK HOLES - EMERGENT RADIATION SPECTRUM 3
     ROTATING (KERR) BLACK-HOLES
        ASTROPHYS J             189(2):343        74         20R

8. THORNE KS
     DISK-ACCRETION ONTO A BLACK-HOLE 2 EVOLUTION OF HOLE
        ASTROPHYS J             191(2):507        74         19R

9. WALD R
     GEDANKEN EXPERIMENTS TO DESTROY A BLACK-HOLE
        ANN PHYSICS             82(2):548         74         24R
```

Figure 5.5 Concept search.

mechanism of biological activity, in vitro testing, clinical testing, and study of toxicity and side effects.

Concept Search

Figure 5.5 is a typical citation search for information on a concept. Such a search, when possible at all by traditional methods, may require numerous lookups. The variety and changes of terminology in most concepts can be quite tricky. The concept in this example is the use of Kerr geometry to describe the astronomical phenomenon of black holes. The researcher is presumed to know nothing more about the subject of black holes than what he had read in a short paper by J. M. Bardeen that was published in *Nature* in 1970. He is interested in identifying the general literature on black holes, but he is especially interested in the use of Kerr geometry to study the phenomenon. Starting with the only paper he knows, the Bardeen paper (#1 in Figure 5.5), he conducts a simple citation search in the 1974 *SCI*. The *Citation Index* section identifies eight papers, six of which (#3, #4, #5, #7, #8, and #9), from their descriptions in the *Source Index,* seem to be relevant. The other two (#2 and #6)

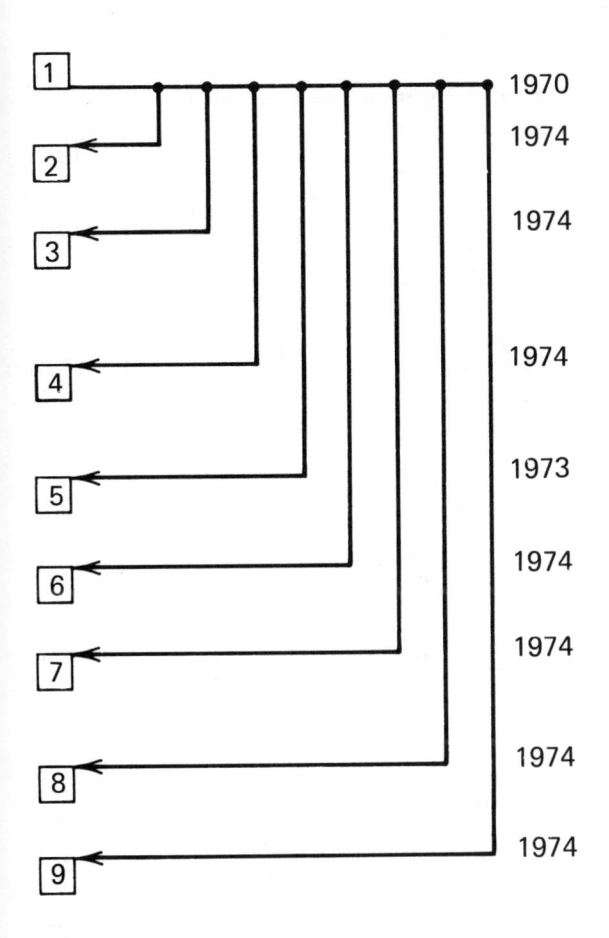

```
1 ────•──•──•──•──•──•──  1970
                          1974
2 ←────┘  │  │  │  │  │
          │  │  │  │  │   1974
3 ←───────┘  │  │  │  │
             │  │  │  │   1974
4 ←──────────┘  │  │  │
                │  │  │   1973
5 ←─────────────┘  │  │
                   │  │   1974
6 ←────────────────┘  │
                      │   1974
7 ←───────────────────┘
                          1974
8 ←───────────────────────┘
                          1974
9 ←───────────────────────┘
```

are at least on related subjects. Since they cite the Bardeen paper, they probably will be useful. Three of the papers (#3, #5, and #6) contain a total of 241 references. These are likely to cover a significant portion, if not all of the literature on both black holes and the role of Kerr geometry in defining them.

Specific Question Search

Searches concerned with answering a specific question usually require sifting through a lot of material. It can be very time-consuming to identify those papers that deal specifically with the question. Figure 5.6 show how a citation index performs on this kind of problem. The question is whether Rae's theory predicting the existence of repetitive DNA sequences has been confirmed. The search is conducted in the 1973 *Citation Index* of *SCI*. The citation for Rae's original paper (#1 in Figure 5.6) is the starting point. Fifteen papers are identified as having cited the Rae paper. Five of them (#3, #8, #10, #12, and #15) have titles that indicate that they are describing repetitive DNA sequences in one type of organism or another. Thus the question is answered, without even consulting the papers themselves.

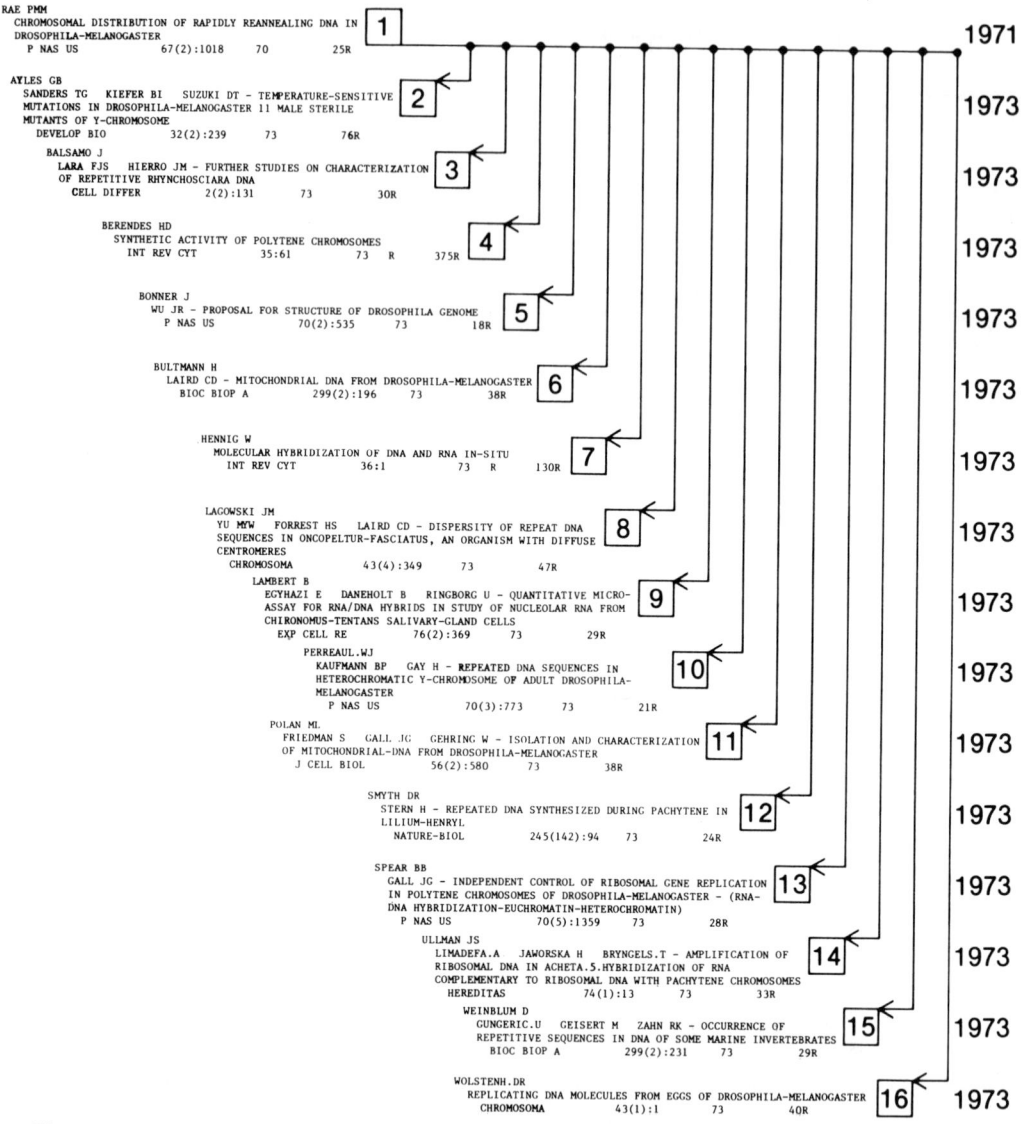

```
RAE PMM
    CHROMOSOMAL DISTRIBUTION OF RAPIDLY REANNEALING DNA IN
  DROSOPHILA-MELANOGASTER                                    [1]                                              1971
    P NAS US          67(2):1018      70        25R

  AYLES GB
    SANDERS TG   KIEFER BI   SUZUKI DT - TEMPERATURE-SENSITIVE
  MUTATIONS IN DROSOPHILA-MELANOGASTER 11 MALE STERILE        [2]                                             1973
  MUTANTS OF Y-CHROMOSOME
    DEVELOP BIO       32(2):239        73        76R

        BALSAMO J
          LARA FJS   HIERRO JM - FURTHER STUDIES ON CHARACTERIZATION    [3]                                   1973
        OF REPETITIVE RHYNCHOSCIARA DNA
          CELL DIFFER       2(2):131        73        30R

            BERENDES HD
              SYNTHETIC ACTIVITY OF POLYTENE CHROMOSOMES              [4]                                     1973
              INT REV CYT        35:61        73    R      375R

              BONNER J
                WU JR - PROPOSAL FOR STRUCTURE OF DROSOPHILA GENOME        [5]                                1973
                P NAS US         70(2):535      73         18R

                BULTMANN H
                  LAIRD CD - MITOCHONDRIAL DNA FROM DROSOPHILA-MELANOGASTER  [6]                              1973
                  BIOC BIOP A        299(2):196      73        38R

                    HENNIG W
                      MOLECULAR HYBRIDIZATION OF DNA AND RNA IN-SITU       [7]                                1973
                      INT REV CYT       36:1         73     R    130R

                    LAGOWSKI JM
                      YU MYW    FORREST HS    LAIRD CD - DISPERSITY OF REPEAT DNA   [8]                       1973
                    SEQUENCES IN ONCOPELTUR-FASCIATUS, AN ORGANISM WITH DIFFUSE
                    CENTROMERES
                      CHROMOSOMA        43(4):349      73       47R

                      LAMBERT B
                        EGYHAZI E   DANEHOLT B   RINGBORG U - QUANTITATIVE MICRO-    [9]                      1973
                      ASSAY FOR RNA/DNA HYBRIDS IN STUDY OF NUCLEOLAR RNA FROM
                      CHIRONOMUS-TENTANS SALIVARY-GLAND CELLS
                        EXP CELL RE       76(2):369      73       29R

                        PERREAUL.WJ
                          KAUFMANN BP   GAY H - REPEATED DNA SEQUENCES IN    [10]                             1973
                        HETEROCHROMATIC Y-CHROMOSOME OF ADULT DROSOPHILA-
                        MELANOGASTER
                          P NAS US       70(3):773      73       21R

                        POLAN ML
                          FRIEDMAN S   GALL JG   GEHRING W - ISOLATION AND CHARACTERIZATION  [11]             1973
                        OF MITOCHONDRIAL-DNA FROM DROSOPHILA-MELANOGASTER
                          J CELL BIOL      56(2):580      73       38R

                          SMYTH DR
                            STERN H - REPEATED DNA SYNTHESIZED DURING PACHYTENE IN    [12]                    1973
                          LILIUM-HENRYI
                            NATURE-BIOL       245(142):94      73       24R

                            SPEAR BB
                              GALL JG - INDEPENDENT CONTROL OF RIBOSOMAL GENE REPLICATION  [13]               1973
                            IN POLYTENE CHROMOSOMES OF DROSOPHILA-MELANOGASTER - (RNA-
                            DNA HYBRIDIZATION-EUCHROMATIN-HETEROCHROMATIN)
                              P NAS US        70(5):1359     73       28R

                              ULLMAN JS
                                LIMADEFA.A   JAWORSKA H   BRYNGELS.T - AMPLIFICATION OF   [14]                1973
                              RIBOSOMAL DNA IN ACHETA.5.HYBRIDIZATION OF RNA
                              COMPLEMENTARY TO RIBOSOMAL DNA WITH PACHYTENE CHROMOSOMES
                                HEREDITAS        74(1):13       73       33R

                                WEINBLUM D
                                  GUNGERIC.U   GEISERT M   ZAHN RK - OCCURRENCE OF     [15]                   1973
                                REPETITIVE SEQUENCES IN DNA OF SOME MARINE INVERTEBRATES
                                  BIOC BIOP A        299(2):231      73       29R

                                  WOLSTENH.DR
                                    REPLICATING DNA MOLECULES FROM EGGS OF DROSOPHILA-MELANOGASTER  [16]      1973
                                    CHROMOSOMA        43(1):1       73       40R
```

Figure 5.6 Specific-question search.

MultiDisciplinary Search

There are two different types of multidisciplinary searches. The most common is when the search is expected to cover more than one discipline, which usually requires more than one discipline-oriented index. How that kind of search can be handled by a single, multidisciplinary citation index is shown in Figure 5.7.

In this example, a manufacturer of chemical additives that are used for the cryogenic storage of biological material is interested in some basic market research. Specifically, he wants to know if his products are being applied more broadly than expected. He also asks how well they are performing in biological and agricultural

The Citation Index as a Search Tool 53

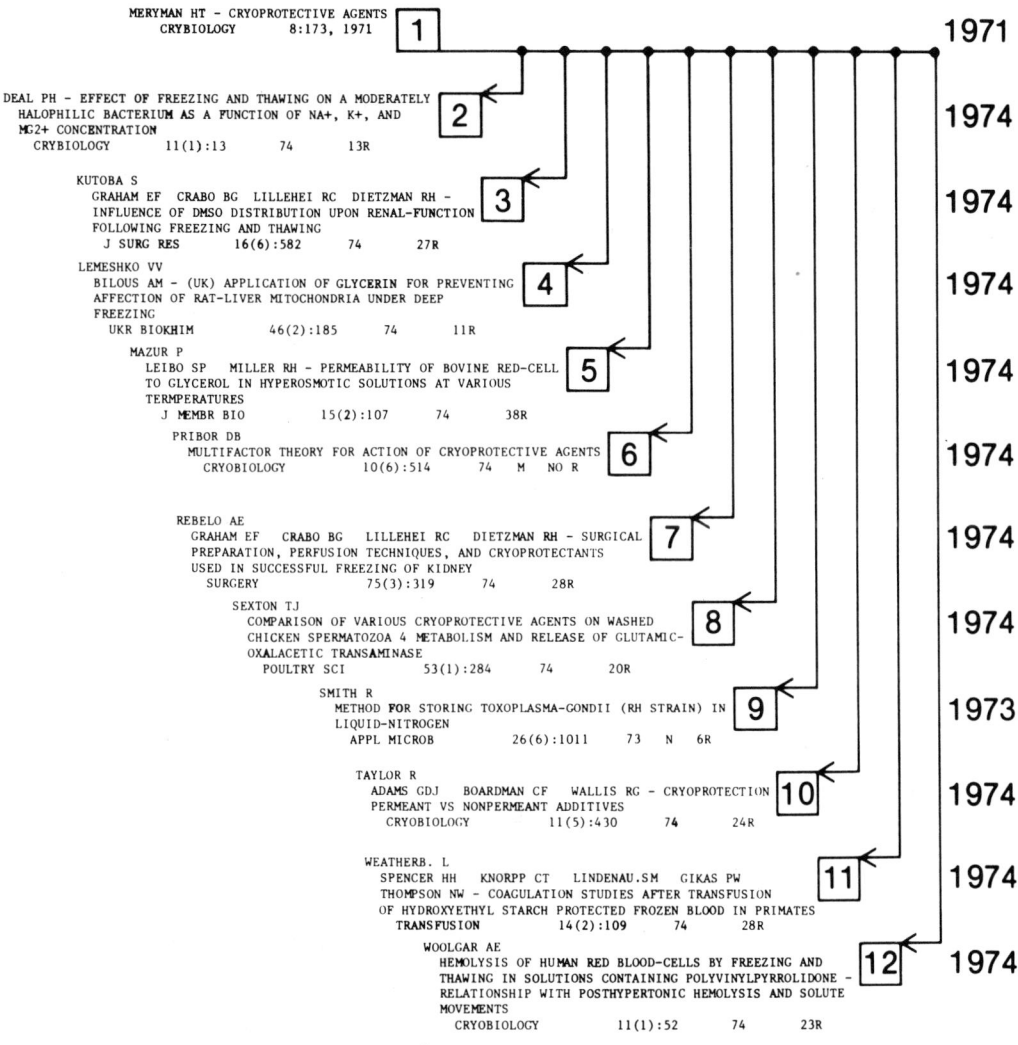

```
MERYMAN HT - CRYOPROTECTIVE AGENTS
    CRYBIOLOGY        8:173, 1971        [1]                                    1971

DEAL PH - EFFECT OF FREEZING AND THAWING ON A MODERATELY
HALOPHILIC BACTERIUM AS A FUNCTION OF NA+, K+, AND    [2]                       1974
MG2+ CONCENTRATION
    CRYBIOLOGY      11(1):13      74      13R

    KUTOBA S
      GRAHAM EF   CRABO BG   LILLEHEI RC   DIETZMAN RH -
      INFLUENCE OF DMSO DISTRIBUTION UPON RENAL-FUNCTION  [3]                   1974
      FOLLOWING FREEZING AND THAWING
          J SURG RES      16(6):582      74      27R
    LEMESHKO VV
      BILOUS AM - (UK) APPLICATION OF GLYCERIN FOR PREVENTING  [4]              1974
      AFFECTION OF RAT-LIVER MITOCHONDRIA UNDER DEEP
      FREEZING
          UKR BIOKHIM      46(2):185      74      11R
        MAZUR P
          LEIBO SP   MILLER RH - PERMEABILITY OF BOVINE RED-CELL  [5]           1974
          TO GLYCEROL IN HYPEROSMOTIC SOLUTIONS AT VARIOUS
          TERMPERATURES
              J MEMBR BIO      15(2):107      74      38R
          PRIBOR DB
            MULTIFACTOR THEORY FOR ACTION OF CRYOPROTECTIVE AGENTS  [6]         1974
                CRYOBIOLOGY      10(6):514      74    M    NO R

        REBELO AE
          GRAHAM EF   CRABO BG   LILLEHEI RC   DIETZMAN RH - SURGICAL  [7]      1974
          PREPARATION, PERFUSION TECHNIQUES, AND CRYOPROTECTANTS
          USED IN SUCCESSFUL FREEZING OF KIDNEY
              SURGERY      75(3):319      74      28R
              SEXTON TJ
                COMPARISON OF VARIOUS CRYOPROTECTIVE AGENTS ON WASHED  [8]      1974
                CHICKEN SPERMATOZOA 4 METABOLISM AND RELEASE OF GLUTAMIC-
                OXALACETIC TRANSAMINASE
                    POULTRY SCI      53(1):284      74      20R
                SMITH R
                  METHOD FOR STORING TOXOPLASMA-GONDII (RH STRAIN) IN  [9]      1973
                  LIQUID-NITROGEN
                      APPL MICROB      26(6):1011      73    N    6R
                  TAYLOR R
                    ADAMS GDJ   BOARDMAN CF   WALLIS RG - CRYOPROTECTION  [10]  1974
                    PERMEANT VS NONPERMEANT ADDITIVES
                        CRYOBIOLOGY      11(5):430      74      24R
                  WEATHERB. L
                    SPENCER HH   KNORPP CT   LINDENAU.SM   GIKAS PW    [11]     1974
                    THOMPSON NW - COAGULATION STUDIES AFTER TRANSFUSION
                    OF HYDROXYETHYL STARCH PROTECTED FROZEN BLOOD IN PRIMATES
                        TRANSFUSION      14(2):109      74      28R
                    WOOLGAR AE
                      HEMOLYSIS OF HUMAN RED BLOOD-CELLS BY FREEZING AND  [12]  1974
                      THAWING IN SOLUTIONS CONTAINING POLYVINYLPYRROLIDONE -
                      RELATIONSHIP WITH POSTHYPERTONIC HEMOLYSIS AND SOLUTE
                      MOVEMENTS
                          CRYOBIOLOGY      11(1):52      74      23R
```

Figure 5.7 Overt multidisciplinary search.

applications. The citation search conducted to answer these questions starts with a single, known paper by H. T. Meryman (#1 in Figure 5.7) that was published in 1971. The 1974 *SCI Citation Index* entry for that paper identifies the 11 citing papers listed in Figure 5.7. The papers identified were published in a fairly broad range of journals: *Cryobiology, Journal of Surgical Research, Ukrainskii Biokhimicheskii Zhurnal, Journal of Membrane Biology, Surgery, Poultry Science, Applied Microbiology,* and *Transfusion.* Moreover, the range of specialties from which the papers come is equally as broad: two are on bacterial storage, two on renal function and the preservation of kidneys, one on mitochondria, three on the preservation and storage of red blood cells, two on the performance of cryoprotective agents, and one on the preservation of sperm.

Finding the same diverse range of papers in conventional indexes would have required separate searches under two or three main subject headings in at least two,

54 *Citation Indexing*

and most likely three, separate indexes. In addition, the selection of appropriate subject headings for each of the searches would have called for a thorough understanding of the linguistic structure of each index. A fair estimate of the time needed to conduct such a search in conventional indexes is three hours. The citation search shown in Figure 5.7 took 20 minutes.

The second kind of multidisciplinary search is one that is focused on the literature of a single discipline or specialty, but that turns out to uncover something useful from outside that literature. This type of search, of course, is unique to a multidisciplinary citation index.

Figure 5.8 is an example of such a search. It might be conducted by a plant geneticist writing a state-of-the-art review of plant hybridization. One of the references he collects is to a 1972 paper by P. S. Carlson on interspecific hybridization, which usually cannot be achieved by conventional sexual methods of reproduction. Using the citation of that paper (#1 in Figure 5.8) as a search term in the 1974 *SCI Citation Index,* the researcher finds 42 papers. Six of them (*#12, #20, #23, #24, #25,* and *#41*) have titles that indicate they are on the subject of the genetic fusion of different species. The titles of another seven (*#2, #7, #8, #14, #29, #36,* and *#43*) imply that they may deal with the same subject. The remaining 29 papers appear to deal mostly with the techniques of separation, fusion, and regeneration that would have to be perfected before interspecific plant hybrids can actually be created. In reading the papers, he finds that the work has its origins in the viral immunology research being done in molecular biology, a specialty that, until this development, had little to do with applied plant genetics.

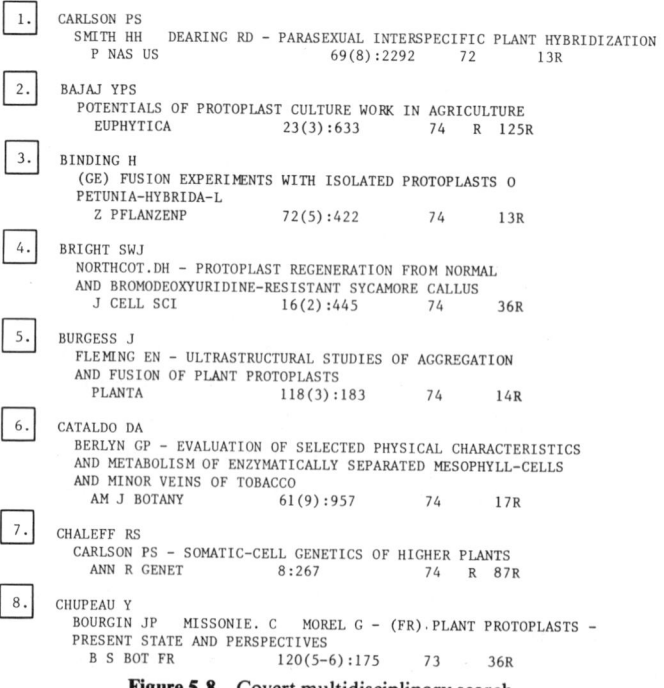

```
1.  CARLSON PS
      SMITH HH    DEARING RD - PARASEXUAL INTERSPECIFIC PLANT HYBRIDIZATION
        P NAS US                69(8):2292        72           13R

2.  BAJAJ YPS
      POTENTIALS OF PROTOPLAST CULTURE WORK IN AGRICULTURE
        EUPHYTICA               23(3):633         74       R   125R

3.  BINDING H
      (GE) FUSION EXPERIMENTS WITH ISOLATED PROTOPLASTS O
      PETUNIA-HYBRIDA-L
        Z PFLANZENP             72(5):422         74           13R

4.  BRIGHT SWJ
      NORTHCOT.DH - PROTOPLAST REGENERATION FROM NORMAL
      AND BROMODEOXYURIDINE-RESISTANT SYCAMORE CALLUS
        J CELL SCI              16(2):445         74           36R

5.  BURGESS J
      FLEMING EN - ULTRASTRUCTURAL STUDIES OF AGGREGATION
      AND FUSION OF PLANT PROTOPLASTS
        PLANTA                  118(3):183        74           14R

6.  CATALDO DA
      BERLYN GP - EVALUATION OF SELECTED PHYSICAL CHARACTERISTICS
      AND METABOLISM OF ENZYMATICALLY SEPARATED MESOPHYLL-CELLS
      AND MINOR VEINS OF TOBACCO
        AM J BOTANY             61(9):957         74           17R

7.  CHALEFF RS
      CARLSON PS - SOMATIC-CELL GENETICS OF HIGHER PLANTS
        ANN R GENET             8:267             74       R   87R

8.  CHUPEAU Y
      BOURGIN JP   MISSONIE. C   MOREL G - (FR) PLANT PROTOPLASTS -
      PRESENT STATE AND PERSPECTIVES
        B S BOT FR              120(5-6):175      73           36R
```

Figure 5.8 Covert multidisciplinary search.

9. CHUPEAU Y
   BOURGIN JP   MISSONIE. C   DORION N   MOREL G - (FR)
   PREPARATION AND CULTURE OF VARIOUS NICOTIANA PROTOPLASTS
      CR AC SCI D   278(12):1565   74   11R

10. COCKING EC
    POWER JB   EVANS PK   SAFWAT F   FREARSON EM   HAYWARD C
    BERRY SF   GEORGE D - NATURALLY OCCURRING DIFFERENTIAL DRUG
    SENSITIVITIES OF CULTURED, PLANT PROTOPLASTS
       PLANT SCI L   3(5):341   74   24R

11. CONSTABE. F
    KIRKPATR. JW   GAMBORG OL - CALLUS FORMATION FROM
    MESOPHYLL PROTOPLASTS OF PISUM-SATIVUM
       CAN J BOTAN   51(11):2105   73   8R

12. DULIEU H
    COMBINATION OF CELL AND TISSUE-CULTURE WITH MUTAGENESIS
    FOR INDUCTION AND ISOLATION OF MORPHOLOGICAL OR DEVEL-
    OPMENTAL MUTANTS
       PHYTOMORPH   22(3-4):283   72   76R

13. FOWKE LC
    BECHHANS. CW   GAMBORG OL - ELECTRON-MICROSCOPIC
    OBSERVATIONS OF CELL REGENERATION FROM CULTURED
    PROTOPLASTS OF AMMI-VISNAGA
       PROTOPLASMA   79(1-2):235   74   43R

14. GAMBORG OL
    MILLER RA - ISOLATION, CULTURE, AND USES OF PLANT
    PROTOPLASTS
       CAN J BOTAN   51(10):1795   73   42R

15. GILES KL
    COMPLEMENTATION BY PROTOPLAST FUSION USING MUTANT
    STRAINS OF MAIZE
       PLANT CEL P   15(2):281   74   4R

16. GLIMELIU. K
    WALLIN A   ERIKSSON T - AGGLUTINATING EFFECTS OF
    CONCANAVALIN-A ON ISOLATED PROTOPLASTS OF DAUCUS-
    CAROTA
       PHYSL PLANT   31(3):225   74   35R

17. GREEN CE
    PHILLIPS RL   KLEESE RA - TISSUE-CULTURES OF MAIZE
    (ZEA-MAYS-L) - INITIATION, MAINTENANCE, AND ORGANIC
    GROWTH-FACTORS
       CROP SCI   14(1):54   74   36R

18. GROUT BWW
    COUTTS RHA - ADDITIVES FOR ENHANCEMENT OF FUSION AND
    ENDOCYTOSIS IN HIGHER PLANT PROTOPLASTS - ELECTROPHORETIC
    STUDY
       PLANT SCI L   2(6):397   74   14R

19. HANKE DE
    NORTHCOT. DH - CELL-WALL FORMATION BY SOYBEAN CALLUS
    PROTOPLASTS
       J CELL SCI   14(1):29   74   34R

20. HEYN RF
    RORSCH A   SCHILPER. RA - PROSPECTS IN GENETIC ENGINEERING
    OF PLANTS
       Q REV BIOPH   7(1):35   74   R 92R

21. HOTTA Y
    MIKSCHE JP - RIBOSOMAL-RNA GENES IN 4 CONIFEROUS SPECIES
       CELL DIFFER   2(6):299   74   23R

22. KAMEYA T
    EFFECTS OF GELATIN ON AGGREGATION OF PROTOPLASTS FROM
    HIGHER-PLANTS
       PLANTA   115(1):77   73   N 7R

23. KANAZAWA KI
    IMAI A - PARASEXUAL-SEXUAL HYBRIDIZATION-HERITABLE
    TRANSFORMATION OF GERM-CELLS IN CHIMERIC MICE
       JAP J EXP M   44(3):227   74   33R

24. KAO KN
    MICHAYLU. MR - METHOD FOR HIGH-FREQUENCY INTERGENERI
    FUSION OF PLANT PROTOPLASTS
       PLANTA   115(4):355   74   18R

Figure 5.8 (continued)

25. KAO KN
    CONSTABE. F   MICHAYLU MR   GAMBORG OL – PLANT PROTOPLAST
    FUSION AND GROWTH OF INTERGENERIC HYBRI CELLS
        PLANTA   120(3):215   74   17R

26. KARTHA KK
    MICHAYLU. MR   KAO KN   GAMBORG OL   CONSTABE. F
    CALLUS FORMATION AND PLANT REGENERATION FROM
    MESOPHYLL PROTOPLASTS OF RAPE PLANTS (BRASSICA-
    NAPUS L CV ZEPHYR)
        PLANT SCI L   3(4):265   74   26R

27. KAWASHIM. N
    TANABE Y   IWAI S – SIMILARITIES AND DIFFERENCES IN
    PRIMARY STRUCTURE OF FRACTION 1 PROTEINS IN GENUS-
    NICOTIANA
        BIOC BIOP A   371(2):417   74   16R

28. KELLER WA
    MELCHERS G – EFFECT OF HIGH PH AND CALCIUM ON TOBACCO
    LEAF PROTOPLAST FUSION
        Z NATURFO C   C 28(11-1):737   73   32R

29. MCCOMB JA
    NEW TECHNIQUES FOR PLANT BREEDING
        J AUS I AGR   40(1):3   74   170R

30. POIRIERH. S
    RAO PS   HARADA H – CULTURE OF MESOPHYLL PROTOPLAST
    AND STEM SEGMENTS OF ANTIRRHINUM-MAJUS (SNAPDRAGON) –
    GROWTH AND ORGANIZATION OF EMBRYOIDS
        J EXP BOT   25(87):752   74   14R

31. PRAT R
    (FR) STUDIES ON PROTOPLASTS .2. ULTRASTRUCTURE OF
    ISOLATED PROTOPLAST AND CELL-WALL REGENERATION
        J MICROSCOP   18(1):65   73   67R

32. SAKANO K
    KUNG SD   WILDMAN SG – IDENTIFICATION OF SEVERAL
    CHLOROPLAST DNA GENES WHICH CODE FOR LARGE SUBUNIT
    OF NICOTIANA FRACTION 1 PROTEINS
        MOL G GENET   130(2):91   74   9R

33. SCHIEDER O
    (GE) FUSION EXPERIMENTS WITH PROTOPLASTS OF MUTANTS
    FROM SHAEROCARPOS-DONNELLII AUST
        BIOC PHY PF   165(4):433   74   N 8R

34. SHARP WR
    CALDAS LS   CROCOMO OJ   MONACO LC   CARVALHO A
    PRODUCTION OF COFFEA-ARABICA CALLUS OF 3 PLOIDY
    LEVELS AND SUBSEQUENT MORPHOGENESIS
        PHYTON   31(2):67   73   17R

35. SMITH HH
    MODEL SYSTEMS FOR SOMATIC-CELL PLANT GENETICS
        BIOSCIENCE   24(5):269   74   104R

36. TAKEBE I
    (JA) PLANT PROTOPLASTS-ISOLATION, ACTIVITY, AND
    APPLICATION
        SEIKAGAKU   46(1):22   74   52R

37. UCHIMIYA H
    MURASHIG. T – EVALUATION OF PARAMETERS IN ISOLATION OF
    VIABLE PROTOPLASTS FROM CULTURED TOBACCO CELLS
        PLANT PHYSL   54(6):936   74   18R

38. USUI H
    MAEDA M   ITO M – HIGH-FREQUENCY OF SPONTANEOUS FUSION
    IN PROTOPLASTS FROM VARIOUS PLANT-TISSUES
        BOTAN MAG   87(1006):179   74   N 6R

39. VASIL V
    VASIL IK – REGENERATION OF TOBACCO AND PETUNIA PLANTS
    FROM PROTOPLASTS AND CULTURE OF CORN PROTOPLASTS
        IN VITRO   10(1-2):83   74   58R

40. WALLIN A
    GLIMELIU. K   ERIKSSON T – INDUCTION OF AGGREGATION AND
    FUSION OF DAUCUS-CAROTA PROTOPLASTS BY POLYETHYLENE-GLYCOL
        Z PFLANZENP   74(1):64   74   26R

Figure 5.8 (continued)

The Citation Index as a Search Tool 57

41. WIDDUS R
AULT CR - PROGRESS IN RESEARCH RELATED TO GENETIC
ENGINEERING AND LIFE SYNTHESIS
INT REV CYT   38:7   74   R   282R

42. WINTON LL
PARHAM RA   JOHNSON MA   EINSPAHR DW - TREE IMPROVEMENT
BY CALLUS, CELL AND PROTOPLAST CULTURE
TAPPI   57(12):151   74   N   8R

43. WITTWER SH
MAXIMUM PRODUCTION OF FOOD CROPS
BIOSCIENCE   24(4):216   74   R   134R

Figure 5.8 (continued)

Quick State-of-the-Art Search

Sometimes an exhaustive view of the literature is unnecessary; all that is needed is a quick review of the state of the art. Figure 5.9 shows a search, on the subject of hemoglobin binding, whose object is to identify papers that can provide a fast overview of the subject. The arbitrary criterion set for such papers is that they have more

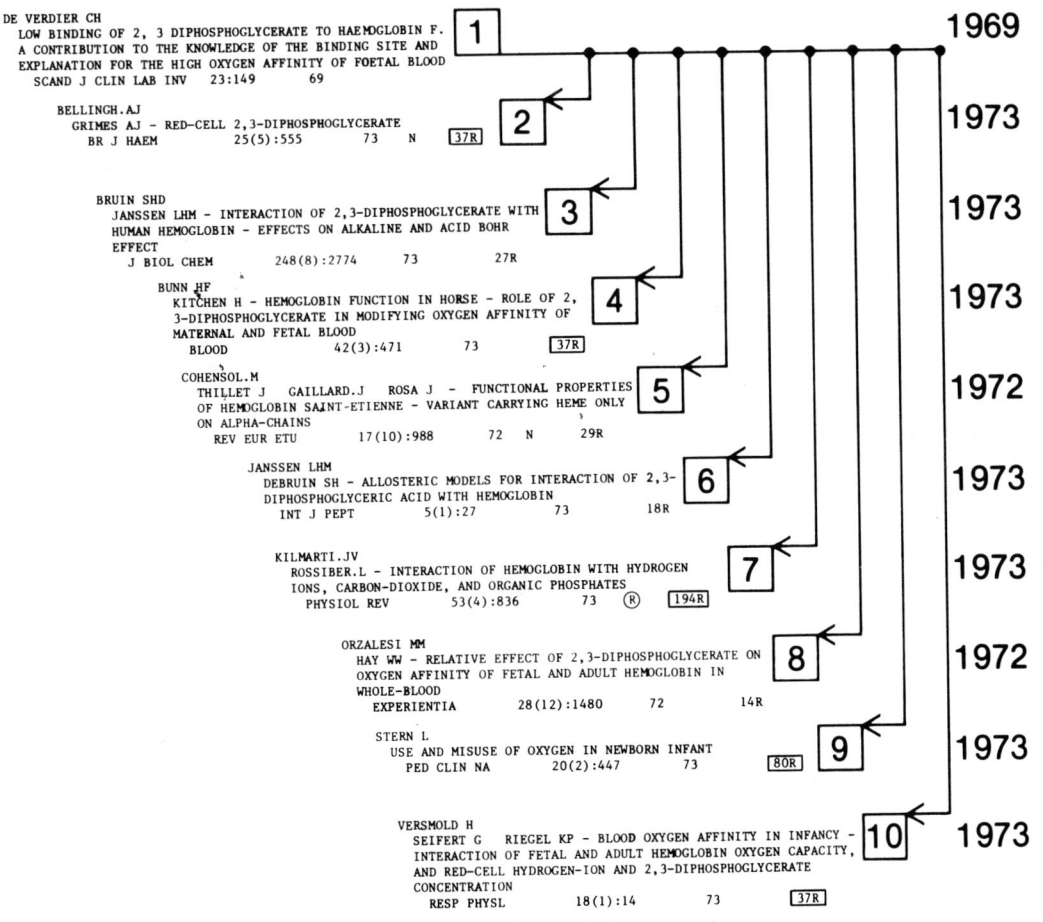

DE VERDIER CH
LOW BINDING OF 2,3 DIPHOSPHOGLYCERATE TO HAEMOGLOBIN F.
A CONTRIBUTION TO THE KNOWLEDGE OF THE BINDING SITE AND
EXPLANATION FOR THE HIGH OXYGEN AFFINITY OF FOETAL BLOOD
SCAND J CLIN LAB INV   23:149   69   **1**   1969

BELLINGH.AJ
GRIMES AJ - RED-CELL 2,3-DIPHOSPHOGLYCERATE
BR J HAEM   25(5):555   73   N   37R   **2**   1973

BRUIN SHD
JANSSEN LHM - INTERACTION OF 2,3-DIPHOSPHOGLYCERATE WITH
HUMAN HEMOGLOBIN - EFFECTS ON ALKALINE AND ACID BOHR
EFFECT
J BIOL CHEM   248(8):2774   73   27R   **3**   1973

BUNN HF
KITCHEN H - HEMOGLOBIN FUNCTION IN HORSE - ROLE OF 2,
3-DIPHOSPHOGLYCERATE IN MODIFYING OXYGEN AFFINITY OF
MATERNAL AND FETAL BLOOD
BLOOD   42(3):471   73   37R   **4**   1973

COHENSOL.M
THILLET J   GAILLARD.J   ROSA J - FUNCTIONAL PROPERTIES
OF HEMOGLOBIN SAINT-ETIENNE - VARIANT CARRYING HEME ONLY
ON ALPHA-CHAINS
REV EUR ETU   17(10):988   72   N   29R   **5**   1972

JANSSEN LHM
DEBRUIN SH - ALLOSTERIC MODELS FOR INTERACTION OF 2,3-
DIPHOSPHOGLYCERIC ACID WITH HEMOGLOBIN
INT J PEPT   5(1):27   73   18R   **6**   1973

KILMARTI.JV
ROSSIBER.L - INTERACTION OF HEMOGLOBIN WITH HYDROGEN
IONS, CARBON-DIOXIDE, AND ORGANIC PHOSPHATES
PHYSIOL REV   53(4):836   73   R   194R   **7**   1973

ORZALESI MM
HAY WW - RELATIVE EFFECT OF 2,3-DIPHOSPHOGLYCERATE ON
OXYGEN AFFINITY OF FETAL AND ADULT HEMOGLOBIN IN
WHOLE-BLOOD
EXPERIENTIA   28(12):1480   72   14R   **8**   1972

STERN L
USE AND MISUSE OF OXYGEN IN NEWBORN INFANT
PED CLIN NA   20(2):447   73   80R   **9**   1973

VERSMOLD H
SEIFERT G   RIEGEL KP - BLOOD OXYGEN AFFINITY IN INFANCY -
INTERACTION OF FETAL AND ADULT HEMOGLOBIN OXYGEN CAPACITY,
AND RED-CELL HYDROGEN-ION AND 2,3-DIPHOSPHOGLYCERATE
CONCENTRATION
RESP PHYSL   18(1):14   73   37R   **10**   1973

Figure 5.9 Quick state-of-the-art search.

58 *Citation Indexing*

than 30 references. The starting point for the search is a paper by C. H. De Verdier (#1 in Figure 5.9) from the researcher's reprint file. The 1973 *SCI Citation Index* identified nine papers on the subject. Five of them (#2, #4, #7, #9, and #10) are shown (see squares in Figure 5.9) to have more than 30 references. Their titles indicate that they are all relevant to the subject of the search. One of the five (#7) is identified as a formal review paper (see circle in Figure 5.9), and the others have enough references to make the researcher think they might be useful for review purposes.

Comprehensive Bibliography Search

The most exhaustive type of search is the one conducted to develop a comprehensive bibliography, which should provide a definitive look at the literature of a given subject. Normally, this type of search calls for the use of several indexes to achieve the degree of thoroughness required.

Figure 5.10 shows the first two cycles of a citation search to produce a bibliography on the subject of serum measurements of iron and ferritin and their roles in diagnosing pathological conditions. The search begins in the 1974 *SCI Citation Index,* with the citation of a paper written in 1965 by D. S. Young for the *Journal of Clinical Pathology* on a method for measuring serum iron. Eighteen papers are shown to have cited the Young paper. Nine of them (#3, #4, #5, #6, #11, #12, #13, #14, #18) appear from their titles to be relevant. In addition, each of them also provides, in its bibliography, reference citations on which the search can be continued through additional cycles.

For example, the paper by D. A. Lipschitz (#12) contains in its bibliography a reference to a paper by K. R. Reissman (#20). When the search continues on the citation for that paper, the 1974 *Citation Index* identifies five more papers (#21 through #25), three of which (#23, #24, and #25) have titles that indicate they are relevant.

The search can be continued in this way through as many cycles as is needed to

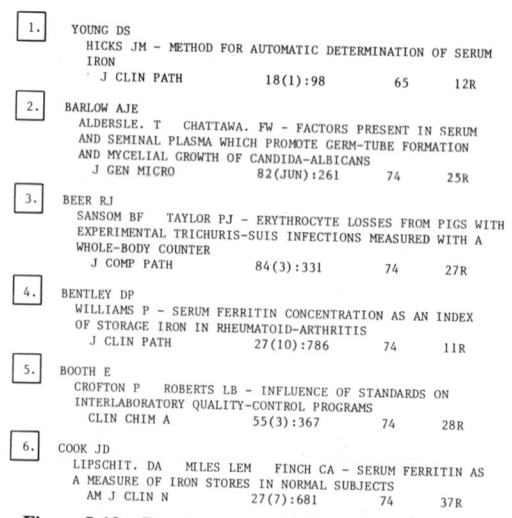

```
1.  YOUNG DS
       HICKS JM - METHOD FOR AUTOMATIC DETERMINATION OF SERUM
       IRON
        J CLIN PATH          18(1):98         65        12R
2.  BARLOW AJE
       ALDERSLE. T   CHATTAWA. FW - FACTORS PRESENT IN SERUM
       AND SEMINAL PLASMA WHICH PROMOTE GERM-TUBE FORMATION
       AND MYCELIAL GROWTH OF CANDIDA-ALBICANS
           J GEN MICRO       82(JUN):261      74        25R
3.  BEER RJ
       SANSOM BF    TAYLOR PJ - ERYTHROCYTE LOSSES FROM PIGS WITH
       EXPERIMENTAL TRICHURIS-SUIS INFECTIONS MEASURED WITH A
       WHOLE-BODY COUNTER
           J COMP PATH       84(3):331        74        27R
4.  BENTLEY DP
       WILLIAMS P - SERUM FERRITIN CONCENTRATION AS AN INDEX
       OF STORAGE IRON IN RHEUMATOID-ARTHRITIS
           J CLIN PATH       27(10):786       74        11R
5.  BOOTH E
       CROFTON P    ROBERTS LB - INFLUENCE OF STANDARDS ON
       INTERLABORATORY QUALITY-CONTROL PROGRAMS
           CLIN CHIM A       55(3):367        74        28R
6.  COOK JD
       LIPSCHIT. DA    MILES LEM    FINCH CA - SERUM FERRITIN AS
       A MEASURE OF IRON STORES IN NORMAL SUBJECTS
           AM J CLIN N       27(7):681        74        37R
```

Figure 5.10   Development-of-bibliography search.

7. CRANE GG
   JONES P   DELANEY A   KELLY A   MACGREGO. A   LECHE J -
   PATHOGENESIS OF ANEMIA IN COASTAL NEW GUINEANS
   AM J CLIN N   27(10):1079   74   39R

8. FLYNN FV
   PIPER KAJ   GARCIAWE. P   MCPHERSO. K   HEALY MJR -
   FREQUENCY DISTRIBUTIONS OF COMMONLY DETERMINED BLOOD-
   CONSTITUENTS IN HEALTHY BLOOD-DONORS
   CLIN CHIM A   52(2):163   74   16R

9. KUMAR R
   FERROKINETIC STUDIES - RED-CELL IRON UTILIZATION AND
   RED-CELL IRON TURNOVER - IN ANEMIA OF CHRONIC INFECTION
   I J MED RES   62(1):53   74   17R

10. LIEDEN G
    ADOLFSSO. L - PHYSICAL WORK CAPACITY IN BLOOD-DONORS
    SC J CL INV   34(1):37   74   18R

11. LIEDEN G
    IRON STATE IN REGULAR BLOOD-DONORS
    SC J HAEMAT   11(5):342   73   37R

12. LIPSCHIT. DA
    COOK JD   FINCH CA - CLINICAL EVALUATION OF SERUM
    FERRITIN AS AN INDEX OF IRON STORES
    N ENG J MED   290(22):1213   74   11R

13. MCCLEAN SW
    PURDY WC - COULOMETRIC DETERMINATION OF SERUM IRON
    ANALYT CHIM   69(2):425   74   16R

14. MEGRAW RE
    HRITZ AM   BABSON AL   CARROLL JJ - SINGLE-TUBE TECHNIQUE
    FOR SERUM TOTAL IRON AND TOTAL IRON-BINDING CAPACITY
    CLIN BIOCH   6(4):266   73   9R

15. NAETS JP
    WITTEK M - EFFECT OF STARVATION ON RESPONSE TO
    ERYTHROPOIETIN IN RAT
    ACT HAEMAT   52(3):141   74   12R

16. RAMSAY CA
    MAGNUS IA   TURNBULL A   BAKER H - TREATMENT OF PORPHYRIA
    CUTANEA-TARDA BY VENESECTION
    Q J MED   43(169):1   74   36R

17. SKJAELAA. P
    HALVORSE. S - DETERMINATION AND PHYSIOLOGIC EFFECTS OF
    ERYTHROPOIESIS INHIBITORS
    J LA CL MED   83(4):625   74   15R

18. SUMMERS M
    WORWOOD M   JACOBS A - FERRITIN IN NORMAL ERYTHROCYTES,
    LYMPHOCYTES, POLYMORPHS, AND MONOCYTES
    BR J HAEM   28(1):19   74   15R

19. WORWOOD M
    SUMMERS M   MILLER F   JACOBS A   WHITTAKE. JA - FERRITIN
    IN BLOOD-CELLS FROM NORMAL SUBJECTS AND PATIENTS WITH
    LEUKEMIA
    BR J HAEM   28(1):27   74   15R

20. REISSMANN KR
    DIETRICH MR - ON THE PRESENCE OF FERRITIN IN THE PERIPHERAL
    BLOOD OF PATIENTS WITH HEPATOCELLULAR DISEASE
    J CLIN INVEST   35:588   56

21. ESHHAR Z
    ORDER SE   KATZ DH - FERRITIN, A HODGKINS-DISEASE ASSOCIATED
    ANTIGEN
    P NAS US   71(10):3956   74   22R

22. LIPSCHIT. DA
    COOK JD   FINCH CA - CLINICAL EVALUATION OF SERUM FERRITIN
    AS AN INDEX OF IRON STORES
    N ENG J MED   290(22):1213   74   11R

23. MARCUS DM
    ZINBERG N - ISOLATION OF FERRITIN FROM HUMAN MAMMARY AND
    PANCREATIC CARCINOMAS BY MEANS OF ANTIBODY IMMUNOADSORBENTS
    ARCH BIOCH   162(2):493   74   45R

24. MILES LEM
    LIPSCHIT. DA   BIEBER CP   COOK JD - MEASUREMENT OF SERUM
    FERRITIN BY A 2-SITE IMMUNORADIOMETRIC ASSAY
    ANALYT BIOC   61(1):209   74   32R

25. UNGER A
    HERSHKO C - HEPATOCELLULAR UPTAKE OF FERRITIN IN RAT
    BR J HAEM   28(2):169   74   29R

Figure 5.10 (continued)

produce a definitive bibliography. Though the example is limited to searches of only the 1974 *SCI*, every citation used to search the literature of that year can be used to search the literature of the preceding years. You can go back as far as the oldest publication year involved—at least until 1961, when *SCI* starts. Such multiyear, cycling would produce a comprehensive bibliography of all the significant papers on the subject.

MACHINE SEARCHES

As with all other types of indexes, citation indexes can be searched by machine. Numerous organizations, including national and multinational information utilities, make the *SCI* and *SSCI* data bases available for this purpose. The advantage of machine searches is that the searcher is required only to supply the search instructions; the computer performs the lookups and prints out the results. This can be a very significant advantage on extensive searches, such as in the last example.

The strategy in machine searches is basically the same as in manual searches. Starting with a target document, the search identifies every paper that has cited the document. There are some variations on this approach in which the search is conducted on a set of target documents. One variation, developed by Schiminovich (6) for classifying a data base, but used successfully by Bichteler and Parsons (7) for retrieval, uses the bibliography of a paper considered representative of the subject of interest as the set of target documents. In another variation, Bichteler and Eaton substitute a custom-designed set of target documents (8) for an existing bibliography. They also rank the retrieved papers by the number of citations they have in common with the target set.

Many of the organizations that use the *SCI* and *SSCI* data bases for machine searches have extended their utility beyond retrospective search into the area of current awareness. The *SCI*, in fact, was the basis for the first commercially available selective-dissemination-of-information (SDI) service for monitoring the current literature on a personalized basis. Called *ASCA* (9), an acronym for *Automatic Subject Citation Alert,* this service searches each weekly addition to the *SCI* data base for papers that match the interests of subscribers. Subscriber interests are specified in what are called "profiles." *ASCA* profiles include both source- and reference-type search terms. One may wish to be informed as to what is being published in given journals, or one may want to know what a given organization or author is publishing. The search can also involve screening article titles for specific subject terms, word phrases, or word stems. In addition to these source-type questions, that is, questions based on the citing work, one can search for material that cites given authors or published works. Thus, *ASCA* profiles can include cited-author, cited-book, cited-journal, or cited-article search terms. The ability to identify material by these citation linkages is an important and unique feature of the service (10). In fact, it has been so useful as a technique for monitoring the literature that a majority of the research organizations and libraries that use the weekly *SCI* computer tapes do so much more often for current-awareness purposes than for retrospective searches.

REFERENCES

1. **Cawkell, A. E.** "*Science Citation Index;* Effectiveness in Locating Articles in the Anaesthetics Field: 'Perturbation of Ion Transport'." *British Journal of Anaesthesia,* **43**:814, 1971.
2. **Cawkell, A. E.** "Search Strategies Using the *Science Citation Index.*" In Houghton, B. (ed.). *Computer-Based Information Retrieval Systems* (London: Clive Bingley Ltd., 1968). Pp. 27-44.
3. **Cawkell, A. E.** "Search Strategy, Construction, and Use of Citation Networks With a Socio-Scientific Example; Amorphous Semiconductors and S. R. Ovshinsky." *Journal of the American Society for Information Science,* **24**:265-269, 1973.
4. **Garfield, E. and Sher, I. H.** "Diagonal Display—A New Technique for Graphic Representation of Complex Topological Networks," Final Report (Philadelphia: Institute for Scientific Information, Air Force Office of Scientific Research, Contract AF49(638)-1547, September 1967).
5. **Williams, J. F. and Ping, V. M.** "A Study of the Access to the Scholarly Record from a Hospital Health Science Core Collection." *Bulletin of the Medical Library Association,* **61**:408-415, 1973.
6. **Schiminovich, S.** "Automatic Classification and Retrieval of Documents by Means of a Bibliographic Pattern Discovery Algorithm." *Information Storage and Retrieval,* **6**:417-435, May 1971.
7. **Bichteler, J. and Parsons, R. G.** "Document Retrieval by Means of an Automatic Classification Algorithm for Citations."*Information Storage and Retrieval,* **10**:267-278, July/August 1974.
8. **Bichteler, J. and Eaton, E. A.** "Comparing Two Algorithms for Document Retrieval Using Citation Links." *Journal of the American Society for Information Science,* **28**:192-195, July 1977.
9. **Garfield, E.** "ASCA, ASCATOPICS, and Cyclic AMP." In *Essays of an Information Scientist,* Vol. 1 (Philadelphia: ISI Press, 1977). Pp. 217-218.
10. **Garfield, E.** "Kudos for ISI's ASCA Service From Abroad." *Essays of an Information Scientist,* Vol. 1 (Philadelphia: ISI Press, 1977). P. 130.

Chapter Six

A Science-Management Tool

Although it was developed primarily for bibliographic purposes, and in spite of its recognized utility as a search tool, the most important application of citation indexing may prove to be nonbibliographic. If the literature of science reflects the activities of science, a comprehensive, multidisciplinary citation index can provide an interesting view of these activities. This view can shed some useful light on both the structure of science and the process of scientific development. In this regard, the *SCI* data base is being used to do such things as evaluate the research role of individual journals, scientists, organizations, and communities; define the relationship between journals and between journals and fields of study; measure the impact of current research; provide early warnings of important, new interdisciplinary relationships; spot fields of study whose rate of progress suddenly begins accelerating; and define the sequence of developments that led to major scientific advances.

What the *SCI* data base brings to those kinds of problems is the ability to define two measures of scientific activity: the citation rates (how often cited) of authors, papers, and journals and the number of citation links between both given papers and given journals. Quantitative, objective, and fundamental, these measures are useful tools in managing science—not in the detailed sense of defining research objectives, routes, and timetables, but in the general sense of allocating resources and measuring progress.

QUALITATIVE MEASURE

The science-mangement applications of the *SCI* data base began with the simplest measure: citation rates. Underlying their use is the obvious need for some objective measure of the contributions made by individual researchers, papers, journals, programs, regions, and nations. Because they reflect the number of times individual scientists consider a given document important enough to cite it in their own work, citation rates appear to be such a measure. Certainly they provide the qualitative factor that is so glaringly absent from simple publication counts. By weighting individual publications on the basis of use by the scientific community, they add an important qualitative dimension to the publication record that is generally accepted as an analog, though an imperfect one, of research effort.

Admittedly, the nature of the quality that citation rates measure is elusive. It has been described variously as "significance," "impact," "utility," and "effectiveness," but no one has succeeded in defining it in more tangible terms. Nevertheless, two things are known about the quality that citation rates measure that make citation analysis a useful technique. One is that it is a positive quality; it generally reflects credit on the scientific work involved. The other is that it plays a significant role in the formation of peer opinions. The existence of these two characteristics are derived from a sizeable number of studies that show a strong, positive correlation between citation rates and peer judgments.

There are a number of theoretical objections raised about the use of citation rates as a measure of scientific quality (1). A person's rate could conceivably be inflated by self-citations. A paper might be cited frequently in refutation or as a negative example. There is no precise way of relating the citation rate of a co-authored paper to the contributions made by individual authors. A prestigious journal might draw more citations than a less prestigious one by providing more visibility. Primordial papers on methods that have been widely adopted tend to be cited with uncommon frequency, though it is debatable whether a methodological contribution is as important as a new theory, a conceptual insight, or an experimental finding. Then too, there is the problem of sloppy, and even biased, bibliographic practices (2). Not everyone cites all the obvious, classical antecedents or is conscientious about citing all the sources actually used. Not everyone conducts an exhaustive literature search or uses all the sources that should have been used. Not everyone limits references to only material that was actually read. And not everyone is objective about who is cited: some people cite a publication to make a friend look better, to flatter a superior, or to wrap themselves in the cloak of scholarship.

The validation studies done were designed to determine whether these factors negated, in fact as well as theory, citation rates as a general measure of scientific quality. The basic studies concentrated on papers and authors, which are closely intertwined. Any measure of the utility of a paper is also implicitly a measure of the work the author has done and is reporting. Since there is no other objective measure of scientific quality, the studies compared the judgments inferred from citation rates with the various forms of subjective peer judgments.

A study performed at ISI used the judgment of the Nobel Prize committees as a base line (3). The subjects of the study were the 1962 and 1963 winners of the Nobel Prize in physics, chemistry, and medicine. The rate at which their work had been cited was taken from the 1961 edition of *SCI* to eliminate any influence the award might have on their popularity as cited authors.

We found that the work of these authors was cited 30 times more frequently than the average for their fields. The average rate was 5.51 citations per author, as compared with 169 citations per Nobel Prize winner. Since Nobel Prize winners tend to publish more frequently than other scientists, we discounted the effect of frequency on the total rate by working out the average citation rate per paper for each author.

The Nobel Prize winners had an average citation rate per paper of 2.9, whereas their colleagues' rate was 1.57. The study showed, therefore, that quality judgments based on citation counts correlate very well with the judgments made by the Nobel Prize committees.

This study was repeated and extended in 1977, when we compiled the 1961–1975 citation rates of all Nobel Prize winners in science since 1950 (4). The list of Nobel laureates (see Figure 6.1) contained 162 names. The citation records of these scientists range from a high of 18,888 (L. D. Landau) to a low of 79 (J. H. D. Jensen), with a median rate of 1910. Only 6 of the laureates had citation counts under 200, and all of them did their award-winning research well before the advent of *SCI* in 1961. Thirty-eight received between 100 and 999 citations; 34, between 1000 and 1999; 21, between 2000 and 2999; 16, between 3000 and 3999; and 43 received over 4000 citations in the 15-year period. As a group they average 2877 citations. Taking the average of the authors listed in the 1970–1974 *SCI* cumulation for comparison purposes, we found that the average cited author could be expected to have accumulated less than 50 citations over the 15-year period.

In addition to determining whether honored scientists are also highly cited scientists, we looked at the corollary question too: Are highly cited scientists also honored scientists? Initially, we compiled a list of the 50 most-cited primary authors in 1967 (5). Six of them turned out to be Nobel Prize winners, and six more have been awarded Nobel Prizes since the study. In 1977 we extended the study to the 250 most-cited primary authors between 1961 and 1975 (4). Listed in Figure 6.2, 42 (17%) of them turned out to be Nobel laureates. Of the 250 most-cited primary authors, 151 (over 60%) have received the recognition of being elected to at least one national academy of science. Only 95 of them (38%) have won neither of these two honors. That doesn't mean, of course, that those 95 are unrecognized; if we had looked at the full range of awards, we most likely would have found that all of them had received recognition in one form or another.

K. E. Clark tested the accuracy of citation counts as a measure of quality in the field of psychology (6) by asking a panel of experts to list the people who they felt had made the most significant contribution to their specialties. He then measured the quality of the work done by the people listed by such criteria as citation counts, number of papers published, income, and number and quality of their students. The citation counts had the strongest correlation with the judgment of the panel.

Bayer and Folger used a sample of 467 biochemistry doctorates granted in 1967 and 1968 to determine, indirectly, how well citation counts correlated with peer judgments about the quality of educational institutions (7). The peer judgments were taken from a previous study in which a group of 152 biochemists were asked to rank the same departments that had granted the doctorates. Bayer and Folger then counted the citations received by each of the graduates and found that there was a strong correlation between the frequency of citation and the quality of the graduating institutions as ranked by professionals in the field.

Orr and Kassab compared citation rates against the peer judgments implied by the editorial rating of papers submitted for publication (8). The results were the same: there was a high correlation between citation counts and the judgments of the

PHYSICS

Name	Country*	Total Citations 1961-1975	Name	Country*	Total Citations 1961-1975
1950 Powell C	Britain	247	1964 Prokhorov AM	U.S.S.R.	1,031
1951 Crockcroft JD	Britain	93	Townes CH	U.S.	2,570
Walton E	Ireland	112	1965 **Feynman RP**	U.S.	6,031
1952 Bloch F	U.S.	2,188	**Schwinger JS**	U.S.	4,855
Purcell EM	U.S.	577	Tomonaga S	Japan	236
1953 Zernike F	Netherlands	467	1966 Kastler A	France	570
1954 **Born M**	Germany	9,206	1967 **Bethe HA**	U.S.	7,718
Bothe W	Germany	201	1968 Alvarez LW	U.S.	331
1955 Kusch P	U.S.	459	1969 **Gell-Mann M**	U.S.	9,669
Lamb WE Jr.	U.S.	1,625	1970 Alfvén HOG	Sweden	1,909
1956 **Bardeen J**	U.S.	4,788	Neel LEF	France	3,070
Brattain W	U.S.	303	1971 Gabor D	Britain	1,749
Shockley W	U.S.	3,571	1972 **Bardeen J**	U.S.	4,788
1957 **Lee TD**	U.S.	4,879	Cooper LN	U.S.	323
Yang CN	U.S.	1,728	Schrieffer JR	U.S.	1,472
1958 Cherenkov PA	U.S.S.R.	84	1973 Esaki L	Japan	747
Frank IM	U.S.S.R.	274	Giaever I	U.S.	695
Tamm IY	U.S.S.R.	1,144	Josephson B	Britain	1,265
1959 Chamberlain O	U.S.	236	1974 Hewish A	Britain	766
Segrè E	U.S.	493	Ryle M	Britain	890
1960 Glaser D	U.S.	343	1975 Bohr AN	Denmark	3,517
1961 Hofstadter R	U.S.	1,686	Mottelson BR	Denmark	1,362
Mössbauer R	Germany	436	Rainwater J	U.S.	300
1962 **Landau LD**	U.S.S.R.	18,888	1976 Richter B	U.S.	205
1963 Jensen JHD	Germany	79	Ting SCC	U.S.	303
Mayer MG	U.S.	290	1977 **Anderson PW**	U.S.	6,787
Wigner EP	U.S.	4,948	**Mott NF**	Britain	10,473
1964 **Basov NG**	U.S.S.R.	4,320	Van Vleck JH	U.S.	5,449

CHEMISTRY

Name	Country*	Total Citations 1961-1975	Name	Country*	Total Citations 1961-1975
1950 Alder K	Germany	4,450	1959 Heyrovsky J	Czech	1,418
Diels O	Germany	1,372	1960 Libby WF	U.S.	832
1951 McMillan EM	U.S.	97	1961 Calvin M	U.S.	2,713
Seaborg G	U.S.	638	1962 Kendrew JC	Britain	1,654
1952 Martin AJP	Britain	777	**Perutz MF**	Britain	4,263
Synge R	Britain	417	1963 **Natta G**	Italy	5,735
1953 Staudinger H	Germany	3,325	Ziegler K	Germany	3,258
1954 **Pauling LC**	U.S.	15,662	1964 Hodgkin DMC	Britain	359
1955 Du Vigneaud V	U.S.	1,470	1965 **Woodward RB**	U.S.	7,069
1956 Hinshelwood C	Britain	476	1966 **Mulliken RS**	U.S.	10,508
Semenov N	U.S.S.R.	1,257	1967 **Eigen M**	Germany	4,980
1957 Todd A	Britain	275	Norrish RGW	Britain	980
1958 Sanger F	Britain	3,716	Porter G	Britain	3,202

Figure 6.1 Nobel prize winners since 1950 in physics, chemistry, and physiology or medicine. Total citations from 1961 to 1975 based on data from the *Science Citation Index*. Names in bold type also rank among the 250 most cited primary authors from 1961 to 1975.

CHEMISTRY (continued)

Name	Country*	Total Citations 1961-1975	Name	Country*	Total Citations 1961-1975
1968 Onsager L	U.S.	3,569	1973 **Fischer E**	Germany	4,788
1969 **Barton DHR**	Britain	8,135	Wilkinson G	Britain	967
Hassel O	Norway	1,113	1974 **Flory PJ**	U.S.	10,247
1970 Leloir LF	Argentina	2,221	1975 Cornforth JW	Australia	2,378
1971 Herzberg G	Canada	13,110	Prelog V	Switzerland	2,229
1972 Anfinsen CB	U.S.	2,286	1976 Lipscomb WN	U.S.	1,443
Moore S	U.S.	8,167	1977 **Prigogine I**	Belgium	4,681
Stein WH	U.S.	1,274			

PHYSIOLOGY OR MEDICINE

1950 Hench PS	U.S.	316	1965 **Monod J**	France	4,791
Kendall EC	U.S.	179	1966 Huggins CB	U.S.	3,808
Reichstein T	Switzerland	1,178	Rous FP	U.S.	1,396
1951 Theiler M	South Africa	206	1967 **Granit RA**	Sweden	4,629
1952 Waksman SA	U.S.	2,291	Hartline HK	U.S.	1,183
1953 Lipmann FA	U.S.	2,038	Wald G	U.S.	3,002
Krebs HA	Britain	7,657	1968 Holley RW	U.S.	2,296
1954 Enders JF	U.S.	1,193	Khorana HG	U.S.	1,651
Robbins FC	U.S.	584	Nirenberg MW	U.S.	1,916
Weller TH	U.S.	1,972	1969 Delbruck M	U.S.	498
1955 Theorell AHT	Sweden	3,150	Hershey AD	U.S.	2,039
1956 Cournand AF	U.S.	1,263	Luria SE	U.S.	1,876
Forssmann W	Germany	637	1970 **Axelrod J**	U.S.	6,973
Richards D	U.S.	668	**Katz B**	Britain	4,690
1957 Bovet D	Italy	1,219	**von Euler U**	Sweden	8,728
1958 Beadle GW	U.S.	948	1971 **Sutherland EW**	U.S.	5,150
Lederberg J	U.S.	3,138	1972 Edelman GM	U.S.	3,414
Tatum EL	U.S.	285	Porter RR	Britain	2,528
1959 **Kornberg A**	U.S.	4,548	1973 von Frisch K	Germany	955
Ochoa S	U.S.	2,425	Lorenz KZ	Germany	1,560
1960 **Burnet FM**	Australia	5,553	Tinbergen N	Netherlands	1,205
Medawar PB	Britain	2,600	1974 **DeDuve C**	Belgium	8,445
1961 von Békésy G	U.S.	1,960	Claude A	U.S.	493
1962 Crick FHC	Britain	2,524	**Palade GE**	U.S.	5,969
Watson JD	U.S.	2,437	1975 Baltimore D	U.S.	2,543
Wilkins MHF	Britain	745	Dulbecco R	U.S.	4,005
Eccles JC	Australia	10,104	Temin HM	U.S.	3,168
1963 **Hodgkin AL**	Britain	7,500	1976 Blumberg BS	U.S.	3,555
Huxley AF	Britain	2,115	Gajdusek DC	U.S.	1,318
1964 Bloch K	U.S.	1,456	1977 Guillemin R	U.S.	2,395
Lynen F	Germany	3,020	Schally A	U.S.	2,985
1965 **Jacob F**	France	7,101	Yalow R	U.S.	3,658
Lwoff A	France	2,111			

* Citizenship of recipient at time of award.

Figure 6.1 (continued)

Name	Total Citations 1961-1975	National Academy	Name	Total Citations 1961-1975	National Academy
Abragam A	6,769	France	Brodie BB	7,493	U.S.
Abramowitz M	5,108		Brown HC	16,623	U.S.
Abrikosov AA	5,429	U.S.S.R.	Brown JB	4,074	
Albert A	8,664		Buckingham AD	4,332	U.K.
Allinger NL	4,140		Budzikiewicz H	5,089	
Allison AC	6,105		Bunnett JF	4,370	
Anden NE	5,147		Burn JH	5,650	U.K.
Anderson PW (77P)	6,787	U.S.	**Burnet FM** (60M)	5,553	U.K., U.S.
Andrews P	4,485		Burton K	6,913	U.K.
Arnon DI	4,323	U.S.	Busing WR	5,066	
Axelrod J (70M)	6,973	U.S.	Carlson LA	4,282	
Baker BR	5,395		Carlsson A	7,697	
Bardeen J (56P) (72P)	4,788	U.S., U.K.	Cattell RB	4,190	
			Chance B	16,306	U.S.
Barrer RM	5,230	U.K.	Chandrasekhar S	8,179	U.S., U.K.
Bartlett PD	5,180	U.S.	Chapman S	5,235	U.K., U.S.
Barton DHR (69C)	7,763	U.K., U.S.	Chatt J	6,692	U.K.
Basolo F	4,083		Clementi E	5,684	
Basov NG (64 P)	4,320	U.S.S.R.	Cohen MH	4,808	
Bates DR	6,925	U.K.	Conney AH	5,151	
Bell RP	4,400	U.K., U.S.	Cope AC	5,269	
Bellamy LJ	10,736		Corey EJ	9,901	U.S.
Bellman RE	5,678		Cotton FA	12,901	U.S.
Bender ML	4,924	U.S.	Coulson CA	6,569	U.K.
Benson SW	5,319		Courant R	4,154	
Bergstrom S	4,473	Sweden, U.S.	Cram DJ	6,148	U.S.
Berson SA	4,486		Cromer DT	5,418	
Bethe HA (67P)	7,718	U.S., U.K.	Cruickshank DWJ	4,512	
Beutler E	5,636	U.S.	Cuatrecasas P	4,484	
Billingham RE	6 269	U.K.	Curtis DR	4,794	
Birch AJ	4,339	U.K.	Dacie JV	4,323	U.K.
Bjorken JD	4,264	U.S.	Dalgarno A	5,365	U.K.
Bloembergen N	5,234	U.S.	Davis BJ	7,074	
Born M (54 P)	9,206	U.S.	Dawson RMC	4,125	
Bourbaki N	4,860		**DeDuve C** (74 M)	8,445	U.S., Belgium
Boyer PD	6,906	U.S.	DeRobertis E	4,801	
Brachet J	5,956	U.S., U.K. France	Dewar MJS	9,800	U.K.
			Dische Z	7,874	U.S.
Braunwald E	4,980	U.S.	Dixon M	6,331	U.K.
Bray GA	8,012		Djerassi C	8,520	U.S.
Bridgman PW (46P)	5,053	U.S., U.K.	Doering WVE	4,253	U.S.

CONTINUED

Figure 6.2 Incidence of Nobel Prizes and memberships in national academies of science among the 250 most cited primary authors from 1961 to 1975. Citation rates are based on data from the *Science Citation Index*. Nobel laureates appear in bold type, followed by year and category of prize: P = physics, C = chemistry, M = physiology or medicine. Membership in national academies of science include correspondents, fellows, foreign members, and foreign associates.

Name	Total Citations 1961-1975	National Academy	Name	Total Citations 1961-1975	National Academy
Dole VP	5,902		Hirs CHW	4,578	
Duncan DB	4,153		Hirschfelder JO	7,033	U.S.
Eagle H	6,498	U.S.	**Hodgkin AL** (63 M)	7,500	U.K., U.S.
Eccles J C (63M)	10,104	U.K., U.S.	Horner L	4,469	
Eigen M (67C)	4,980	U.K., U.S.	House HO	4,393	
Eliel EL	8,615	U.S.	Hubel DH	4,640	U.S.
Erdelyi A	5,978	U.K.	Huisgen R	9,309	F.R.G., G.D.R.
Eysenck HJ	5,241		Huxley HE	4,073	U.K.
Fahey JL	4,724		Ingold CK	4,198	
Falck B	4,275		Jackman LM	4,927	
Farquhar MG	4,525		**Jacob F** (65 M)	7,101	U.K. U.S., France
Fawcett DW	6,236	U.S.			
Feigl F	4,074		Jaffé HH	5,106	
Feldberg W	4,762	U.K.	Johnson HL	4,117	U.S.
Feynman RP (65P)	6,031	U.S., U.K	Jorgensen CK	6,049	Denmark
Fieser LF	9,392	U.S.	Kabat EA	7,529	U.S.
Fischer EO (73C)	4,788		Karnovsky MJ	5,616	
Fisher ME	4,289	U.K.	Karplus M	5,770	U.S.
Fisher RA	8,336	U.K.	Kato T	4,138	
Fiske CH	8,249		Katritzky AR	4,704	
Flory PJ (74 C)	10,247	U.S.	**Katz B** (70 M)	4,690	U.K., U.S.
Folch J	9,693		Keilin D	4,121	
Fraenkel-Conrat H	4,376	U.S.	Kety SS	4,594	U.S.
Fredrickson DS	6,897	U.S.	King RB	5,109	
Freud S	8,490	U.K.	Kirkwood JG	4,084	U.S.
Friedel J	4,325	France	Kittel C	5,591	U.S.
Gell-Mann M (69 P)	9,669	U.S.	Klein G	4,430	U.S.
Gilman H	7,849	U.S., U.K.	Klotz IM	4,151	U.S.
Ginzburg VL	6,834	U.S.S.R.	Kolthoff IM	9,697	U.S.
Glasstone S	5,080		**Kornberg A** (59 M)	4,548	U.S., U.K.
Gomori G	7,136		**Krebs HA** (53 M)	7,.657	U.K., U.S.
Good RA	4,607	U.S.	Kubo R	4,232	U.S.
Goodman LS	5,627	U.S.	**Kuhn R** (38C)	7,488	
Goodwin TW	4,727	U.K.	**Landau LD** (62 P)	18,888	U.S.S.R.
Gornall AG	5,921	Canada	**Lee T D** (57 P)	4,879	U.S.
Grabar P	4,717		Lehninger AL	5,507	U.S.
Granit RA (67 M)	4,629	U.K., U.S., Sweden	Lemieux RU	4,619	Canada, U.K.
			Levine S	4,035	
Green DE	4,708	U.S.	Lineweaver H	5,202	
Gutowsky HS	4,286	U.S.	Löwdin PO	5,060	Sweden, Norway
Hansen M	5,262	U.S.			
Harned HS	4,960	U.S.	Lowry OH	58,304	U.S.
Herbert V	4,106		Luft JH	8,926	
Herzberg G (71 C)	13,110	U.S., U.K., Canada	Marmur J	6,475	
			McConnell HM	5,490	U.S.

Figure 6.2 (continued)

referees on a total of 5000 documents that had been submitted to two biomedical journals over a period of five years.

Still another test of the correlation between peer judgments of quality and citation rates was performed by Virgo (9). Her study had nine subject experts, from the

Name	Total Citations 1961-1975	National Academy	Name	Total Citations 1961-1975	National Academy
McKusick VA	4,181		Seitz F	5,396	U.S.
Miller JFA	6,371	U.K.	Selye H	8,928	Canada
Millonig G	4,106		Seyferth D	4,462	
Mitchell P	4,086	U.K.	Sillen LG	4,375	
Monod J (65 M)	4,791	U.S.	Skou JC	4,127	
Moore S (72 C)	8,167	U.S.	Slater JC	7,587	U.S.
Morse PM	5,089	U.S.	Smith HW	6,946	
Mott NF (77 P)	10,473	U.K., U.S.	Smithies O	6,192	U.S.
Muller A	4,500		Snedecor GW	14,762	
Müller E	4,664	U.S.	Somogyi M	4,465	
Mulliken RS (66 C)	10,508	U.S., U.K.	Spackman DH	6,889	
Nakamoto K	5,132		Spitzer L	4,238	U.S.
Natta G (63 C)	5,735	Italy, France, U.S.S.R.	Stahl E	6,252	
			Steel RGD	5,100	
			Streitwieser A	7,511	U.S.
Nesmeyanov AN	6,783	U.S.S.R., U.K.	**Sutherland EW** (71 M)	5,150	
			Taft RW	5,083	
Newman MS	4,730	U.S.	Tanford C	5,934	U.S.
Novikoff AB	7,662	U.S.	Udenfriend S	5,039	U.S.
Olah GA	8,311	U.S.	Umbriet WW	5,229	
Ouchterlony O	5,986		Van Slyke DD	4,282	
Palade GE (74 M)	5,969		**Van Vleck JH** (77 P)	5,449	U.S., U.K., France
Pauling L (54 C) (62 Peace)	15,662	U.S., France, U.K., U.S.S.R.	**von Euler US** (70M)	8,728	U.S., U.K.
			Walling C	5,590	U.S.
Pearse AGE	10,522		**Warburg O** (31 M)	7,463	U.K.
Perutz MF (62 C)	4,263	U.K., U.S., France	Warren L	4,303	
			Watson ML	4,176	
Pople JA	15,135	U.K.	Weber G	8,319	U.S.
Prigogine I (77C)	4,681	U.S.	Weber K	5,823	
Racker E	4,567	U.S.	Weinberg S	6,306	U.S.
Reed LJ	4,290	U.S.	Weiss P	4,048	U.S.
Reynolds ES	10,115		Wiberg KB	5,461	U.S.
Roberts JD	4,501	U.S.	Wieland T	4,423	
Robinson RA	5,543		Wigglesworth VB	4,489	U.K., U.S.
Rose ME	4,127		**Wigner EP** (63P)	4,948	U.S., U.K.
Rossini FD	4,105	U.S.	Wilson EB	5,139	U.S.
Russell GA	5,933		Winer BJ	5,145	
Sabatini DD	6,205		Winstein S	7,884	
Scatchard G	4,191		Wittig G	6,079	France
Scheidegger JJ	4,159		**Woodward RB** (65 C)	7,069	U.S., U.K.
Schneider WC	7,029		Zachariasen WH	4,050	U.S.
Schwarzenbach G	4,618		Zeldovich YB	4,794	U.S.S.R.
Schwinger J (65 P)	4,855	U.S.	Ziman JM	4,499	U.K.
Seeger A	4,757		Zimmerman HE	4,217	

Figure 6.2 (continued)

fields of surgery and radiology, select papers relevant to their research and then rate five pairs of them in two different ways. The individual papers in each pair were ranked by relative importance, and all the papers were rated on a quality scale of 1 to 5. The citation frequency of each paper turned out to correlate with the relative ranking of each pair of papers at least as well as the ratings by a second set of subject experts. In addition, when Virgo attempted to determine which of 10 objective and seven subjective variables associated with the papers correlated with the scale rating of 1 to 5, she found that a combination of two citation measures was the only one that did. In fact, the correlation was even stronger than the one between citation frequency and the relative ranking of the pairs of papers. One of the measures was the citation rate achieved by the paper. The other was the average citation rate per item published achieved by the publishing journal.

A study conducted by ISI for the Air Force Office of Scientific Research (AFOSR) proved the same point about citation counts, while demonstrating one of the applications of the measure. The study consisted of counting the citations received during 1965–1966 by papers that were published in 1964 on research sponsored by the AFOSR. The purpose of the study was to see how well the AFOSR was doing in selecting projects to support; that was the application side of the coin. The other side was that the AFOSR had a rather rigorous process for screening the proposals it received for research support. They used outside referees, panels from in-house laboratories, and other methods to select the best of the proposals. In other words, they had a rather elaborate system of peer judgments for measuring the quality of the scientists and proposals they considered supporting.

In comparing the citation counts of the papers published from AFOSR-supported research against the citation counts of a random sample of papers taken from the same journals, the study showed that the AFOSR-supported papers that were cited at least once drew an average of 2.10 citations versus 1.63 citations for the control papers that had been cited at least once. From the Air Force viewpoint, this finding confirmed the effectiveness of their selection process. From the viewpoint of those interested in an objective measure of scientific performance, however, it also confirmed, once again, that there is a high correlation between citation counts and peer judgments on the subject of scientific quality.

What all the studies show, therefore, is that of all the variables that can influence citation rates, the scientific quality of the work published is the dominant one. Sloppy, biased bibliographic practice is a random variable that tends to get canceled out. The same thing cannot be said for the variables of exposure, prestige, coauthors, and nature of the references. They are not random; they do not get canceled out. They must be considered in any citation analysis of a person or a paper, and they negate any quality judgments that might be made on the basis of small differences in citation rates. But the evidence shows that these variables are not strong enough in their influence to explain large differences in citation counts. Apparently, only differences in quality and impact account for that.

CITATION INSIGHTS

The ability of citation counts to provide a rough, but objective and useful, relative measure of scientific quality promises to have some profound implications. Following in the steps of the Air Force, other government agencies are using citation analysis to improve their ability to define what is going on in scientific fields of interest. A study conducted by ISI for the National Science Foundation on the characteristics of frequently cited papers in chemistry is typical.

Some of the main findings of the study were:

1. Seventy percent of the heavily cited (10 times or more in the year studied) items were published during the preceding 10 years.
2. The items most heavily cited, particularly by applied chemists, tended to be books that were published early in the 10-year time frame.
3. Theoretical papers dominated the list of the 50 most frequently cited items. Experimental methodology was the next most frequently cited type of subject matter.
4. The central specialty of chemistry was molecular orbital theory.
5. A high percentage of highly cited chemists were receiving NSF support, and the amount of support NSF was providing to the most highly cited ones was substantially higher than the average NSF award.

This view of the inner workings of the science of chemistry was enlightening enough for the National Science Foundation to extend its investigation to include the engineering sciences, and to take a closer look at the cross-disciplinary papers in chemistry.

Similar citation studies, looking at similar characteristics, have been conducted for other government agencies—including the National Institute of Mental Health, the National Cancer Institute, and the Consiglio Nationale delle Ricerche (CNR) in Italy. The National Institute of Mental Health was concerned with measuring the output of its research grants. The National Cancer Institute was looking for statistical data that would help it evaluate proposals for the support of cancer centers. CNR was looking for information on the life sciences that would have a bearing on a variety of science-policy decisions.

Citation rates of individual papers, or groups of papers that define given fields, are also being used to identify research areas marked by sudden spurts of activity. Price has used the *SCI* to develop an average citation-rate curve that can be used as a base line for spotting groups of papers whose rate is higher, increasing faster, or more enduring (10). A study of the literature on pulsars (11) suggests that these characteristics typify an emerging field.

At the opposite end of the spectrum from Price's macro views of science, citation counts are being used by others to provide a micro view of individual scientists. At least one major university has reversed a decision to refuse tenure after a citation analysis was done of the applicant's work. In another, much more public case (12), citation analysis was used to support a formal legal challenge of a tenure decision. The challenge came from a female biochemist, who was denied tenure at the same time it was granted to two male colleagues. She claims they are no better qualifed than she. The claim has been quantified by Robert E. Davies, a biochemist at the University of Pennsylvania, who was asked to testify as an expert witness on tenure procedures. Davies and two operations-research specialists, Nancy L. Geller and

John S. De Cani, have developed a way of estimating the lifetime citation rates of a given paper (13). The technique, Davies claims, is a careful one, which compensates for such disturbing variables as self-citation, derogatory citations, multiple authorships, prestige of the publishing journal, and tendency for papers on widely useful methods to be heavily cited. According to Davies and his colleagues, citation measures show that the research work of the biochemist who was denied tenure is superior to the two faculty members who received it and, in fact, is on a par with the full professors in the department. The evidence, however, did not prevent the court from rejecting the claim.

STRUCTURAL RELATIONSHIPS

Studies of the citation links between papers are providing still different views of science. In his work on the sociology of science, Price has shown that the distribution of references by the age of cited papers provides a way of distinguishing between hard science, soft science, and the humanities—each of which is built on a different social system and progresses in a different manner and at a different rate (14). He did this by developing an immediacy index, which describes the percent of total references that cite literature published in the last five years. In analyzing the material published by journals in a number of fields, he found that their immediacy-index rating agreed with intuitive judgments about what is hard science, soft science, and the humanities. Journals of physics and biochemistry have an immediacy index of 60 to 70%. Journals in the field of radiology show a 54 to 58% index value. The *American Sociological Review* has an index of 46.5%, and journals dealing with the study of literature as an art form are all less than 10%.

Earlier (10), Price had shown that the literature of any given field is made up of two segments: the archival literature and the recent literature that describes the research front of the field. His work on the age of references led him to conclude that the frequency with which authors cite the research-front literature is a measure of the "hardness" of the field.

Another way in which citation links between papers can help shed some light on the sociology of science is by providing a graphic, detailed picture of the history of major scientific developments. This application is not as far advanced as some of the other citation techniques used in sociological studies, but its potential is at least as great.

Working under a contract from the Air Force Office of Scientific Research, ISI has already used the *SCI* data base to construct a network diagram (see Figure 6.3) that defines the particular sequence of research events that culminated in the discovery of the DNA code (15). Definition is in terms of the key research events, their relative importance, chronological sequence, and relationships to each other. The key events were taken from the Asimov book, *The Genetic Code* (16). Each was represented by one or more of the published papers in which the research of the event was originally described. The relative importance of the events was measured by the number of times each paper was cited. The relationships between events were defined by the citation links between the papers representing the events.

To test the accuracy of the network, we constructed another diagram of the same development that was based entirely on the Asimov account. In this network, the relationships shown are those described by Asimov.

The citation network confirmed 65% of the relationships described by Asimov. And when the events in the citation network were weighted on the basis of the number and type of citation links, the one that scored the highest was the same one that Asimov judged to be the single most important contribution.

The citation analysis did more than just duplicate most of the account that Asimov had put together from a remarkable memory. It also added some insights into what happened by identifying 31 relationships and one event that Asimov did not mention. The event was identified not by the citation network, but by the citation index from which the network was developed. The index showed every paper cited by the papers representing the Asimov events. This view of the development process identified 26 authors who were cited by "event" authors, but who were not mentioned by Asimov. Four of those authors were cited for work that played an important role in the development and verification of the DNA-code theory. The work of at least one of the four seems to have been sufficiently critical to be included in the Asimov account.

The study made four significant points about the use of citation analysis for historical research. First, the relationships that a citation analysis shows among the components of a given body of work correspond very well to the relationships perceived by a scientist of Asimov's rank. Second, a citation analysis can identify significant relationships and events that even a remarkable memory might forget, or that traditional techniques of historical research might miss. Third, a graphic presentation of the sequence of events is superior to a narrative presentation for the purposes of historical and sociological analyses. And fourth, the manual construction of network diagrams, named "historiographs," was much too laborious for them to ever become widely used.

The last point led to additional research, which is still continuing, into the feasibility of computer-generated historiographs. Such a development is, at the very least, technologically feasible. Given the continuing rapid development of computer technology, economic feasibility looks promising, which makes it likely that some time in the intermediate future science historians and sociologists will be able to sit at a computer terminal and generate historiographs from a citation-index data base as easily as they now perform ordinary literature searches.

Citation links show just as useful a picture of the present as of the past. A research program at ISI is using citation links to graphically depict the high activity areas of science (17). Several types of citation counts also are involved in this process. Straight citation counts are used to identify the highly cited items in a given year. Co-citation counts, the number of times a pair of papers has been cited by individual source papers that year, are used to organize the papers into clusters and show the relationships between clusters. A cluster consists of all the papers linked by co-cita-

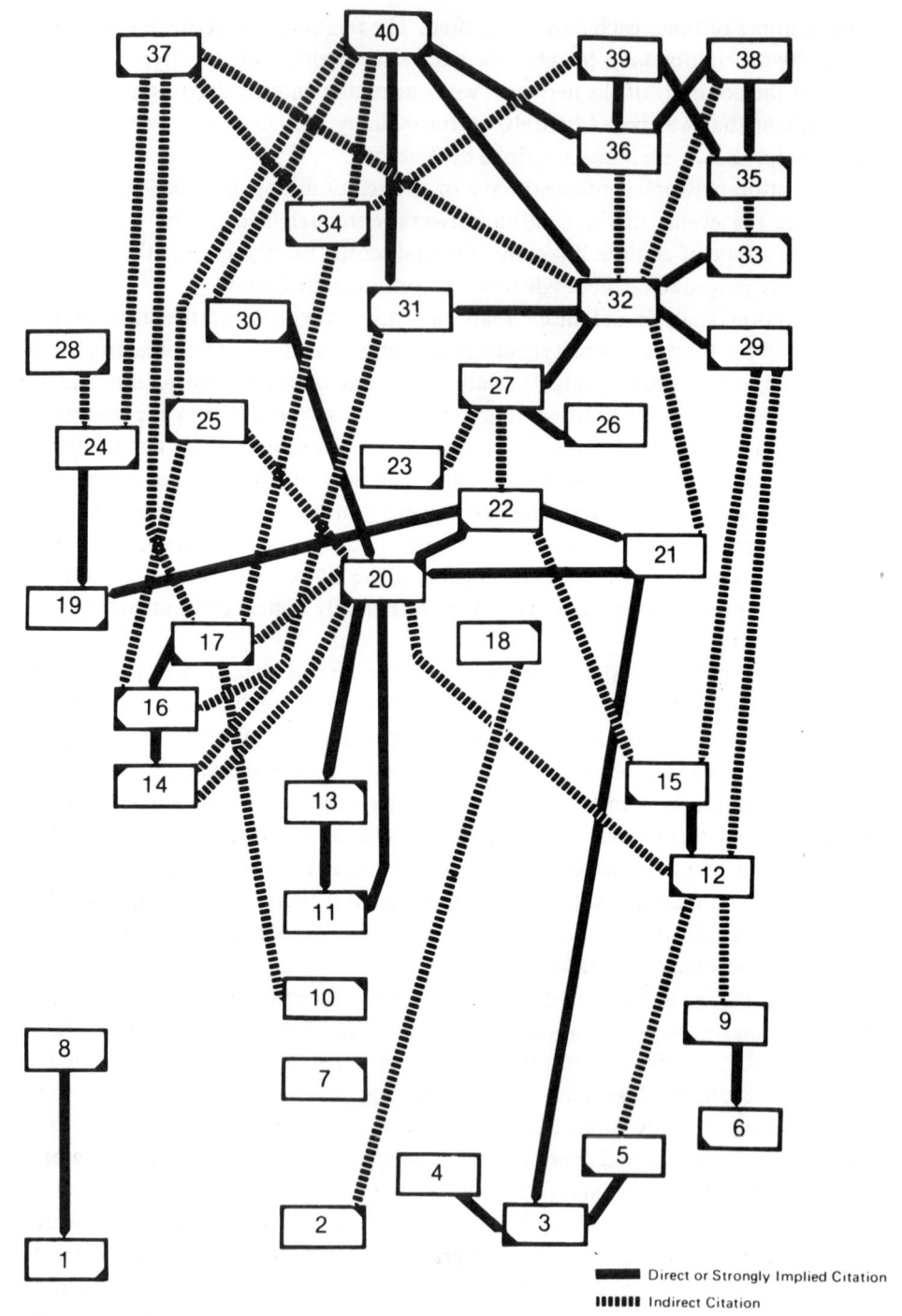

Figure 6.3 Historiograph of DNA development.

KEY

1. Braconnot 1820
2. Mendel 1865
3. Miescher 1871
4. Flemming 1879
5. Kossel 1886
6. Fischer and Piloty 1891
7. DeVries 1900
8. Fischer 1907
9. Levene and Jacobs 1909
10. Muller 1926
11. Griffith 1928
12. Levene with Mori and London 1929
13. Alloway 1932
14. Stanley 1935
15. Levene and Tipson 1935
16. Bawden and Pirie 1936-1937
17. Caspersson and Schultz 1938-1939
18. Beadle and Tatum 1941
19. Martin and Synge 1943-1944
20. Avery, MacLeod, and McCarty 1944
21. Chargaff 1947
22. Chargaff 1950
23. Pauling and Corey 1950-1951
24. Sanger 1951-1953
25. Hershey and Chase 1952
26. Wilkins 1953
27. Watson and Crick 1953
28. DuVigneaud 1953
29. Todd 1955
30. Palade 1954-1956
31. Fraenkel-Conrat 1955-1957
32. Ochoa 1955-1956
33. Kornberg 1956-1957
34. Hoagland 1957-1958
35. Jacob and Monod 1960-1961
36. Hurwitz 1960
37. Dintzis 1961
38. Novelli 1961-1962
39. Allfrey and Mirsky 1962
40. Nirenberg and Matthaei 1961-1962

tions at a frequency level equal to or greater than a given threshold. In other words, every paper in a cluster has been co-cited with at least one other paper in the cluster n times (threshold level) or more. Co-citation links below the threshold level are used to show the relationships between clusters.

When the titles of the papers in each cluster are analyzed, they are found to have certain words and concepts in common that suggest names descriptive of the type of research being reported. These cluster names seem to describe coherent scientific specialties. Authors of some of the cluster papers, with whom the names and contents of the clusters have been checked, confirmed that the names are, in fact, descriptive of their specialty and that the papers in the clusters represent the core literature of the specialty.

Except for the analysis of the paper titles and the naming of the clusters, this entire process is automatic. In other words, what we have developed is a computer model capable of mapping the structure of science in terms of its most active specialties. By changing the threshold levels of the citation and co-citation counts that qualify papers for inclusion in the model and its clusters, we can change the resolution of the map. The lower the threshold, the broader the view (see Figure 6.4); the higher the threshold, the narrower and sharper the view (see Figure 6.5).

The specialty viewpoint seems to be very useful. For one thing, it is detailed enough to be sensitive to the subtle changes that take place in scientific research from year to year. Maps of the biomedical group of clusters derived from the literature of 1972 and 1973 (Figure 6.6) showed significant changes in the relative importance of several specialties, shifts in the relationships between specialties, and the emergence of an important, new specialty.

The detail level and responsiveness of specialties seem well suited to a system for classifying scientific literature hierarchically by subject. The effectiveness of an indexing/retrieval system built on an hierarchy of subject classifications is a function

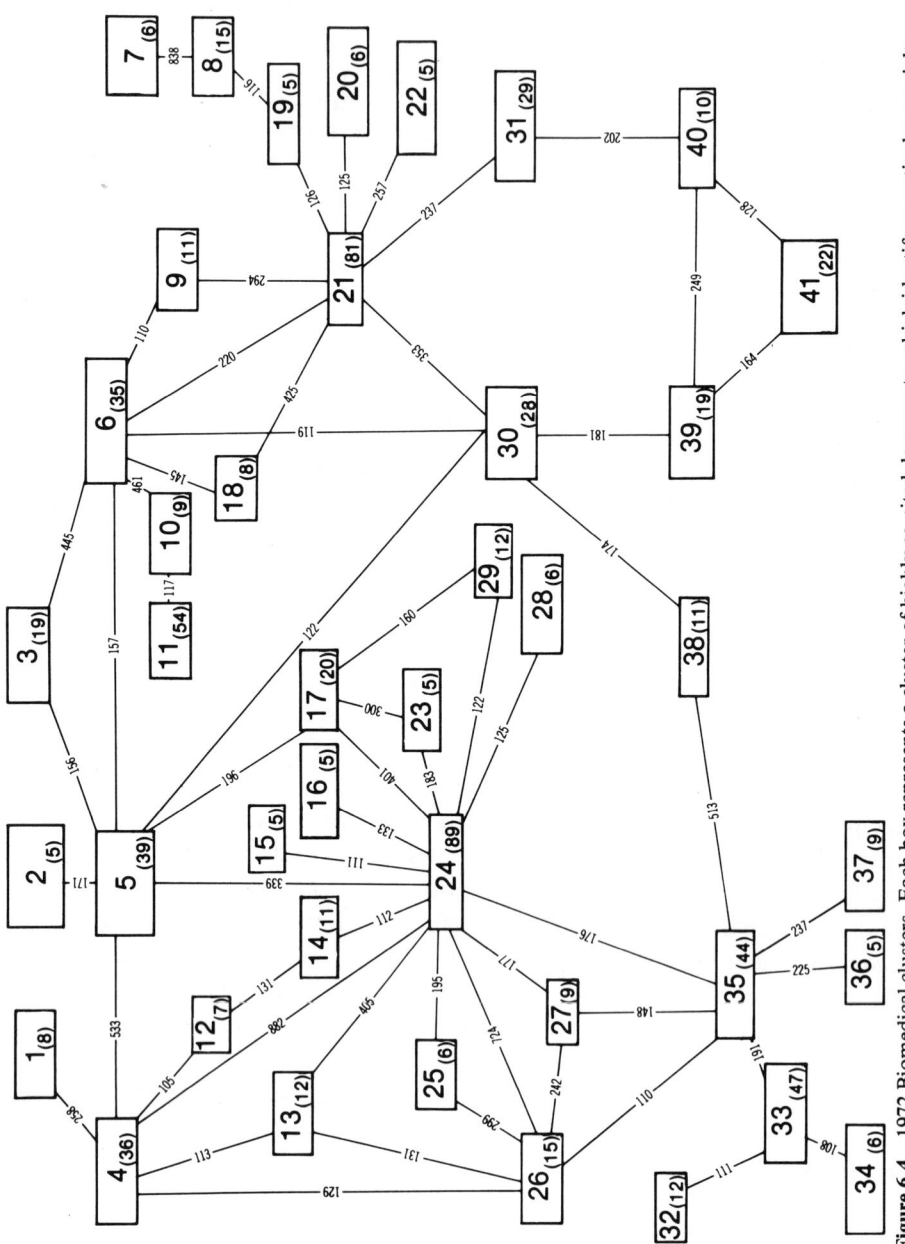

Figure 6.4 1972 Biomedical clusters. Each box represents a cluster of highly co-cited documents, which identify a particular specialty. The number in parentheses in each box indicates the number of co-cited documents in the cluster. The numbers on the lines connecting the boxes indicate the frequency with which documents in both clusters were co-cited.

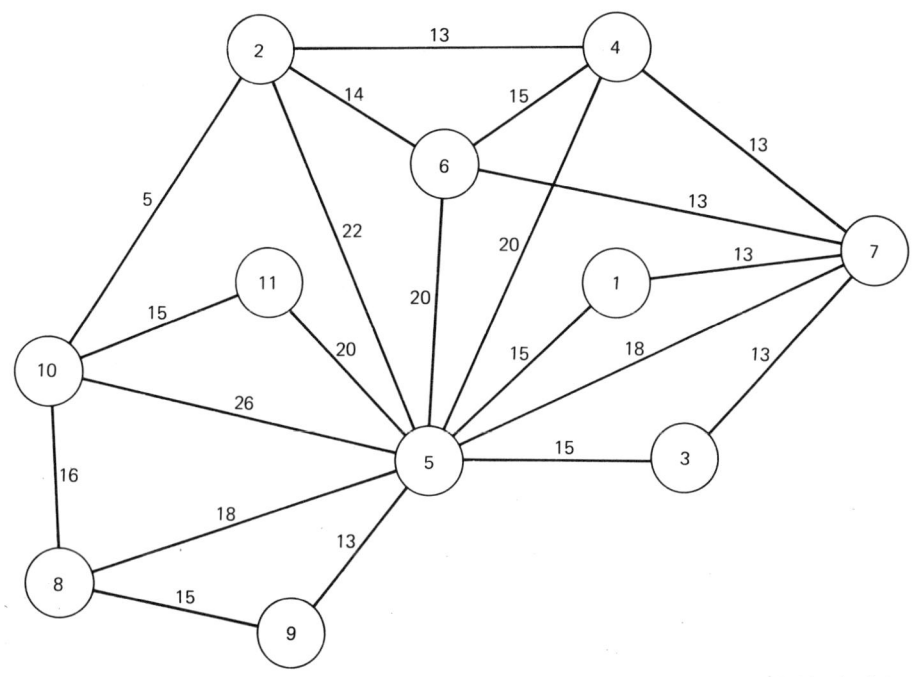

Figure 6.5 FSH and LH releasing hormone cluster in 1972. Each node represents a highly cited document. The numbers on the lines connecting pairs of nodes indicate the number of times the pairs of documents were co-cited.

KEY TO AUTHORS AND PUBLICATION YEARS OF NODAL PAPERS:

1. Amoss 1971
2. Baba 1971
3. Burbus 1971
4. Geiger 1971
5. Matsuo 1971
6. Matsuo 1971
7. Monahan 1971
8. Niswender 1968
9. Ramirez 1963
10. Schally 1971
11. Schally 1971

---

of how close the subject headings and their hierarchical relationships match reality. In the case of science, reality consists of the basic units of research and the relationships between them. Constructing such an hierarchy of descriptive terms is one of the primary difficulties in developing a useful classification system. Keeping the heirarchy current in the face of constant change is the other one.

The computer model of scientific specialties derived from the *SCI* data base may offer a way around these difficulties. The specialties defined by the model seem to be the basic units of research in the scientific process, and the relationships shown between them seem to correspond to the logical structure of the process. Equally as important, the automated nature of the model makes it practical to update the classification scheme yearly to keep pace with the dynamics of the process.

Theoretically, it should be possible to build an automatic classification system from the *SCI* model of scientific specialties. Such a system would automatically classify papers by their references, according to the cluster in which the reference

78 *Citation Indexing*

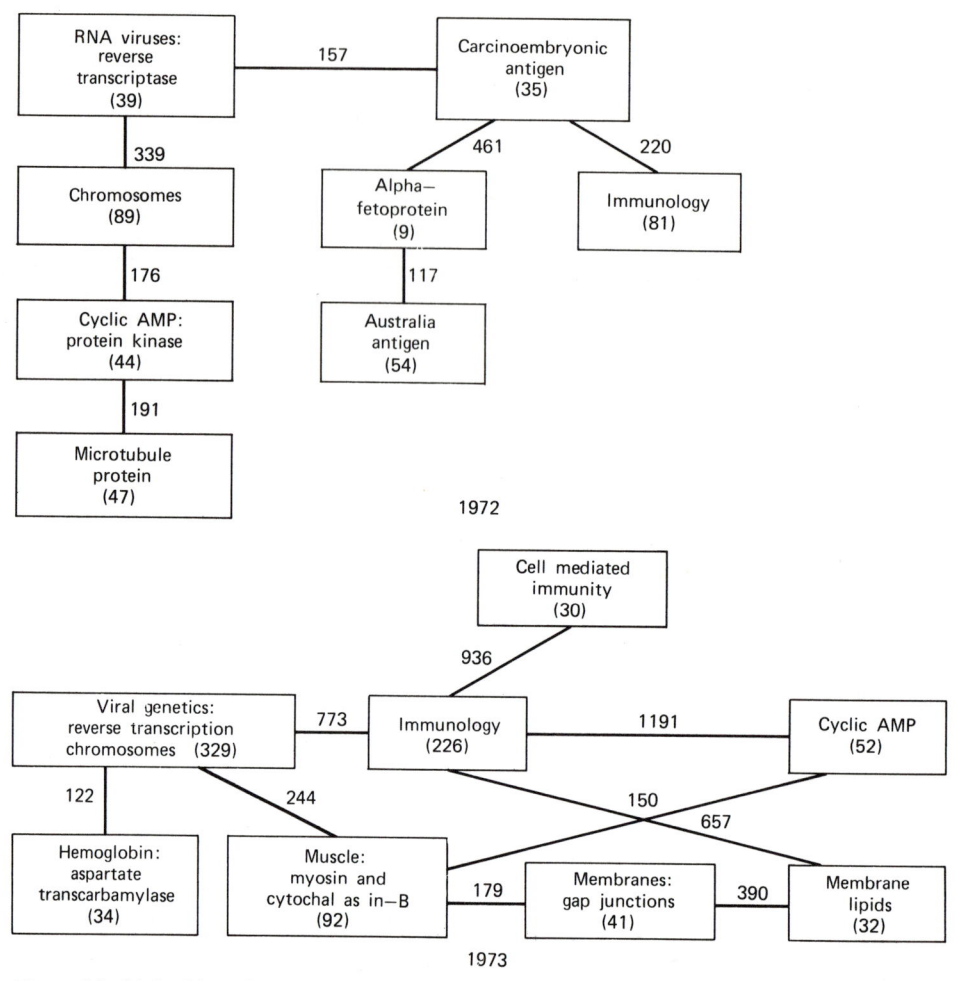

Figure 6.6 Major biomedical clusters in 1972 and 1973. Each box represents a cluster of highly co-cited documents on the subject of the specialty shown. The number in each box indicates the number of documents in the cluster. The numbers on the lines connecting boxes indicate the frequency with which documents in both clusters have been cited together.

citations are found. Research on such a system is being conducted at ISI.

There is one more area of science management in which citation counts and links are useful. The *SCI* data base shows measures not only for authors and papers, but also for journals. This information is published as a part of the *SCI* under the name *Journal Citation Reports*.

Journal Citation Reports® provides the following data on the source journals covered by *SCI:*

1. How often each journal is cited.
2. How many items it publishes.
3. How often (on an average) each item is cited, which is called "impact factor."
4. How often (on an average) each item is cited during the year of its publication, which is called "immediacy index."

5. The source journals responsible for the references to each journal, the number of references received from each, and how they were distributed by the publication years of cited issues.
6. The number of references each journal published, to what journals, and how the references were distributed by the publication years of cited issues.

As with all other citation measures, the ones given for journals are not absolute. Citation counts measure only one aspect of journal performance: that of disseminating research findings that are useful to scientists. They say nothing about a journal's performance in disseminating general news about a given area of scientific activity. And even at that, the citation counts can be influenced by such factors as the reputation of authors published, the controversiality of the subject matter, the journal's circulation, its reprint policies, and the coverage by indexing and abstracting services.

Nevertheless, as with authors and papers, a large difference in the citation counts of two journals indicates a significant difference in the quality of the research results they publish. Librarians concerned with the cost effectiveness of their journal collections, researchers and teachers who have to compile reading lists for given subject areas, journal editors looking for a way of measuring their performance against competition, and scientists doing research on one aspect or another of the scientific process, all find the journal citation counts useful.

For librarians and people doing general science studies, the citation links between journals are also useful. By showing what journals cite what journals, and with what frequency, the *Journal Citation Reports* makes it possible to define the core and tail of the literature on any given subject, model journal networks, and to gauge the degree of interdisciplinary interaction in a proposed research project. Essentially, the data from *Journal Citation Reports* can be used to do all the things I have been talking about in regard to the management of science—the only difference being that the view is of science at the journal level of detail.

The citation-index view of the literature, then, extends deeply into the structure and dynamics of the scientific process itself. With the help of a computer, this view can be used to measure, define, and model the process at the level of individuals, papers, and journals. For those concerned with the study and management of science, that array of capabilities suggests some intriguing possibilities.

REFERENCES

1. **Aaronson, S.** "The Footnotes of Science." *Mosaic,* **6:**23–27, 1975.
2. **Martino, J.P.** "Citation Indexing for Research and Development Management." *IEEE Transactions on Engineering Management,* **EM-18:** 146–151, 1971.
3. **Sher, I. H., and Garfield, E.** "New Tools for Improving and Evaluating the Effectiveness of Research." In Yovits, M. C., Gilford, D.M., Wilcox R.H., Stavely, E., and Lemer H.D. L (eds.) *Research Program Effectiveness* (New York: Gordon and Breach, 1966), Pp. 135–146.
4. **Garfield, E.** "The 250 Most-Cited Primary Authors, 1961–1975. Part II. The Correlation between Citedness, Nobel Prizes, and Academy Memberships." *Current Contents,* No. 50: 5–16, December 12, 1977.

5. **Garfield, E.** "Citation Indexing for Studying Science." *Nature,* **227:**669–671, 1970.
6. **Clark, K.E.** "The APA Study of Psychologists." *American Psychologist,* **9:**117–120, 1954.
7. **Bayer, A.E. and Folger, J.** "Some Correlates of a Citation Measure of Productivity in Science." *Sociology of Education,* **39:**383–390, 1966.
8. **Orr, R.H. and Kassab, J.L.** "Peer Group Judgments on Scientific Merit: Editorial Refereeing." (Washington, D.C.: Congress of the International Federation of Documentation, October 15, 1965.)
9. **Virgo, J. A.** "A Statistical Procedure for Evaluating the Importance of Scientific Papers." *The Library Quarterly,* **47:**415–430, 1977.
10. **Price D.J.D.** "Networks of Scientific Papers." *Science,* **149:**510–515, 1967.
11. **Meadows, A.J.** "The Citation Characteristics of Astronomical Research Literature." *Journal of Documentation,* **23:**28–33, 1967.
12. **Wade, N.** "Citation Analysis: A New Tool for Science Administrators." *Science,* **188:**429–432, 1975.
13. **Geller, N.L., de Cani, J.S., and Davies, R. E.** "Lifetime Citation Rates as a Basis for Comparisons Within a Scientific Field." In Goldfield, E.D. (ed.) *American Statistical Association Proceedings of the Social Statistics Section.* (Washington, D.C.: American Statistical Association, 1975). Pp. 429–433.
14. **Price D.J.D.** "Citation Measures of Hard Science, Soft Science, Technology, and Non-Science." In Nelson, C.E. and Pollock, D.K. (eds). *Communication Among Scientists and Engineers* (Lexington, Mass.: D.C. Heath, 1970). Pp. 3–22.
15. **Garfield, E., Sher, I., and Torpie, R.J.** *The Use of Citation Data in Writing the History of Science* (Philadelphia: Institute for Scientific Information, 1964). 86 pp.
16. **Asimov, I.** *The Genetic Code* (New York: New American Library, 1962). 187 pp.
17. **Garfield, E., Malin, M.V., and Small, H.** "A System for Automatic Classification of Scientific Literature." *Journal of Indian Institute of Science,* **57:**61–74, 1975.

Chapter Seven

Citation Analysis as a Method of Historical Research into Science

The use of citation analysis in research on the history of science is based on a literary model of the scientific process. In this model, scientific work is represented by the papers written and published to report it, and the relationships between discrete pieces of work are represented by the references in the papers. Price, one of the leading contributors to the model, has taken this view of the scientific process to the point of defining scientific papers as the chief product of a scientist's work, and a scientist as one who writes scientific papers (1). Though the literary model is certainly a gross simplification of the scientific process, it seems to provide a functional view of that process that is both accurate and useful. Price has used it in a series of studies that have produced a number of insights into how science works and the ways in which it differs from, and interacts with, technology (1-4). Small and Griffith have used it to define the specialities that make up the leading edge of scientific development (5, 6), and I have used it to clarify the interactions between broad fields of research (7).

The accuracy and productivity of the model for historical studies was tested and proved in 1964 in a study conducted for the Air Force Office of Scientific Research (8). That study was concerned with determining whether citation analysis could be used to develop an accurate and useful network diagram of the cumulative research that led to a given scientific breakthrough.

The idea was not entirely a new one. Bernal had used the network diagram technique in 1953 to show the antecedents and consequences of Pasteur's discovery of molecular asymmetry but had not based it on citation analysis (9). The potential usefulness of references for historical research was suggested in 1955 (10). Then, in 1960, Dr. Gordon Allen put together the two ideas of references and diagrams with the illustration shown in Figure 7.1. A picture of the chronological and citation relationships among the papers in a bibliography on the staining of nucleic acids, the

82 *Citation Indexing*

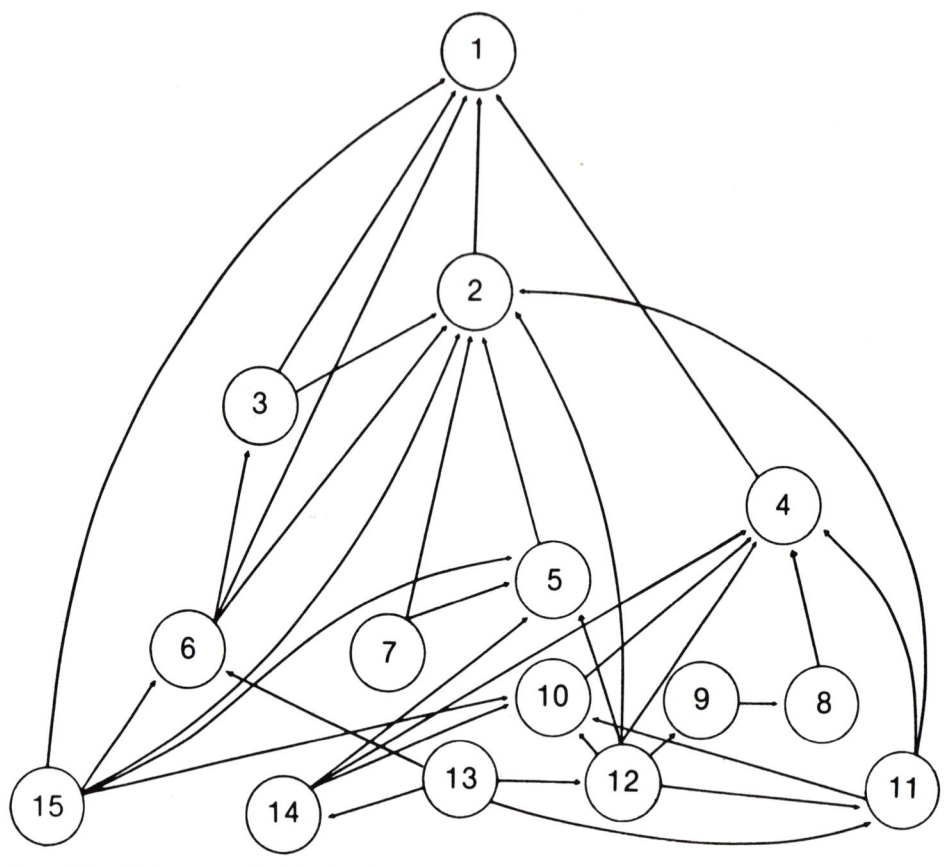

Figure 7.1 Citation network of the development of nucleic-acid staining.

KEY

1. Rabinowitch 1941
2. Michaelis 1947
3. Michaelis 1950
4. Zanker 1952
5. Northland 1954
6. Lawley 1956
7. Peacocke 1956
8. Appel 1958
9. Appel 1958
10. Steiner 1958
11. Steiner 1959
12. Bradley 1959
13. Bradley 1959
14. Bradley 1960
15. Loeser 1960

---

diagram uses circles arranged vertically in chronological order to represent papers and has arrows to represent the references between papers. Though Allen had not intended it, the resulting network diagram struck me as being a concise, easily understood outline of the historical development of the staining methodology. That observation led directly to the idea of using references to diagram the research dynamics of a given scientific development over time (11). According to the literary model of the scientific process, that type of analysis and presentation could be expected to be very useful to science historians. Bernal (12), Price (13), Leake (14), and Shryock (15) agreed that the idea had merit. The study for the Air Force was designed to determine how much.

ESTABLISHING A BASE LINE

To test the historical accuracy of citation analysis, we needed a base line—a recent scientific breakthrough whose history had been analyzed and documented by a recognized authority. We chose as our base line *The Genetic Code,* by Dr. Isaac Asimov (16), a clear, concise account of more than a century of complex research that led, eventually, to the development and validation of the DNA theory of genetic coding that controls protein synthesis.

The study strategy was simple: produce a network diagram of the events and relationships described by Asimov, produce a second diagram from the references in the papers that reported the Asimov events, compare the two to see how closely they match, and perform a thorough citation analysis of the papers to see whether they identify any important events or relationships missed by Asimov. How the strategy was implemented is shown in Figure 7.2.

The first task was to analyze Asmiov's account of the development to identify the

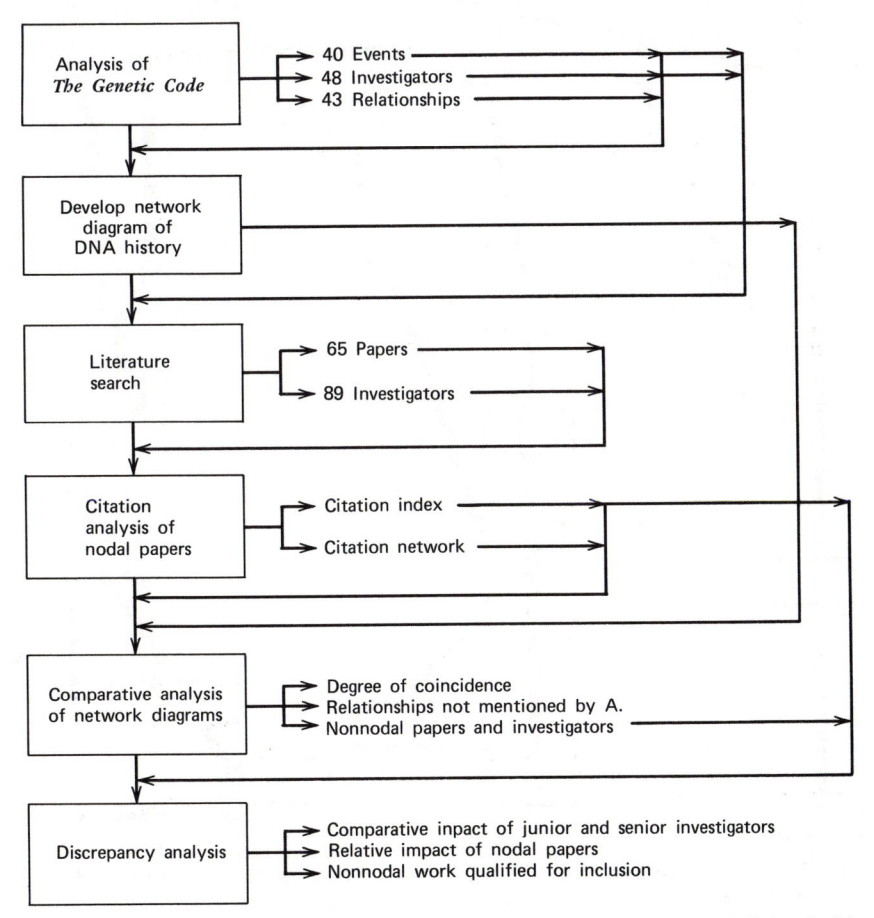

Figure 7.2 Flowchart of major tasks in study to validate use of citation analysis in defining the history of scientific development.

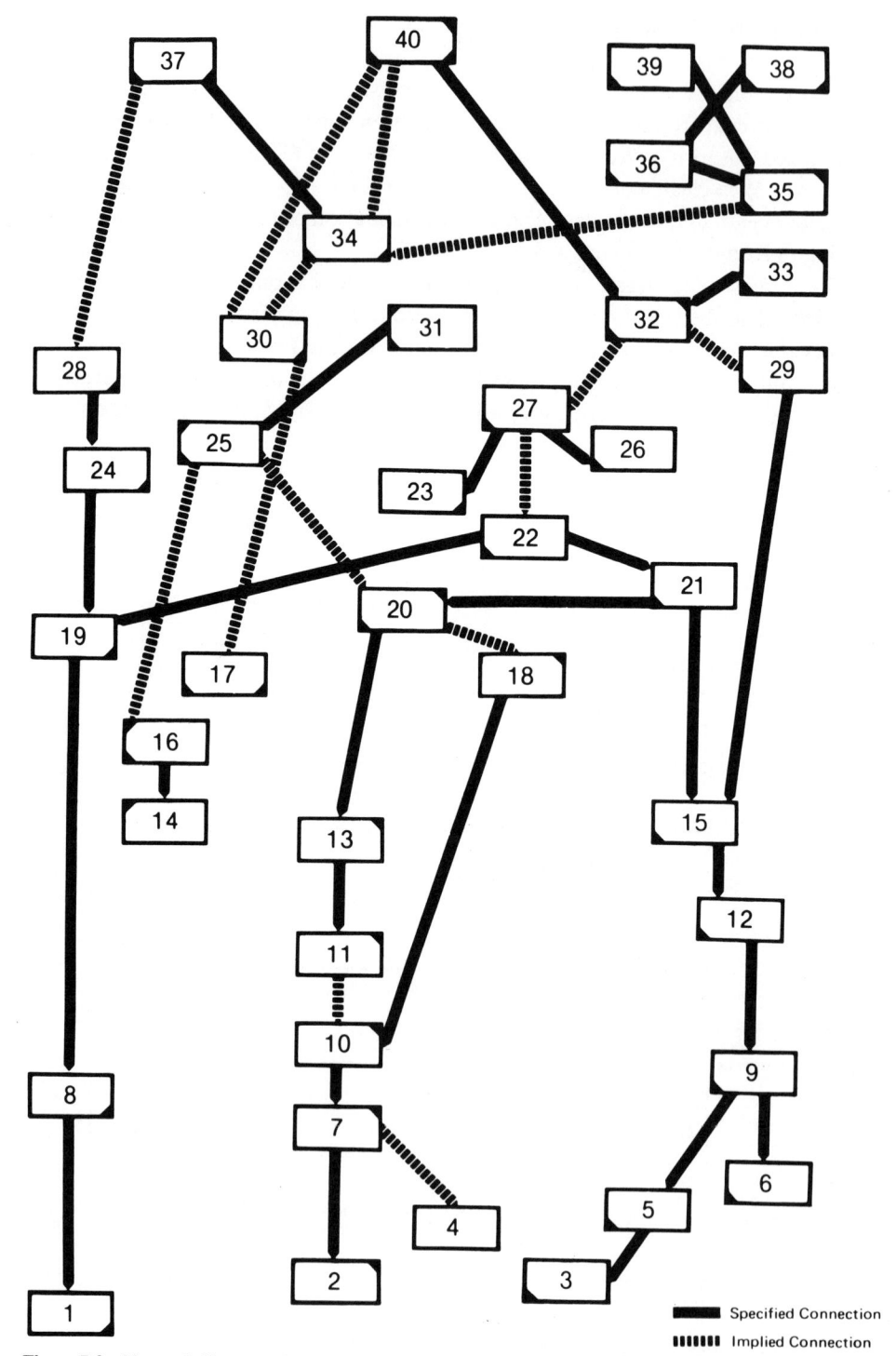

Figure 7.3 Network diagram of how DNA theory was developed and proved, as defined by I. Asimov in *The Genetic Code*.

KEY

1. Braconnot 1820
2. Mendel 1865
3. Miescher 1871
4. Flemming 1879
5. Kossel 1886
6. Fischer and Piloty 1891
7. DeVries 1900
8. Fischer 1907
9. Levene and Jacobs 1909
10. Muller 1926
11. Griffith 1928
12. Levene with Mori and London 1929
13. Alloway 1932
14. Stanley 1935
15. Levene and Tipson 1935
16. Bawden and Pirie 1936-1937
17. Caspersson and Schultz 1938-1939
18. Beadle and Tatum 1941
19. Martin and Synge 1943-1944
20. Avery, MacLeod, and McCarty 1944
21. Chargaff 1947
22. Chargaff 1950
23. Pauling and Corey 1950-1951
24. Sanger 1951-1953
25. Hershey and Chase 1952
26. Wilkins 1953
27. Watson and Crick 1953
28. DuVigneaud 1953
29. Todd 1955
30. Palade 1954-1956
31. Fraenkel-Conrat 1955-1957
32. Ochoa 1955-1956
33. Kornberg 1956-1957
34. Hoagland 1957-1958
35. Jacob and Monod 1960-1961
36. Hurwitz 1960
37. Dintzis 1961
38. Novelli 1961-1962
39. Allfrey and Mirsky 1962
40. Nirenberg and Matthaei 1961-1962

research events and relationships he described. Forty events were found, ranging in time from 1820 to 1962. The descriptions of 36 of them included the names of the investigators involved; the remaining four did not, but they did give enough other information for us to be able to identify the investigators. Asimov also identified 29 relationships between events and implied the existence of another 14.

All 40 events and 43 relationships were then laid out in a network diagram (Figure 7.3) in which the nodes represent events and the arrows between nodes represent research relationships. Each node is numbered and identifies the name of the investigator credited with the research, the years covered by the research, and the general type of research. The type of research is shown by the corner code, which distinguishes between genetics, protein chemistry, nucleic acid chemistry, and virology. The nodes are grouped by type of research along three vertical lines to show the development and evolution of the three oldest research fronts. Protein chemistry events are on the left, nucleic acid chemistry on the right, and genetics in the middle. The diagram shows each of them as having been distinctly separate lines of research in the nineteenth century (bottom of diagram) and then combining to form molecular biology about the middle of this century (middle and top of diagram).

THE CITATION-BASED NETWORK

Developing a network diagram from the references of the papers that reported the nodal events began with an extensive literature search to determine which papers should be used. The search was conducted, on the names of investigators and subjects obtained and derived from the Asimov book, in a number of major indexes, namely *Chemical Abstracts, Current List of Medical Literature,* and *Index Medicus.*

Though there was no problem in finding papers on the subjects of the nodal events, there was one in finding the particular papers that first reported the events as Asimov described them. The problem was one of judgment. Certain events were reported in a number of papers, all of which had to be analyzed thoroughly by subject specialists to determine which one was the first to report the particular research described by Asimov. Generally, the most difficult choices were posed by the events that took place after 1945, which is when scientists began the practice of publishing significant results in several journals concurrently and of publishing the results of multistage research a stage at a time. One paper chosen, for example, was the thirty-second of a series.

Strict adherence to the self-imposed rule that the papers selected be the first to report the events as Asimov defined them was an important convention in the methodology of the study. A number of events were first reported in papers with few references and later elaborated on in papers containing extensive bibliographies. The Watson and Crick discovery of the molecular configuration of DNA, for example, was announced in two articles, published in *Nature,* with minimal bibliographies. Within the year, however, Watson and Rich published a paper on the same subject, in the *Proceedings of the National Academy of Sciences U.S.,* that had a much more extensive bibliography. By always selecting representative papers on the basis of first announcement rather than length of bibliography, the study team made the test of the citation analysis technique considerably more rigorous than it might have been. As a result, the citation-based network that was developed is a demonstration not of how much historical detail citation analysis can define, but of whether it can define at least enough to be useful in the study of science history.

The literature search and review produced a total of 65 papers, which reported the nodal events, and 89 investigators, who were credited with authorship of the papers. These papers and investigators were the basis of the citation analysis that was performed to develop the alternative network diagram.

For the purposes of this analysis, a citation index (see excerpt in Figure 7.4) was developed from the 65 nodal papers. The primary entries in the index were the reference citations from the 65 papers. Under each entry were listed the nodal papers that cited it.

Using the nodal citation index to identify reference connections between papers, the network diagram shown in Figure 7.5 was developed and promptly named a "historiograph" ("historiogram" might have been more appropriate). The nodes are the Asimov events. The arrows connecting the nodes, however, reflect the relationships between events that are identified not by Asimov, but by the references in the nodal papers. Some of the connections are strong ones, consisting of references with a formal citation to another nodal paper, to a relevant nonnodal paper by a nodal author, or to a nonnodal paper by the citing author that, in turn, cites a nodal paper. In other words, all the strong connections are explicit references, though some are through an intermediate self-citation, to papers by nodal authors that are on the subject of nodal events. Other connections are weaker, consisting of

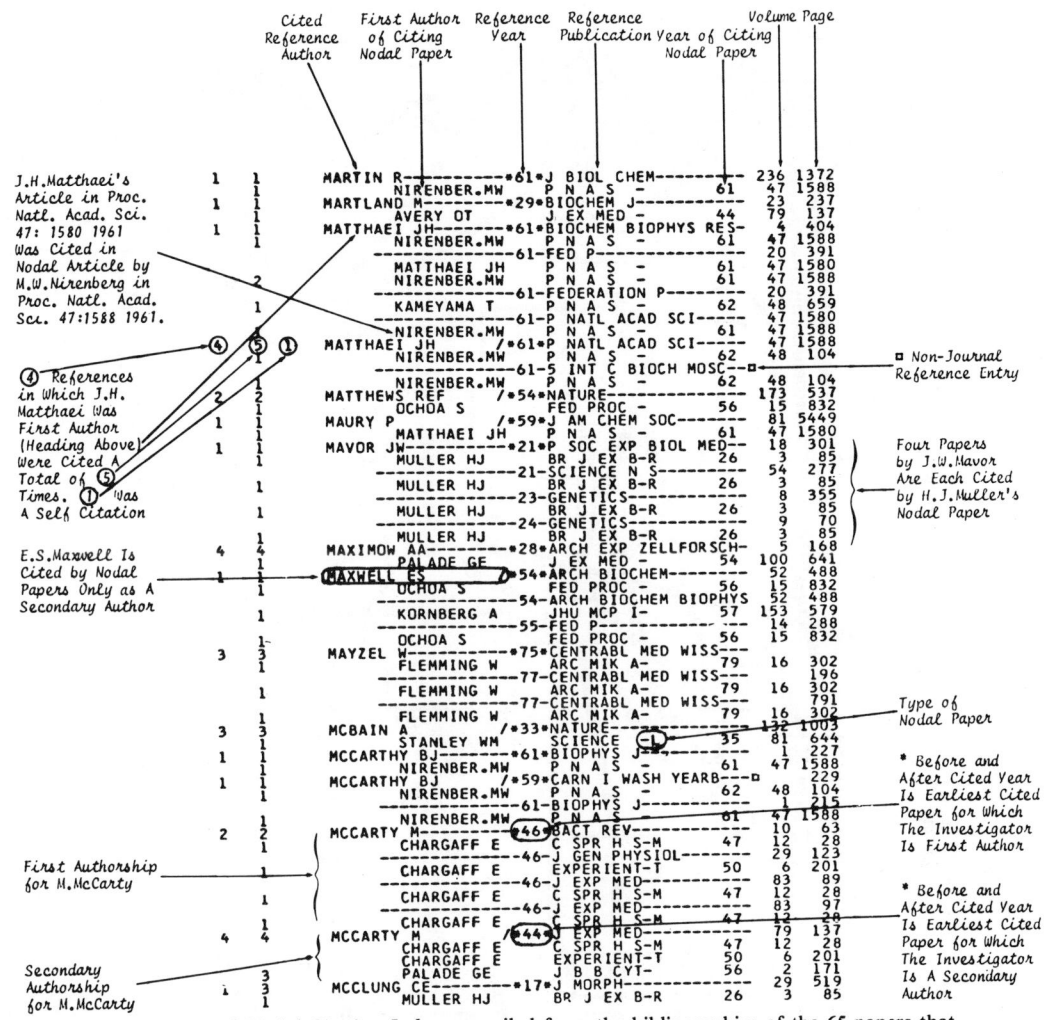

Figure 7.4 Excerpt of *Nodal Citation Index,* compiled from the bibliographies of the 65 papers that reported the events specified by I. Asimov in his history of the DNA theory.

acknowledgments of the relevant work of another nodal author without explicitly citing a particular paper, or references to papers by nonnodal authors that, in turn, cite a nodal paper.

The citation analysis performed to identify relationships was far from exhaustive. First of all, the nodal citation index was compiled only from the papers chosen to represent the nodal events. As mentioned earlier, these papers were only a fraction of what had been written to report some of the nodal events. If all the relevant papers by nodal authors had been included in the citation index, many more relationships between nodal events might have been identified. Second, the effort to uncover the relationships identified by even the limited citation index that was used concentrated primarily on looking for direct connections between nodal papers, regardless of whether the reference included a formal citation or stopped with an acknowledgment in the text. For economic reasons the search for indirect citations,

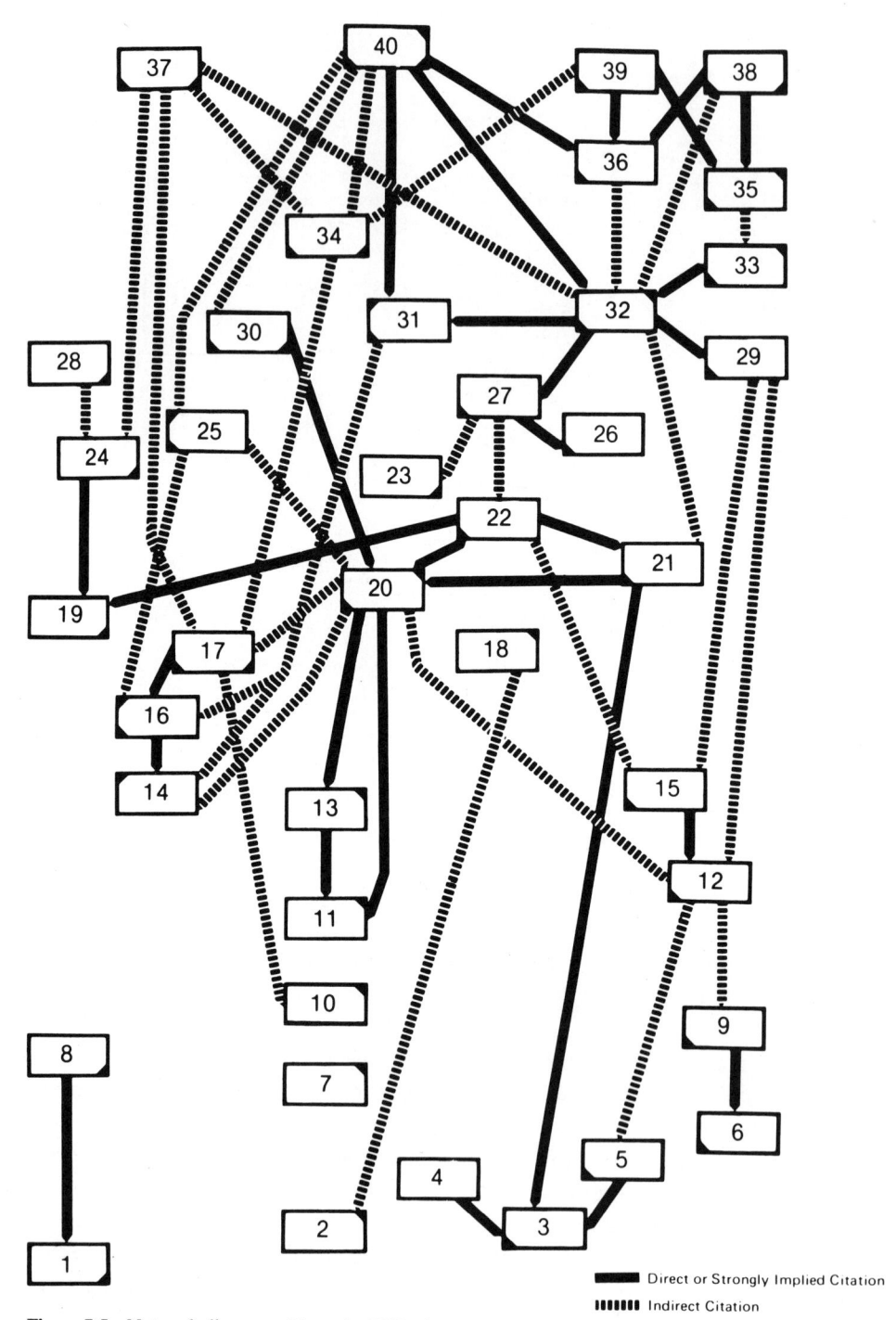

Figure 7.5 Network diagram of how the DNA theory was developed and proved, as defined by the citation connections among the nodal papers.

KEY

1. Braconnot 1820
2. Mendel 1865
3. Miescher 1871
4. Flemming 1879
5. Kossel 1886
6. Fischer and Piloty 1891
7. DeVries 1900
8. Fischer 1907
9. Levene and Jacobs 1909
10. Muller 1926
11. Griffith 1928
12. Levene with Mori and London 1929
13. Alloway 1932
14. Stanley 1935
15. Levene and Tipson 1935
16. Bawden and Pirie 1936-1937
17. Caspersson and Schultz 1938-1939
18. Beadle and Tatum 1941
19. Martin and Synge 1943-1944
20. Avery, MacLeod, and McCarty 1944
21. Chargaff 1947
22. Chargaff 1950
23. Pauling and Corey 1950-1951
24. Sanger 1951-1953
25. Hershey and Chase 1952
26. Wilkins 1953
27. Watson and Crick 1953
28. DuVigneaud 1953
29. Todd 1955
30. Palade 1954-1956
31. Fraenkel-Conrat 1955-1957
32. Ochoa 1955-1956
33. Kornberg 1956-1957
34. Hoagland 1957-1958
35. Jacob and Monod 1960-1961
36. Hurwitz 1960
37. Dintzis 1961
38. Novelli 1961-1962
39. Allfrey and Mirsky 1962
40. Nirenberg and Matthaei 1961-1962

made through an intermediate reference, was conducted only in cases where no direct links existed. While this approach did not reduce the number of nodal events that could be linked together, it did understate the strength of some of the connections.

Despite these limitations, the citation analysis identified a total of 59 relationships between nodal events, and all but 11 of them were identified by strong reference links.

COMPARATIVE ANALYSIS

A comparative analysis of the historiographs produced from the Asimov account and the citation analysis turned up a number of similarities and differences. First, the similarities:

The most important similarity was that the historiograph produced from the citation analysis duplicated 65% of the relationships in the one produced from the Asimov account (28/43). The degree of coincidence was even greater for the relationships that Asimov considered important enough to specify in full detail. The citation-based historiograph duplicated 72% of them (21/29).

Two other points of similarity had to do with judgments made or implied about the relative originality and importance of the events. The citation historiograph showed 11 events that were not connected to any earlier work, which suggested that they were significant departures from earlier work, marked by an exceptional degree of originality, and probably of fundamental importance to the overall line of research. In some cases, the research independence is more apparent that real; it can be explained by the fact that the earlier a work appears on a chronological scale that stretches back to the middle of the nineteenth century, the lower the probability that it will contain references to earlier work. Nevertheless, the citation historiograph's implication that these 11 events were historically independent coincided closely with Asimov's judgment. He related only four of them to earlier work, which means that his judgment confirms 64% of the inferences about fundamental importance that could be made from the citation historiograph. An analysis of the papers that reported the 11 events showed that all of them did, in fact, involve highly original work that opened up productive new directions.

The second similarity of judgment was more explicit. Asimov singled out one particular event as probably being the single most important contribution to the overall effort. To test the citation analysis against this judgment, we calculated citation weights for all the nodes. The weight assigned to each node reflected the number and type of reference links to and from all the other nodes in the network. The nodal event with the highest citation weight turned out to be the same one that Asimov had judged to be the most important.

The major point of difference between the two historiographs was that the one based on citation analysis identified 31 relationships not noted by Asimov. These relationships ranged in strength from perfunctory acknowledgment of earlier work to strong research dependency.

Other differences were apparent when the Asimov historiograph was compared with the nodal citation index, which identified a number of papers and investigators neither implied nor mentioned by Asimov. The papers were on work that did not correspond to any of the nodal events but that were important enough to have been cited by nodal papers. Some of the investigators Asimov failed to mention consisted of the authors of these nonnodal papers; the rest were uncredited coauthors of nodal papers. These points of discrepancy were analyzed in more detail to see if citation counts could be taken further as a measure of the impact of scientific work, and if citation analysis could identify any major contributions that Asimov had not.

DISCREPANCY ANALYSIS

The test of citation counts as a measure of impact was built around the 41 coauthors of nodal papers who Asimov did not credit. By not crediting them, he implied that their work had less impact than the work of those he did credit. The 1961 *SCI* was used to find out whether this implied difference was reflected in the citation record compiled that year for the two groups of investigators.

The citation record put together for each investigator was based on all papers cited in 1961 (not just nodal papers) and consisted of the following data:

1. Number of times cited.
2. Number of times cited by nonnodal authors.
3. Number of self-citations.
4. Number of times cited by the coauthors of their nodal papers.

5. Number of times cited by other nodal authors.
6. Publication date of the earliest paper cited.

Averages were then worked out for each class of investigators.

The analysis showed that the investigators credited by Asimov and designated as "senior" were more heavily cited than those who had not been credited by him and had been designated as "junior." In all but three cases, the junior investigators were cited less frequently than the senior investigator with whom they shared the authorship of a nodal paper. The three exceptions were all a matter of special circumstance: In one case, the junior and senior investigators were coauthors in a series of heavily cited papers, including the nodal paper, in which the junior investigator was listed more often as the first author. In another case, the junior investigator, again, was listed as first author on the nodal paper, which was a heavily cited one. And in the third case, the junior investigator had been publishing much longer than the senior one; when the papers published prior to the earliest cited paper of the senior investigator were excluded from the comparison, the senior investigator turned out to be cited more frequently.

The averages quantified the extent of the difference between the two groups. The 48 senior investigators each were cited an average of 112 times, while the average per junior investigator was only 41.6. These rates are put into perspective by a 5.5 average for all the reference authors listed in the 1961 *SCI* and a 169 average for the 13 winners of the Nobel Prize for physics, chemistry, and medicine in 1962 and 1963.

Since the analysis showed that citation counts did, in fact, reflect the type of gross judgment Asimov implied about the relative impact of scientific work, it was extended to see if citation rates could provide a more precise measure. This extension of the analysis was based on the assumption that the work reported in nodal papers probably had more impact than all, or most, other work reported by the authors. The question to be answered was whether the citation rates of the nodal papers reflected this level of quality.

Again, the 1961 *SCI* was the source of the citation data used. This time, however, the comparison was not between investigators, but between all the cited papers—nodal and nonnodal—in which each investigator was listed as the first author. The comparison was made by ranking each author's papers by the number of times they had been cited in 1961, and then examining the listing for each author to see where the nodal paper ranked relative to the others. A finding that a significant percentage of the nodal papers ranked first in their listings would indicate that citation counts might be a way of identifying what work by a given scientist has had the greatest impact.

There were a number of factors that made the results of this analysis more indicative than definitive. One was that the analysis was based on citation data taken from the single year of 1961. Because authors tend to cite recent literature more frequently than older material, this approach produced a bias that is inversely proportional to age. This tendency means that the older a paper is, the lower it is likely to rank relative to more recent papers. The analysis confirmed the pattern when the average citation rate per nodal paper was computed for three different time periods: the average was 15.1 for articles published from 1951—1961, 5.5 for those published from 1930—1950, and only 1.1 for those published from 1820—1929. The total number of citations to all the papers in the earliest time period was so low, in fact, that there was doubt about their statistical significance.

Another factor distorting the results of the analysis was that the nodal papers were the earliest report of the Asimov events, but not always the most substantive. A number of authors went on to write comprehensive reviews of their nodal work that were much more heavily cited than their initial reports.

Then, too, it was reasonable to expect that some investigators would continue to do outstanding work that generated even more interest than their nodal research. This, of course, turned out to be the case in a few instances.

Despite these negative factors, the analysis showed that 61% of the nodal papers ranked as either the first or second most highly cited of the material published by their first author. As expected, the results were highly time sensitive. Only 35% of the nodal papers published prior to 1941 ranked as the first or second highest cited. But that ranking was achieved by 77% of the papers published after 1940. In fact, 54% of those published between 1941 and 1961 ranked as the most highly cited papers produced by the investigators listed as first authors.

The analysis concerned with identifying overlooked developments that qualified for inclusion in the Asimov account focused on the nonnodal papers and authors that were cited by at least three different nodes of the citation-based historiograph. They were identified by the nodal citation index.

Only one paper met that criterion. It also matched the primary citation characteristics of the nodal papers: its author had been cited in the 1961 *SCI* a total of 172 times, which was higher than the 112 citations averaged by the senior nodal investigators, and this particular paper was the most highly cited of his works. When the paper was reviewed, however, it was found to describe an experimental method that, though useful, probably was not important enough in the historical scheme of things to have been mentioned by Asimov.

The second step in the analysis dug a little deeper by identifying all the nonnodal authors who had been cited by at least three different nodes, but not for any one paper. This uncovered 26 investigators who merited additional study. Twenty-five of them were cited in the 1961 *SCI* more frequently than the average of 41.6 for the junior nodal authors. Thirteen of them were cited more frequently than the 112 average for the senior nodal investigators. And four of the 13 were cited by nodal authors for papers that ranked either first or second in citation rate relative to the rest of the reference citations listed for them in the 1961 *SCI*. Since these four papers matched the primary citation characteristics of the nodal papers, they were selected for individual analysis.

The individual analysis showed that two of the papers described methods, one a reaction, and one a phenomenon that provided an explanation of RNA replication in the absence of DNA. Though important, the methods and reaction probably were not sufficiently critical to the development and proof of the DNA theory to have been mentioned by Asimov. The last paper, however, was a different story. RNA replication in the absence of DNA challenged the entire DNA theory. Work that brought that capability into the framework of the DNA theory certainly seemed to have a place in the history of the basic science involved. Asimov agreed with that conclusion in later discussions.

LESS EFFORT, MORE RESULTS

So the citation analysis ended up uncovering an event of importance that had been overlooked in a history written from memory by a scientist/writer whose memory is acknowledged to be phenomenal. Equally important, the study showed that citation analysis, even at a level considerably less than exhaustive, provides a way of identifying key events, their chronology, relationships, and relative importance, and that it is a very useful tool in working out the history of a given scientific effort. It could well be, in fact, that the technique is even more useful than the DNA study indicates. When the *SCI* data base has been expanded to cover the literature back as far as 1900, it will be possible to see whether the ability to analyze a much larger percentage of the important journal sources produces a significantly greater degree of historical definition.

Another aspect of the utility of citation analysis as a research method is that it is mechanistic. A computer can be used to compile a citation index from the bibliographic inputs, do much of the analysis needed to identify relationships and relative importance, and even produce historiographs [17]. An on-line system for performing these functions in an interactive mode has already been developed at ISI [18]. Even if the role of the computer is minimized to nothing more than the compilation of the index, the method is still mechanistic (algorithmic) in the sense that it consists of procedures that require no special knowledge or talents in either history or the subject being researched.

The historiograph in Figure 7.6 makes the point very nicely. An update of the DNA history that had been done in the 1964 study, it was produced by an assistant of mine, working under my direction, in 1968. Neither of us were historians, nor knew anything about genetics. Yet, it is quite accurate as far as it goes, which is to show the major advances in genetics since 1960.

The procedure we used was considerably simpler than the one followed in 1964 to test the validity of the method. Our starting point was a list of approximately three dozen papers obtained from a review of the 1967 literature on the subject [19]. Using these papers as our source documents, we compiled a citation index of their bibliographies [20]. The index consisted of several hundred papers, which we reduced to the 28 most important by the simple method of eliminating all that had been cited less than five times. To validate the importance of these papers, we checked them out in the 1967 *SCI* to see whether their relatively high citation rate was maintained within the broader framework of the approximately 304,000 source

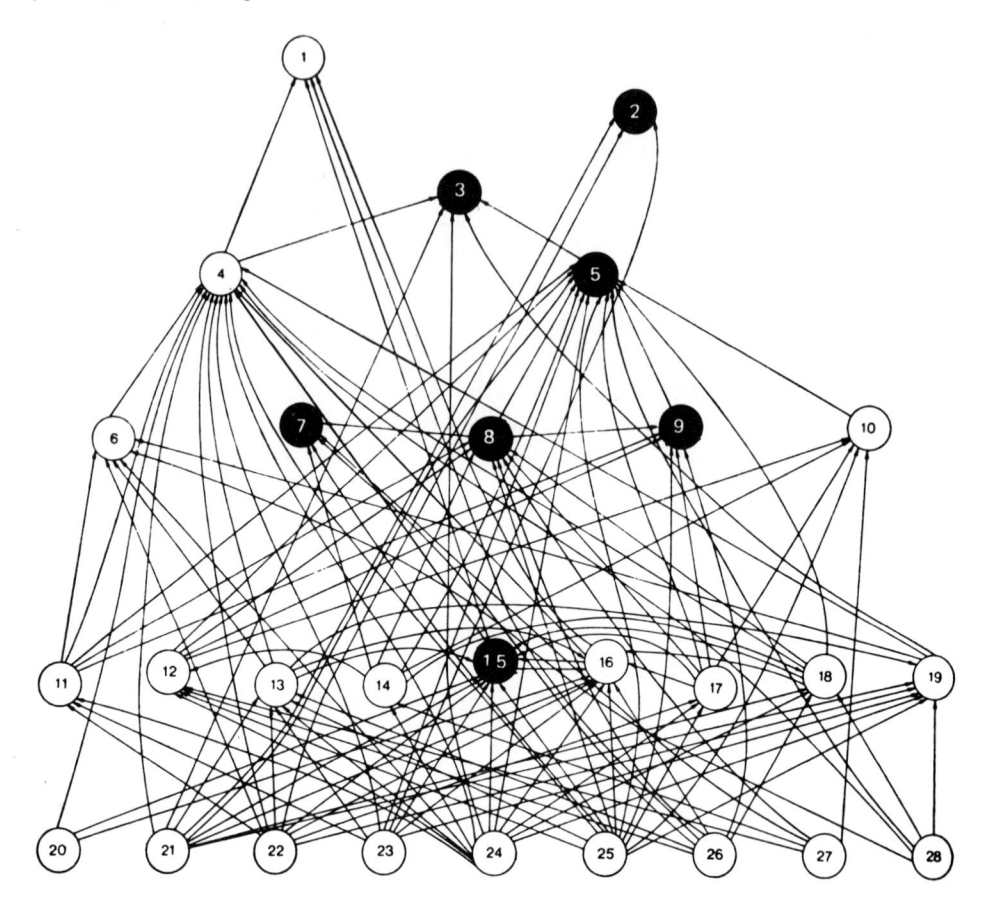

1, Sheehan 1958; 2, Bray 1960; 3, Nirenberg 1961; 4, Marcker 1964; 5, Nirenberg 1964; 6, Marcker 1965; 7, Brenner 1965; 8, Khorana 1965; 9, Nirenberg 1965; 10, Khorana 1965; 11, Marcker 1966; 12, Khorana 1966; 13, Marcker 1966; 14, Khorana 1966; 15, Adams 1966; 16, Webster 1966; 17, Nirenberg 1966; 18, Ochoa 1966; 19, Nakamoto 1966; 20, Berberich 1967; 21, Lucas-Leonard 1967; 22, Caskey 1967; 23, Ochoa 1967; 24, Khorana 1967; 25, Nirenberg 1967; 26, Ochoa 1967; 27, Khorana 1967; 28, Ochoa 1967.

Figure 7.6 Historiograph of the major advances in genetics between 1958 and 1967, based on a citation analysis of a review of the 1967 literature. Each circle represents a paper cited five or more times by the papers listed in the bibliography of the review. The papers represented by solid black circles were cited 15 times or more in the 1967 *SCI*.

items from which that edition of *SCI* was compiled. They were, and the citation index was used to draw the historiograph shown in Figure 7.6. A bibliography of its nodal papers is shown in Figure 7.7.

Spanning the 10-year period from 1958 through 1967, this historiograph certainly does not fill in completely everything that happened since the earlier study, but it does provide a useful outline of the core work done in that time period. If the analysis had been expanded to the literature of each of the intervening years between the two studies, the picture would have been proportionately more comprehensive.

node
1. SHEEHAN, J. C. and YANG, D. M. (1958), The use of N-formylamino acids in peptide synthesis. *J. Amer. Chem. Soc.*, 80, 1154.
2. BRAY, G. A. (1960), A simple efficient liquid scintillator for counting acqueous solutions in a liquid scintillation counter. *Analyt. Biochem.*, 1, 279.
3. NIRENBERG, M. and MATTHAEI, J. H. (1961), The dependence of cell-free protein synthesis in E. coli upon naturally occurring or synthetic polyribonucleotides. *Proc. nat. Acad. Sci. (Wash.)*, 47, 1588.
4. MARCKER, K. A. and SANGER, F. (1964), N-formylmethionyl-sRNA. *J. molec. Biol.*, 8, 835.
5. NIRENBERG, M. and LEDER, P. (1964), RNA codewords and protein synthesis-effect of trinucleotides upon binding of sRNA to ribosomes. *Science*, 145, 1399.
6. MARCKER, K. (1965), Formation of N-formyl-methionyl-sRNA. *J. molec. Biol.*, 14, 63.
7. BRENNER, S., STRETTON, A. O. W. and KAPLAN, S. (1965), Genetic code — nonsense triplets for chain termination and their suppression. *Nature*, 206, 994.
8. SOLL, D., OHTSUKA, E., JONES, D. S., LOHRMANN, R., HAYATSU, H., NISHIMURA, S. and KHORANA, H. G. (1965), Studies on polynucleotides. 49. Stimulation of binding of aminoacyl-SRNAS to ribosomes by ribotrinucleotides and a survey of codon assignments for 20 amino acids. *Proc. nat. Acad. Sci. (Wash.)*, 54, 1378.
9. NIRENBERG, M., LEDER, P., BERNFIELD, M., BRIMACOMBE, R., TRUPIN, J., ROTTMAN, F. and O'NEAL, C. (1965), RNA codewords and protein synthesis. 7. On general nature of RNA code. *Proc. nat. Acad. Sci. (Wash.)*, 53, 1161.
10. NISHIMURA, S., JONES, D. S., OHTSUKA, E., HAYATSU, H., JACOB, T. M. and KHORANA, H. G. (1965), Studies on polynucleotides. 47. *In vitro* synthesis of homopeptides as directed by a ribopolynucleotide containing a repeating trinucleotide sequence — new codon sequences of lysine glutamic acid and arginine. *J. molec. Biol.*, 13, 283.
11. BRETSCHER, M. S. and MARCKER, K. A. (1966), Polypetidyl-s-ribonucleic acid and aminoacyl-s-ribonucleic acid binding sites on ribosomes. *Nature*, 211, 380.
12. JONES, D. S., NISHIMURA, S. and KHORANA, H. G. (1966), Studies on polynucleotides. 56. Further syntheses in vitro of copolypeptides containing 2 amino acids in alternating sequence dependent upon DNA-like polymers containing 2 nucleotides in alternating sequence. *J. molec. Biol.*, 16, 454.
13. CLARK, B. F. C. and MARCKER, K. A. (1966), N-formyl-methionyl-s-ribonuclei cacid and chain initiation in protein biosynthesis — polypeptide synthesis directed by a bacteriophage ribonucleic acid in a cell-free system. *Nature*, 211, 378.
14. MORGAN, A. R., WELLS, R. D. and KHORANA, H. G. (1966), Studies on polynucleotides. 59. Further codon assignments from amino acid incorporations directed by ribopolynucleotides containing repeating trinucleotide sequences. *Proc. nat. Acad. Sci. (Wash.)*, 56, 1899.
15. ADAMS, J. M. and CAPECCHI, M. R. (1966), N-formylmethionyl-sRNA as initiator of protein synthesis. *Proc. nat. Acad. Sci. (Wash.)*, 55, 147.
16. WEBSTER, R. E., ENGELHARDT, D. L. and ZINDER, N. (1966), In vitro protein synthesis — chain initiation. *Proc. nat. Acad. Sci. (Wash.)*, 55, 155.
17. KELLOGG, D. A., DOCTOR, B. P., LOEBEL, J. E. and NIRENBERG, M. (1966), RNA codons and protein synthesis. 9. Synonym codon recognition by multiple species of valine-, alanine-, and methionine-sRNA. *Proc. nat. Acad. Sci. (Wash.)*, 55, 912.
18. STANLEY, W. M., SALAS, M., WAHBA, A. J. and OCHOA, S. (1966), Translation of genetic message — factors in initiation of protein synthesis. *Proc. nat. Acad. Sci. (Wash.)*, 56, 290.
19. NAKAMOTO, T. and KOLAKOFSKY, D. (1966), A possible mechanism for initiation of protein synthesis. *Proc. nat. Acad. Sci. (Wash.)*, 55, 606.
20. BERBERICH, M. A., KOVACH, J. S. and GOLDBERGER, R. F. (1967), Chain initiation in a polycistronic message — sequential versus simultaneous derepression of enzymes for histidine biosynthesis in Salmonella typhimurium. *Proc. nat. Acad. Sci. (Wash.)*, 57, 1857.
21. LUCAS-LENARD, J. and LIPMANN, F. (1967), Initiation of polyphenylalanine synthesis by N-acetylphenylalanyl/sRNA. *Proc. nat. Acad. Sci. (Wash.)*, 57, 1050.
22. CASKEY, C. T., REDFIELD, B. and WEISSBACH, H. (1967), Formylation of guinea pig liver methionyl-sRNA. *Arch. Biochem.*, 120, 119.
23. SALAS, M., HILLE, M. B., LAST, J. A., WAHBA, A. J. and OCHOA, S. (1967), Translation of genetic message. 2. Effect of initiation factors on binding of formyl-methionyl-tRNA to ribosomes. *Proc. nat. Acad. Sci. (Wash.)*, 57, 387.
24. GHOSH, H. P., SÖLL, D. and KHORANA, H. G. (1967), Studies on polynucleotides. 67. Initiation of protein synthesis in vitro as studied by using ribopolynucleotides with repeating nucleotide sequences as messengers. *J. molec. Biol.*, 25, 275.
25. MARSHALL, R. E., CASKEY, C. T. and NIRENBERG, M. (1967), Fine structure of RNA codewords recognized by bacterial amphibian and mammalian transfer RNA. *Science*, 155, 820.
26. LAST, J. A., STANLEY, W. M., SALAS, M., HILLE, M. B., WAHBA, A. J. and OCHOA, S. (1967), Translation of genetic message. 4. UAA as a chain termination codon. *Proc. nat. Acad. Sci. (Wash.)*, 57, 1062.
27. KÖSSEL, H., MORGAN, A. R. and KHORANA, H. G. (1967), Studies of polynucleotides. 73. Synthesis in vitro of polypeptides containing repeating tetrapeptide sequences dependent upon DNA-like polymers containing repeating tetranucleotide sequences — direction of reading of messenger RNA. *J. molec. Biol.*, 26, 449.
28. SALAS, M., MILLER, M. J., WAHBA, A. J. and OCHOA, S. (1967), Translation of genetic message. 5. Effect of Mg^{++} and formylation of methionine in protein synthesis. *Proc. nat. Acad. Sci. (Wash.)*, 57, 1865.

Figure 7.7 Bibliography of the nodal papers in the historiograph of the major advances in genetics between 1958 and 1967.

Citation analysis, then, seems to be a method that greatly simplifies the effort involved in constructing the sequence of events and web of relationships that serve as the starting point for the evaluations, interpretations, and explanations that are the essence of historical research.

There is, of course, one factor that limits the application of citation analysis in history-of-science studies. Bibliographic citation has been an established convention of scientific publication only since the early part of the twentieth century. The further back in time a study goes beyond that point, the less realistic the picture produced by citation analysis. In historical studies dealing with developments since the first quarter of this century, however, citation analysis is a method that seems to be able to simplify the research process and increase the research results.

REFERENCES

1. **Price, D.J.D.** "Is Technology Historically Independent of Science? A Study in Statistical Historiography." *Technology & Culture,* 1:553-568, 1965.
2. **Price, D.J.D.** "Networks of Scientific Papers." *Science,* 149:510-515, 1967.
3. **Price, D.J.D.** "Citation Measures of Hard Science, Soft Science, Technology, and Non-Science." In Nelson, C.E. and Pollock, D.K. (eds). *Communication Among Scientists and Engineers* (Lexington Mass.: D.C. Heath, 1970). Pp. 3-22.
4. **Price, D.J.D.** *Little Science, Big Science* (New York: Columbia University Press, 1963). 119 pp.
5. **Small, H.G. and Griffith, B.C.** "The Structure of Scientific Literature, I: Identifying and Graphing Specialties." *Science Studies,* 4:17-40, 1974.
6. **Griffith, B.C., Small, H.G., Stonehill, J.A., and Dey, S.** "The Structure of Scientific Literatures, II: Toward a Macro- and Micro-structure for Science." *Science Studies,* 4:339-365, 1974.
7. **Garfield, E.** "Journal Citation Studies 1: What is the Core Literature of Biochemistry as Compared to the Core of Chemistry?" *Essays of an Information Scientist,* Vol. 1 (Philadelphia: ISI Press, 1977). Pp. 262-265.

   Garfield, E. "Journal Citation Studies 2: What is the Core Literature of Chemical Physics?" *Essays of an Information Scientist,* Vol. 1 (Philadelphia: ISI Press, 1977). Pp. 274-277.

   Garfield, E. "Journal Citation Studies 3: *Journal of Experimental Medicine* Compared With *Journal of Immunology,* or How Much of a Clinician is the Immunologist?" *Essays of an Information Scientist,* Vol. 1 (Philadelphia: ISI Press, 1977). Pp. 326-329

   Garfield, E. "Journal Citation Studies 4: The Literature Cited in Rheumatology is Not Much Different From That of Other Specialties." *Essays of an Information Scientist,* Vol. 1 (Philadelphia: ISI Press, 1977). Pp. 338-341.

   Garfield, E. "Journal Citation Studies 5: Is Paleontology a Life or a Physical Science? *JCI* Reveals Gap in Coverage of Paleontology and Need for Better Small Journal Statistics." *Essays of an Information Scientist,* Vol. 1 (Philadelphia: ISI Press, 1977). Pp. 423-424.

   Garfield E. "Journal Citation Studies 6: *Journal of Clinical* Investigation: How Much Clinical and How Much Investigation?" *Essays of an Information Scientist,* Vol. 2 (Philadelphia: ISI Press, 1977). Pp. 13-16.

   Garfield, E. "Journal Citation Studies 10: Geology and Geophysics." *Essays of an Information Scientist,* Vol. 2 (Philadelphia: ISI Press, 1977). Pp. 102-106.

   Garfield, E. "Journal Citation Studies 14: Wherein We Observe That Physicists Cite Different Physics Journals Than Other People." *Essays of an Information Scientist,* Vol. 2 (Philadelphia: ISI Press, 1977). Pp. 154-157.

Garfield, E. "Journal Citation Studies 15: Cancer Journals and Articles." *Essays of an Information Scientist,* Vol. 2 (Philadelphia: ISI Press, 1977). Pp. 160–167.

Garfield, E. "Journal Citation Studies 19: Psychology and Behavior Journals." *Essays of an Information Scientist,* Vol. 2 (Philadelphia: ISI Press, 1977). Pp. 231–235

Garfield, E. "Journal Citation Studies 20: Agriculture Journals and the Agricultural Literature." *Essays of an Information Scientist,* Vol. 2 (Philadelphia: ISI Press, 1977). Pp. 272–278.

Garfield, E. "Journal Citation Studies 21: Engineering Journals." *Essays of an Information Scientist,* Vol. 2 (Philadelphia: ISI Press, 1977). Pp. 304–309.

8. **Garfield, E., Sher, I., and Torpie, R.J.** *The Use of Citation Data in Writing the History of Science* (Philadelphia: Institute for Scientific Information, 1964). 86 pp.
9. **Bernal, J.D.** *Science and Industry in the Nineteenth Century* (London: Routledge, Kegan Paul Ltd., 1953), P. 23.
10. **Garfield, E.** "Citation Indexes for Science." *Science,* 122:108–111, 1955.
11. **Garfield, E.** "Citation Indexes in Sociological and Historical Research." *American Documentation,* 14:289–291, 1963.
12. **Bernal, J.D.** Private communication, March 1962.
13. **Price, D.J.D.** Private communication, March 1962.
14. **Leake, C.D.** Private communication, August 1962.
15. **Shryock, R.** Private conversation, September 1962.
16. **Asimov, I.** *The Genetic Code* (New York: New American Library, 1963). 187 pp.
17. **Garfield, E., and Sher, I.H.** *Diagonal Display—A New Technique for Graphic Representation of Complex Topological Networks* (Philadelphia: Institute for Scientific Information, 1967). 94 pp.
18. **Yermish, I.** *"A Citation-Based Interactive Associative Information Retrieval System."* (Philadelphia: University of Pennsylvania, Ph.D. dissertation, 1975). 278 pp. mimeogr.
19. **Sadgopal, A.** "Genetic Code After the Excitement."*Advances in Genetics,* 14:325–404.
20. **Garfield, E.** "Citation Indexing, Historio-Bibliography, and the Sociology of Science." *Proceedings of the Third International Congress of Medical Librarianship,* Amsterdam, May 1969, Davis, K.E. and Sweeney, W.D. (eds.) (Amsterdam: Excerpta Medica, 1970). pp. 187–204. Reprinted in: **Garfield, E.** *Essays of an Information Scientist,*Vol. 1 (Philadelphia: ISI Press, 1977). Pp. 158–174.

Chapter Eight

Mapping the Structure of Science

Conceptually, there is not much distance between diagraming the intellectual structure of an historical line of research and doing the same thing for the whole of contemporary science. If, as the DNA-history study showed (1), citation analysis can be used to define the intellectual relationships between past research events, there is no obvious reason why it cannot be used to do the same thing for current ones. In other words, what the DNA-history study validated was not just a methodology for exploring the history of science but a methodology for defining the intellectual structure of science, past or present.

The structure of science is an intriguing subject to those who study science as a system. Beyond the intuitively comfortable hypothesis that science is a mosaic of small units, rather than a structural monolith, there are many more questions than answers. What is the nature of the basic units in the mosaic structure? How do they relate to each other? Are the intellectual and social structures similar? Are they made up of the same basic units? What is the relationship between them? Is there a variety of configurations at the infrastructure level? How dynamic are the configurations? Is there a relationship between configuration and research performance? Can structural analysis help us make more effective science policy decisions?

A number of studies during the first half of the 1970s began examining some of these questions in a systematic manner. Most of them provide evidence that specialties are the basic intellectual and social unit of the scientific mosaic. Crawford (2) described how the specialty of sleep research is built around the communications between a small group of key individuals and research centers. Griffith and Mullins (3) have shown that small, socially coherent groups are capable of producing major changes within disciplines. Crane's work on specialties in rural sociology and mathematics has led her to the idea of specialties forming a structure that can be mapped (4).

As might be expected, citation analysis has played a prominent and productive role in the attempt to define the structure of science. Building on the conceptual foundations of the literary model of science that was validated by the DNA history study, Price has used citation patterns to explore the structure of physics (5) and one of its specialties (6). Narin, working at a more general level, is using the citation patterns between journals to define the disciplinary structure of science (7). Goffman (8), Jahn (9), and Small (10) have all shown that a specialty is defined by a few critically important papers that appear early in its history. Small and Griffith (11) (12) have gone so far as to produce a map that showed all the high-activity specialties in the natural sciences. Small, on his own, has extended this work to produce a similar map of the social sciences (13) and a five-year series of maps that show the evolution of a single, biomedical specialty, collagen research (14).

The mapping studies by Small and Griffith deserve special attention. They represent the most sophisticated attempt made, as of the mid-1970s, to use citation analysis to define the structure of science on the scale and at the level of detail needed for science policy purposes. On the one hand, their method seems capable of depicting all the major scientific specialties in a single, coherent structure. On the other hand, it offers a range of resolution broad enough to permit the detailed examination of any substructure level that is appropriate to the questions an investigator may choose to pose. This combination of scale and variable resolution produces a functional capability, for analytical purposes, that is analogous to an automated design system in which a computer is used to display a product at all production levels, from final configuration down through the entire hierarchy of subassemblies. If the structures depicted by the Small-Griffith approach are validated as being reasonably realistic, the search for the structure of science will end, and the development of structural analysis techniques that produce functional insights will begin.

CO-CITATION CLUSTERING

The first study by Small and Griffith (11) was designed to test two hypotheses. One was that science is made up of a structure of specialties that can be defined by objective means. The other was that a particular citation measure of the common intellectual interest between two documents was a practical way of defining the structure.

The measure they used was co-citation strength, which is the number of documents that have cited a given pair of documents. Co-citation strength is a creative reversal of Kessler's bibliographic coupling concept (15), which uses the number of references a given pair of documents have in common to measure the similarity of their subject matter. The shortcoming of bibliographic coupling in structural studies of science is that the structure, presumably, is dynamic over time, whereas bibliographic coupling is a fixed measure. (Once a document is published, its references do not change.) In contrast, co-citation strength reflects the frequency of being cited, which is a characteristic that is variable over time. The rationale behind the use of co-citation strength was that its variability was caused by shifts in research focus and relationships (16). I.V. Marshakova also noted this characteristic in her paper on using reference citations for literature classification (17).

To test these hypotheses, Small and Griffith worked out the method shown in Figure 8.1 for identifying clusters of papers that are linked by specific levels of co-citation strength. The processing is done by computer. The initial input to the processing cycle is a calendar increment (quarter, semiannual, annual) of the *SCI* or *SSCI* data base, depending on whether the study is concerned with the natural or social sciences.

Processing begins with extracting a highly cited subset of the data base, which includes both reference and source citations. Setting the threshold of citation frequency that will qualify documents for inclusion in the subset is an important matter of judgment. On the one hand, the threshold should be set low enough to pick up all the documents that could be considered, by the measure of citation frequency, the core of the scientific literature. This core material is representative of the full spectrum of significant research activity. On the other hand, the threshold must be set high enough to exclude documents that do not add anything to the definition of research areas, and may even obscure some of them.

Regardless of the citation-frequency threshold set, the product of the first processing step is a citation index of highly cited documents and the papers that cited them. In the second step, this material is sorted to produce a source-item index of the highly cited documents. In other words, the highly cited documents are organized by the source papers that cited them, so co-citation links can be identified.

All pairs of documents that have been cited by the same source paper (co-cited) are then extracted, and the documents in each pair are arranged in alphabetical sequence. The result is a list of document pairs in which each pair appears in only one of the two sequences that are possible: as AB, but not as BA. The pair list is then put into alphabetical order, which brings together all identical pairs.

To reduce the number of records that must be processed, the alphabetically ordered pair list is consolidated. The number of times each pair appears is counted, the total is recorded next to the first record of the pair, and all duplicate records are deleted.

The next step is to duplicate the consolidated pair list, but with the document sequence of each pair reversed: AB becomes BA.

The two consolidated pair lists are then combined and put into alphabetical order, producing a master list of co-cited pairs on which all pairs that have a single document in common are batched together.

The last step in the procedure is running the master list of co-cited pairs through a clustering routine that aggregates clusters of documents by sequentially linking together all pairs that have at least one document in common. Starting with one pair, say AB, the clustering routine links it to all pairs that include A. It then links to that aggregation all pairs that include a given document that has been linked to A. That procedure is repeated, document by document, until there are no pairs left on the master list that have one of the aggregated documents in common.

At that point, the routine has produced a cluster of documents that are related,

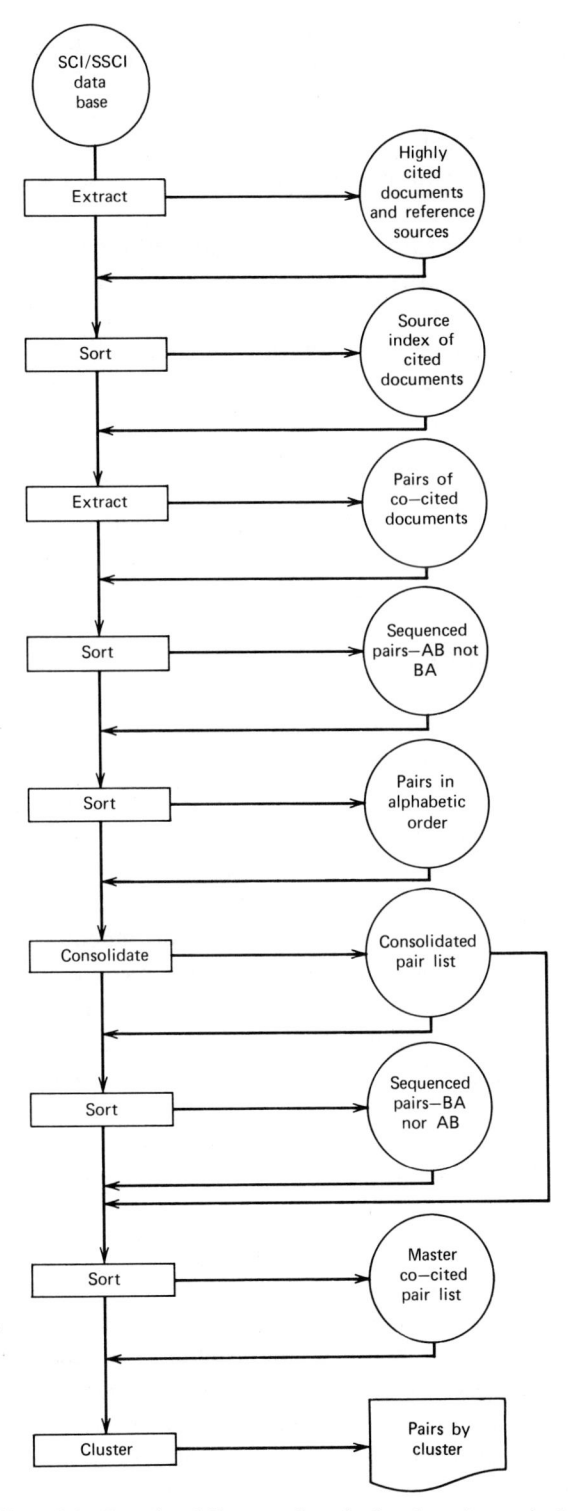

Figure 8.1 Functional diagram of co-citation clustering method.

either directly or indirectly, by co-citation. It then goes through the same operation for each of the unassigned pairs until all the entries on the master list either have been clustered or have been found to be isolated from all the clusters.

The output of the clustering routine is a printout of the pairs contained in each cluster, along with their co-citation strengths, and a list of the isolated pairs that do not fit into any clusters.

The resolution of the clustering operation, in terms of the research scope defined by the papers in individual clusters, can be controlled by setting a threshold for the co-citation frequency that qualifies a pair for inclusion in the clustering routine. Every pair on the master list has a co-citation frequency of at least one, so a co-citation threshold of one would qualify every pair on the list for clustering. As the threshold is raised, however, fewer pairs qualify, and membership in a cluster becomes more exclusive. Because a reduction in the number of pairs in a cluster reduces the potential for subject diversity, raising the cluster threshold has the effect of defining the intellectual scope of the cluster more narrowly—or, increasing cluster resolution.

NATURAL SCIENCE STRUCTURES

The first application of this methodology was in the natural sciences. The data base used was the first quarter of the 1972 *SCI,* consisting of 867,600 reference citations and 93,800 source citations. The source papers came from approximately 2400 journals, which cover just about all the disciplines in the natural sciences.

The threshold set for selecting the subset of highly cited documents from which the master pair list would be derived was a citation frequency of 10. The subset obtained with this threshold contained 1832 reference documents and 16,927 source papers. Out of a possible 1.7 million pairs that could have been formed from the reference documents, they yielded only 20,414. The yield as a percent of potential, which is a measure of the integration of the subset, worked out to a low 1.2%, indicating that the intellectual relationships in the subset were loosely structured. The co-citation strength of the 20,414 pairs ranged from 1 to 81, with 1.78 being the average—another indication of the looseness of the subset structure. On the other hand, all but 18 of the reference documents were included in at least one pair—an indication that, though the structure may be a loose one, there is a definite structural potential.

The subset was clustered at three co-citation threshold levels: 3, 6, and 10. Figure 8.2 shows the number of pairs that qualified for clustering at each of the levels, the number of unique documents in the pairs, and the number of unique documents that did not qualify (isolated cases). Figure 8.3 shows how the clusters at each level were distributed by size and the number of cited documents in each size category. Clusters consisting of only two documents are, of course, not clusters at all, but individual pairs that met the co-citation threshold but did not link to any other pairs. Ignoring them, the number of clusters formed at each level was:

Level	No. of Distinct Pairs	No. of Documents Paired	No. of Isolated Documents
3	3,067	1,310	522
6	791	594	1,238
10	213	193	1,639

Figure 8.2 Co-citation pairs that qualified for clustering.

Cluster Size in Papers	NO. OF CLUSTERS Levels 3	6	10	NO. OF CITED ITEMS Levels 3	6	10
2	71	60	21	142	120	42
3	13	17	3	39	51	9
4	9	11	6	36	44	24
5	7	5	3	35	25	15
6	5	2	4	30	12	24
7	1	1	1	7	7	7
8		3			24	
9	2	1		18	9	
10	1	2		10	20	
11						
12	1	1		12	12	
13						
14						
15	1			15		
16						
17		1			17	
18						
19						
20						
26		1			26	
27		1			27	
32	1			32		
41	1			41		
72			1			72
92	1			92		
200		1			200	
801	1			801		
Total	115	107	39	1,310	594	193

Figure 8.3 Distribution of clusters by number of cited documents.

103

- Level 3: 44 clusters.
- Level 6: 47 clusters.
- Level 10: 18 clusters.

The largest cluster at each of the three levels consists of documents on biomedical research: 801 at level 3, 200 at level 6, and 72 at level 10. This cluster accounts for 61% of all the documents that qualified for clustering at level 3, 34% at level 6, and 37% at level 10. The large drop that takes place in the percent of documents accounted for by the biomedical cluster when the threshold is raised from 3 to 6 suggests that the cluster is rather loosely linked. The fact that the percentage does not drop further when the threshold is raised to 10, however, suggests that a number of the links are quite strong.

Figure 8.4 identifies the 10 largest clusters at level 3. Each is described by a name derived from the titles of its documents, the number of documents and pairs it contains, its integration level (percent of potential pairs), and the average publication date of its documents. The three largest clusters (at all levels, in fact) were *biomedicine, chemistry,* and *nuclear physics.* Again, low integration levels imply that they are very loosely structured. This time, the inference was confirmed by an examination of the documents: each cluster was found to contain several sets of documents on subjects considerably more specialized than the cluster designation. The list also shows clearly the relationship between cluster size and specialization: as the cluster size decreases, the subject matter of its documents becomes more specialized.

With the exception of *biomedicine* and *chemistry,* which describe disciplines, the names assigned to the clusters formed at level 3 all identified specialty areas of research. Since the names were derived from the titles of cluster documents, this finding suggests that the clusters represent the specialties that some researchers think are the basic structural units of science. Analysis of the documents in clusters formed at the other two levels produced similar results.

The relationship between clusters and specialties was further examined by analyz-

	No. of Documents	No. of Pairs	Percentage Connectedness	Average Date
Biomedicine	801	2,205	0.69	1963.3
Chemistry	92	291	7	1962.5
Nuclear physics	41	59	7	1964.3
Particle physics	32	99	20	1968.1
Australia antigen	15	70	66	1969.0
Crystal structure of enzymes	12	30	45	1968.0
Plate tectonics	10	35	78	1967.8
Virally transformed cells	9	25	69	1964.2
Nuclear magnetic resonance	9	8	22	1957.0
Neurophysiology of vision	7	14	66	1963.1

Figure 8.4 Ten largest clusters at level 3.

ing the structure and interactions of a few of the clusters. For this analysis, the network of documents in the *nuclear physics* and *particle physics* clusters formed at level 3 were drawn as simple block diagrams. This had the effect of dramatizing the structural difference that is indicated by the disparate integration levels of the two clusters (Figure 8.4). *Nuclear physics,* which had an integration level of only 7% was quite easy to diagram (Figure 8.5), using blocks to represent its documents and lines between the blocks to represent the strength of the co-citation linkages between documents. However, when it came to the *particle physics* cluster, with an integration level of 20%, this diagraming method was only partially successful (Figure 8.6). Twenty-one of its documents were so tightly linked that it would have been impossible to distinguish between the connecting lines.

To find out if the structures of the two clusters were logically consistent, word profiles were constructed for each document from the titles of the papers that cited it. The rationale behind this method of analyzing the contents of the cluster documents is the same one that underlies the use of citation counts as a measure of research utility: the usefulness of a document is an attribute conferred by the authors who cite it. It follows, then, that an effective way of generally identifying the useful content of the document is by defining the subject matter of the citing papers. Analyzing the title words of the citing papers is the easiest way of doing that.

The profile for each cluster document consisted of the four words most frequently used in the titles of the papers that cited it. The frequency rate of each word also was included in the profiles. With these profiles in the appropriate diagram boxes (Figures 8.7 and 8.8), it was possible to analyze the logical consistency of the clusters. What was being looked at were word patterns: consistency between linked boxes, differences between unlinked ones, and a logical progression of change over a series of linked boxes.

The patterns found seemed to be logically consistent for the specialties of nuclear and particle physics. For example, in the *nuclear physics* cluster, the groups of papers linked together at the top, slightly to the right of center, all have profiles in which the word "scattering" is prominent. As you move down the vertical line of linked documents in the center of the cluster, the profiles describe a progression that goes from nuclear reaction to fission. Conversely, the profiles for unlinked documents are properly dissimilar.

The same type of consistency exists in the *particle physics* cluster. At the bottom, the profiles describe work on current algebras and broken chiral symmetry. As you move up, they introduce applications of the Veneziano model; and, at the top, in the large box containing the tightly linked documents that defied diagraming, they shift to the vocabulary used to describe work in inclusive reactions and the internal structure of elementary particles.

More evidence of the physics clusters being representative of the specialties implied by their names was provided when they were both reclustered at a co-citation threshold level of 1. At that level of commonality, the two clusters were linked at the points shown by the dashed lines on Figures 8.5 through 8.8. Most of the connections were made between the "scattering" work in *nuclear physics* and the loosely structured tail of *particle physics*. The appropriateness of this connection was con-

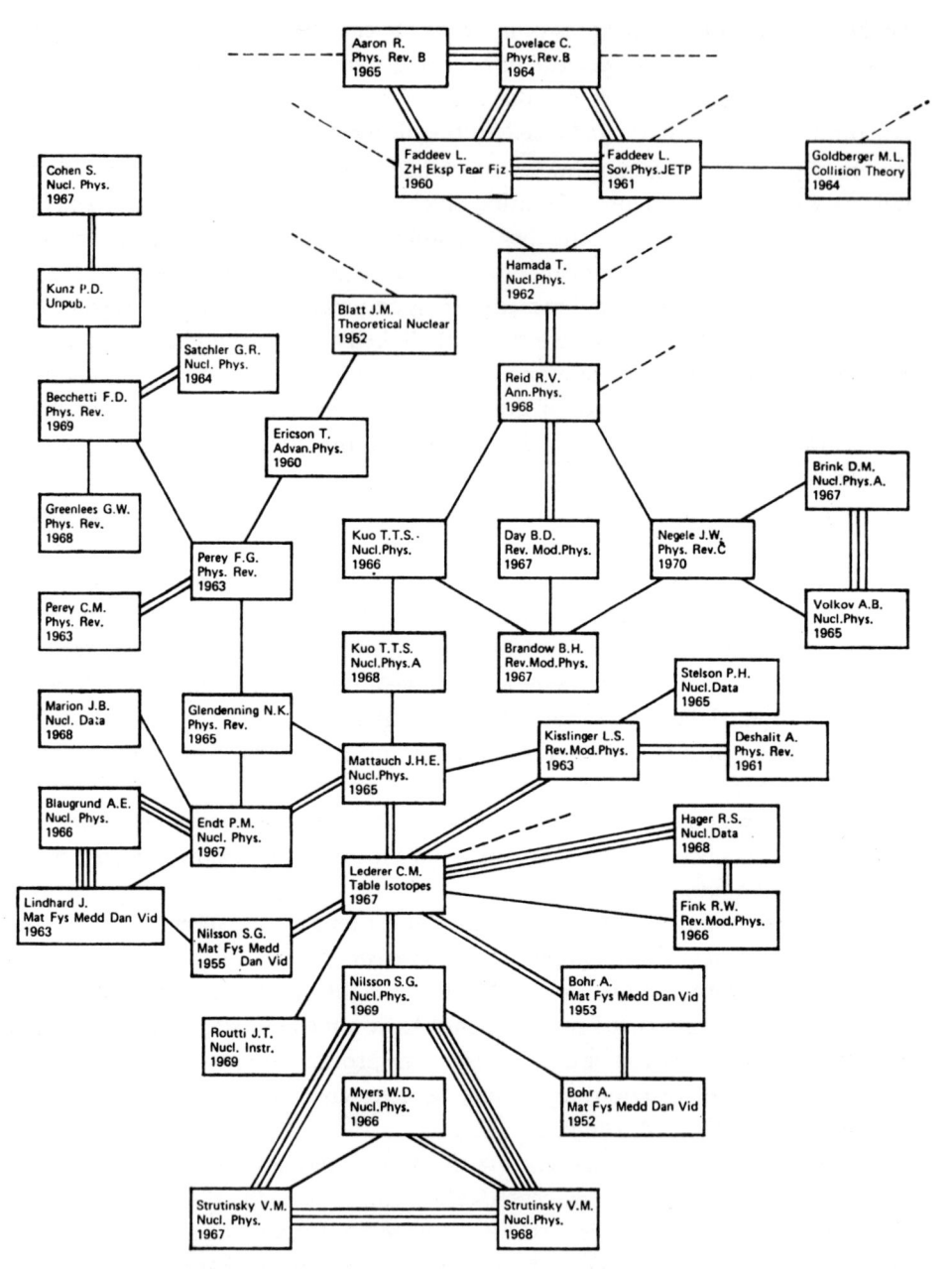

Figure 8.5 Block diagram of level 3 *nuclear physics* cluster. Each box represents a cited document, which is identified by the name of the first author, the title of the journal or book, and the year. Connecting lines between boxes indicate co-citation links, with the number of lines proportional to the strength of the linkages according to the following scale:

Number of Lines	Co-citation Strength
1	3
2	4–5
3	6–8
4	9–12

Dashed lines indicate points at which the cluster links to the *particle physics* cluster below level 3.

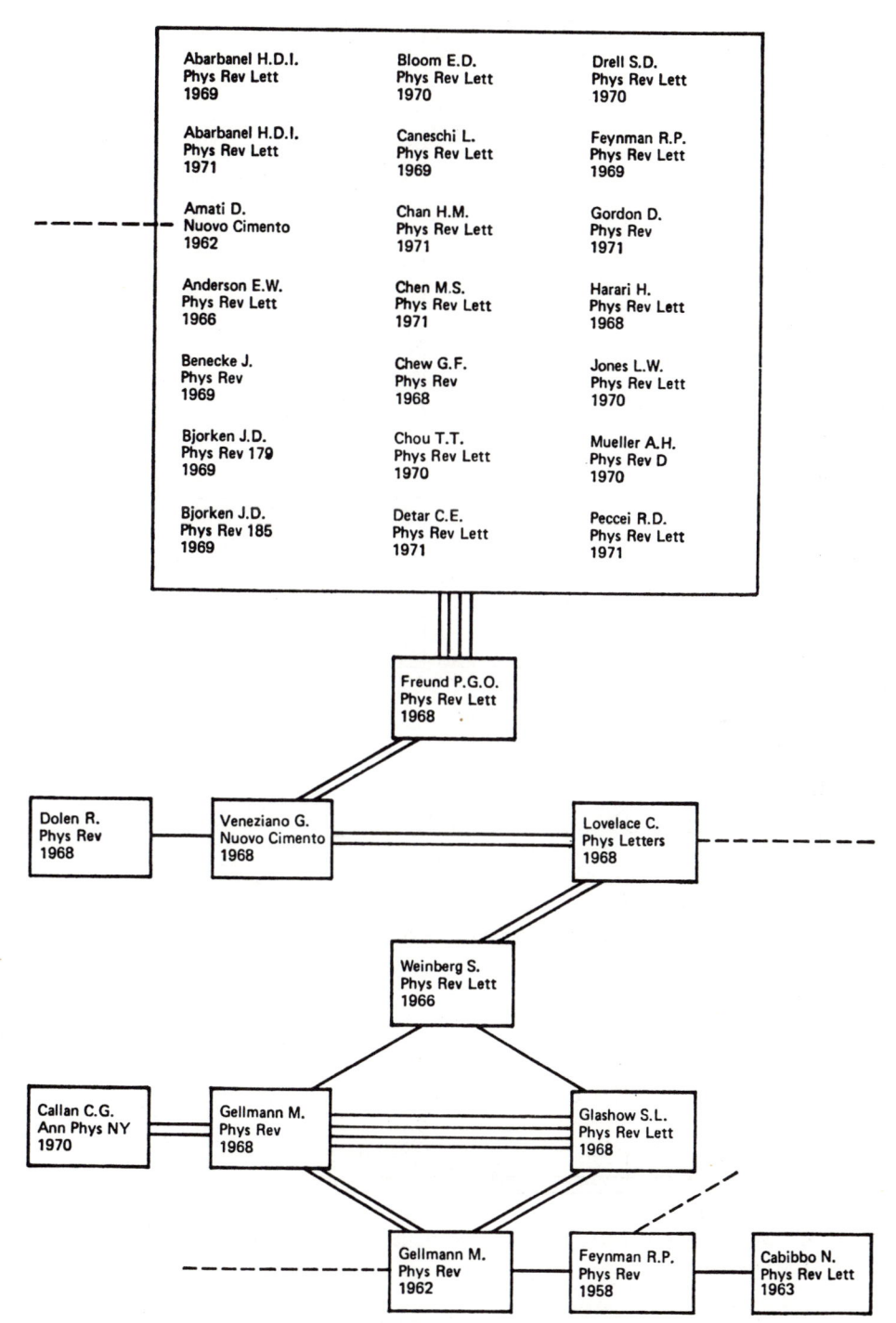

Figure 8.6 Block diagram of level 3 *particle physics* cluster. Documents and co-citation linkages are indicated as in Figure 8.5, with the exception of large box at the top. The co-citation linkages between the 21 documents listed in that box were too strong to depict with lines. The dashed lines indicate co-citation linkages to the *numclear physics* cluster below level 3.

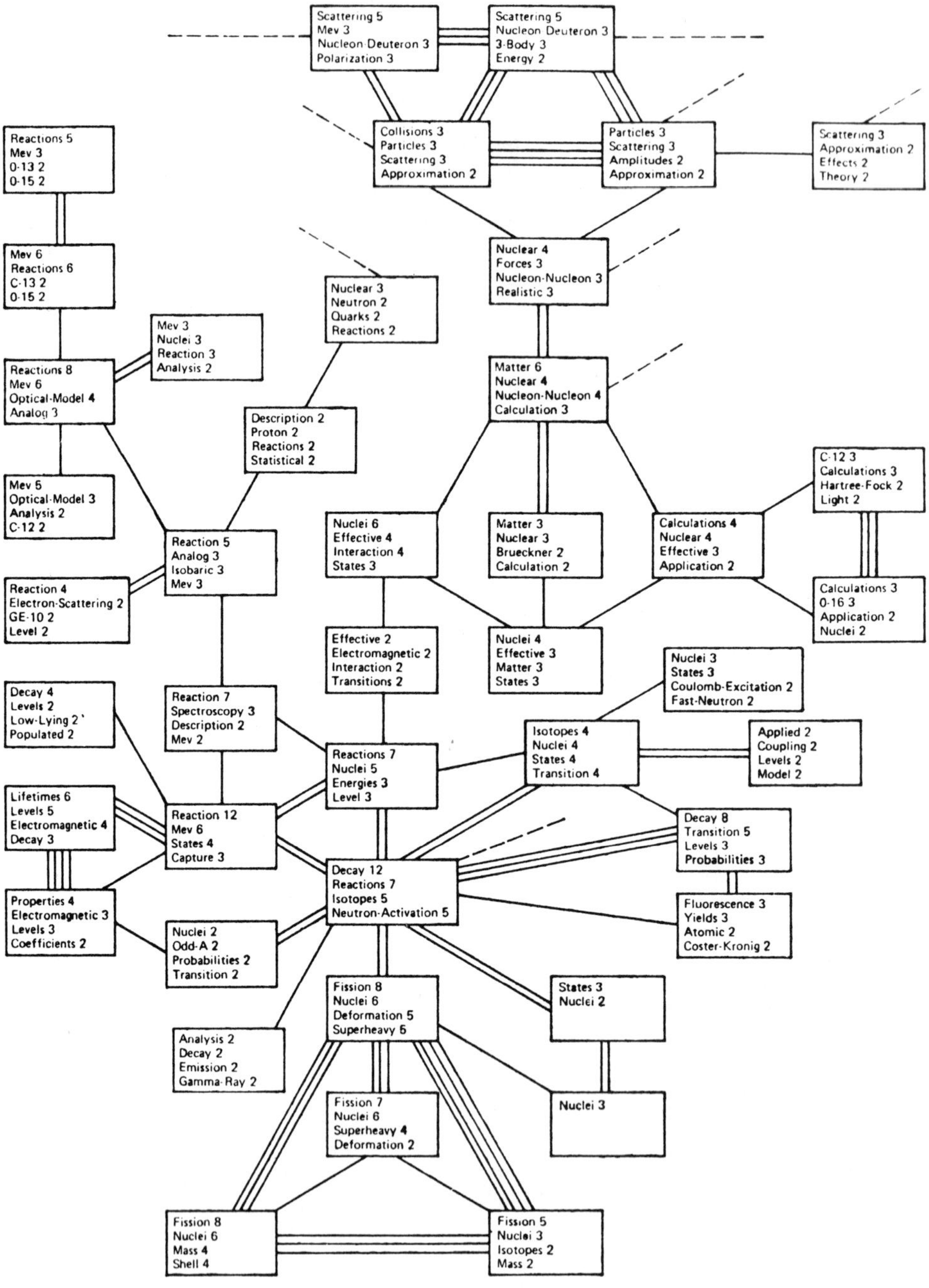

108 *Citation Indexing*

Figure 8.7 Word profiles of level 3 *nuclear physics* cluster. Numbers following the words indicate frequency of occurrence.

firmed by the author of one of the articles that formed the connection—a review article on final-state interactions—who wrote, "The main subject of this review article is a chapter of physics which is recognized as common ground for nuclear physics and what is currently known as particle physics."

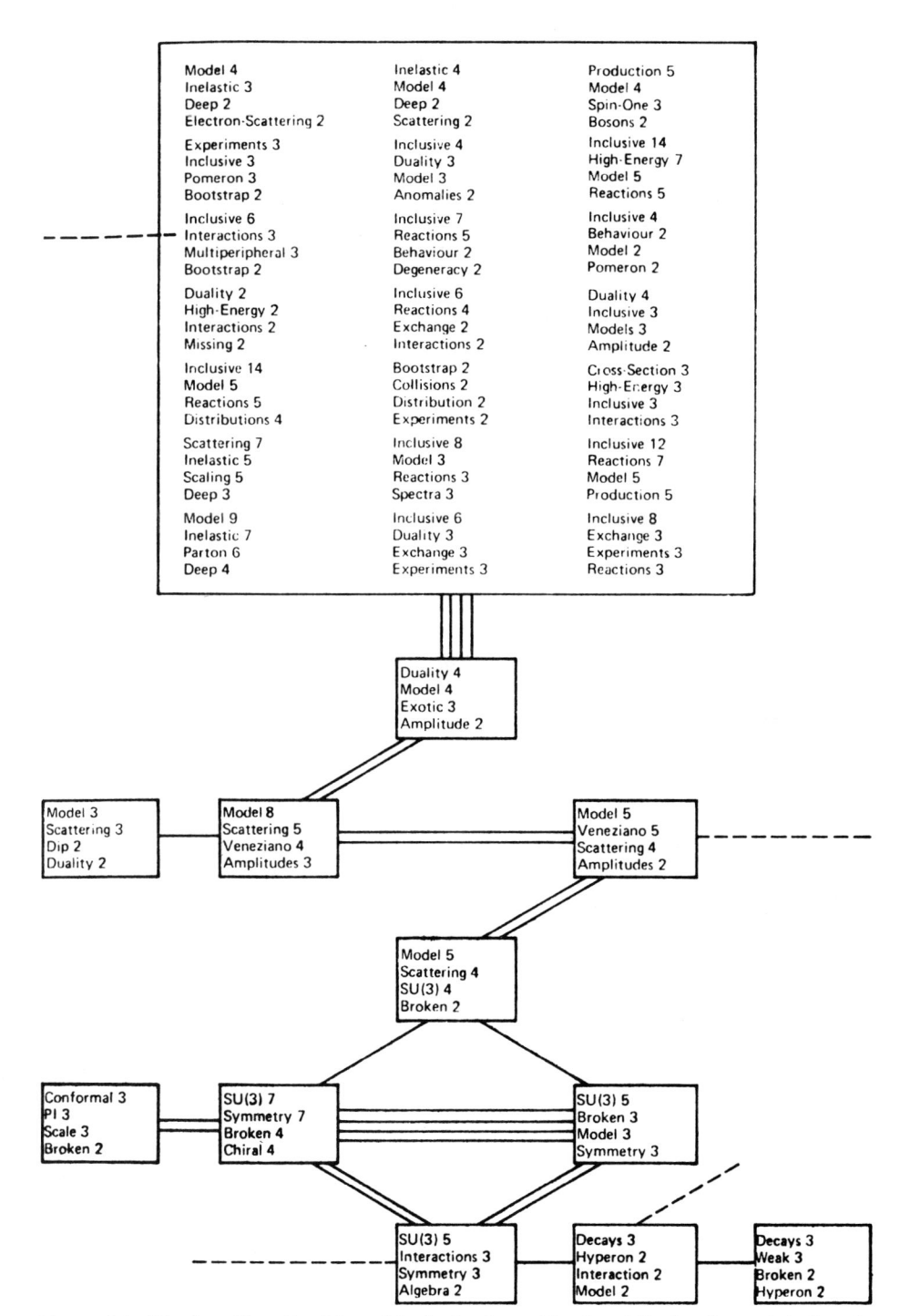

```
Model 4              Inelastic 4        Production 5
Inelastic 3          Model 4            Model 4
Deep 2               Deep 2             Spin-One 3
Electron-Scattering 2 Scattering 2      Bosons 2

Experiments 3        Inclusive 4        Inclusive 14
Inclusive 3          Duality 3          High-Energy 7
Pomeron 3            Model 3            Model 5
Bootstrap 2          Anomalies 2        Reactions 5

Inclusive 6          Inclusive 7        Inclusive 4
Interactions 3       Reactions 5        Behaviour 2
Multiperipheral 3    Behaviour 2        Model 2
Bootstrap 2          Degeneracy 2       Pomeron 2

Duality 2            Inclusive 6        Duality 4
High-Energy 2        Reactions 4        Inclusive 3
Interactions 2       Exchange 2         Models 3
Missing 2            Interactions 2     Amplitude 2

Inclusive 14         Bootstrap 2        Cross-Section 3
Model 5              Collisions 2       High-Energy 3
Reactions 5          Distribution 2     Inclusive 3
Distributions 4      Experiments 2      Interactions 3

Scattering 7         Inclusive 8        Inclusive 12
Inelastic 5          Model 3            Reactions 7
Scaling 5            Reactions 3        Model 5
Deep 3               Spectra 3          Production 5

Model 9              Inclusive 6        Inclusive 8
Inelastic 7          Duality 3          Exchange 3
Parton 6             Exchange 3         Experiments 3
Deep 4               Experiments 3      Reactions 3
```

Duality 4
Model 4
Exotic 3
Amplitude 2

Model 3   Model 8   Model 5
Scattering 3   Scattering 5   Veneziano 5
Dip 2   Veneziano 4   Scattering 4
Duality 2   Amplitudes 3   Amplitudes 2

Model 5
Scattering 4
SU(3) 4
Broken 2

Conformal 3   SU(3) 7   SU(3) 5
PI 3   Symmetry 7   Broken 3
Scale 3   Broken 4   Model 3
Broken 2   Chiral 4   Symmetry 3

                   SU(3) 5   Decays 3   Decays 3
                   Interactions 3   Hyperon 2   Weak 3
                   Symmetry 3   Interaction 2   Broken 2
                   Algebra 2   Model 2   Hyperon 2

Figure 8.8 Word profiles of level 3 *particle physics* cluster. Numbers following the words indicate frequency of occurrence.

A similar attempt to see where one of the level 6 clusters connected at a lower threshold level involved a cluster named *reverse transcription*. That, too, tied into an appropriate structural point: earlier work in molecular biology.

The *biomedicine* cluster, being the largest of the two anomalies that were disciplinary in scope, also was examined in detail. Though it was steadily reduced in size as the co-citation threshold was raised, it seemed to resist attempts to break it into clusters as compact and sharply focused as most of the others. At level 10, it still contained 72 papers that had more of the diversity of a discipline than the focus of a specialty. An analysis of the highly co-cited papers at that level revealed the problem: all but two of the 31 documents that had the highest co-citation rates were methodology papers.

Several strategies, involving the removal of increasingly large subsets of the documents from the clustering data base, were tried to determine the structural role of the methodology documents. Only when all of them were removed and the remaining documents were clustered at level 4 did the individual biomedical specialties emerge. The result was 74 clusters, each one with the intellectual focus of a specialty.

The analysis of the biomedical cluster showed, then, that it had two structures: a conceptual one of specialties and a methodological one of techniques, with the methodological one functioning as a superstructure that tended to link together specialties that had little more in common than a set of shared techniques.

The finding of the dual structure in *biomedicine* was, in comparison, the least of what the study produced. Of more fundamental importance were the findings that co-citation clustering succeeded in identifying groups of papers that were linked by a common intellectual interest, and that the clusters of documents produced by that method seemed to correspond to the specialties that are said to make up the mosaic structure of science. In fact, the study provided the first large-scale evidence of the notion that science is a network of specialties, and that the network can be viewed through the literature.

The study's evidence in support of these two assertions is quite strong. The clustering patterns found certainly were not inevitable. There was a distinct possibility that none of the highly cited papers would be co-cited, or that none of the co-cited pairs would link together. Alternatively, the study could have found the interaction between all areas of research (and the co-citation links between documents) to be so strong that all the highly cited documents formed one gigantic cluster even at high co-citation threshold levels.

The clustering method used in the study, in fact, was biased in favor of producing the second alternative. Because it clusters on the strength of only one link between two pairs, it has a tendency to string together objects that have little in common. Yet, this tendency was evident only at the very low co-citation levels; through most of the threshold range, there was a realistic amount of discrimination. There is no doubt, therefore, that the clusters produced were intrinsic to the data, rather than the methodology.

Though the evidence for the clusters being representative of specialties was considerably less conclusive, it certainly was consistent and encouraging. The clusters of documents fit expectations of how specialties should look and behave. Typically, they consisted of a core of discovery papers, surrounded by others describing work built on the original discoveries. The word analysis showed that their internal structure was logical. And the way the intellectual scope of clusters varied with the cocitation threshold level was consistent with the theory that the specialties of science create a heirarchical structure that forms an all-encompassing mosaic pattern of interaction at the lowest level.

Aside from the obvious importance of these structural findings, the study was significant also for the methodology it demonstrated. Citation analysis has two distinct advantages over the more traditional methods of exploring the structure of science through its literature. One is that much of it can be automated—a characteristic that makes it practical to study science on a scale large enough to distinguish between special and universal characteristics and to make valid comparisons from one specialty to another. The functional practicality of the method also makes it feasible to repeat studies frequently enough to closely monitor changes over time.

The second advantage of citation analysis is its objectivity. Other methods for studying specialty behavior from the literature are based on subjective judgments about what comprises the literature of the specialty. In co-citation clustering, this judgment is made algorithmically from the hard data of citation relationships, which are specified on a massive and inclusive scale by the population of publishing scientists.

MAPPING SPECIALTIES

The success in using co-citation clustering to identify specialties led to the next logical step of using the same technique to map them (12). To do this, Small and Griffith extended their methodology in the way shown in Figure 8.9.

Mapping the specialties picks up where defining them leaves off. The clustering routine can produce a list of clustered documents organized by cluster number. This list is matched against the master list of co-cited pairs, and all the documents on the pair list that appear on the cluster list are tagged with the appropriate cluster number. All the rest, which are part of pairs that have not been co-cited frequently enough to be clustered, are left untagged. The result of the matching and tagging operation, therefore, is to divide the pair list into three classes: those pairs in which both documents have the same cluster number; those in which the two documents have different cluster numbers; and those in which only one of the documents, or neither, has a cluster number.

Document pairs with the same two cluster numbers are those co-cited frequently enough to have an intracluster relationship. Those that have two different cluster numbers have not been co-cited frequently enough to qualify for an intracluster relationship, but they do have an intercluster relationship. Those pairs in which only one document, or neither, has a cluster number are those that have no relationship at all with the clusters formed at the co-citation threshold used.

The first two classes, of course, are the ones used in mapping the specialties.

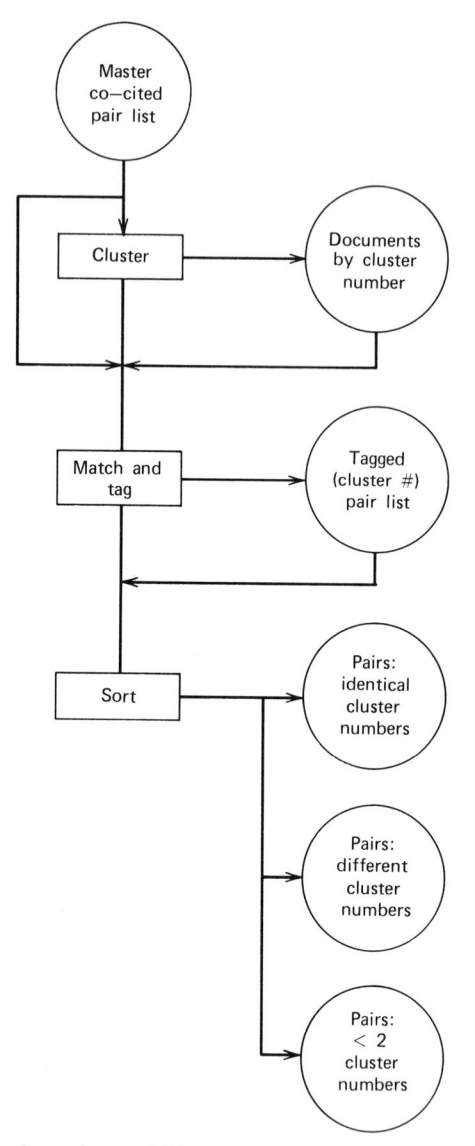

Figure 8.9 Methodology of mapping specialties.

Those pairs with intracluster links represent the contents of the individual clusters. Those with intercluster links provide a co-citation measure of the relationship between clusters. Together, they can be used to map the specialties in a number of ways.

Figure 8.10 is one of the ways. A simple network diagram, its nodes represent individual clusters. The number in each node corresponds to the number of the cluster. Those clusters that contain three or more documents are identified in Figure 8.11, which also shows the number of documents they contain. The lines connecting the nodes represent co-citation links between the clusters. The figures beside the lines represent the strength of those links. Each of the figures is the cumulative

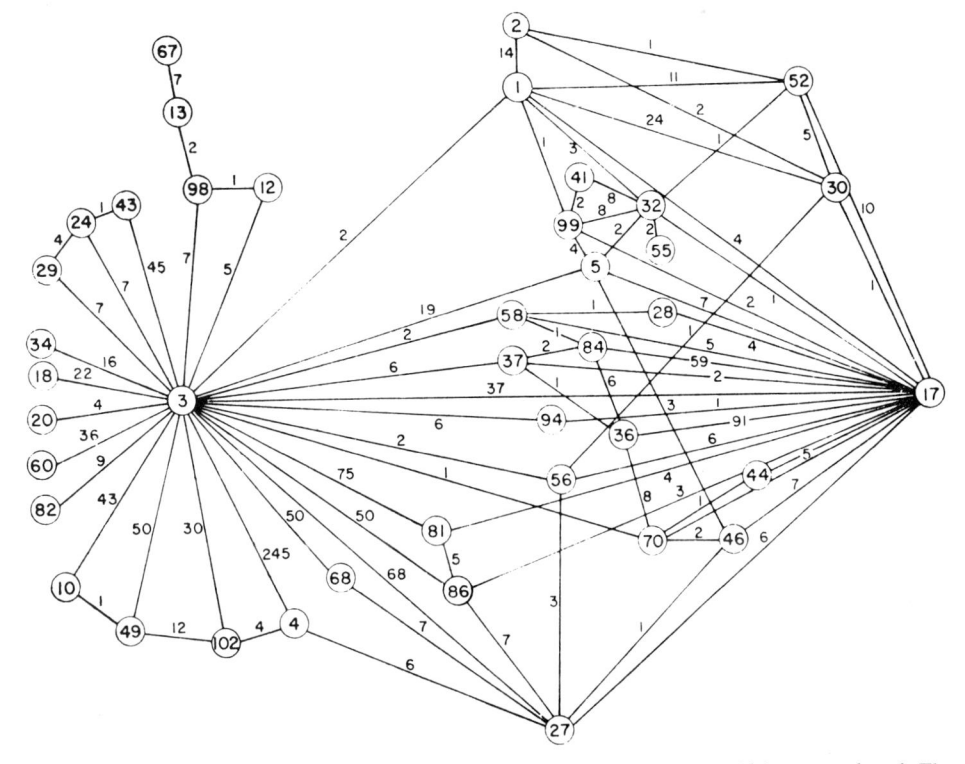

Figure 8.10 Network diagram of level 3 clusters. Circles represent clusters, which are numbered. The lines connecting clusters indicate co-citation links. The numbers on the lines indicate the strength of the links.

number of times unique pairs with a document in each of the two clusters have been co-cited. The co-citation strength of each unique pair that contributes to the total is, of course, lower than the co-citation threshold used for clustering.

The data base from which Figure 8.10 was produced is the same one used in the initial study to test the co-citation clustering technique: the first quarter of the 1972 *SCI*. The nodes are the clusters produced when all the documents in this data base that had been cited at least 10 times were clustered at a co-citation threshold level of 3.

The picture Figure 8.10 provides of the natural sciences is a logically comfortable one. It shows three disciplinary poles: *physics* (clusters #1 and #2, with 73 documents), *chemistry* (#17, with 92 documents), and *biomedicine* (#3, with 801 documents). Most of the specialties are connected to the *biomedicine* and *chemistry* poles and are small, which may be an intrinsic characteristic of scientific specialties. A large number of the ones that are connected to *biomedicine* have no connections to any other part of the natural sciences. In contrast, the specialties linked to *chemistry* are also connected to either *physics* or *biomedicine*. This pattern suggests that chemistry functions as a critical point of integration for much of the natural sciences—a hypothesis that is supported further by the very weak connection between *physics* and *biomedicine*.

Cluster No.	No. of Documents	Description
1	41	nuclear structure physics
2	32	particle physics
3	801	biomedicine
4	9	virally transformed cells
5	9	nuclear magnetic resonance (spin relaxation)
10	15	Australia antigen (viral hepatitis)
12	4	multivariate statistics
13	10	plate tectonics
17	92	chemistry (crystallography, molecular orbital theory, nuclear spin polarization)
18	3	bacterial susceptibility to antibiotics
20	3	kidney transplantation
24	3	psychology (arousal expectancy)
27	12	crystal structure of enzymes
28	4	radiationless transitions
29	7	neurophysiology of vision
30	4	nuclear reaction theory
32	5	solid state physics (theory of alloys)
34	5	renin
36	4	ligand field theory (charge transfer)
37	5	organic chemistry (substituent effects)
41	5	solid state physics (semiconductors, band theory)
43	6	Parkinsonism (treatment with L-dopa)
44	3	carbanion chemistry
46	6	nuclear magnetic resonance (paramagnetic shift reagents)
49	6	viral leukaemia
52	6	atomic physics (self-consistent fields)
55	3	solid state physics (critical phenomena)
56	5	computer science (minimization methods)
58	3	chemistry of singlet oxygen (photo-oxygenation reactions)
60	3	radioimmunology (fsh)
67	3	geology (origin of basalt magmas)
68	3	protein conformation (circular dichroism)
70	3	chemistry (dipole moments, Ising model)
81	5	transfer RNA
82	4	marihuana chemistry
84	4	chemistry (cycloadditions)
86	4	stereochemistry of nucleic acids
94	3	light scattering (biological cells)
98	5	numerical taxonomy (multidimensional scaling)
99	3	solid state physics (lattice theory)
102	4	cancer (detection with immunofluorescence)

Figure 8.11 Description of level 3 clusters with at least three documents.

There are only three obvious anomalies on this map of the natural science specialties, and all of them can be explained. *Plate tectonics* (#13) is attached, though indirectly, to *biomedicine*. This unlikely link between the earth sciences and biomedicine is created by a methodology [*numerical taxonomy, multidimensional scaling* (#98)] that is common to both. *Computer sciences* (#56) is linked, though weakly, to *biomedicine* (#3), *chemistry* (#17), *nuclear reaction theory* (#30), and the *crystal structure of enzymes* (#27), but not, as one would expect, to mathematics. The reason for this is that the citation threshold of 10 was too high to pick up very much of the mathematics literature, which uses references more sparingly than most of the rest of the natural sciences. That situation precluded the possibility of *computer sciences* connecting to anything other than its major application areas.

The third anomaly is the continued appearance of macroclusters that encompass several specialties. The *biomedicine* and *chemistry* clusters are this type. In their first study, when Small and Griffith investigated this phenomenon by analyzing the *biomedicine* cluster, they found that a superstructure of methods documents held together multiple substructures of conceptual papers that otherwise would have formed separate specialty clusters. In their second study, they extended their investigation by mapping the methodological superstructure and specialty substructures within the *biomedicine* cluster.

The methodological superstructure is shown in Figure 8.12 as a spatial display in which the documents are depicted as points that are plotted on a two-dimensional scale. The distance between points is inversely proportional to the strength of the co-citation links between them (the stronger the links, the shorter the distance). Pictured on the display are 28 of the 29 methods papers that were found to be holding together relatively disparate specialties. The missing paper is one by O. H. Lowry on a method for measuring proteins. It was left off the map because it was so highly co-cited with each of the other documents that all the points ended up in the same location when plotted on a two-dimensional, proximity scale.

The logical structure of the diagram can be derived from the titles of the documents involved. The six papers at the top, reading down from Karnovsky to Reynolds, all deal with electron microscopy. The three papers directly below them, by Bartlett, Chen, and Folch, are all on the measurement of phosphorous, particularly lipids. The measurement of lipids, as well as sugars, ACTH, and proteins, is the subject of the three papers in the center by Fiske, Gornall, and Dubois. The two papers to the right of center, lying above and below the horizontal axis, by Burton and Marmur, are on the measurement of DNA. The three papers by Ellman, Ornstein, and Davis, which lie on an arc beneath and to the left of the central group, are on the separation of organic materials by electrophoresis. Separation by molecular weight, using ultracentrifugation, is the subject of the large group of papers that straddle the vertical axis at the bottom. To the right of them are a number of older, classical methods papers.

There is, then, a definite logic to the structure. As shown in the lower right-hand corner of Figure 8.12, the subject matter begins at the top with electron microscopy methods for dealing with relatively large biochemical structures and progresses to methods concerned with the separation of very small structures (molecular in scale) at the bottom.

The major specialty substructures that were held together by the methodological superstructure are shown in Figure 8.13. When the 29 methods papers were removed from the data base, and the remaining 772 documents were clustered at a co-citation threshold level of 4, 74 clusters were produced. Forty-six of them, the ones shown in Figure 8.13, were interlinked at a co-citation strength of at least three. The size and

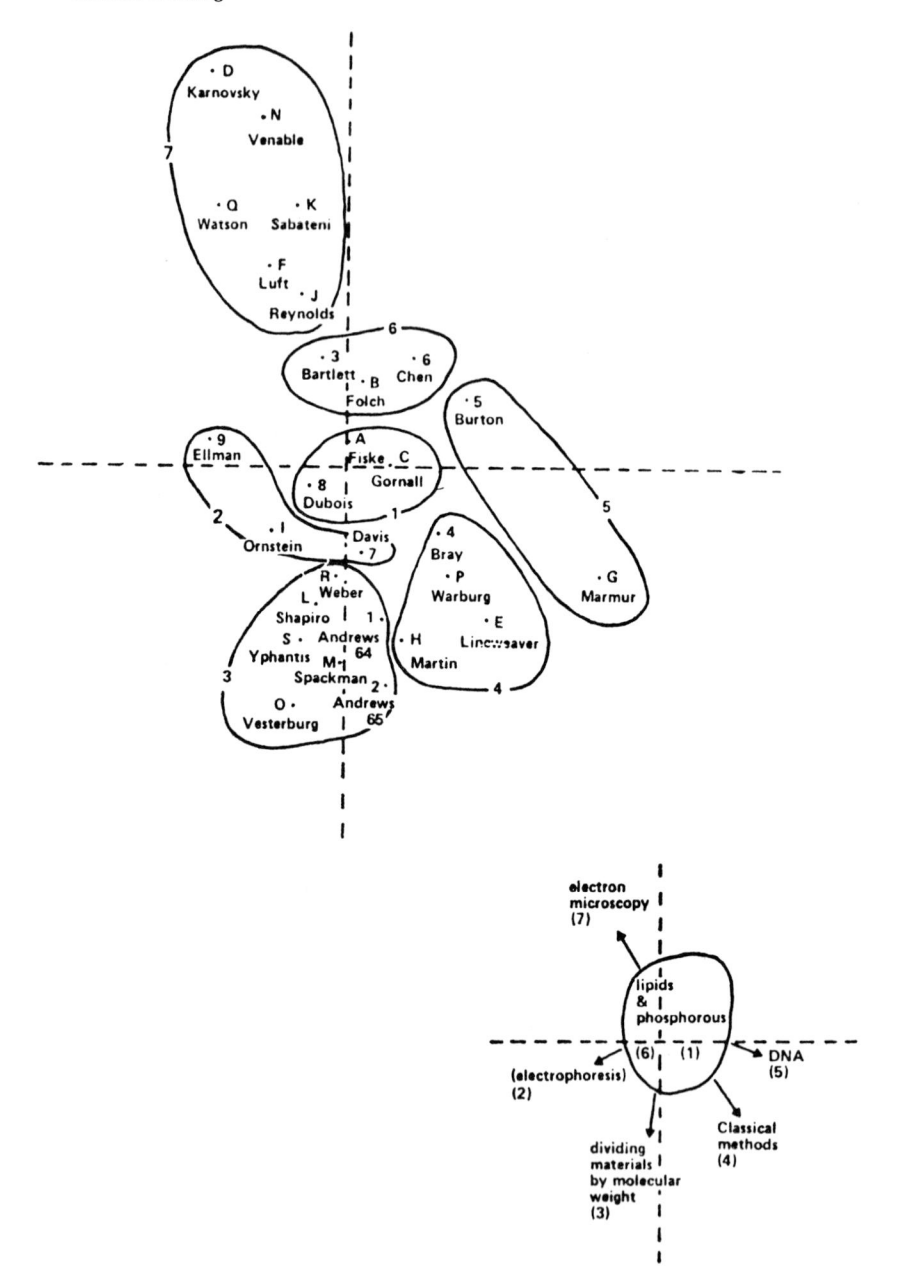

Figure 8.12 Spatial display of *biomedicine* methods papers. The papers are indicated by dots and identified by the name of the first author. The free-form shapes enclosing groups of papers represent clusters. The diagram at lower right shows the logical relationships between the clusters.

names of the interlinked clusters that defined at least four documents are shown in Figure 8.14. The names were derived from the titles of both the documents in the clusters and the papers that cited them.

The majority of the specialty clusters formed a very loose, treelike structure that, again, was logically consistent. For example, *immunology* (#9) was properly linked to both *cancer research, reverse transcription* (#10) and *structure of im-*

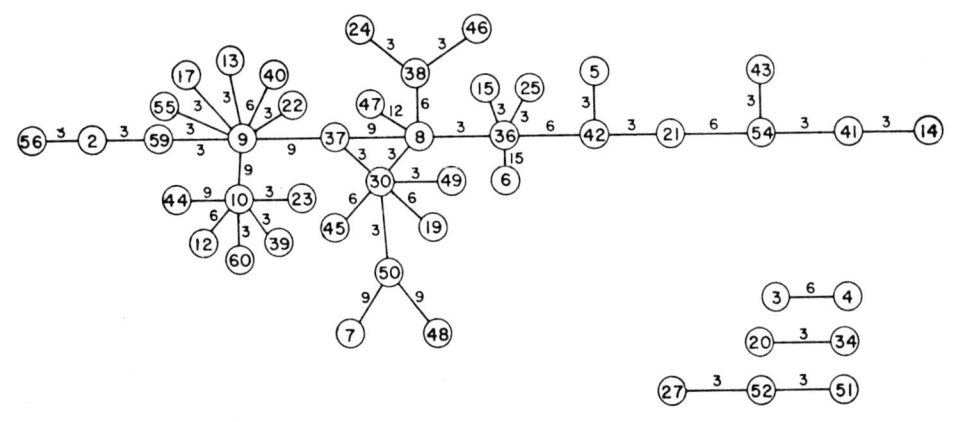

Figure 8.13 Network diagram of the major *biomedicine* specialty clusters. Circles represent clusters; the lines connecting circles represent co-citation links; numbers on the lines represent the strength of the links.

Cluster No.	No. of Documents	Description
1	15	fat transport in lipoproteins
2	9	radioimmunoassay of hormones
6	6	transport across cell membranes
7	4	fibrinogen, defibrination
8	34	protein structure, allosteric systems
9	65	immunology
10	57	cancer research, reverse transcription
11	11	human chromosomes, fluorescence patterns
12	4	mitochondrial DNA
13	6	lymphocyte stimulation
14	6	bactericidal capacity of leukocytes
15	8	muscle
16	5	digitalis intoxication
19	7	cellular hypersensitivity
20	16	platelet function
23	5	RNA polymerase, cyclic re-use
24	18	cyclic AMP
25	5	intracellular transport of secretory proteins
26	7	myosin structure
29	4	biomembrane lipids
30	15	secretory IGA, polypeptide chains
33	10	microsomal enzyme induction
36	17	erythrocyte membranes
37	14	structure of immunoglobulins
39	4	RNA metabolism
40	4	genetic control of antibody response
41	4	cell junctions, ultrastructure
42	4	water transport in biological membranes
44	4	bacterial DNA
47	6	carbohydrate metabolizing enzymes
51	4	glucogenic amino acids, metabolism
61	9	bio-statistics
62	17	biogenic monamines, effect on brain

Figure 8.14 Description of *biomedicine* specialty clusters with at least four documents.

munoglobulins (#37). And the specialities around *protein structure, allosteric systems* (8) were appropriately biochemical in nature.

The relationship between the specialty and methodological structures also was tested and found to be logically consistent. The seven groups of methods documents were treated as clusters and added to the list of documents from the specialty clusters. When the combined cluster list was matched with the master list of co-cited pairs, every one of the specialty clusters, even the 28 that had no other structural connections (so were not shown in Figure 8.13), linked to a logical methods cluster, and those specialty clusters that were strongly linked to each other were found to connect to the same region of the methodological superstructure map shown in Figure 8.12.

Additional evidence of consistency was found by examining pairs containing only one document that was tagged with a cluster number. Many of the tagged documents in these pairs linked to a methodological cluster, and almost all that did turned out to be methods papers. When these additional methods papers were plotted on the methodological superstructure map shown in Figure 8.12, their co-citation links placed them in the appropriate subject regions.

The dual structure of the *biomedicine* macrocluster may be unusual. If so, the structural analysis of most macroclusters will involve considerably less data manipulation than was required for *biomedicine*. At least that was the case with *cancer research, reverse transcription,* a macrocluster of 57 documents that ranged over several specialties. The specialties within it were identified and mapped simply by clustering the 57 documents at a co-citation level of 6 and then plotting the results as a spatial diagram (Figure 8.15). Each cluster is represented by a circle whose diameter is inversely proportional to the average co-citation strength inside the cluster (the smaller the diameter, the higher the average co-citation strength). The distance between clusters is inversely proportional to the average strength of their co-citation links (the shorter the distance, the greater the strength).

In Figure 8.15, all clusters of less than three documents and all intercluster links weaker than an average of 0.5 have been removed. What remains is a loosely structured eight-cluster network that has three distinct poles: *reverse transcription (RNA dependent DNA polymerase), gel electrophoresis of RNA,* and *DNA/RNA hybridization.* The most tightly integrated cluster is *reverse transcription* (#12), which interacts very strongly with *RNA tumor viruses, breast cancer* (#9) and, somewhat less strongly, with *DNA Polymerase* (#11) and *polyadenylic acid, RNA viruses* (#3).

VALIDATION STUDIES

This initial work has been followed by a number of other studies to determine how closely co-citation clusters match specialties. The studies have tested cluster behavior over time, and at different levels of abstraction, against various theories and perceptions of the mosaic of science.

Working from the 1972 and 1973 annual editions of *SCI,* Small produced

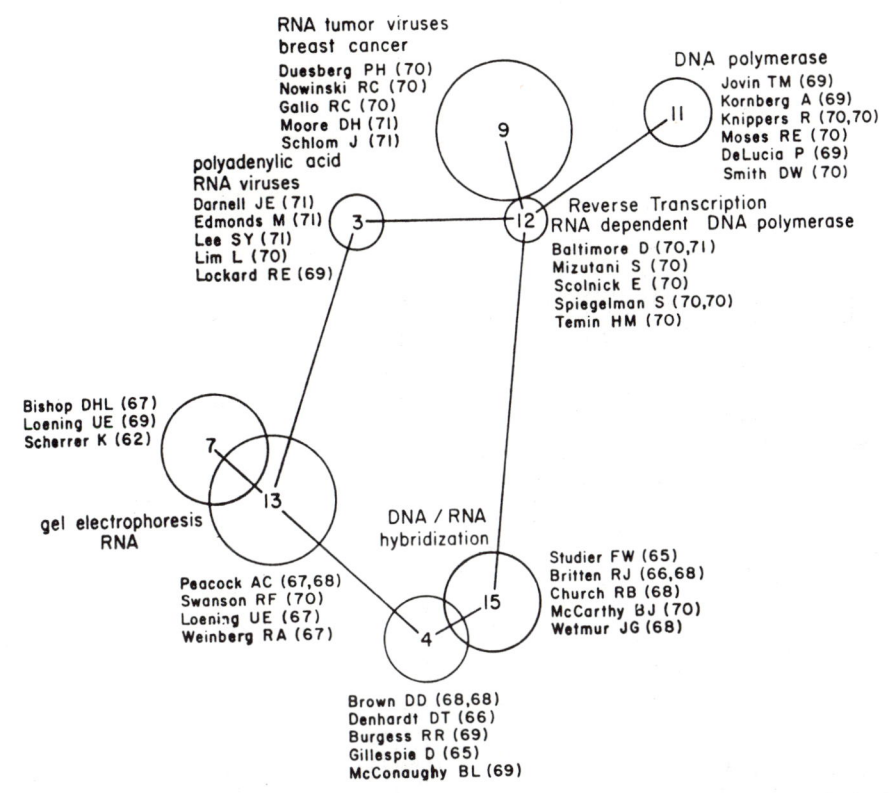

Figure 8.15 Spatial diagram of *cancer research, reverse transcription* macrocluster. Each circle represents a cluster. Cluster documents are identified by the name of the first author and the year of publication. Terms adjacent to clusters approximate the subject matter of the documents.

evidence that the structure of the biomedical clusters, and their behavior from one year to the next, matches the general perception of what is happening in the biomedical specialties. Since they were annuals, the data bases used for this study were considerably larger and more comprehensive than the quarterly one used for the initial clustering studies. The 1972 annual data base consisted of 2.6 million reference citations; the 1973, 2.7 million. A citation-frequency threshold of 15 was used to select a subset of documents that were paired and, then, clustered at a co-citation threshold level of 11. A total of some 900 clusters were produced from the 1972 and 1973 data, of which approximately 65% were identified as biomedical.

Figures 8.16 and 8.17 show, in map form, the biomedical clusters in each of the two years that contained at least three documents and were linked at a co-citation strength of at least 100. The parenthetical numbers in the boxes on the maps indicate the size of the cluster in documents, while the ones in the lines linking the clusters show the co-citation strength of the links.

The 1972 map (Figure 8.16) showed biomedicine as being dominated (in terms of number of documents) by four specialty areas: *RNA viruses, reverse transcriptase*

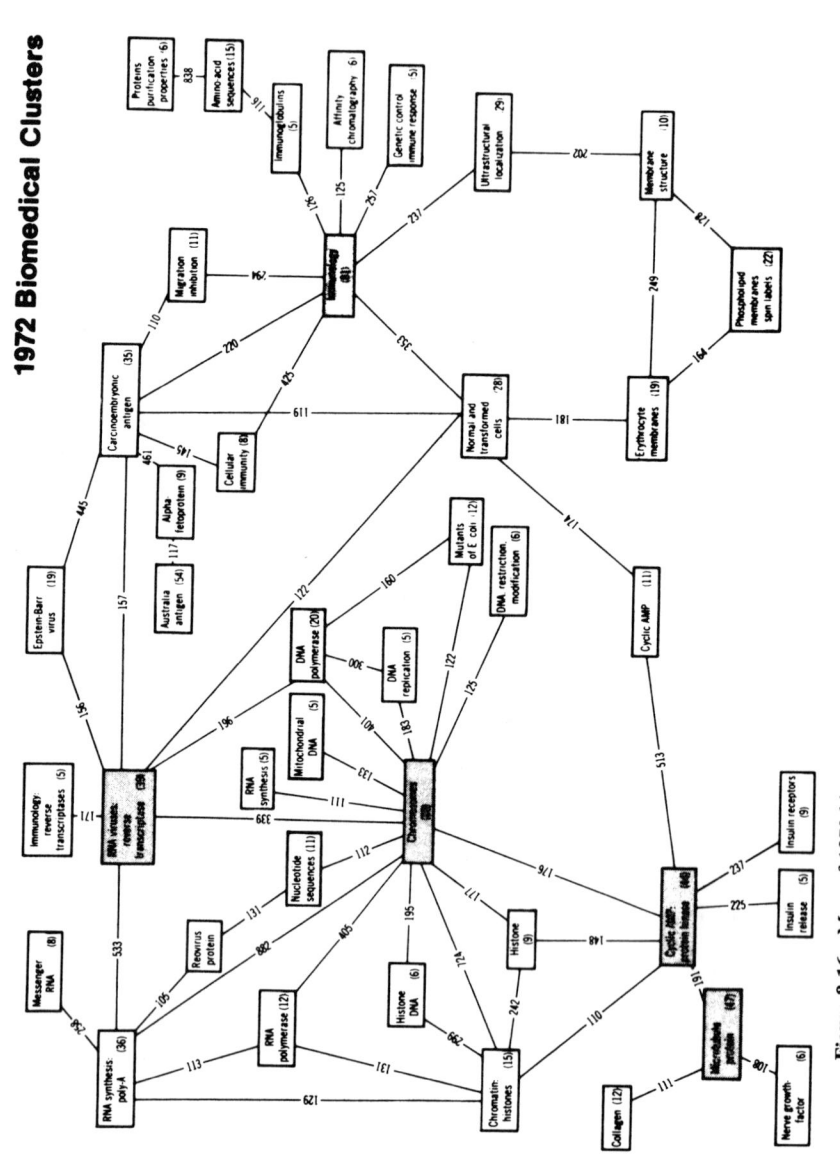

Figure 8.16 Map of 1972 biomedical clusters. Boxes represent clusters. Parenthetical numbers in boxes indicate the number of documents in clusters. Co-citation links between clusters are shown by connecting lines; strength of links is shown by numbers in lines.

1973 Biomedical Clusters

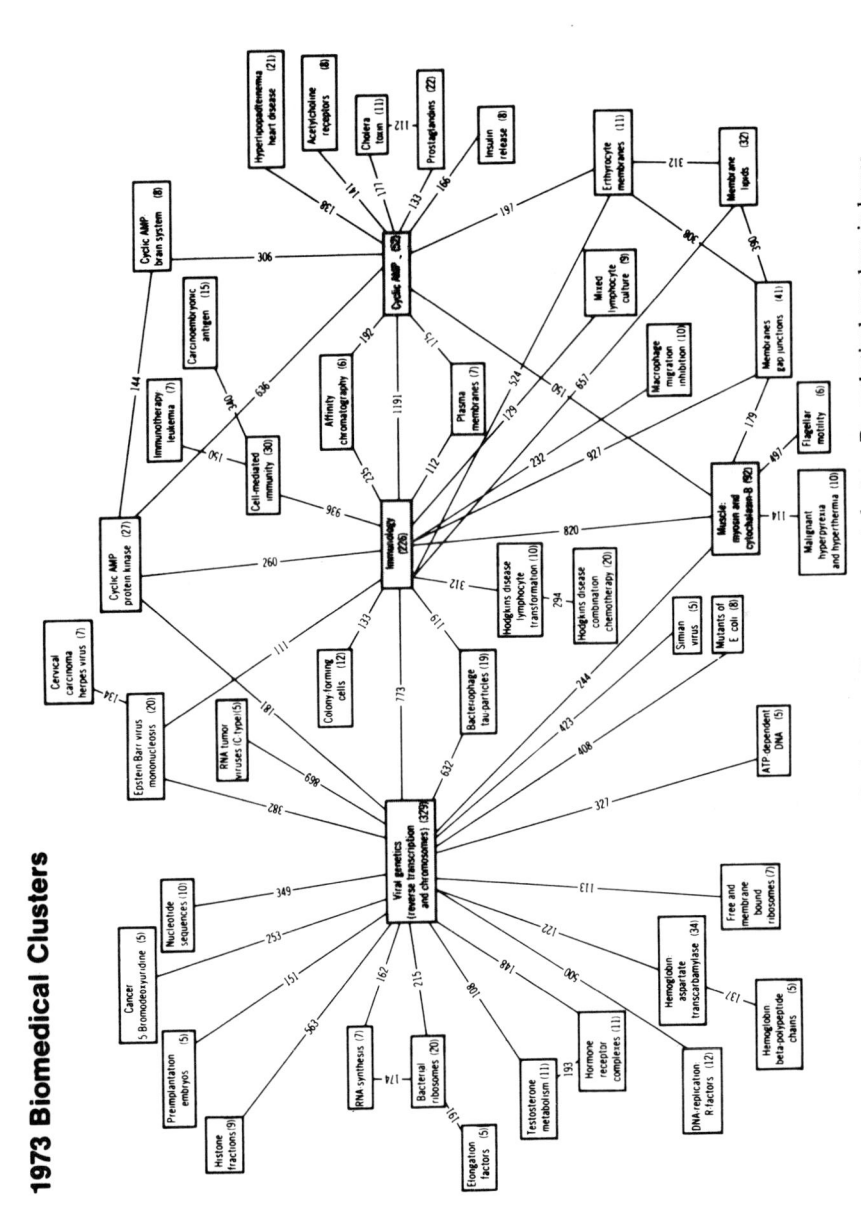

Figure 8.17 Map of 1973 biomedical clusters. Boxes represent clusters. Parenthetical numbers in boxes indicate the number of cluster documents. Co-citation links between clusters are shown by connecting lines; strength of links is shown by numbers in lines.

and *chromosomes* (5 and 34), *immunology* (27), *biological membranes* (39, 40, 41), and *cyclic AMP: protein kinase* and *microtubule protein* (35). By 1973 (Figure 8.17) *chromosomes; RNA viruses, reverse transcriptase;* and several smaller specialties concerned with the genetics of viruses have coalesced into *viral genetics,* which dominates the map. *Immunology* has grown and established a strong link with *viral genetics.* A direct, very strong link also has evolved between *immunology* and *cyclic AMP*; and *microtubule protein* has been transformed into *muscle, myosin and cytochalasin-B,* which is not only one of the four major specialties but which also is linked to each of the other three.

Small also tested the logic of the biomedical structure at the more abstract level of disciplines. Using the 1973 *SCI* data base of 2.7 million reference citations, he selected those that met a citation frequency threshold of 15, clustered them at a co-citation level of 7, and calculated the co-citation links between clusters. The result is the map of five natural science disciplines shown in Figure 8.18. It agrees reasonably well with the major features of the specialty map of the natural sciences produced from the *SCI* data on the first quarter of 1972 (Figure 8.10). *Biomedicine, chemistry,* and *physics,* which were the three major poles of the specialty map, account for three of the five disciplines identified. Also, as on the specialty map, *chemistry* is the only one of the three that is strongly linked to almost all areas, showing up again as the integration point for the natural sciences. Besides these similarities, other interesting features are that at the disciplinary level of abstraction, *physics* is still distinctly multipolar and *crystallography,* through strongly linked to *chemistry,* shows up as a separate discipline.

The most intensive validation effort made to date has involved detailed studies of a number of specialties over a period of time. Small looked at the behavior of 30 dif-

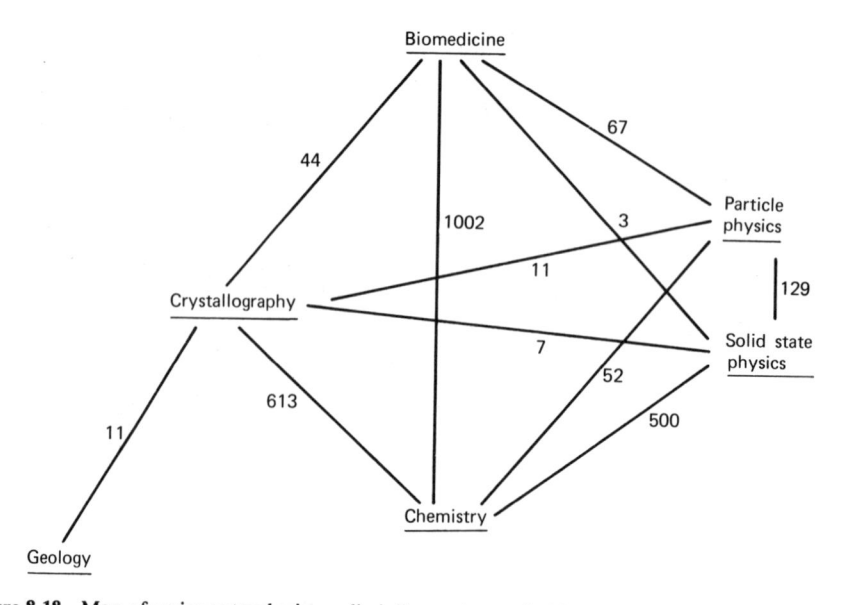

Figure 8.18 Map of major natural science disciplinary clusters in 1973. Numbers beside connecting lines indicate strength of co-citation links.

ferent specialty clusters during the four years of 1970-1973. Though his analysis is still incomplete, there are some interesting initial observations. One is cluster behavior that is consistent with the findings of a number of sociometric and historical studies (18, 19) that specialties can change or emerge very suddenly—in biomedicine, within six months after the publication of a keystone discovery paper (20). Also interesting is the finding that the average continuity rate of documents over the four-year period was 40%, which suggests that the intellectual fermentation of science proceeds at a slow boil. That figure, however, is only the average for the 30 specialties; the range of continuity rates is quite broad. In one-third of the specialties, all but one or two of the documents in the first-year cluster were gone by the fourth year. If high turnover rate (of documents) can be correlated with the revolutionary shifts of research focus theorized by Kuhn (21), this finding suggests that specialties average one revolution every 12 years. Another interesting facet of the change process is that documents tended to move in and out of the clusters in multiples, rather than one at a time. Change on this scale might be a sign that the leadership within the specialty has shifted from one group of researchers to another.

A much more complete picture of cluster behavior over time, and how that behavior matches the real-world events within the specialty, was produced by Small from a study of the literature on collagen research during the five-year period running from 1970 through 1974 (14).

Collagen is a large, triple-helical, protein molecule in the human body whose functional role is to form fibers that attach to tendons and joints and line arterial walls. The primary constituent of connective tissue, it is the most abundant protein in the body. Despite its ubiquity, collagen had the general reputation, for many years, of being a rather unexciting research subject. Until the 1960s, the consensus was that collagen was an inert material, and all the research was concerned with defining its structural characteristics. Initially, beginning in the 1920s, electron diffraction was the primary methodology used in the structural studies. In the 1950s, X-ray diffraction considerably increased the power of structural analysis and produced a molecular picture of collagen as being a triple-stranded, helical coil. Two of the strands, named alpha-1, were biochemically identical. The third was different, so was named alpha-2.

Most of the work in the 1960s was devoted to defining the structures of the strands. During this period, there was a switch to biochemical methodologies to work out amino acid sequences and to define the nature and composition of the linkages connecting the strands. The carboxymethyl cellulose chromatography column (CMC column) was used to separate the molecular chains, and cyanogen bromide (CNBr) was used to divide the chain into appropriate subunits.

A discovery, in 1969, of a genetically distinctive type of collagen that consisted of only the two alpha-1 strands set off a search for other types of collagen. Work during 1970 and 1971 confirmed a theory that predicted the existence of a soluble, precursor type of collagen, which eventually was named "procollagen." This discovery produced a radical shift in the research orientation of the specialty. Though the structural studies continued, the main focus of collagen research shifted to understanding the stability and biosynthesis of the collagen molecule.

The intellectual shift was accompanied by a sociological one. What had been considered a dull specialty suddenly became an exciting one. What had been a small, very cohesive area of biochemical research began growing in size and scope, generating subspecialities and attracting MD's working on the clinical medicine problems of aging, heart and lung disease, cancer, and arthritis. The cooperation that is often so typical of small specialties was replaced by the competition that is often typical of the larger ones.

That is the history of collagen as gleaned from its literature and conversations with its researchers. The version of the most recent part of that history that was derived from citation analysis is shown in Figures 8.19 through 8.23. The clusters, which were generated from the *SCI* data base at a citation-frequency threshold of 15, and a co-citation threshold of 11, are shown as contour maps. The documents of a cluster are represented by dots, whose relative locations have been plotted, by a metric-scaling algorithm, according to co-citation frequencies. In general, the proximity of each dot to all the rest is inversely proportional to their co-citation strength (the stronger the co-citation link, the closer the proximity). The contour lines are drawn to provide a height scale that is directly proportional to the citation frequency of each document. A bibliography of all the papers shown in the series of cluster maps appears in Figure 8.24.

The 1970 cluster (Figure 8.19) reflects a research orientation that is exclusively structural. Piez 1963, the most highly cited document, defines the structure of the

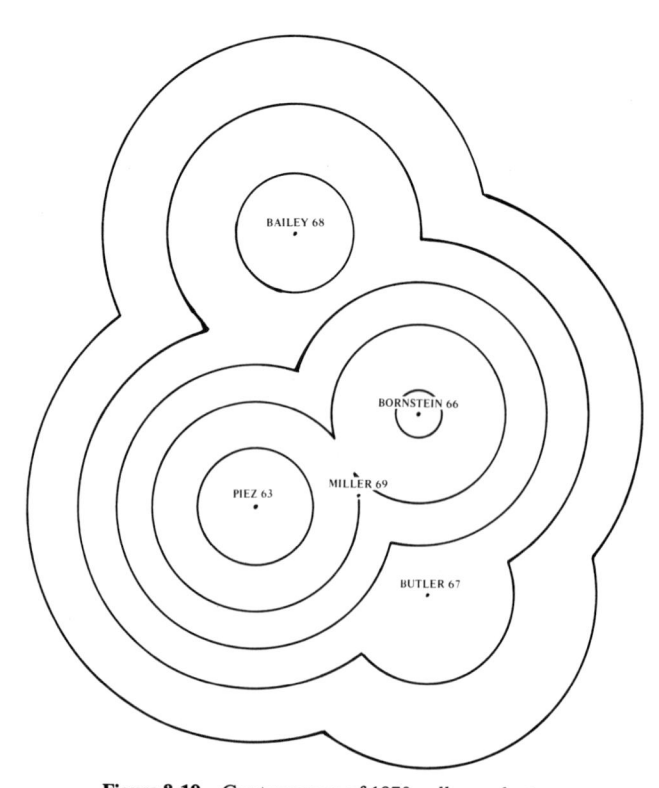

Figure 8.19 Contour map of 1970 *collagen* cluster.

alpha-1 chain. Bornstein 1966, the second most highly cited document, describes the nature of the links between chains. Butler 1967 and Miller 1969, whose proximity to each other reflects frequent co-citation, both discussed the same general aspects of the alpha-1 structure—the primary difference between them being that one used bone collagen for his studies whereas the other used skin collagen. Bailey 1968 also reports on a structural study, one that produced a catalog of the amino acids on the collagen cross-links. This document is set apart somewhat from the rest because the work it describes differs enough from the rest to make co-citation with the other documents relatively infrequent.

The 1971 cluster (Figure 8.20) is identical to that of 1970, except for the disappearance of Bailey 1968. The research continues to be exclusively structural.

The 1972 cluster (Figure 8.21) shows a major change. Suddenly there are two distinctly separate areas of collagen research. One is the structural research from past years, represented in the right-hand region by the documents from the 1971 cluster, plus one new entry: Rauterberg 1971, which describes work similar to that done by Butler 1967 and Miller 1969, except that the collagen analyzed is from a different source. The other area of research, represented by a completely new set of papers in the left-hand region, is concerned with the biosynthesis of collagen. This area is dominated by Layman 1971 and Bellamy 1971. Layman 1971 was the first to report the discovery of the new type of collagen that was later to be named procollagen. Bellamy 1971 was the one who named it, and the first to characterize it as the precursor to collagen. Müller 1971 was the first to determine whether the synthesis of collagen from procollagen took place inside or outside the cell. Dehm 1971

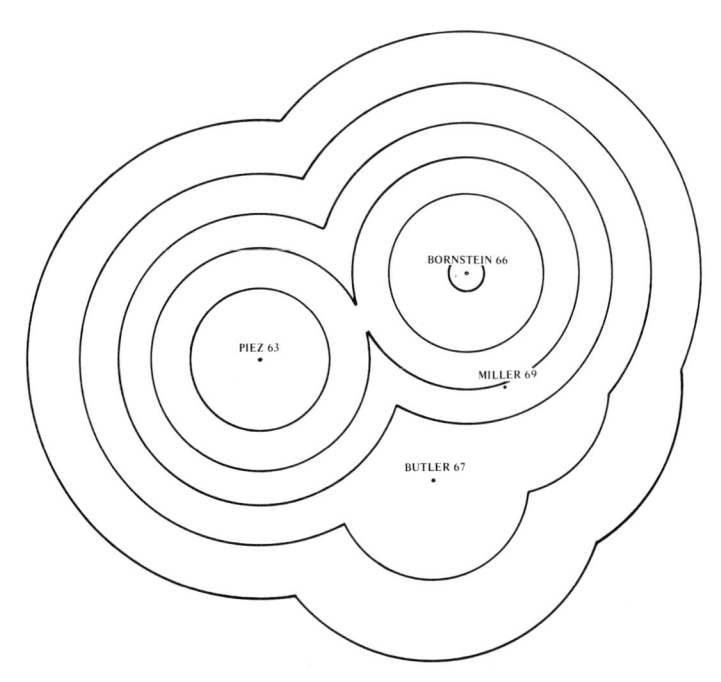

Figure 8.20 Contour map of 1971 *collagen* cluster.

126 *Citation Indexing*

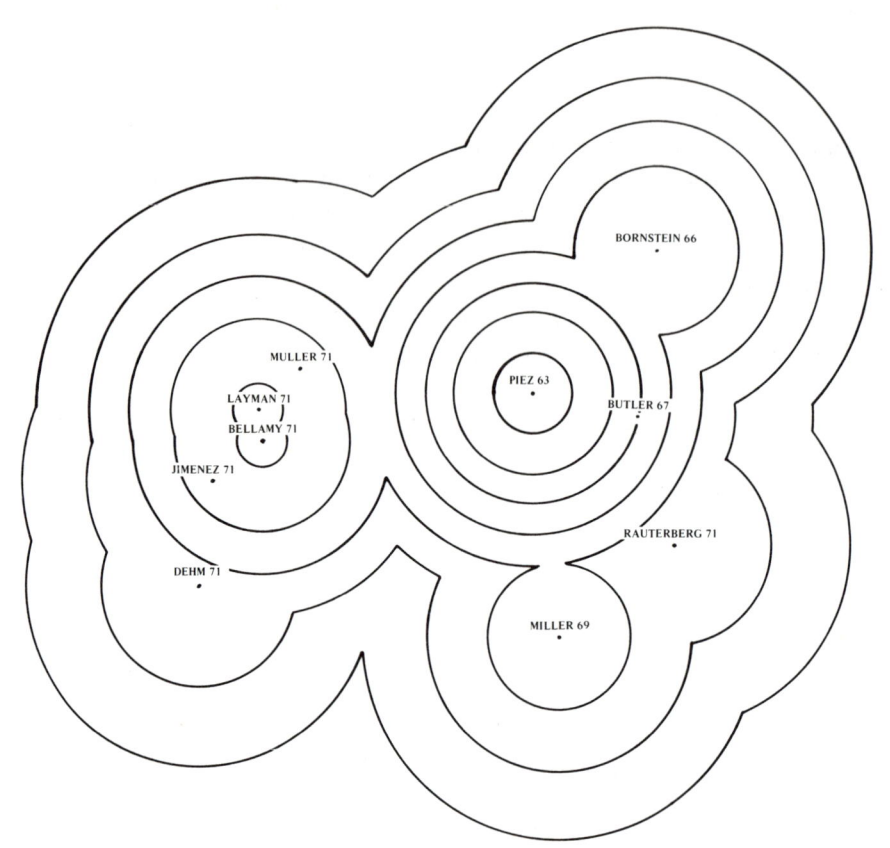

Figure 8.21 Contour map of 1972 *collagen* cluster.

described the preparation of a matrix of free cells that plays an important methodological role in biosynthesis studies. Jimenez 1971 used this methodology to determine the molecular size of procollagen.

An interesting characteristic of the series of new documents on biosynthesis is that they are all only one year old. The achievement of a high citation rate within a year after publication may be a sign of a discovery paper that has enough intellectual energy to change the state of a specialty.

The 1973 cluster (Figure 8.22) shows a return to a single research orientation, but that orientation now is biosynthesis. All the structural work has disappeared. The original work on procollagen has been retained, and new documents on the subject have appeared. Layman 1971 now clearly dominates the cluster, with Bellamy 1971 close by. Two new papers—Bornstein 1972 and Dehm 1972—have pushed Møller 1971 to the periphery, with studies on the cystine content of procollagen. A second group of new papers to the right of Layman, consisting of Stark 1971, Lenaers 1971, and Lapiere 1971, deal with the investigations of a Belgian laboratory into a cattle disease suspected of being caused by procollagen. Again, the currency of the cluster is still remarkable. None of the documents is more than two years old.

The 1974 cluster (Figure 8.23) shows a major increase in the size of the specialty.

Mapping the Structure of Science 127

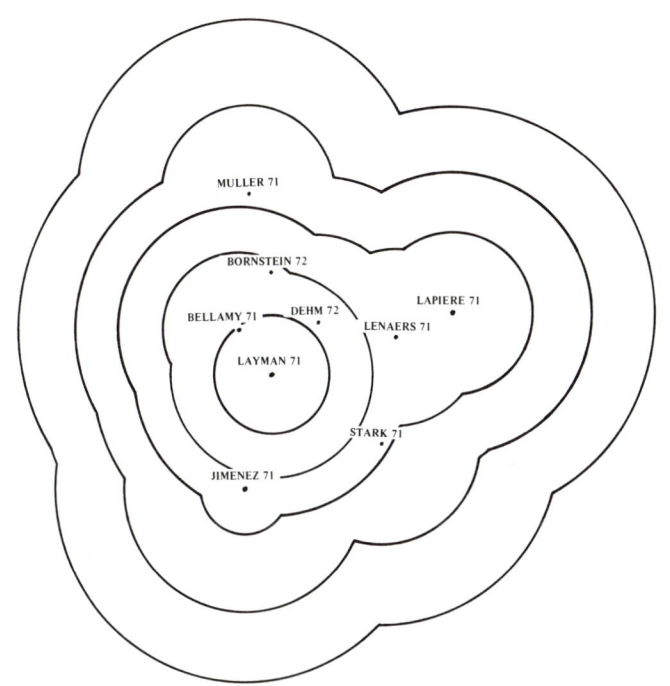

Figure 8.22 Contour map of 1973 *collagen* cluster.

The cluster is now almost three times its 1973 size, with the number of documents having increased from 9 to 24, and it identifies three relatively separate research fronts.

The group of five documents at the lower right are on the stabilization of collagen by hydroxyproline. Built on the existence and characterization of procollagen, this work represents the first major advance made possible by the original discovery of procollagen. The fact that it came only two years after the original research is a sign of rapid research growth and change. Typically, four of the five papers are only one year old, and the fifth is only two.

The central region of the cluster contains the original work on procollagen. Still dominated by Layman 1971, it has been expanded by three new documents.

The group of papers to the left of Layman 1971 are on genetically distinctive types of collagen—work that until this point had formed a cluster separate from the main line of collagen research. (This cluster was easily identifiable as a separate branch of work on collagen as early as 1972, but no one thought to look for more than one collagen cluster.) It is dominated by Miller, who discovered, in 1969, a form of collagen composed of only the two alpha-1 strands. This discovery set off the search for other types of collagen that culminated in the identification of procollagen. The appearance of this work in the main collagen cluster suggests that the relationship between research on genetic variations of collagen and the characterization of procollagen became considerably stronger in 1974.

Two papers in the 1974 cluster are somewhat removed from all three research

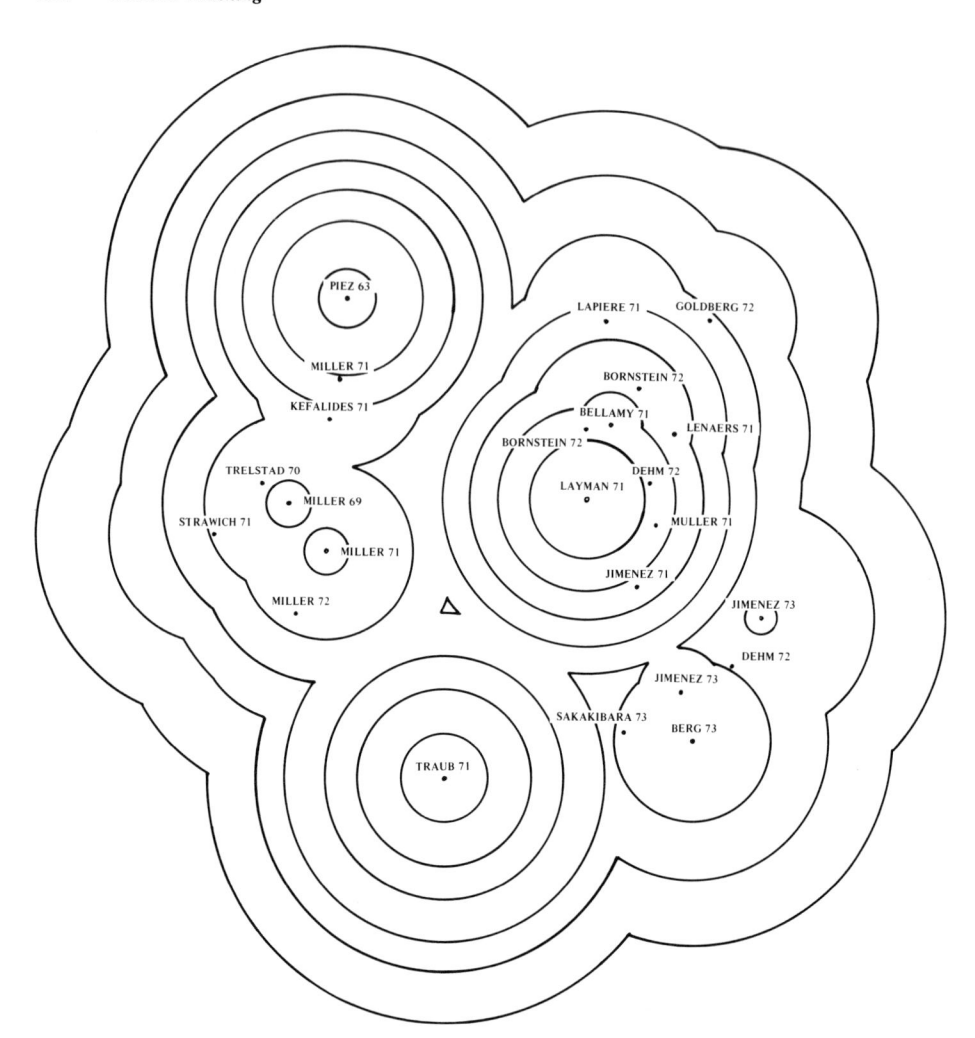

Figure 8.23 Contour map of 1974 *collagen* cluster.

fronts. The reason, it turns out, is not that they are unrelated to any of the fronts, but that they are related to all of them, rather than to any single one. Piez 1963 is the same document that was so prominent in the 1970–1971 clusters and then disappeared in 1973, when the research emphasis shifted from structural studies to biosynthesis. A landmark paper on structure, it has reappeared as a highly cited paper in 1974 because it is methodologically important to all the research fronts. Traub 1971 is a new paper that borders on all three of the fronts because it is a comprehensive review of the state of the art of the entire specialty.

Figure 8.24 Bibliography of documents in *collagen* cluster from 1970–1974.

Bailey, A. J. and **Peach, C. M.** "Isolation and Structural Identification of a Labile Intermolecular Crosslink in Collagen." *Biochemical and Biophysical Research Communications,* **33**(5):812-819, 1968.

Bellamy, G. and **Bornstein, P.** "Evidence for Procollagen, a Biosynthetic Precursor of Collagen." *Proc. Nat. Acad. Sci. USA,* **68**(6):1138-1142, 1971.

Berg, R. A. and **Prockop, D. J.** "The Thermal Transition of a Non-hydroxylated Form of Collagen—Evidence for a Role for Hydroxyproline in Stabilizing the Triple-helix of Collagen." *Biochemical and Biophysical Research Communications,* **52**(1):115-120, 1973.

Bornstein, P. and **Piez, K. A.** "The Nature of the Intramolecular Cross-links in Collagen—the Separation and Characterization of Peptides from the Cross-link Region of Rat Skin Collagen." *Biochemistry,* **5**(11):3460-3473, 1966.

Bornstein, P., Ehrlich, H. P. and **Wyke, A. W.** "Procollagen: Conversion of the Precursor to Collagen by a Neutral Protease." *Science,* **175**:544-546, 1972.

Bornstein, P., Von Der Mark, K., Wyke, A. W., Ehrlich, H. P., and **Monson, J. M.** "Characterization of the Pro-q1 Chain of Procollagen." *Journal of Biological Chemistry,* **247** (9):2808-2813, 1972.

Butler, W. T., Piez, K. A. and **Bornstein, P.** "Isolation and Characterization of the Cyanogen Bromide Peptides from the q1 chain of Rat Skin Collagen." *Biochemistry,* **6**(12):3771-3780, 1967.

Dehm, P. and **Prockop, D. J.** "Synthesis and Extrusion of Collagen by Freshly Isolated Cells from Chick Embryo Tendon." *Biochimica et Biophysica Acta,* **240**:358-369, 1971.

Dehm, P., Jimenez, S.A., Olsen, B.R., and **Prockop, D.J.** "A Transport Form of Collagen from Embryonic Tendon: Electron Microscopic Demonstration of an NH_2-terminal Extension and Evidence Suggesting the Presence of Cystine in the Molecule." *Proc. Nat. Acad. Sci. USA,* **69**(1):60-64, 1972.

Dehm, P. and **Prockop, D.J.** "Time Lag in the Secretion of Collagen by Matrix-Free Tendon Cells and Inhibition of the Secretory Process by Colchicine and Vinblastine." *Biochimica et Biophysica Acta,* **264**:375-382, 1972.

Goldberg, B., Epstein, E.H., Jr., and **Sherr, C.J.** "Precursors of Collagen Secreted by Cultured Human Fibroblasts." *Proc. Nat. Acad. Sci. USA,* **69**(12):3655-3659, 1972.

Jimenez, S.A., Dehm, P., and **Prockop, D.J.** "Further Evidence for a Transport Form of Collagen—Its Extrusion and Extracellular Conversion to Tropocollagen in Embryonic Tendon." *FEBS Letters,* **17**(2):245-248, 1971.

Jimenez, S.A., Dehm, P., Olsen, B.R., and **Prockop, D.J.** "Intracellular Collagen and Protocollagen From Embryonic Tendon Cells." *Journal of Biological Chemistry,* **248**(2):720-729, 1973.

Jimenez, S.A., Harsch, M., and **Rosenbloom, J.** "Hydroxyproline Stabilizes the Triple Helix of Chick Tendon." *Biochemical and Biophysical Research Communications,* **52**(1):106-114, 1973.

Kefalides, N. A. "Isolation of a Collagen from Basement Membranes Containing

Figure 8.24 (continued)

Three Identical q-chains." *Biochemical and Biophysical Research Communications,* **45**(1): 226-234, 1971.

Lapiere, C.M., Lenaers, A. and **Kohn, L.D.** "Procollagen Peptidase: an Enzyme Excising the Coordination Peptides of Procollagen." *Proc. Nat. Acad. Sci. USA,* **68**(12): 3054-3058, 1971.

Layman, D.L., McGoodwin, E.B. and **Martin, G.R.** "The Nature of the Collagen Synthesized by Cultured Human Fibroblasts." *Proc. Nat. Acad. Sci. USA,* **68**(2): 454-458, 1971.

Lenaers, A., Ansay, M., Nusgens, B.V., and **Lapiere, C.M.** "Collagen Made of Extended q-chains, Procollagen, in Genetically Defective Dermatosparaxic Calves." *Eur. J. Biochem.,* **23**: 533-543, 1971.

Miller, E.J., Lane, J.M., and **Piez, K.A.** "Isolation and Characterization of the Peptides Derived from the q1 Chain of Chick Bone Collagen after Cyanogen Bromide Cleavage." *Biochemistry,* **8**(1): 30-39, 1969.

Miller, E.J. and **Matukas, V.J.** "Chick Cartilage Collagen: a New Type of q1 Chain Not Present in Bone or Skin of the Species." *Proc. Nat. Acad. Sci. USA,* **64**: 1264-1268, 1969.

Miller, J. "Isolation and Characterization of a Collagen from Chick Cartilage Containing Three Identical q Chains." *Biochemistry,* **10**(9): 1652-1659, 1971.

Miller, E.J., Epstein, E.H., Jr., and **Piez, K.A.** "Identification of Three Genetically Distinct Collagens by Cyanogen Bromide Cleavage of Insoluble Human Skin and Cartilage Collagen." *Biochemical and Biophysical Research Communications,* **42**(6): 1024-1029, 1971.

Miller, E.J. "Structural Studies on Cartilage Collagen Employing Limited Cleavage and Solubilization with Pepsin." *Biochemistry,* **11**(26): 4903-4909, 1972.

Müller, P.K., McGoodwin, E., and **Martin, G.R.** "Studies on protocollagen: Identification of a Precursor of Proto q1." *Biochemical and Biophysical Research Communications,* **44**(1): 110-117, 1971.

Piez, K.A., Eigner, E.A., and **Lewis, M.S.** "The Chromatographic Separation and Amino Acid Composition of the Subunits of Several Collagens." *Biochemistry,* **2**: 58-66, 1963.

Rauterberg, R. and **Kuhn, K.** "Acid Soluble Calf Skin Collagen—Characterization of the Peptides Obtained by Cyanogen Bromide Cleavage of its q1-chain." *Eur. J. Biochem.,* **19**: 398-407, 1971.

Sakakibara, S., Inouye, K., Shudo, K., Kishida, Y., Kobayashi, Y., and **Prockop, D.J.** "Synthesis of (Pro-Hyp-Gly)$_n$ of Defined Molecular Weights—Evidence for the Stabilization of Collagen Triple Helix by Hydroxypyroline." *Biochimica et Biophysica Acta,* **303**: 198-202, 1973.

Stark, M., Lenaers, A., Lapiere, C., and **Kuhn, K.** "Electronoptical Studies of Procollagen from the Skin of Dermatosparaxic Calves." *FEBS Letters,* **18**(2): 225-227, 1971.

Strawich, E. and **Nimni, M.E.** "Properties of a Collagen Molecule Containing Three Identical Components Extracted from Bovine Articular Cartilage." *Biochemistry,* **10**(21): 3905-3911, 1971.

Figure 8.24 (continued)

Mapping the Structure of Science 131

Traub, W. and **Piez, K.A.** "The Chemistry and Structure of Collagen." *Adv. Protein Chem.*, **25**: 243-352, 1971.

Trelstad, R.L., Kang, A.H., Igarashi, S., And Gross, J. "Isolation of Two Distinct Collagens from Chick Cartilage." *Biochemistry,* **9**(25): 4993-4998, 1970.

Figure 8.24 (continued)

One abstract, but revealing, quantitative measure of the five years of activity shown by the collagen clusters is a stability index, which is computed by dividing the number of documents that survive n years by the number of unique documents that appear in the cluster over the same period of time. The stability index for the collagen clusters over two- and three-year periods is shown in Figure 8.25.

	70-71	71-72	72-73	73-74
Stability Index	.80	.31	.32	.44

	70-71-72	71-72-73	72-73-74
	.29	0	.20

Figure 8.25 Stability index for *collagen* cluster from 1970-1974.

Since the major conceptual shift in collagen research first showed up in the third year (1972) of the five years studied, the stability index is considerably lower for the successive three-year periods than it is for the two-year ones. In the 1971-1973 period, which brackets the emergence of the biosynthesis research front, the stability index is zero; not one of the papers in the 1971 cluster survived the two following years. In the 1972-74 period, the stability index rebounded to only .20, despite the fact that the biosynthesis front had emerged in 1972. In other words, even after the appearance of the discovery papers that provided the foundation for the new conceptual direction, the combination of turnover and net increase in core documents kept the stability index low, which suggests that the new research front remained very dynamic.

The same picture is shown, though not as dramatically, by the stability-index measures of successive two-year periods. It dropped from a high of .80 during 1970-1971, before the biosynthesis research was published, to a low of .31 during the 1971-1972 period, which included the last year in which all the work was structural and the first year in which biosynthesis emerged as an important research front. Continuity was barely any stronger during 1972-1973, when the structural work disappeared completely from the cluster, and rose to only .44, well below the presynthesis days, during the last two years.

PEER VALIDATION

Both a qualitative and quantitative analysis of the collagen cluster, then, characterized the five-year period as one in which the intellectual focus of the specialty changed completely, producing a major increase in size and development rate. This picture seemed to fit the general history of the specialty that had been put together from a review of the literature and conversations with several collagen researchers. But to test it more precisely, and in more detail, Small (14) surveyed 24 collagen researchers who had published papers in 1973 that cited at least one of the documents in the 1973 cluster.

The survey was conducted by mail. The researchers surveyed were not told anything at all about the citation analysis that had been performed, or about any of the data produced by the analysis. They were simply asked to respond to a few questions about the recent history of collagen research. The only impact that the citation analysis had upon the survey—and it was both subtle and indirect—was that it provided the underlying hypothesis that there was a specialty of collagen research. Eleven of the researchers surveyed responded completely, which confirmed that the specialty did exist and was properly named.

The survey, which was conducted at the end of 1974, asked four questions:

1. What were the most important scientific advances in collagen research during the past five years?
2. What papers were the first to describe the advances identified in question 1?
3. Whom do you regard as the leading investigator in collagen research?
4. Has collagen research undergone a major change or conceptual shift in the last five years? Please explain.

The responses to these questions are summarized in Figures 8.26 through 8.29.

In the first question, the respondents identified five advances that they considered important (Figure 8.26). All of them, except for the work on genetic defects, were identified by the citation analysis. The work on the sequencing of collagen chains was done prior to 1970, which put it outside the time frame of the study, but still was identified by papers in the 1970 cluster. The two advances that were most visible in the citation analysis—the discoveries of procollagen and genetically distinctive types of collagen—also turned out to be the only ones on which there was substantial agreement among the researchers.

Advance or Development	Number of Responses
1. Procollagen, a biosynthetic precursor molecule	11(100%)
2. Genetic types of collagen	10
3. Sequencing of collagen chains	5
4. Genetic defects of collagen metabolism in hereditary diseases	5
5. Stabilization of collagen by hydroxyproline	4

Figure 8.26 Responses to question about the most important advances in collagen research.

When it came to identifying the papers that first reported these advances, the respondents singled out 32 papers, 14 of which appeared in at least one cluster.

However, only nine of the 32 papers were mentioned by at least two respondents. Shown in Figure 8.27, along with the annual clusters in which they appeared, all but one of those nine papers were picked up by the citation analysis. The missing paper was Pinnell 1972, which described genetic defects of collagen metabolism—the one advance missed by the citation analysis. Again, as in the case of the advances, those papers about which there was the most agreement were all identified by the citation analysis.

Paper (First author, Year)	Mentions	Years in Cluster 70 71 72 73 74	Subject
1. Layman 1971	7	X X X	Procollagen
2. Bellamy 1971	7	X X X	Procollagen
3. Miller 1969	6	X X X	Genetic types
4. Jimenez 1973	3	X	Hydroxyproline
5. Berg 1973	3	X	Hydroxyproline
6. Jimenez 1971	2	X X X	Procollagen
7. Miller 1971	2	X X	Genetic types
8. Kefalides 1971	2	X	Genetic types
9. Pinnell 1972	2		Hereditary disease

Figure 8. 27 Responses to question about the papers that reported the most important advances in collagen research. Twenty-three other papers received one mention. Six of these appeared in the cluster.

In checking back to determine why the Pinnell work was missed, Small found that the first year it could have been included (1973), it made the citation-frequency threshold of 15, but did not make the co-citation threshold of 11. The next year (1974), the Pinnell paper was cited fewer than 15 times, so it did not qualify for the data base subset from which document pairs were extracted for clustering. The threshold levels set obviously are very critical to how comprehensive a picture citation analysis can produce of the activity in a specialty.

When asked to identify the leading investigators in collagen research, the respondents identified 24 people, 15 of whom appeared in the clusters as authors or coauthors of at least one paper. Figure 8.28 shows the ones who were mentioned at least twice and the number of cluster papers they were associated with. Ten of the 13 were associated with at least one paper, and there is a general correlation between the number of times they were mentioned by their peers and the number of cluster

Investigator	Number of Mentions	Number of Authorships on Clustered Papers
1. Bornstein	11	5
2. Miller	10	5
3. Prockop	9	7
4. Piez	9	6
5. Martin	9	2
6. Kahn	7	2
7. Gross	7	1
8. Viez	3	0
9. Bailey	2	1
10. Rosenbloom	2	1
11. Trelstad	2	1
12. Fessler	2	0
13. Ballop	2	0

Figure 8. 28 Responses to question about the leading investigators in collagen research. Eleven other investigators received one mention. Five of these appeared in the cluster.

papers that identified them. Interestingly enough, however, the correlation does not hold for those who were mentioned by their peers less than twice. Four investigators who were named by their peers less than twice (two, in fact, were not mentioned at all) were involved in writing at least three cluster papers. One of those who was not mentioned at all was an author of five highly cited papers. This finding suggests that many of the cluster authors are young, upcoming scientists whose reputation among their peers has not yet caught up with their work. In this sense, citation measurements of researcher prominence may be a leading indicator of peer judgment. More evidence of this is found in the fact that the cluster papers identified roughly twice as many researchers as the respondents, and many of them were young, relatively junior (in terms of experience) coauthors.

The response to the last question of whether there had been a major conceptual shift in the specialty and, if so, what precipitated it, is summarized in Figure 8.29. Ten of the 11 respondents said that a major change had taken place. As for the reason for the change, the discovery of procollagen was credited nine times; the discovery of genetically different collagen, five times; and the work on genetic defects, twice. Again, the experts working in the field agreed with the citation analysis. They confirmed the shift shown by the clusters, and they attributed the shift to the two developments that changed the size and configuration of the clusters.

| Yes: 10 | |
| No: 1 | |
Reason for shift	Number of Responses
1. Concern with collagen biosynthesis via procollagen	9
2. Concern with genetically different collagens	5
3. Concern with genetic defects in collagen metabolism	2

Figure 8.29 Responses to question about major conceptual shifts in collagen research.

Overall, the survey of collagen researchers produced a five-year history of the specialty that matched the one derived from citation data. This result strengthens the hypothesis that clusters formed by this particular type of citation analysis correspond to scientific specialties and that the cluster characteristics provide a usefully accurate picture of the intellectual nature of the specialty, the rate and direction of its evolution, and the number and identity of its key people.

EXAMINING THE SOCIAL SCIENCES

While the major concern of these initial studies has been the development and validation of the methodology, Small also has demonstrated the universality of the methodology by using it to produce a coherent, though still unproved, picture of the structure underlying the social sciences.

Citation analysis, of one type or another, is not new in studies of the social sciences. Jaspars and Ackermans have used the citation patterns between journals to determine how well social psychology performs as a link between psychology and sociology (22). Lin has used the same patterns to study the relationship between sociology journals and institutions (23). Clark (24) and Myers (25) have both used citation rates to measure the eminence of psychologists. Citation data also has played a role in studies of the dynamics of two specialties in sociology. S. Cole used it to define the changes in deviance (26), while J. Cole and H. Zuckerman examined the sociology of science (27). In addition, the INFROSS project at Bath University has used citation relationships between journals and age distributions of references in extensive studies of the information-transfer patterns and requirements of the social sciences (28).

Since all these studies have established a correlation between citation patterns and the reality of the social sciences, it was reasonable to assume that the co-citation clustering technique might very well produce a coherent picture of the structure of the social sciences. Nevertheless, the outcome of the Small study (13) was far from certain. What Small was attempting was quite different, in both kind and degree, from all the previous studies. His was the first to use citation data to generate a large-scale map of all the social science specialties, and the size of the sample he used was several orders of magnitude bigger than any previous one.

The sample used was the *SSCI* data base for the three years from 1972–1974—a total of approximately 1.2 million unique, cited documents. A citation-frequency threshold of 10 produced a set of 14,110 documents, from which 830,042 co-cited pairs were extracted for clustering. The primary clustering was done at four co-citation threshold levels: 11, 13, 16, and 20.

The methodology of this study differed from the preceding ones in a single, but significant respect: the measure of co-citation strength. Rather than using the simple measure of the number of times a pair of documents was co-cited, the measure was normalized to take into account the total citation rate of the pair. A co-citation strength of 11, then, indicates that the co-citation rate of a pair is 11% of its total citation rate. This standard was applied also to the co-citation threshold levels set for qualifying pairs of documents for clustering: the clustering levels of 11, 13, 16, and 20 that were used in the study represent a ratio of co-citations to citations, rather than a simple co-citation count. In other words, to qualify for clustering at level 11, a pair of documents had to have a co-citation-to-citation ratio of at least 11%.

This change was adopted for two reasons. First of all, computing co-citation strength as a function of the citation rate makes the co-citation threshold less restrictive, which permits fields of relatively low activity to become visible. Second, it represses the methodological superstructures that tend to aggregate groups of individual specialties into macroclusters. The reason for this effect is that the highly co-cited methodology papers are generally co-cited with a large number of partner documents, which means that the co-citation strength achieved with any one document is a relatively small part of its total citation rate. The result of these two effects is a greater number of clusters and a more realistic distribution of cluster sizes.

Using this more refined methodology, the study explored the social sciences at three different structural levels: that of individual specialties, groups of closely related specialties, and a multidisciplinary aggregate of all specialties. In addition, the basic structural characteristics of the social sciences were compared with those of the natural sciences.

For the comparative analysis, the three-year sample of 14,110 cited social science documents that qualified for pairing by meeting the citation-frequency threshold of 10 was compared to a one-year sample (1973 *SCI*) of 15,973 cited natural science documents that qualified for pairing by meeting a citation-frequency threshold of 15. The difference in the citation-frequency thresholds used was intended to keep the data bases from which pairs were extracted as close as possible in size.

The major difference seen between the two structures was that the social sciences were much more tightly integrated. This was shown by several measures, the major one being the ratio of actual to potential pairs. By this measure, the degree of integration for the social sciences was 83% versus 56% for the natural sciences.

Other measures of cohesiveness showed the same sort of difference. The mean number of co-citation linkages per document was 117.8 for the social sciences versus 89.7 for the natural sciences. The nodal number of linkages per document was 57 for the social sciences versus 35 for the natural sciences. The same pattern held when the co-citation links between clusters formed at level 16 were worked out: 3.4% of the potential linkages between social-science clusters at that level were realized versus 2% for the natural sciences, and the mean number of linkages per social science cluster was 41.2 versus 32 for the natural science clusters.

Aside from this evidence of a greater degree of interaction between social science specialties, the only other obvious sign of a significant difference between the social and natural sciences was in the age of the cluster documents. The mean date for the natural science documents was 1969.6 versus 1966.5 for the social sciences. This finding is consistent with the often-heard opinion that the social sciences change more slowly than the natural sciences and that the concepts underlying its research are older.

In all other ways, the structures of the two parts of science appear to be much the same. The most significant similarity is that the specialty area of research seems to be the basic structural unit in both.

One view of the structure of the social sciences at a specialty level of detail is shown in Figure 8.30. This map was produced by clustering the data base of document pairs at a co-citation threshold level of 16%, and then reclustering the clusters (rather than the documents in the clusters) that had been cited at least 100 times at co-citation threshold levels of 20% and 10%.

In a sense, then, the map is a composite. The large network of specialties connected by solid lines was produced when the level 16 clusters were reclustered at level 20. The four ovals around the perimeter are separate networks, formed at level 20, that are shown in macrocluster form to fit them onto the map. They connected to the large network at the positions shown by the dotted lines only when the reclustering level was dropped from 20 to 10.

Another bit of perspective that is useful in interpreting the map is the fact that the level 16 clustering of co-cited document pairs produced 143 clusters that had been cited at least 100 times. When these specialties were reclustered at level 20, 47 of them formed the solid line network, which consists of psychology (mostly social, but with some experimental) and sociology. The only other networks of significant size that were formed were the ones shown in ovals as macroclusters: a 20 cluster network on *memory and learning; a three cluster network on multidimensional scaling;* a five cluster network on *psychiatry*; and a three cluster network on *counseling,* which is really a secondary psychiatry network. Not shown is a network of three clusters on law.

On the one hand, the fact that all the networks link together at a reclustering level of 10 is a demonstration of the relatively high degree of integration in the social sciences. The level 10 network accounted for 70% of the 143 clusters originally created.

On the other hand, considering the high degree of integration, the fact that the *memory and learning* and *psychiatry* networks did not link to the main one until the co-citation threshold was dropped to 10 suggests that there are major conceptual and methodological differences between the specialties in these areas of research and the ones in social psychology and sociology. In retrospect, that does not seem very surprising in the case of *psychiatry*. However, it is surprising in the case of *memory and learning,* which is something one would expect to be in the mainstream of psychology.

The map also suggests that many of the social science specialties are highly problem oriented and employ a broad mix of scientific skills. For example, when the documents in the *organizational structure* cluster were examined, they were found to be a mix of material on psychology, sociology, and management science. Consistent with this characteristic, there are no specialties that can clearly be defined as social psychology. The type of work normally described by these names is scattered throughout the dominant psychology-sociology network.

What the map does not show, and its absence is somewhat conspicuous, is work in the areas of economics and political science. This gap was caused by the decision to recluster only those specialties whose documents had been cited at least 100 times. Characterized by low publication rates and low citation levels, economics and political science failed to qualify.

To provide a more comprehensive view of the social sciences structure, it was mapped a second time with the same technique used to map the natural sciences. Simply clustering the data base of co-cited pairs at a co-citation frequency threshold of 11% produced a map that was more inclusive and that struck a different balance between aggregation and differentiation. The result was a consolidation of most of the psychology clusters that dominated Figure 8.30 and the identification of specialties in economics, political science, psychoanalysis, and sociology that were missing from that map.

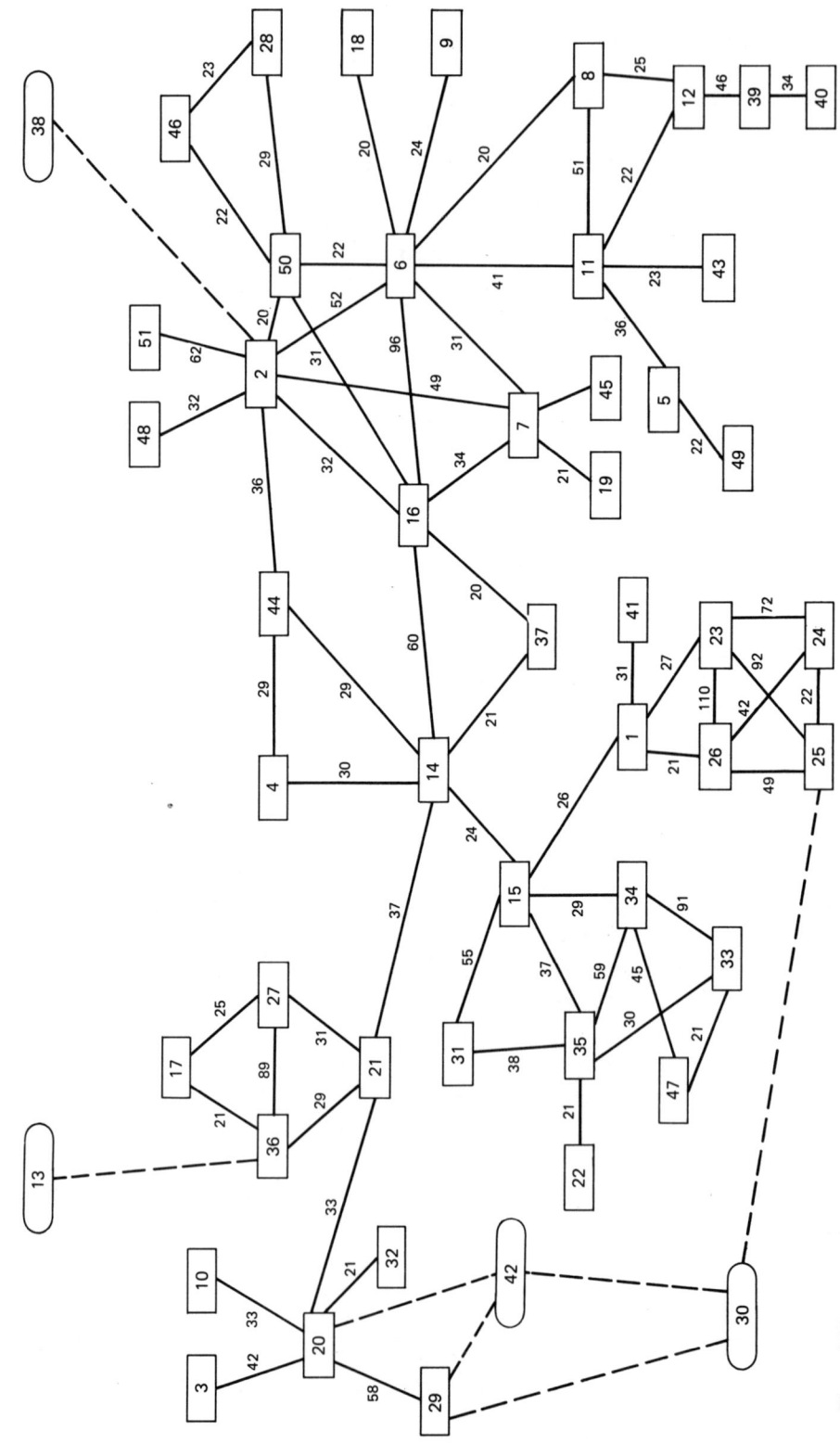

Figure 8.30. Map of major social sciences clusters from 1972–1974 data base.

KEY

1. Achievement motivation
2. Anxiety reduction
3. Attitude and behavior
4. Attitude change
5. Avoidance learning
6. Behavior modification
7. Behavior therapy
8. Behavioral contrast
9. Childhood psychosis
10. Cognitive balance
11. Concurrent reinforcement
12. Contrast in conditioning
13. Counseling
14. Equity theory
15. Expectancy theory predictions
16. Helping behavior
17. Human territoriality
18. Hyperactive children
19. Hypothalamic feeding
20. Impression formation
21. Interpersonal attraction
22. Leadership style
23. Locus of control
24. Locus of control, activism
25. Locus of control, alienation
26. Locus of Control, internal-external
27. Man-made environments
28. Mass-media violence
29. Measurement of human judgment
30. Memory and learning
31. Motivation and job satisfaction
32. Multiple-cue learning
33. Organizational decision making
34. Organizational structure
35. Organizational theory, management
36. Personal space
37. Prisoners dilemma
38. Psychiatry
39. Reinforcement in conditioning
40. Reward magnitude
41. Risky shift
42. Scaling, multidimensional
43. Schedule-induced behaviors
44. Self perception
45. Sexual behavior
46. Social aggression
47. Social participation in organization
48. State-trait model, anxiety
49. Taste-aversion learning
50. Television imitation
51. Treatment of phobias

The 20 largest clusters from the second, more inclusive map are shown in Figure 8.31, where they have been plotted as a series of points on a two-dimensional scale. The distance between points is inversely proportional to the strength of the co-citation links that join them (the closer the points, the stronger the co-citation links between them). The dominant cluster is *psychology,* which occupies the central position on the map. A number of separate psychology specialties, mostly clinical in nature, appear in the upper-right quadrant. Specialties in economics, political science, management, and sociology appear in the lower-left quadrant.

The most striking feature of the configuration of this map is the clear distinction it makes between the behavior of individuals and the behavior of groups. The specialties concerned with individual behavior are located in the upper-right quadrant, while those concerned with group behavior are in the lower left. This results in a well defined polar axis, similar to the one formed in the natural sciences by medicine, biology, chemistry, and physics, in that order. There is evidence that if co-citation clustering were used to produce a combined map of the social and natural sciences, the linear structure of the two would match, with the clinical psychology research on individuals (upper-right quadrant) leading into medicine.

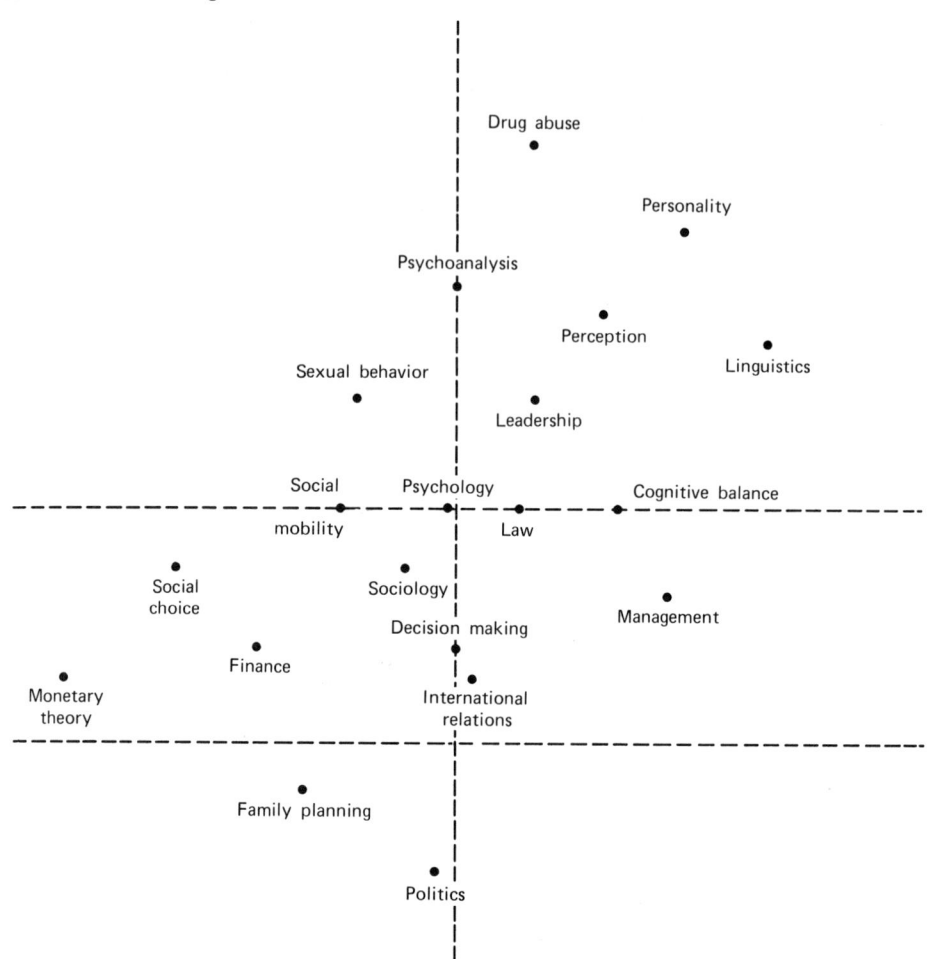

Figure 8.31 Two-dimensional plot of 20 largest social science clusters at level 11.

At the opposite end of the structural spectrum, the co-citation clustering methodology produced the same type of picture of individual social science specialties as it did of the ones in the natural sciences. Figure 8.32 shows an example: a specialty named *free recall,* which is one of the components of the *memory and learning* macrocluster on the social sciences map in Figure 8.30. Each box represents a document, which is described by the name of its author, the year and journal in which it was published, and the number of times it was cited. This shows the work on *free recall* as being dominated by five men: Craik, Glanzer, Waugh, Atkinson, and Rundus.

Figure 8.33 is an example of what was shown at an intermediate point on the structural scale. The subject is *memory and learning,* the macrocluster in which *free recall* is found. This view of the macrocluster was produced by identifying all the level 16 clusters that had at least 50 co-citation links to *free recall,* representing each one with a circle whose diameter is proportionately scaled to the number of times it was cited and then plotting them on a two-dimensional scale so that the overlap between circles is proportional to the strength of the co-citation links between clusters.

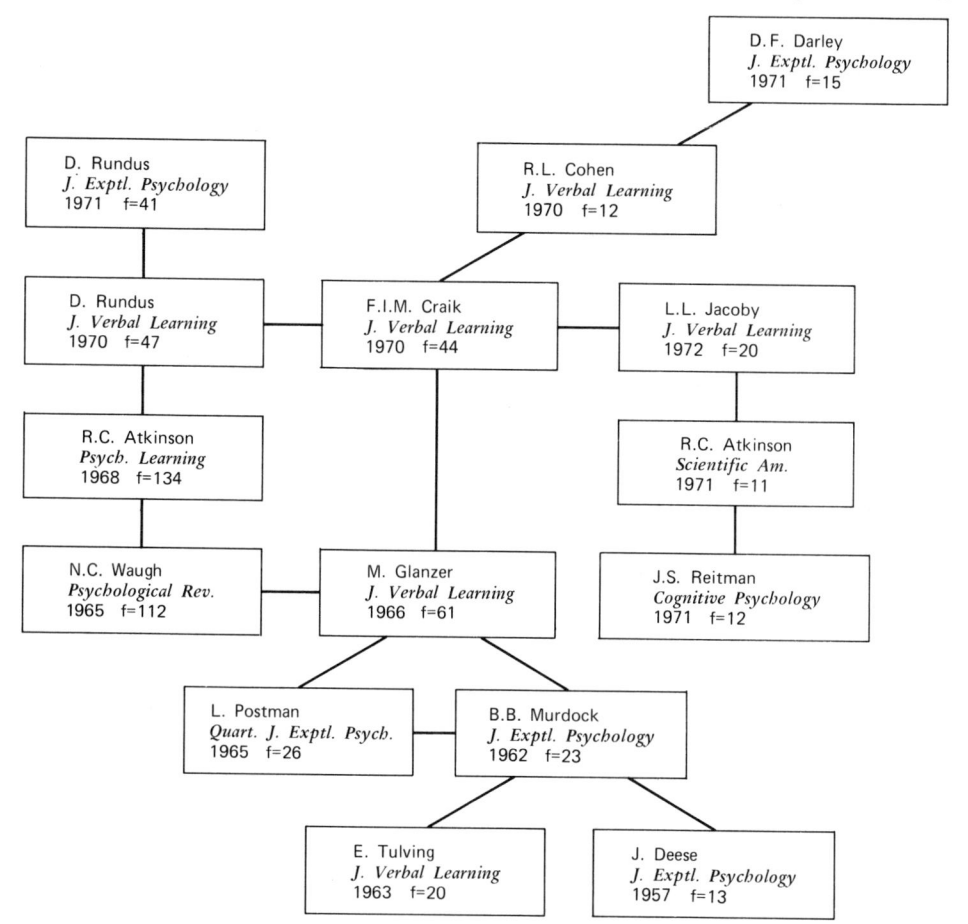

Figure 8.32 Block diagram of *free recall* cluster. Each block represents a document, which is described by the name of its author, the year and journal in which it was published, and the number of times it was cited from 1972–1974.

The result shows a very tightly structured set of 11 specialties in which *free recall* lies close to the center.

One of the interesting byproducts of this structural study of the social sciences is a list of the 26 documents that were cited most frequently during the 1972-1974 period (Figure 8.34). All of them were cited at least 200 times during the three-year period.

The most striking feature of this list is that all but three of the documents are books, which is consistent with the evidence and opinions that the ideas and concepts that support the research fronts in the social sciences are older than those found in the natural sciences. Another characteristic of the list that is consistent with the structural studies is the dominance of psychology. At least 15 of the 26 items on the list could be classified as belonging to that discipline. The overriding methodological importance of statistics in the social sciences is reflected by two texts on that subject being the two most frequently cited items on the list.

142 *Citation Indexing*

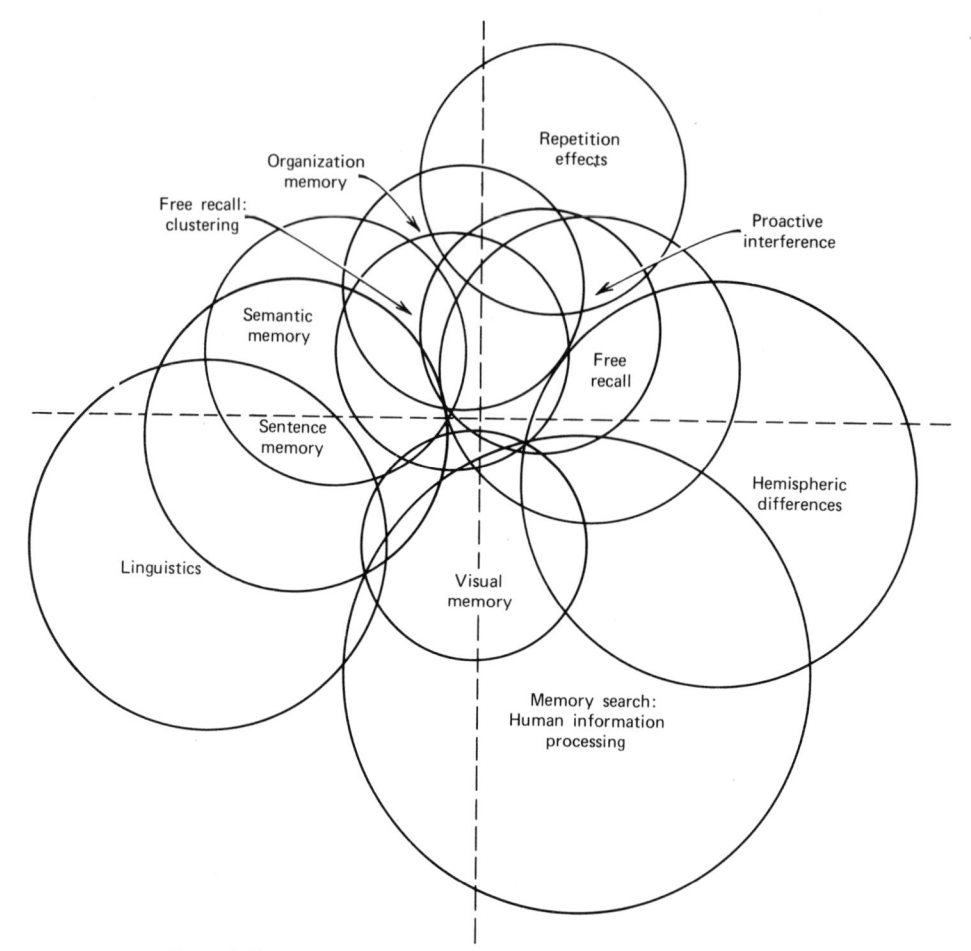

Figure 8.33 Spatial diagram of *memory and learning* macrocluster.

IMPLICATIONS

The ultimate implications of this series of studies are, of course, still uncertain, but they could be highly significant. Although Price has long hypothesized that science, despite its complexity, must be a two-dimensional spatial system (29), the co-citation maps of the natural and social sciences are the first confirmation of that hypothesis. Price, for one, thinks the confirmation has important theoretical and practical implications for scientific communication, particularly as it pertains to the number and subject scope of primary journals and to indexing systems (30). One very practical communications implication that ISI already is seriously working on is the development of an *Atlas of Science* that provides the same type of graphic, two-dimensional guide to the intellectual world of science as the traditional atlases do to the physical world (31).

Beyond that, the evidence produced by these initial studies suggests that the literature model of science may have led us to a methodology that will permit the

Author	Title	Year	Citation Frequency 1927-1974
Winer, B.J.	Statistical Principles in Experimental Design	62	1333
Siegel, S.	Nonparametric Statistics for the Behavioral Sciences	56	1020
Osgood, C.E.	Measurement of Meaning	57	480
Bandura, A.	Principles of Behavior Modification	69	422
Chomsky, N.	Aspects of the Theory Syntax	65	382
Rotter, J.B.	Psychological Monographs	66	381
Neisser, U.	Cognitive Psychology	67	334
Festinger, L.	Theory of Cognitive Dissonance	57	328
Heider, F.	Psychology of Interpersonal Relations	58	315
Merton, R.K.	Social Theory and Social Structure	57	313
Hollingshead, A.B.	Social Class and Mental Illness	58	303
Coleman, J.S.	Equality of Educational Opportunity	66	296
Hays, W.L.	Statistics for Psychologists	63	283
Rokeach, M.	Open and Closed Mind	60	277
Wolpe, J.	Psychotherapy by Reciprocal Inhibition	58	275
Toffler, A.	Future Stock	70	268
Adorno, T.W.	Authoritarian Personality	50	240
Jensen, A.R.	How Much Can We Boost IQ and Scholastic Achievement	69	226
Witkin, H.A.	Psychological Differentiation	62	219
Kuhn, T.S.	Structure of Scientific Revolutions	62	217
Thorndike, E.L.	Teachers' Word Book of Thirty Thousand Words	44	217
Parsons, T.	Social System	51	214
Skinner, B.F.	Beyond Freedom & Dignity	71	208
Miller, G.A.	The Magic number Seven: Plus or Minus Two	56	203
Katz, D.	Social Psychology of Organizations	66	202
Fenichel, O.	Psychoanalytic Theory of Neurosis	45	201

Figure 8.34 List of social science documents cited at least 200 times from 1972 to 1974.

systematic investigation and objective definition, through structural analysis, of the status, dynamics, and underlying processes of science. But a lot of work is required to make that case conclusive.

There is no doubt that co-citation clustering has uncovered a structure in science. What is in doubt is the nature of that structure—whether it is the fundamental one of specialties that has been predicted, and is expected to produce informative insights. The studies conducted so far indicate that it is.

The collagen study proved that the cluster that appeared to represent the specialty of collagen research did, in fact, do so—at least to the extent that the changes that took place in its size, configuration, and intellectual content over time were accurate indicators of the state of the specialty as seen by the researchers who knew it best. But that study proves the validity of only one set of clusters. Similar success in a statistically significant number of specialty studies is needed to conclusively prove that all the clusters are representative of specialties.

Assuming that the clusters do represent specialties, the next step is to determine what types of information can be derived from them. The stability index, for example, must be validated as a measure of the rate of intellectual change in a specialty; and, if it is, it must also be calibrated so that we know what degree of change in the index is significant and the nature of the significance.

Furthermore, the emergence of a series of very recent papers describing a different research front must be validated as a signal of a major conceptual shift. And it must be determined whether there is a limit to the number of research fronts that can be contained in a single cluster before one of them is spun off to form a new independent specialty.

Cluster configurations must be studied to see if there is any relationship between the size and shape of clusters and the status of the specialty. It is possible that defining the status of science can be reduced to a pattern-recognition problem.

Another relationship that must be explored is the one between the intellectual structure of a specialty and its social structure. It is hard to imagine that the picture co-citation clusters produce of intellectual structures is completely divorced from social factors. But in what specific way are they related? Do the authors of the cluster documents represent the "invisible college" upon which the specialty is built? Does a change in these authors signal a change in the membership of that college? Is the size of the cluster related to whether communication within the specialty is informal and open or formal and guarded?

Once all these things are determined, cluster analysis can be employed, first, to test and further develop theories of specialty behavior and, then, to apply these theories to the job of characterizing the mosaic of science in ways that will be useful to the people who must make science policy decisions.

There is already much to test. At a general level, there are three hypothetical models of the dynamics of science that suggest particular patterns of specialty behavior. Kuhn thinks scientific change takes place in revolutionary spurts, interspersed with periods of stability (21). Popper sees it as proceeding at a continuous, rather than intermittent, revolutionary pace (32). And Toulmin sees the change as being continuous and evolutionary (33).

At the more detailed level, there are such things as Crane's observation that the growth in the size of a specialty seems to follow, rather than precede, innovation (4)—a pattern that certainly was seen in the collagen clusters, which did not expand dramatically in size until three years after the publication of the discovery papers that opened up a major, new research front. Another characteristic of specialty behavior that is important to study is the aging process. Is there a shift from basic to applied research as a specialty ages, or is there just a temporary increase in size and scope that is limited by a tendency for application work to achieve independent specialty status? And that question is but a part of a bigger, more important aspect of specialty behavior. Is there a universal life cycle for specialties—a cycle of birth, growth, and decay? If so, it would simplify the job of determining which of the three general models of science is most accurate.

In other words, there is still much validation, characterization, and application work to be done before anything definite can be said about the impact that co-citation clustering will have on the study and management of science. To facilitate the work, ISI is developing an on-line computer-based system that will permit researchers to work with the *SCI* and *SSCI* data bases in an interactive mode to produce and analyze diagrams of specialty clusters at all points on the structural scale. The storage-and-retrieval subsystem already is operational and has demonstrated a functional capability and efficiency that can considerably reduce the time and cost of performing citation analyses (34). The National Science Foundation is financing the development of the graphic sybsystem as part of their continuing interest in the potential of citation analysis as a science policy tool.

In his famous book, *The Structure of Scientific Revolutions* (21), Kuhn wrote,

". . . if I am right that each scientific revolution alters the historical perspective of the community that experiences it, then that change of perspective should affect the structure of post-revolutionary text-books and research publications. One such effect—a shift in the distribution of the technical literature cited in the footnotes to research reports—ought to be studied as a possible index to the occurrence of revolutions."

Co-citation analysis promises to produce an index that does that and more.

REFERENCES

1. **Garfield, E., Sher, I. and Torpie, R.J.** *The Use of Citation Data in Writing the History of Science* (Philadelphia: Institute for Scientific Information, 1964). 86 pp.
2. **Crawford, S.** "Informal Communication among Scientists in Sleep Research." *Journal of the American Society for Information Science,* 22:301–310, 1971.
3. **Griffith, B.C. and Mullins, N.C.** "Coherent Social Groups in Scientific Change," *Science,* 177:959–964, 1972.
4. **Crane, D.** *Invisible Colleges: Diffusion of Knowledge in Scientific Communities* (Chicago: University of Chicago Press, 1972). Pp. 2131
5. **Price, D.J.D.** Unpublished studies (New Haven: Yale University, 1964–1967).
6. **Price, D.J.D.** "Networks of Scientific Papers." *Science,* 149:510–515, 1967.
7. **Narin, F., Carpenter, M. and Berlt, N.C.** "Inter-relationships of Scientific Journals." *Journal of the American Society for Information Science,* 23:323–331, 1972; **Carpenter, M. and Narin, F.** "Clustering of Scientific Journals." (In press).

8. **Goffman, W.** "Mathematical Approach to the Spread of Scientific Ideas—The History of Mast Cell Research." *Nature,* **212:**449-452, 1966.
9. **Jahn, M.** *Changes with Growth of the Scientific Literature of Two Biomedical Specialties.* (Philadelphia: Drexel University, MS thesis, 1972). 64 pp.
10. **Small, H.** *Nuclear Physics in the Physical Review 1927-1940.* Unpublished report of a study at the American Institute of Physics, 1970.
11. **Small, H.G. and Griffith, B.C.** "The Structure of Scientific Literature, I: Identifying and Graphing Specialties." *Science Studies,* **4:**17-40, 1974.
12. **Griffith, B.C., Small, H.G., Stonehill, J.A., and Dey, S.** "The Structure of Scientific Literature, II: Toward a Macro- and Micro-structure for Science." *Science Studies,* **4:**339-365, 1974.
13. **Small, H.G.** *Mapping the Specialty Structure of the Social Sciences Using the Social Sciences Citation Index.* Unpublished report of a study for the National Science Foundation, 1975.
14. **Small, H.G.** "A Co-Citation Model of a Scientific Specialty: A Longitudinal Study of Collagen Research." *Social Studies of Science,* **7:**139-166, 1977.
15. **Kessler, M.M.** "Bibliographic Coupling Between Scientific Papers." *American Documentation,* **14:**10-25, 1963.
16. **Small, H.G.** "Co-Citation in the Scientific Literature: A New Measure of the Relationship Between Two Documents." *Journal of the American Society for Information Science,* **24:**265-269, 1973.
17. **Marshakova, I.V.** "Bibliographic Coupling System Based on Cited References (*Science Citation Index*)." *Nauchno Tekhnicheskaya, Informatsiza Seriya,* **2:**3-8, 1973.
18. **Goffman, W.** "A Mathematical Method of Analyzing the Growth of a Scientific Discipline." *Journal of the Association for Computing Machinery,* **18:**173-185, 1971.
19. **Magyar, G.** "Bibliometric Analysis of a New Research Sub-field." *Journal of Documentation,* **30:**32-50, 1974.
20. **Griffith, B.C.** "On the Nature of Social Science and Its Literature." *CACUL Newsletter,* **4:**195-229, January 16, 1973.
21. **Kuhn, T.S.** *The Structure of Scientific Revolutions* (Chicago: University of Chicago Press, 1962). Pp. 172
22. **Jaspars, J.M.F. and Ackermans, E.** "The Interdisciplinary Character of Social Psychology." *Sociologia Neerlandica,* **4:**62-79, 1966-1967.
23. **Lin, N.** "Stratification of the Formal Communication System in American Sociology." *American Sociologist,* **9:**199-206, 1974.
24. **Clark, K.E.** *America's Psychologists: A Survey of a Growing Profession* (Washington, D.C.: American Psychological Association, 1957). Pp. 247
25. **Myers, C.R.** "Journal Citations and Scientific Eminence in Contemporary Psychology." *American Psychologist,* **25:**1041-1048, 1970.
26. **Cole, S.** "The Growth of Scientific Knowledge: Theories of Deviance as a Case Study." In Coser, L.A. (ed.). *The Idea of Social Structure: Papers in Honor of Robert K. Merton* (New York: Harcourt, Brace, Jovanovich, 1975). Pp. 175-220.
27. **Cole, J.R. and Zuckerman, H.** "The Emergence of a Scientific Specialty: The Self-exemplifying Case of the Sociology of Science." In Coser, L.A. (ed.). *The Idea of Social Structure: Papers in Honor of Robert K. Merton* (New York: Harcourt, Brace, Jovanovich, 1975). Pp. 139-174.
28. **Bath University Library.** "The Use of Citation Linkages and Networks for information Retrieval in the Social Sciences." Working Paper #6, *Design of information Systems in the Social Sciences* (March 1973). See also Working Paper #11 on journal clustering.
29. **Price, D.J.D.** "Science: The Science of Scientists." *Medical Opinon and Review,* **1:**88-97, 1966.
30. **Price, D.J.D.** "Society's Needs in Scientific and Technical Information." *Ciencia da Informacao, Rio de Janeiro,* **3:**97-103, 1974.
31. **Garfield, E.** "ISI's Atlas of Science May Help Students in Choice of Career in Science." *Essays of an Information Scientist,* Vol. 2 (Philadelphia: ISI Press, 1977) 311-314.
32. **Popper K.** "Normal Science and Its Dangers." In Lakatos, I. and Musgrave, A. (eds.). *Criticism and the Growth of Knowledge* (Cambridge: Cambridge University Press 1970). Pp. 51-58.

33. **Toulmin, S.** *Human Understanding: The Collective Use and Evolution of Concepts* (Princeton: Princeton University Press, 1972).
34. **Yermish, I.** *"A Citation-Based Interactive Associative Information Retrieval System.* (Philadelphia: University of Pennsylvania Ph.D dissertation, 1975). 278 pp., mimeogr.

Chapter Nine

Citation Analysis of Scientific Journals

Citation analysis is used to study the journals of science as well as the people and work of science. The citation links between scientific papers, technical notes, reviews, and, in some cases, meeting abstracts provide a quantitative picture of journal utility and relationships that is useful in many ways. For example, it may be used by editors trying to determine their competitive position, information scientists studying the structure of the literature, librarians managing journal collections, sociologists attempting to define the structure of science itself, and every researcher who has a need to identify useful journals when the interaction between specialties or disciplines pushes him or her beyond the borders of familiar territory.

The citation picture of journals is subject to the same qualifications as all other citation pictures. Based only on what scientists say about utility and relationships in their choice of references, it is not definitive. For one thing, citation links show only how frequently and where published research is used. How good a measure that is of a journal's utility and relationships varies according to the function of the journal. For those whose primary function is to keep scientists informed about what is going on in a general news sense, and that publish few research reports or reviews, it is a measure of little, if any, relevance. On the other hand, citation links provide a very relevant measure of the utility and relationships of journals whose primary function is to communicate research results. Even in these cases, however, the citation picture is not a definitive one, simply because scientific merit is not always the sole reason an author will cite a paper published in a particular journal. Such factors as the reputation of the cited author and the visibility, prestige, and accessibility of the cited journal may affect, to a greater or lesser degree, the work an author chooses to cite. Because of these qualifications, citation pictures of journals have to be used with the same care and intelligence as any other type of citation picture: they must be applied only where they are relevant, and they must be interpreted within the framework of the decision to be made or the hypothesis to be examined.

A CITATION VIEW OF JOURNALS

The preceding qualifications notwithstanding, citation analysis provides a number of interesting and useful insights into the network of journals that function as the primary, formal communications medium of science. The insights come from five different citation measures.

The basic one is the citation rate of a journal: the number of times it has been cited. There are several different ways this figure can be calculated. It can consist of all the references to the cited journal, with even duplicate references from the same source article counting as separate citation links. At the other extreme, the citation rate of a journal can consist of only the number of source articles that cited the journal, with multiple references (even different ones) from the same source article counting only as a single citation link. Somewhere between these two extremes lies a third type of citation rate that consists of the number of references to the cited journal, but that discounts duplicate references from the same source article, so they count as only a single citation link. The third type of citation rate is the one used at ISI.

Another citation measure is the impact factor, which is the average citation rate of a journal's articles. The purpose of the impact factor is to discount the advantage in citation potential that larger/older journals have over smaller/younger journals because they publish more material. Again, there are several different ways of calculating the impact-factor measure, which is basically a ratio between the citation rate of the journal and its citation potential. The difference between the various ways lies in the way these two parameters are defined. Citation rate can consist of either the number of times cited or the number of items cited. The citation potential can consist of either the number of citable items published or the number of cited items published. At ISI, citation rate is defined as the number of times cited, while citation potential is defined as the number of citable items published. The impact factor we use, therefore, is the number of times a journal was cited, divided by the number of citable articles the journal published.

There also are two measures of how frequently journals cite themselves. One is the self-citing rate, which shows what percentage of a journal's references cite articles it published. The other is the self-cited rate, which shows what percent of citations received by a journal originated in articles published by the journal.

It is hard to say anything very definitive about these two measures because their analytical role has not been worked out. They are being used primarily in studies to determine the significance of self-citation practices. Some observers look upon self-citation as a self-serving practice, particularly when authors cite their own work. On the other hand, it is easy to justify the practice as being nothing more than a manifestation of the perfectly normal tendency of a scientist to build on his or her own work. Certainly, the practice is common; although precise figures are difficult to develop, it would be safe to say that some 10 to 20% of all references cite prior work of the source author. The significance of self-citations at the journal level also is uncertain. Preliminary studies at ISI (1) show that among the top 20 most cited journals, the self-cited rate was generally lower than the self-citing rate. This means that the references these journals published to their own articles were a smaller percentage of the citations they received than they were of the references they published. However, when the focus of the study was switched to the group of journals that ranked from 500 to 520 in terms of citation rate, the reverse was found to be true: their self-cited rate tended to be higher than the self-citing rate. The reason for this reversal is not yet clear, but self-citation rates seem to say something about the newness, size, and isolation of the intellectual universe in which a journal operates.

The fifth citation measure is an immediacy index, which is a way of showing how rapidly a journal's material is picked up and used. This measure, too, can be calculated in several different ways, but the basic parameter used in all of them is the number of citations received by articles during the year in which they were published. This parameter can be shown either as a percent of the total number of citations received (citation rate) or as a percent of the total number of citeable articles published (citation potential). ISI's immediacy index consists of the latter.

DATA BASE OF JOURNAL CITATION MEASURES

All five of these measures are published in the *Journal Citation Reports* (*JCR*™*) section of *SCI* for the thousands of cited and source journals covered by the index (2). The first issue of *JCR* was published in the 1975 *SCI* but reflected the 1974 citation record of the journals covered. The record was based on 4,248,065 citations from the references of approximately 400,000 source items published in the 1974 issues of some 2400 source journals. The references provided citation data on more than 2500 cited journals.

The citation data for these journals is organized into three separate, but related, packages. The first is the Journal Ranking Package, which consists of six sections. Section I (see Figure 9.1) is an alphabetic listing, by title abbreviation, of 2630 cited journals for which it shows:

- The total number of times cited (citation rate).
- The number of citations to articles published in 1972 and 1973 (by individual year and in aggregate).
- The number of items published (citation potential) in 1972 and 1973 (by individual year and in aggregate).
- The impact factor.
- The number of citations to articles published in 1974.
- The number of items published in 1974.
- The immediacy index.

The entry for *Acta Anaesthetica Scandinavica* in Figure 9.1, then, shows that references cited it 287 times; 25 of those references cited articles published in 1973

---

*A trademark of the Institute for Scientific Information.

Specimen

	JOURNAL RANKING PACKAGE	J O U R N A L C I T A T I O N R E P O R T S										SECTION 1	PAGE 1
		JOURNALS IN ALPHABETICAL ORDER											
	JOURNAL TITLE	<------CITATIONS IN 1974 TO------>				<--SOURCE ITEMS IN-->			IMPACT FACTOR	CITATIONS IN 1974 TO 1974 ITEMS	SOURCE ITEMS IN 1974	IMMEDIACY INDEX	
		ALL YEARS	1973	1972	73+72	1973	1972	73+72					
1	A GRAEFES A KLIN E O	647	72	52	124	90	78	168	0.738	24	123	0.195	
2	A VAN LEEUW J MICROB	557	47	53	100	62	55	117	0.855	15	63	0.238	
3	AAPG BULL	1639	151	203	354	145	158	303	1.168	29	161	0.180	
4	ABRASIVE ENG	1	0	0	0	25	35	60	0.000	0	24	0.000	
5	ACCOUNTS CHEM RES	2738	326	555	881	63	56	119	7.403	65	62	1.048	
6	ACTA AGRON HUNG	43	6	2	8	54	60	114	0.070	1	93	0.011	
7	ACTA ALLERGOL	334	40	44	84	33	39	72	1.167	9	40	0.225	
8	ACTA ANAESTH SCAND	287	25	37	62	54	48	102	0.608	8	61	0.131	
9	ACTA ANAT	1212	47	84	131	141	142	283	0.463	17	157	0.108	
10	ACTA ASTRONAUTICA	10	0	0	0	40	89	129	0.000	3	94	0.032	
11	ACTA BIOCHIM BIOPHYS	250	15	51	66	32	51	83	0.795	7	46	0.152	
12	ACTA BIOCHIM POL	336	34	31	65	37	37	74	0.878	11	51	0.216	
13	ACTA BIOL CRACOV BOT	48	2	5	7	13	19	32	0.219	1	15	0.067	
14	ACTA BIOL CRACOV ZOO	66	5	2	7	27	23	50	0.140	1	18	0.056	
15	ACTA BIOL HUNG	227	4	15	19	27	43	70	0.271	1	15	0.067	
16	ACTA BIOL MED GER	922	112	189	301	216	228	444	0.678	50	223	0.224	
17	ACTA BOT NEER	465	45	43	88	76	76	152	0.579	16	64	0.250	
18	ACTA CHEM SCAND	8803	472	720	1192	549	595	1144	1.042	165	434	0.380	
19	ACTA CHIM HUNG	904	98	97	195	197	236	433	0.450	29	152	0.191	
20	ACTA CHIR HUNG	54	6	9	15	45	32	77	0.195	3	33	0.091	
21	ACTA CHIR SCAND	1645	64	142	206	142	137	279	0.738	26	133	0.195	
22	ACTA CIENT VENEZ	64	6	14	20	77	101	178	0.112	0	10	0.000	
23	ACTA CRYSTALLOGR	7598	22	18	40	0	0	0		3	0		
24	ACTA CRYSTALLOGR A	1793	241	275	516	141	235	376	1.372	73	166	0.440	
25	ACTA CRYSTALLOGR B	4520	854	984	1838	630	753	1383	1.329	221	635	0.348	
26	ACTA CYTOL	763	98	93	191	81	90	171	1.117	8	73	0.110	
27	ACTA DERMAT-VENEREOL	840	96	122	218	120	84	204	1.069	27	96	0.281	
28	ACTA DIABETOL LAT	281	12	44	56	46	11	57	0.982	3	39	0.077	
29	ACTA ENDOCRINOL PAN	12	0	6	6	8	10	18	0.333	0			
30	ACTA ENDOCRINOL-COP	4909	708	675	1383	251	311	562	2.461	159	278	0.572	
31	ACTA ENTOMOL BOHEMOS	79	15	23	38	51	42	93	0.409	7	44	0.159	
32	ACTA GENET MED GEMEL	122	1	5	6	13	33	46	0.130	0	61	0.000	
33	ACTA GERONTOL	17	11	3	14	25	19	44	0.318	0	0		
34	ACTA HAEMATOL	953	54	11[illegible]	[illegible]65	88	100	188	0.878	1[illegible]	93	0.172	
3[illegible]	[illegible]PATO-GASTRO	[illegible]	25	[illegible]	[illegible]	69	[illegible]	[illegible]	0.418	[illegible]	66	[illegible]	

Figure 9.1 *Journal Citation Reports (JCR)* Journal Ranking Package, Section 1.

152 Citation Indexing

and 37 cited 1972 material, for a total of 62 references to the material published during that two-year period. It published 54 items in 1973, 48 in 1972, and a total of 102 during those two years; its impact factor is 0.608 (62/102); it published 61 articles in 1974 and they were cited eight times to produce an immediacy index value of 0.131 (8/61).

The other five sections of the Journal Ranking Package show all the same data, but the journals are listed in ranked order by the measures of citation rate (Figure 9.2), impact factor (Figure 9.3), immediacy index (Figure 9.4), items published in 1974 (Figure 9.5), and number of times 1972–1973 material was cited (Figure 9.6).

Specimen

Figure 9.2 *Journal Citation Reports (JCR)* Journal Ranking Package, Section 2. Ranking by total citation rate.

Specimen

Figure 9.3 *Journal Citation Reports (JCR)* Journal Ranking Package, Section 3. Ranking by impact factor.

Specimen

Figure 9.4 *Journal Citation Reports (JCR)* Journal Ranking Package, Section 4. Ranking by immediacy index.

Specimen

```
                          JOURNAL CITATION REPORTS

    JOURNAL TITLE      <------CITATIONS IN 1974 TO------>   <--SOURCE ITEMS IN-->   IMPACT    CITATIONS    SOURCE    IMMEDIACY
                       ALL YEARS    1973    1972    73+72     1973    1972   73+72  FACTOR   IN 1974 TO    ITEMS      INDEX
                                                                                              1974 ITEMS   IN 1974
```

Section 5

```
 24  J APPL PHYS---------19277----1509--1766---3275-----1077--1025---2102----1 558--------371------956----0 388
 25  J CHEM SOC CHEM COMM 14454    1856   2597   4453      894  1231   2125    2 096         353      938    0 376
 26  PHYS REV D----------9441----2932--2372---5304-----1033---915---1948----2 723------802------933----0 860
 27  FIZ TVERD TELA       4497     499    562   1061      936   885   1821    0 583         114      919    0 124
 27  SCIENCE-------------47505----5121--6660--11781◄----1026--1151---2177----5 412------1208-----919---►1 314
     SOV PHYS SOLID ST*   2377     143    227    370      936   427   1363    0 271          12      919    0 013
 30  CHEM PHYS LETT------8478----1899--2306---4205-----928---822---1750----2 403------423------896----0 472
 31  BRAIN RES-AMSTERDAM 10227    2012   2510   4522      775   682   1457    3 104         565      893    0 633
```

Figure 9.5 *Journal Citation Reports (JCR)* Journal Ranking Package, Section 5. Ranking by items published in 1974.

Specimen

```
                          JOURNAL CITATION REPORTS

    JOURNAL TITLE      <------CITATIONS IN 1974 TO------>   <--SOURCE ITEMS IN-->   IMPACT    CITATIONS    SOURCE    IMMEDIACY
                       ALL YEARS    1973    1972    73+72     1973    1972   73+72  FACTOR   IN 1974 TO    ITEMS      INDEX
                                                                                              1974 ITEMS   IN 1974
```

Section 6

```
 1  J AM CHEM SOC        98995    7855   9233  17088     1776  2123   3899   4 383        1835     1432    1 281
 2  P NAT ACAD SCI USA--46917----6866--8451--15317-----849---855---1704----8 989-----1268-----1195----1 061
 3  BIOCHIM BIOPHYS ACTA 51491    6409   7720  14129     2314  2215   4529   3 120         946     1910    0 495
 4  J BIOL CHEM---------81354----6319--7366--13685-----1213--1129---2342----5 843-----1352-----1147----1 179
 5  SCIENCE              47505    5121   6660  11781     1026  1151   2177   5 412        1208      919    1 314
 6  J CHEM PHYS---------62041----4496--5966--10462-----1725--1860---3585----2 918-----1022-----1631----0 627
 7  LANCET               37047    5249   5134  10383      646   909   1555   6 677        1971      623    3 164
 8  PHYS REV LETT-------29275----5167--4941--10108-----899--1099---1998----5 059-----1416------960----1 475
```

Figure 9.6 *Journal Citation Reports (JCR)* Journal Ranking Package, Section 6. Ranking by citation rate of 1972-1973 material.

The other two packages are designed to show the relationships between journals as defined by citation patterns. One, the Citing Journal Package, shows the citation patterns of the 2443 source journals covered by *SCI* in 1974: what journals they cited, and with what frequency. The other, the Cited Journal Package, shows the sources of the citations to the 2630 cited journals identified by *SCI* in 1974 and the citation frequency of each source. Both packages also show a distribution of the citations by the publication year of the cited material.

Figure 9.7 shows a sample of the Citing Journal Package. The citing journals are listed in alphabetical order by title abbreviation. The first column shows the journal's impact factor; the second, an abbreviation of its title; and the third, the total number of references it published in its 1974 material. The remaining columns show how these references were distributed by the publication year of the cited material. The journals cited by a given journal are listed beneath it in the same column format: the first showing their impact factor, the second showing their title abbreviation, the third showing the total number of times they were cited, and the rest showing how the references were distributed by the publication year of the cited material. The references of a citing journal, therefore, are distributed by both the journals cited and the publication year of the cited material. The cited journals are listed in descending order of citation frequency, with the last entry consisting of the aggregate total of all journals that were cited fewer than six times. Since one of the cited journals is always the source journal itself (more often than not, it heads the list), the self-citing rate of the source journal can be computed by dividing the number of references to its own material by the total number of references it published.

The entry for *Mathematische Zeitschrift* in Figure 9.7, then shows that:
- It published 1090 references (not including duplicate references from the same source article) in 1974, 26 of which cited 1974 material, 92 of which cited 1973 material, 115 of which cited 1972 material, and so on, with 432 of the references citing material published in 1964 or earlier.
- It cited itself more than any other journal, a total of 151 times.
- The 151 references to its own material were distributed as shown, with five citing 1974 material, 24 citing 1973 material, 18 citing 1972 material, etc., and with 36 citing material it published in 1964 or earlier.
- Of the other journals cited, it cited *Mathematische Annalen* the most frequently: 60 times. Four of the 60 references cited 1974 material, two cited 1973 material, and so on, with more than half of the 60 references citing material published in 1964 or earlier.
- Three hundred fifty-six of its references cited material published by 217 journals that are not identified. These references are distributed by the publication year of the cited material as shown: five to 1974 material, 28 to 1973 material, and so on, with 150 to material published in 1964 or earlier.

What the data in the entry for *Mathematische Zeitschrift* says about the journal is that approximately 40% of its references cited material published in 1964 and earlier (432/1090), that 42.6% of its references cited material published in 1969 or later (464/1090), that its self-citing rate is 13.8% (151/1090), that language presents no barriers to its authors (they cite English, French, German, Russian, and Japanese journals), and that the material it publishes is oriented toward physical and applied mathematics.

Figure 9.8 shows a sample of the Cited Journal Package. The format is the same as that in the Citing Journal Package, though the data and journals describe the number and source of citations received, rather than references published. The cited journals are listed alphabetically by title abbreviation, with the impact factor shown in the column preceding the title and the total number of times cited shown in the column following the title. The rest of the columns distribute the citations received by the publication year of the cited material. The journals that were the sources of the citations are listed beneath each cited journal, along with their impact factor and the number of times they cited it. The source references are distributed by publication year of the cited material. Again, the citations received by a journal are distributed by both their sources and the publication year of the cited material. And the source journals are again listed in descending order of citation frequency, with the last entry consisting of the aggregate total of a group of unidentified journals that were each responsible for fewer than six citations. Since every journal is cited by itself, every cited journal is also listed as one of its own source journals, making it possible to compute its self-cited rate by dividing the number of times it cited itself as a source journal by the number of times it was cited.

The entry in Figure 9.8 for the *American Journal of Physics,* then, shows that:

It was cited 800 times in 1974, with 14 of the references citing material published

Specimen

JOURNAL CITATION REPORTS

PAGE 449

CITING JOURNAL PACKAGE

CITING JOURNAL / CITED JOURNAL	TOTAL	<1974	1974	NUMBER OF TIMES THIS YEAR WAS CITED IN 1973	1972	1971	1970	1969	1968	1967	1966	1965	REST
17 MATH NACHR (CONTINUED)													
ALL OTHER (313)	478	8	17	46	57	35	34	21	22	30	20	188	
23 MATH SCAND========	===215*	===1	===14	===30	===15	===17	===14	===12	===8	===14	===4	===86	
23 MATH SCAND	16	0	3	4	0	0	1	0	0	1	1	6	
1 22 ANN MATH	13	0	0	1	1	2	1	0	0	1	0	7	
2 08 ACTA MATH	8	0	0	1	0	2	0	2	0	0	0	3	
29 ARK MAT	7	0	0	0	1	1	0	0	1	0	0	4	
51 B AM MATH SOC	7	0	1	0	0	0	0	0	0	0	0	5	
48 T AM MATH SOC	6	0	0	0	0	1	0	1	0	1	0	3	
ALL OTHER (90)	158	1	9	24	13	12	12	10	6	10	3	58	
47 MATH Z===============	===1090*	===26	===92	===115	===95	===70	===66	===61	===49	===41	===43	===432	
47 MATH Z	151	5	24	18	12	19	6	9	9	6	7	36	
38 MATH ANN	60	4	2	1	1	0	6	7	1	1	0	34	
48 T AM MATH SOC	46	1	3	1	3	5	6	2	1	2	4	21	
77 J ALGEBRA	40	0	3	10	7	2	5	5	1	4	0	4	
1 22 ANN MATH	37	0	1	1	0	1	3	0	1	2	0	27	
30 P AM MATH SOC	29	0	1	2	5	4	4	2	1	0	0	10	
77 ARCH RATION MECH AN	25	0	0	7	2	0	3	0	1	0	0	4	
47 AM J MATH	24	0	0	0	1	1	2	0	1	0	2	18	
51 B AM MATH SOC	23	0	3	3	2	2	2	0	3	0	0	8	
59 COMMUN PUR APPL MATH	19	0	3	3	3	1	0	0	0	0	2	7	
31 J LOND MATH SOC	19	0	3	4	2	1	0	0	0	0	2	7	
33 COMMENT MATH HELV	18	0	0	2	0	0	2	0	0	1	1	12	
27 PAC J MATH	18	0	2	0	1	1	2	0	1	2	2	8	
31 CAN J MATH	17	0	0	0	0	0	3	1	1	0	2	4	
22 ARCH MATH	16	0	3	2	3	2	2	1	0	1	0	5	
31 ILLINOIS J MATH	16	1	0	0	0	0	0	0	0	2	2	9	
80 INVENT MATH	14	1	0	0	3	2	1	0	4	2	1	0	
2 08 ACTA MATH	13	0	0	0	0	0	1	1	1	1	0	8	
ABH MATH SEM HAMBURG	12	0	1	0	1	0	0	2	0	1	0	7	
CR HEBD ACAD SCI	12	0	1	0	0	2	0	0	0	0	1	6	
FUND MATHEMATICAE	11	1	1	0	1	1	0	0	0	0	0	8	
35 J REINE ANGEW MATH	11	1	0	0	1	1	0	0	0	2	0	6	
53 P LOND MATH SOC	11	0	0	0	0	3	0	3	0	1	1	3	
39 DUKE MATH J	10	0	2	0	0	0	0	0	0	0	1	7	
INDAGATIONES MATH	9	0	0	0	2	0	1	0	0	2	0	4	
J COMB THEORY	8	0	1	1	2	2	1	0	0	1	0	0	
34 MANUSCRIPTA MATH	8	3	4	0	0	0	0	0	0	1	0	0	
J DIFFERENTIAL GEOM	7	0	2	0	0	0	2	2	0	1	0	0	
49 STUD MATH	7	0	0	0	0	0	0	1	0	0	3	3	
TOPOLOGY	7	0	0	2	0	1	0	0	2	0	1	1	
36 ANN I FOURIER	6	2	0	0	0	0	0	0	0	3	0	1	
25 B SOC MATH FR	6	0	0	1	0	1	0	0	2	0	0	3	
J FUNCT ANAL	6	0	3	0	0	0	3	0	0	0	0	0	
30 J MATH SOC JAPAN	6	0	0	0	1	0	1	0	0	1	1	2	
MAT SB	6	0	0	2	0	0	0	1	0	1	0	6	
SOV MATH DOKLADY	6	0	0	0	1	0	0	0	0	0	0	0	
ALL OTHER (217)	356	5	28	40	41	24	15	12	18	9	14	150	

Figure 9.7 *Journal Citation Reports (JCR)* Citing Journal Package.

Specimen

```
                        J O U R N A L   C I T A T I O N   R E P O R T S

                                        CITED JOURNAL PACKAGE                                    PAGE    39

CITED JOURNAL                  <------------NUMBER OF TIMES THIS YEAR WAS CITED IN  1974-->
  CITING JOURNAL         TOTAL  1974 1973 1972 1971 1970 1969 1968 1967 1966 1965  REST

AM J PHARM EDUC (CONTINUED)
 .26  J AM PHARM ASSOC       2     0    0    0    0    2    0    0    0    0    0    0
 .67  PHARMAZIE              2     0    0    1    1    1    0    0    0    0    0    0
      ALL OTHER    (10)     10     0    1    3    1    2    0    2    0    1    0    0

AM J PHYS============    800*  ==14  ==95 =104  ==83 ==77 ==61 ==46 ==40 ==31 ==19  ==230
 .25  AM J PHYS           243     7   60   44   34   14   10   17    5   10    8    34
2.91  J CHEM PHYS          29     0    1    4    2    5    3    3    2    1    1     8
 .99  NUOVO CIMENTO        26     0    2    6    0    5    5    0    1    2    0     8
2.86  PHYS REV B           25     0    0    0    0    0    0    0    1    2    0     8
2.61  PHYS REV A           21     1    0    6    4    1    2    0    2    0    1     3
 .75  LETT NUOVO CIMENTO   18     0    2    3    2    2    1    0    0    0    0     8
2.72  PHYS REV D           17     0    2    3    2    0    1    0    0    0    0    10
 .53  FOUND PHYS           14     1    0    5    2    0    1    1    0    0    0     6
1.55  J APPL PHYS          14     0    1    1    4    4    1    1    0    0    0     2
1.04  J MATH PHYS          13     0    0    0    2    0    4    0    1    0    1     6
2.01  J OPT SOC AM         12     1    0    1    3    4    0    1    0    0    0     2
 .96  PHYSICA              12     0    0    3    2    0    2    0    0    0    0     4
1.19  J PHYS A MATH NUCL G 10     0    0    0    2    5    0    1    0    0    0     2
1.07  IEEE T EDUCATION      9     0    1    0    0    0    1    0    1    0    0     6
 .09  ARCH HIST EXACT SCI   8     0    0    1    2    1    0    1    1    2    0     0
1.74  J MOL SPECTROSC       8     0    0    0    0    0    2    0    0    1    0     5
1.51  USP FIZ NAUK*         8     0    0    0    1    0    1    0    0    0    0     6
1.39  J PHYS CHEM SOLIDS    7     0    0    0    2    0    2    0    0    0    0     3
5.41  SCIENCE               7     1    0    1    3    0    0    1    0    0    1     4
1.94  SOLID STATE COMMUN    7     0    1    2    0    0    0    2    0    0    0     2
4.06  ASTROPHYS J           6     0    0    0    0    1    2    0    2    0    0     1
1.02  INT J QUANT CHEM      6     0    0    0    0    0    1    0    2    0    0     1
2.01  P IEEE ELEC ENG       6     1    0    2    0    3    0    0    0    0    0     1
2.21  P ROY SOC LOND A MAT  6     0    0    0    0    0    0    0    0    0    1     5
1.11  PHYS STATUS SOLIDI B  6     0    1    0    0    0    4    0    0    1    0     1
      ALL OTHER    (153)  262     3   21   22   16   22   23   14   20   13   8    100

AM J PHYS ANTHROPOL==    920*  ==10 =103 =106  ==67 ==79 ==57 ==50 ==38 ==32 ==32  ==346
 .89  AM J PHYS ANTHROPOL 250     2    8   34   23   30   22   16    7   12    8    94
 .69  HUM BIOL             61     0    3   11    0    9    3    4    2    2    3    19
 .52  J HUM EVOL           57     0   10   12    3    9    6    4    4    3    2    16
3.13  J HUM GENET          26     0    4    5    3    3    0    0    1    0    0    10
```

Figure 9.8 *Journal Citation Reports (JCR)* Cited Journal Package.

	3.23	BRIT J CANCER	14	2	1	1	2	3	1	0	1	2	0	1
	.60	ENVIRON PHYSIOL BIOC	14	0	0	2	1	0	0	4	0	1	1	5
	2.80	J LAB CLIN MED	14	0	1	0	2	2	2	3	1	0	0	3
	.82	J PHARMACOL-PARIS	14	0	3	4	0	0	1	2	0	1	0	3
	6.67	LANCET	14	0	4	2	3	1	0	2	1	0	1	0
	.22	ACTA PHYSIOL POL	13	0	0	2	0	0	1	2	2	3	0	3
		ALL OTHER (508)	1770	17	155	239	174	155	180	167	96	102	113	372
	BIOCHEM PHYSIOL VISU		2*	0	2	0	0	0	0	0	0	0	0	0
	2.78	J COMP PHYSIOL	1	0	1	0	0	0	0	0	0	0	0	0
	1.00	Z NATURFORSCH C	1	0	1	0	0	0	0	0	0	0	0	0
73	BIOCHEM SOC TRANS		502*	97	398	7	0	0	0	0	0	0	0	0
	3.62	BIOCHEM J	73	9	64	0	0	0	0	0	0	0	0	0
	.73	BIOCHEM SOC TRANS	38	28	10	0	0	0	0	0	0	0	0	0
	3.12	BIOCHIM BIOPHYS ACTA	29	4	25	0	0	0	0	0	0	0	0	0
	3.04	FEBS LETT	21	5	16	0	0	0	0	0	0	0	0	0
	2.91	J ENDOCRINOL	18	0	17	1	0	0	0	0	0	0	0	0
	3.87	EUR J BIOCHEM	12	2	10	0	0	0	0	0	0	0	0	0
	3.53	J NEUROCHEM	12	6	6	0	0	0	0	0	0	0	0	0
	3.63	NATURE	11	5	6	0	0	0	0	0	0	0	0	0
	3.74	BIOCHEM BIOPH RES CO	8	1	7	0	0	0	0	0	0	0	0	0
	5.84	J BIOL CHEM	8	0	8	0	0	0	0	0	0	0	0	0
	7.50	J MOL BIOL	7	3	4	0	0	0	0	0	0	0	0	0
		ORIGINS LIFE	7	0	6	1	0	0	0	0	0	0	0	0
	.47	GENETIKA*	6	0	6	0	0	0	0	0	0	0	0	0
	2.16	J GEN MICROBIOL	6	0	6	0	0	0	0	0	0	0	0	0
	6.67	LANCET	6	2	4	0	0	0	0	0	0	0	0	0
	1.69	PURE APPL CHEM	6	0	6	0	0	0	0	0	0	0	0	0
		ALL OTHER (131)	234	32	197	5	0	0	0	0	0	0	0	0
	BIOCHEM Z		2420*	0	2	1	0	1	4	2	8	199	165	2038
	3.12	BIOCHIM BIOPHYS ACTA	131	0	0	0	0	0	0	0	0	15	18	98
	5.84	J BIOL CHEM	115	0	0	0	0	0	0	0	0	7	13	95
	3.87	EUR J BIOCHEM	100	0	0	0	0	0	0	0	0	8	10	82
	3.62	BIOCHEM J	77	0	0	0	0	0	0	0	0	11	5	61
		MOL CELL BIOCHEM	73	0	0	0	0	0	0	0	0	1	0	72
	4.71	BIOCHEMISTRY-US	64	0	0	0	0	0	1	0	1	5	1	56
	2.29	H-S Z PHYSIOL CHEM	55	0	0	0	0	0	0	0	0	5	5	45
		ARCH BIOCHEM	52	0	0	0	0	0	0	0	0	5	4	43
	1.71	J BIOCHEM TOKYO	37	0	0	0	0	0	0	0	0	9	3	25
	3.04	FEBS LETT	29	0	0	0	0	0	0	0	0	4	3	22
	3.74	BIOCHEM BIOPH RES CO	27	0	0	0	0	0	1	0	0	1	0	25
	8.98	P NAT ACAD SCI USA	27	0	0	0	0	0	1	0	1	1	1	23
	2.72	J BACTERIOL	26	0	0	0	0	0	0	0	0	5	2	19

Figure 9.8 (continued)

in 1974, 230 citing material published in 1964 or earlier, and the rest being distributed over material published during the years in between.
- It cited itself 243 times and was cited by the *Journal of Chemical Physics* 29 times.
- It has a self-cited rate of 30.4% 243/800).
- Of the citations it received, 28.8% were to material published in 1964 or earlier.
- It was cited as often by *Science* as it was by *Solid State Communications*.

EXPLORATORY STUDIES

Data, of course, is an abstraction. Its utility depends on the types of information that can be derived from it by analysis. A series of studies conducted by ISI demonstrates the most obvious types of information that can be derived from the *JCR* data. Based mostly on a prototype version of the *JCR* that consisted of data from only one quarter of 1969, and that was somewhat less refined (3) than the 1974 data, these studies were not guided by any particular application objective. They were consciously exploratory, with the general purpose of seeing what types of useful information could be uncovered by analyzing citation data on various journals and groups of journals.

There was one exception to this exploratory philosophy. For years, I and a few others had hypothesized that a small fraction of the scientific journals published were responsible for communicating an overwhelming majority of the useful research material reported. The first thing I did with the *JCR* data was to test this

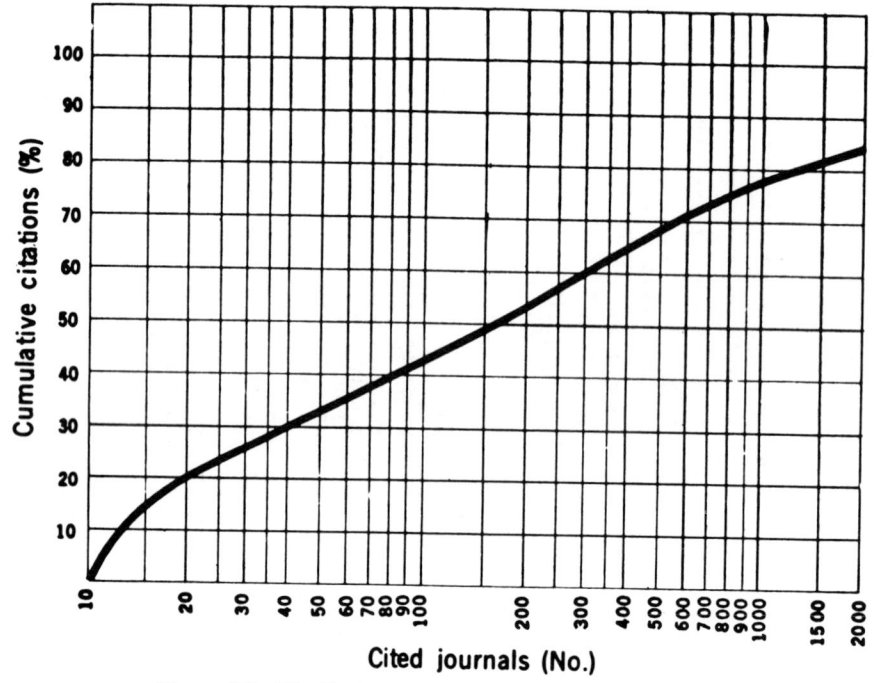

Figure 9.9 Distribution of citations among cited journals.

Item No. (1)	Cited Journal (2)	Times Cited Last Quarter 1969 (3)	1969 Citations to 1967 and 1968 Articles (4)	Articles Published in 1967 and 1968 (5)	Impact Factor (6)
1	J AM CHEM SOC	26323	22156	3946	5.614
2	PHYS REV	20674	20740	5767	3.596
3	J BIOL CHEM	17112	10768	1777	6.059
4	NATURE LONDON	15325	15956	6811	2.342
5	J CHEM SOC	14028	17764	5827	3.048
6	J CHEM PHYS	13690	11696	3738	3.128
7	SCIENCE	9752	11880	3968	2.993
8	BIOCHIM BIOPHYS ACTA	9550	10956	3531	3.102
9	P NAT ACAD SCI USA	8260	11548	1348	8.566
10	BIOCHEM J	7638	6348	2074	3.060
11	LANCET	7617	8164	5496	1.485
12	PHYS REV LETT	6581	11380	2317	4.911
13	CR ACAD SCI	5789	6576	8345	0.788
14	AM J PHYSIOL	5420	3156	1013	3.115
15	J ORG CHEM	5401	5756	2475	2.325
16	J APPL PHYS	5190	5072	2880	1.761
17	P SOC EXP BIOL MED	5079	3468	1920	1.806
18	J MOL BIOL	4982	7340	833	8.811
19	J PHYSIOL LOND	4966	3036	1248	2.432
20	P ROY SOC LOND	4864	1916	621	3.085
21	J CELL BIOL	4813	4596	1357	3.386
22	J CLIN INVEST	4785	3652	1086	3.362
23	J PHYS CHEM	4703	4516	1939	2.329
24	CHEM BER	4541	2128	1037	2.052
25	NEW ENGL J MED	4512	5252	2226	2.359
26	J AM MED ASS	4492	3980	3787	1.050
27	BRIT MED J	4304	4224	6238	0.677
28	SOV PHYS JETP	4295	3400	754	4.509
29	ASTROPHYS J	4271	5440	1167	4.661
30	ANALYT CHEM	4259	2424	1510	1.605
31	J BACTERIOL	4147	4712	1410	3.341
32	BIOCHEMISTRY	4076	6344	1114	5.694
33	NUCL PHYS	4034	6716	2345	2.863
34	PHYS LETT	3943	7160	3034	2.359
35	TETRAHEDRON LETT	3937	8252	2902	2.843
36	J EXP MED	3871	2700	325	8.307
37	ANN NY ACAD SCI	3787	2344	1216	1.927
38	ARCH BIOCHEM BIOPHYS	3689	3776	1169	3.230
39	J GEOPHYS RES	3537	5312	1569	3.385
40	J POLYM SCI	3458	2888	2069	1.395
41	BIOCHEM BIOPHYS RES	3417	5108	1190	4.292
42	FED P	3372	4036	7374	0.547
43	J PHYS	3308	3256	2379	1.368
44	T FARADAY SOC	2922	1808	879	2.056
45	ACTA CRYSTALLOGR	2917	2164	1803	1.200
46	DOKL AKAD NAUK SSSR	2869	2456	5385	0.456
47	J PHARMACOL EXP THER	2781	2020	566	3.568
48	ANGEW CHEM	2728	3660	1251	2.925
49	J IMMUNOL	2627	2992	726	4.121
50	INORG CHEM	2620	3976	1247	3.188
51	SOV PHYS SOLID STATE	2620	2984	1561	1.911
52	CIRCULATION	2601	2624	2160	1.214
53	ENDOCRINOLOGY	2548	2276	783	2.906
54	ACTA CHEM SCAND	2444	1984	943	2.103
55	NUOVO CIMENTO	2431	3436	1938	1.772
56	B SOC CHIM FRANCE	2416	2664	2704	0.985
57	VIROLOGY	2376	2620	584	4.486
58	CANCER RES	2349	2344	814	2.879
59	CAN J CHEM	2280	2392	1182	2.023
60	HELV CHIM ACTA	2249	1524	539	2.827
61	Z NATURFORSCHUNG	2200	2172	1650	1.316
62	AM J MED	2191	1784	395	4.516
63	J LAB CLIN MED	2120	1284	754	1.702
64	TETRAHEDRON	2071	3220	1313	2.452
65	EXP CELL RES	1958	1464	653	2.241
66	LIEBIGS ANN CHEM	1952	768	492	1.560
67	ANN INT MED	1946	1844	1098	1.679
68	PHIL MAG	1943	1180	547	2.157
69	J CLIN ENDOCR METAB	1903	1888	488	3.868
70	J APPL PHYSIOL	1836	1460	643	2.270
71	ACTA PHYSIOL SCAND	1816	1024	413	2.479
72	J PHYS SOC JAP	1786	1768	2074	0.852
73	Z PHYS	1764	1228	844	1.454
74	CIRC RES	1750	1820	432	4.212
75	PHYTOPATHOLOGY	1713	1632	1597	1.021
76	J NAT CANCER I	1668	1672	417	4.009

Figure 9.10 The 152 most frequently cited journals, ranked by frequency of citation in journals covered by *SCI*.

hypothesis. One result of this test is shown in Figure 9.9, a curve of the distribution of citations among cited journals. The curve shows that a core of fewer than 200 journals accounted for the material cited in approximately half the journal references processed for *SCI* in 1969, and that only 2000 or so journals accounted for the material cited in about 84% of them. The data from which the curve was plotted showed that the specific number of journals responsible for the material cited in half the references was 152. It also showed that only 540 journals were cited 1000 or more times that year, and that only 968 journals were cited even 400 times. Another result of this test was a list of the 152 journals that were indentified in 50% of the citations. This list (see Figure 9.10) shows a multidisciplinary mix of journals

Item No. (1)	Cited Journal (2)	Times Cited Last Quarter 1969 (3)	1969 Citations to 1967 and 1968 Articles (4)	Articles Published in 1967 and 1968 (5)	Impact Factor (6)
77	AM J OBSTET GYNECOL	1657	1440	1193	1.207
78	PLANT PHYSIOL	1646	1808	1149	1.573
79	IND ENG CHEM	1644	928	856	1.084
80	ANN SURG	1641	1036	642	1.613
81	B CHEM SOC JAP	1639	2004	1567	1.278
82	EUR J BIOCHEM	1635	1992	501	3.976
83	GENETICS	1618	1340	738	1.815
84	BLOOD	1614	1256	566	2.219
85	P IEEE	1610	1856	756	2.455
86	J OPT SOC AM	1587	1196	1322	0.904
87	ANALYT BIOCHEM	1519	1672	502	3.330
88	J GEN PHYSIOL	1507	1208	407	2.968
89	ARCH INTERN MED	1501	860	486	1.769
90	AM HEART J	1453	1036	539	1.922
91	J EXP PSYCHOL	1449	1152	644	1.788
92	J GEN MICROBIOL	1445	1136	534	2.127
93	J COMP PHYSIOL PSYCH	1444	888	476	1.865
94	J PHYS CHEM SOLIDS	1430	1572	801	1.962
95	CANCER	1416	1224	593	2.064
96	AM J PATHOL	1401	960	529	1.814
97	RUSS J PHYS CHEM	1400	1116	1545	0.722
98	METHODS ENZYMOL	1391	1456	482	3.020
99	J INORG NUCL CHEM	1391	1356	908	1.493
100	PEDIATRICS	1382	1060	709	1.495
101	SURG GYNECOL OBSTET	1374	868	535	1.622
102	ANAT REC	1365	752	1836	0.409
103	REV MOD PHYS	1364	816	189	4.317
104	T MET SOC AIME	1359	1196	901	1.327
105	CAN J PHYS	1352	2156	1019	2.115
106	BRIT J PHARMACOL	1348	1348	507	2.658
107	APPL PHYS LETT	1337	2556	721	3.545
108	PHYS STAT SOLIDI	1329	2192	1485	1.476
109	J ELECTROCHEM SOC	1308	1208	1538	0.785
110	ACTA METALLURG	1304	964	452	2.132
111	PHYS FLUIDS	1304	1548	1050	1.474
112	EXPERIENTIA	1297	1592	1565	1.017
113	GASTROENTEROLOGY	1286	1428	1244	1.147
114	Z ZELLF MIKR ANAT	1286	1800	653	2.756
115	SURGERY	1274	996	790	1.260
116	REV SCI INSTR	1273	968	1148	0.843
117	AM J ROENTGENOL	1272	1044	860	1.213
118	AIAA J	1269	1456	1231	1.182
119	T ASME	1246	800	1332	0.600
120	AM J CARDIOL	1238	1600	737	2.170
121	J HISTOCHEM CYTOCHEM	1229	828	362	2.287
122	J PEDIAT	1229	1076	783	1.374
123	J ACOUST SOC AM	1219	1016	2196	0.462
124	NATURWISSENSCHAFTEN	1218	944	1091	0.865
125	J NUTR	1209	952	489	1.946
126	SPECTROCHIM ACTA	1201	1248	679	1.837
127	Z ANORG ALLG CHEM	1188	580	549	1.056
128	J PERSON SOC PSYCHOL	1186	676	581	1.163
129	RADIOLOGY	1175	1244	835	1.489
130	AM J BOT	1171	644	726	0.887
131	Z PHYS CHEM LEIPZIG	1170	332	252	1.317
132	J CHROMATOGR	1161	1708	1343	1.271
133	HOPPE SEYLERS Z	1145	1412	863	1.636
134	J UROL	1142	656	712	0.921
135	ARCH PATHOL	1138	556	409	1.359
136	ARCH SURG	1134	748	867	0.862
137	AM J DIS CHILD	1127	748	610	1.226
138	ACTA MED SCAND	1112	680	472	1.440
139	ANN PHYSICS	1105	692	224	3.089
140	COLD SPR HARB SYMP	1091	1060	194	5.463
141	J ORGANOMET CHEM	1089	2784	796	3.497
142	PFLUGERS ARCH	1083	896	732	1.224
143	OPT SPECTROSC USSR	1076	1100	814	1.351
144	KLIN WSCHR	1057	800	1198	0.667
145	CHEM IND LOND	1049	648	1703	0.380
146	BER BUNSEN PHYS CHEM	1044	688	771	0.892
147	BIOCHEM PHARMACOL	1030	1292	684	1.888
148	PHYSIOL REV	1022	572	33	17.333
149	J BONE JOINT SURG	1021	500	745	0.671
150	J NEUROPHYSIOL	1015	692	156	4.435
151	CR SOC BIOL	1010	596	1316	0.452
152	REC TRAV CHIM	1010	728	337	2.160

Figure 9.10 (continued)

that makes it obvious that a good, multidisciplinary journal collection need contain no more than a few hundred titles.

These results led to the formulation of the bibliographic law of concentration (4), which goes an important step beyond the Bradford law by stating that the tail of the literature of any one discipline consists, in large part, of the cores of the literature of all other disciplines, and that all the disciplines combined produce a multidisciplinary literature core for all of science that consists of no more than 1000 journals. In fact, this multidisciplinary core might be as small as 500 journals. Though larger collections certainly can be justified in many cases, the single function of providing reasonably cost-effective coverage of the literature most used by research scientists requires no more than 500 to 1,000 journals.

The bibliographic law of concentration has since been validated many times, most notably with an anlysis of 1974 *JCR* data that shows only 206 primary journals and another 78 review journals have an impact factor of three or higher (5). In addition, the same analysis produced a list of the 206 journals that were cited most frequently in 1974 (Figure 9.11) that was just as multidisciplinary as the one of 152 journals produced from the 1969 data.

The more general types of studies of journal-citation patterns explored the following subjects and produced the following results:

A	B	C		D	E	F
1	1	98995	J. Am. chem. Soc.	4.383	17088	3
2	2	91645	*Physical Rev. (5)	2.670	19174	1
3	3	81353	J. biol. Chem.	5.843	13685	6
4	5	75206	*Nature (3)	4.006	18924	2
5	4	66272	*J. chem. Soc. (9)	1.870	12513	7
6	6	62041	*J. chem. Physics	2.918	10462	9
7	8	51491	Biochim. biophys. Acta	3.120	14129	5
8	7	47505	Science	5.412	11781	8
9	9	46917	Proc. natn. Acad. Sci. USA	8.989	15317	4
10	11	37047	Lancet	6.677	10383	10
11	10	31563	Biochem. J.	3.627	4885	23
12	12	29275	Physical Rev. Letters	5.059	10108	11
13	32	27080	Biochemistry	4.711	7325	17
14	25	26726	New Engl. J. Med.	8.364	7385	15
15	22	24768	J. clin. Invest.	6.992	5377	21
16	18	24209	J. molec. Biol.	7.502	6129	18
17	41	23220	Biochem. biophys. Res. Comm.	3.744	8110	12
18	19	22520	J. Physiol. Lond.	4.495	3160	46
19	33	22460	*Nuclear Physics (3)	2.514	7356	16
20	21	22245	*J. Cell Biol. (2)	6.770	3683	38
21	29	22201	Astrophys. J.	4.063	7451	14
22	14	21519	Am. J. Physiol.	2.414	2412	59
23	27	20748	Brit. med. J.	3.556	4829	24
24	36	20699	J. expl Med.	11.874	5557	19
25	15	20539	J. org. Chem.	1.495	3526	40
26	16	19277	J. appl. Physics	1.558	3275	42
27	31	18375	J. Bacteriology	2.727	3809	37
28	30	18190	Analytical Chem.	3.291	4140	32
29	17	18171	Proc. Soc. expl Biol. Med.	1.471	2454	58
30	23	18086	J. phys. Chem.	2.031	2768	54
31	26	17211	J. Am. med. Ass.	3.068	2982	49
32	20	17201	*Proc. R. Soc. (3)	2.350	1114	135
33	13	16782	*C.r. Acad. Sci. (5)	0.529	4247	29
34	35	16509	Tetrahedron Letters	1.777	5004	22
35	38	15970	*Archs Biochem. Biophys. (2)	2.952	3050	48
36	53	15948	Endocrinology	4.337	4098	33
37	49	15826	J. Immunology	5.112	4703	26
38	34	15666	*Physics Letters (2)	2.133	7672	13
39	39	15281	J. geophys. Res.	2.536	3854	36
40	24	14706	*Chem. Ber. (2)	1.506	1353	104
41	37	14668	Ann. N. Y. Acad. Sci.	1.181	1291	113
42	52	14461	Circulation	6.834	4025	34
43	50	14310	Inorg. Chem.	2.457	3589	39
44	45	13911	*Acta crystallographica (3)	1.361	2394	60
45	82	13847	*Eur. J. Biochem. (2)	3.857	4595	27
46	47	13753	J. Pharmacol. expl Ther.	3.576	2026	65
47	42	13072	Fedn Proc.	0.489	4212	30
48	58	12544	Cancer Res.	3.391	3164	45
49	69	11645	*J. clin. Endocr. Metab. (2)	5.170	3443	41
50	43	11459	*J. Physics (7)	1.689	5450	20
51	28	11421	*Zh. eksp. teor. Fiz. (2)	1.565	1607	84
52	57	11371	Virology	3.752	2949	50
53	40	11294	*J. Polym. Sci. (6)	0.964	1565	88
54	65	11127	Exp. Cell Res.	3.014	2788	53
55	48	10756	*Angew. Chem. (2)	4.140	2666	56
56	67	10231	Ann. internal Med.	4.828	2187	63
57	355	10227	Brain Res.	3.104	4522	28

Figure 9.11 Journals most highly cited in 1974. A = rank by 1974 citations. B = rank by 1969 citations. C = total 1974 citations. D = 1974 impact. E = 1974 citations of 1972 and 1973 articles. F = rank by 1974 citations of 1972 and 1973 articles. The citation counts for journal titles marked by an asterisk are aggregates of multiple sections, retitled continuations, translated versions, etc. The number in parentheses after such journals indicates the number of multiple sections, etc., that were included in the aggregate count.

A	B	C		D	E	F
58	87	10206	Analytical Biochem.	2.379	2184	64
59	46	9824	*Dokl. Akad. Nauk SSSR (7)	0.339	1681	81
60	62	9779	Am. J. Med.	4.411	1535	90
61	76	9678	J. natn. Cancer Inst.	3.289	2858	52
62	95	9497	Cancer	2.361	2056	66
63	59	9142	Can. J. Chem.	1.396	1793	73
64	707	9094	FEBS Letters	3.049	4815	25
65	74	9082	Circulation Res.	4.922	1698	79
66	108	9026	*Physica Status Sol. (3)	1.476	3201	44
67	64	8903	Tetrahedron	1.576	1913	69
68	77	8890	Am. J. Obstet. Gynec.	2.100	2236	62
69	78	8835	Plant Physiol.	2.580	1935	68
70	54	8803	*Acta chem. scand. (3)	1.042	1192	124
71	63	8798	J. Lab. clin. Med.	2.802	1132	131
72	113	8693	Gastroenterology	5.394	2260	61
73	107	8625	Appl. Physics Letters	3.220	3246	43
74	70	8619	J. appl. Physiol.	1.780	1184	125
75	481	8478	Applied Physics Letters	2.403	4205	31
76	141	8241	J. organomet. Chem.	2.392	3891	35
77	56	8183	Bull. Soc. chim. France	1.001	1492	96
78	81	7941	Bull. chem. Soc. Japan	0.932	1859	72
79	132	7928	J. Chromatography	2.173	2886	51
80	71	7922	Acta physiol. scand.	2.204	919	170
81	72	7914	J. phys. Soc. Japan	1.132	1500	95
82	61	7860	*Z. Naturforschung (3)	1.070	1503	94
83	192	7794	J. Neurochem.	3.535	2464	57
84	106	7656	*Br. J. Pharmacol.	3.516	1751	77
85	80	7459	Ann. Surgery	2.129	1060	140
86	113	7335	*Cell Tissue Res. (2)	1.961	1761	75
87	122	7183	J. Pediatrics	2.600	1890	70
88	84	7120	Blood	4.319	1529	91
89	60	7117	Helv. chim. Acta	1.649	1034	144
90	68	7063	Philosophical Mag.	1.836	876	178
91	147	7007	Biochem. Pharmacol.	2.023	1689	80
92	100	6951	Pediatrics	2.502	1346	105
93	120	6811	Am. J. Cardiol.	3.704	1889	71
94	276	6788	J. Virology	4.864	3142	47
95	149	6770	*J. Bone Jt Surg. (3)	1.358	729	234
96	73	6662	Z. Physik	1.340	864	182
97	112	6600	Experientia	0.883	1647	83
98	88	6539	J. gen. Physiol.	4.308	741	229
99	51	6362	*Fizika tverd. Tela (2)	0.762	1388	102
100	129	6307	Radiology	1.198	1320	107
101	66	6177	Annln Chemie (J. Liebig)	1.024	432	379
102	89	6066	*Archs internal Med. (2)	2.202	946	163
103	90	5994	Am. Heart J.	1.791	840	188
104	86	5885	J. opt. Soc. Am.	2.016	905	173
105	94	5849	*J. Physics Chem. Solids (2)	1.394	715	239
106	99	5761	J. inorg. nucl. Chem.	0.962	1149	128
107	156	5743	J. Endocrinology	2.919	1757	76
108	217	5683	*J. Pharmaceut. Sci. (3)	1.622	1549	92
109	92	5679	J. gen. Microbiol.	2.160	1136	129
110	115	5675	Surgery	1.559	842	187
111	378	5573	Solid St. Comm.	1.945	2768	55
112	170	5557	Clin. chim. Acta	1.669	1587	86
113	150	5556	J. Neurophysiology	4.537	676	249
114	98	5501	Methods Enzymology	1.765	547	311
115	136	5491	Archs Surgery	1.462	915	171
116	101	5486	Surgery Gynec. Obstet.	1.332	750	226
117	109	5478	J. Electrochem. Soc.	1.053	1098	136
118	55	5474	*Nuovo Cimento (3)	0.994	999	155
119	123	5428	J. acoust. Soc. Am.	1.142	830	195
120	96	5388	Am. J. Pathol.	2.807	856	184
121	91	5388	J. expl Psychol.	1.027	750	226
122	126	5363	*Spectrochim. Acta (3)	1.487	840	188
123	83	5326	Genetics	2.835	995	157
124	158	5197	J. Ultrastruct. Res.	2.709	837	190
125	103	5186	Revs mod. Physics	21.502	731	231
126	121	5167	J. Histochem. Cytochem.	4.005	757	224
127	102	5138	Anat. Rec.	2.884	649	265
128	235	5092	*Zh. obshch. Khim. (2)	0.808	1050	142
129	192	5063	Immunology	2.816	1118	132
130	125	5053	J. Nutrition	1.845	740	230
131	117	5038	Am. J. Roentg. Rad. Ther.	1.008	634	272
132	166	5033	J. Lipid Res.	3.525	719	238
133	134	5031	J. Urology	0.721	776	216
134	194	5000	Life Sciences	2.062	1200	121
135	177	4909	Acta endocrinologica	2.461	1383	103
136	267	4861	J. infect. Dis.	3.040	1669	82
137	75	4847	Phytopathology	1.155	789	210
138	111	4822	Physics Fluids	1.188	972	159
139	116	4801	Rev. scient. Instrum.	1.018	1001	153

Figure 9.11 (continued)

A	B	C		D	E	F
140	160	4767	J. Biochem. Japan	1.715	1079	138
141	184	4707	Nucl. Instrum. Meth.	1.050	1420	100
142	127	4704	Z. anorg. allg. Chem.	1.019	595	286
143	159	4697	J. comp. Neurol.	3.725	771	219
144	105	4656	Can. J. Physics	1.038	774	218
145	168	4655	Lab. Investigation	2.940	932	166
146	133	4604	Hoppe-Seylers Z. physiol.Chem.	2.291	1031	146
147	211	4603	Applied Optics	1.832	1539	89
148	370	4600	Surface Science	3.340	1787	74
149	224	4511	*Comp. Biochem. Physiol. (3)	1.014	1250	116
150	247	4480	Applied Microbiology	1.292	1196	122
151	155	4479	Am. J. clin. Pathol.	1.348	663	255
152	182	4462	Am. J. Surg.	1.183	731	231
153	220	4453	Molecular Physics	2.334	1258	115
154	442	4451	*J. comp. Physiol. (2)	2.782	893	175
155	137	4416	Am. J. Dis. Child.	1.495	809	202
156	162	4393	*Archs Dermatology (3)	1.784	835	192
157	262	4369	Phytochemistry	1.103	1568	87
158	110	4356	Acta Metallurgica	1.705	583	291
159	93	4353	*J. comp. physiol. Psychol. (2)	1.230	663	256
160	140	4348	Cold Spring Harb. Symp.	2.443	623	278
161	139	4347	Ann. Physics	2.128	598	284
162	214	4308	Planta	2.589	1261	114
163	135	4303	Archs Pathology	1.521	508	332
164	85	4277	*Proc. IEEE (2)	2.013	781	215
165	147	4253	Pflugers Arch./Eur. J. Physiol.	1.810	856	184
166	238	4208	*J. Pharmacy Pharmacol. (2)	3.140	1118	132
167	443	4180	*Zh. neorg. Khim (2)	0.523	823	198
168	199	4116	J. Anim. Sci.	1.311	1000	154
169	153	4104	Chem. Revs	11.154	580	293
170	161	4093	J. thorac. cardiovasc. Surg.	1.480	836	191
171	180	4072	*J. cell. Physiol. (2)	3.737	710	240
172	286	4068	J. Reprod. Fert.	2.357	1414	101
173	274	4054	*Transplantation (2)	2.250	1134	130
174	558	4049	Clin. expl Immunol.	4.423	1601	85
175	176	4040	Coll. Czech. chem. Comm.	0.791	831	194
176	169	4031	*Am. Rev. resp. Dis. (3)	1.630	937	165
177	189	4023	Geochim. cosmochim. Acta	4.056	1160	127
178	271	4005	Analytica chim. acta	2.093	1312	110
179	157	4003	*Deut. med. Wschr. (2)	1.022	1025	149
180	148	3996	Physiol. Revs	13.861	499	334
181	138	3993	Acta med. scand.	1.124	508	331
182	195	3952	Diabetes	3.941	863	183
183	97	3932	*Zh. fiz. Khim (2)	0.331	646	266
184	194	3906	Geol. Soc. Am. Bull.	1.674	1026	147
185	364	3899	Astronomy Astrophys.	2.267	2018	67
186	172	3897	J. Dairy Sci.	0.273	569	300
187	218	3892	Neurology	2.181	796	206
188	503	3874	*Int. J. Cancer (2)	4.928	1508	93
189	367	3869	Clinical Chem.	3.195	1460	97
190	171	3864	Am. J. Ophthalmol.	1.389	792	208
190	178	3864	Progr. theor. Physics	1.421	1003	151
192	178	3858	Mon. Not. R. astr. Soc.	2.467	1036	143
193	165	3857	Archs Ophthalmology	1.293	561	302
194	154	3852	J. Fluid Mech.	1.254	617	280
195	146	3827	*Ber. Bunsenges.	1.382	532	319
196	160	3820	J. math. Physics	1.046	632	274
197	339	3777	*J. mednl Chem. (2)	1.444	1196	123
198	369	3726	Gut	3.336	1081	137
199	130	3710	Am. J. Botany	1.378	357	441
200	232	3701	J. Neurosurgery	1.252	636	271
201	204	3699	Scand. J. clin. Lab. Invest.	1.917	644	268
202	249	3673	*Archs Neurol. (2)	2.217	828	228
203	599	3647	*Eur. J. Pharmacol. (2)	2.537	1205	120
204	339	3633	Developmental Biol.	3.384	1242	117
205	196	3561	Arzneimittel-Forschung	0.876	833	193
206	202	3598	*Clin. Sci. mol. Med. (2)	2.474	762	223

Figure 9.11 (continued)

Core Literatures of Chemistry and Biochemistry (6)

Starting with a single leading journal in chemistry and biochemistry, the core literature of each field was defined simply by identifying the journals they cited most frequently. The starting point in chemistry was the *Journal of the American Chemical Society* (*JACS*). The journals it cited most frequently are shown in Figure 9.12. *Biochemistry* was chosen as the starting point for its field, and the journals it cited most frequently are shown in Figure 9.13. In both lists, the journals marked

	Times Cited	Title
1.	14012	*Journal of the American Chemical Society
2.	1920	*Journal of the Chemical Society
3.	1472	*Journal of Organic Chemistry
4.	1376	*Tetrahedron Letters
5.	1036	Chemical Communications
6.	884	*Inorganic Chemistry
7.	820	*Journal of Physical Chemistry
8.	708	*Chemische Berichte
9.	620	*Canadian Journal of Chemistry
10.	568	*Angewandte Chemie
11.	500	*Tetrahedron
12.	400	*Transactions of the Faraday Society
13.	302	*Annalen der Chemie
14.	292	*Journal of Biological Chemistry
15.	252	Bulletin of the Chemical Society of Japan
16.	252	*Helvetica Chimica Acta
17.	240	*Analytical Chemistry
18.	236	*Acta Crystallographica
19.	228	*Accounts of Chemical Research
20.	224	*Chemical Reviews
21.	224	*Journal of Organometallic Chemistry
22.	216	*Acta Chemica Scandinavica
23.	208	Nature
24.	204	*Quarterly Reviews
25.	188	Chemistry and Industry
26.	184	Molecular Physics
27.	180	*Recueil des Travaux Chimiques des Pays-Bas
28.	152	*Biochemistry
29.	144	*Proceedings of the National Academy of Sciences of the United States
30.	140	*Journal of Inorganic and Nuclear Chemistry
31.	120	*Bulletin de la Societe Chimique de France
32.	112	Organic Synthesis
33.	112	Proceedings of the Chemical Society
34.	104	Proceedings of the Royal Society
35.	96	*Biochimica Biophysica Acta
36.	88	*Australian Journal of Chemistry
37.	84	*Biochemical Journal
38.	76	*Advances in Chemistry Series
39.	76	Discussions of the Faraday Society
40.	76	Progress in Physical and Organic Chemistry
41.	76	Gazzetta Chimica Italiana
42.	72	Photochemistry and Photobiology
43.	72	Science
44.	68	Advances in Physical and Organic Chemistry
45.	68	Advances in Organometallic Chemistry
46.	60	*Doklady Akademii Nauk SSSR
47.	60	Physical Review
48.	60	Zhurnal Obshchei Khimii
49.	56	*Comptes Rendus Hebdomadaires des Seances de l'Academie des Sciences
50.	56	Pure and Applied Chemistry

Figure 9.12 Journals cited most frequently by *Journal of the American Chemical Society*. Asterisks identify journals that also are major sources of references to *Journal of the American Chemical Society*.

Citation Analysis of Scientific Journals 165

	Times Cited	Title
1.	2836	*Journal of Biological Chemistry
2.	2204	*Biochemistry
3.	1384	*Journal of the American Chemical Society
4.	1260	*Biochimica Biophysica Acta
5.	1044	*Proceedings of the National Academy of Sciences of the United States
6.	724	*Biochemical Journal
7.	632	*Journal of Molecular Biology
8.	612	*Archives of Biochemistry and Biophysics
9.	540	*Biochemical and Biophysical Research Communications
10.	456	*Nature
11.	340	*Federation Proceedings
12.	312	*Science
13.	264	Methods in Enzymology
14.	184	Advances in Protein Chemistry
15.	184	*Analytical Biochemistry
16.	176	Analytical Chemistry
17.	160	*Journal of Chemical Physics
18.	144	*Annals of the New York Academy of Sciences
19.	136	Annual Review of Biochemistry
20.	132	Biochemische Zeitschrift
21.	128	Journal of the Chemical Society
22.	128	*Journal of Physical Chemistry
23.	124	Acta Chemica Scandinavica
24.	112	*Journal of Experimental Medicine
25.	108	Biophysical Journal
26.	104	*Journal of Immunology
27.	96	*Journal of Biochemistry
28.	92	*Hoppe-Seylers Zeitschrift für physiologische Chemie
29.	92	Cold Spring Harbor Symposia on Quantitative Biology
30.	88	*Journal of Bacteriology
31.	88	*Journal of Organic Chemistry
32.	88	Proceedings of the Royal Society
33.	84	*Biopolymers
34.	84	*European Journal of Biochemistry
35.	81	*Journal of Cell Biology
36.	81	*Journal of Clinical Investigation
37.	72	Chemical Communications
38.	68	Journal of General Physiology
39.	64	Advances in Enzymology
40.	64	Tetrahedron Letters
41.	56	Canadian Journal of Chemistry
42.	52	*Immunochemistry
43.	52	Journal of Lipid Research
44.	44	Chemische Berichte
45.	44	*Proceedings of the Society for Experimental Biology and Medicine
46.	40	Brookhaven Symposia in Biology
47.	40	*Endocrinology
48.	40	Helvetica Chimica Acta
49.	40	Journal of Medicinal Chemistry
50.	36	Journal of Neurochemistry

Figure 9.13 Journals cited most frequently by *Biochemistry*. Asterisks identify journals that also are major sources of references to *Biochemistry*.

with an asterisk not only are cited frequently by the subject journals, but also are among the main sources of citations to the subject journals.

An analysis of the two lists shows two distinctly separate core literatures, with very little overlap between them. *JACS* cites very few biochemical journals, whereas *Biochemistry* cites biochemical and biomedical journals heavily. Both draw on each other, of course, but with *Biochemistry* citing *JACS* much more frequently than the other way around.

Rank	Times Cited	Title
1.	14396	*Journal of Chemical Physics
2.	2728	*Physical Review
3.	1284	*Journal of the American Chemical Society
4.	980	*Journal of Physical Chemistry
5.	872	Proceedings of the Royal Society (London)
6.	540	*Transactions of the Faraday Society
7.	508	*Molecular Physics
8.	496	*Physical Review Letters
9.	436	*Journal of the Chemical Society
10.	344	*Acta Crystallographica
11.	316	Physica
12.	312	Zeitschrift für Physik
13.	308	*Journal of Physics
14.	308	*Journal of the Physical Society of Japan
15.	304	*Journal of Molecular Spectroscopy
16.	296	Reviews of Modern Physics
17.	272	*Canadian Journal of Physics
18.	264	Chemical Physics Letters
19.	256	*Spectrochimica Acta
20.	248	Nature
21.	244	*Journal of Applied Physics
22.	240	*Optika i Spektroskopiya
23.	236	*Inorganic Chemistry
24.	232	*Canadian Journal of Chemistry
25.	232	Review of Scientific Instruments
26.	220	Journal of Mathematical Physics
27.	220	*Zeitschrift für Naturforschung
28.	212	Discussions of the Faraday Society
29.	196	Journal of the Optical Society of America
30.	184	*Journal of the Physics and Chemistry of Solids
31.	164	Bulletin of the American Physical Society
32.	156	Zhurnal Eksperimentalnoi i Teoreticheskoi Fiziki
33.	148	*Bulletin of the Chemical Society of Japan
34.	144	Advances in Chemical Physics
35.	144	Proceedings of the National Academy of Sciences USA
36.	140	Rarefied Gas Dynamics. Proc. Internat. Symp.
37.	140	*Journal de Chimie Physique
38.	124	Journal of Research of the National Bureau of Standards
39.	116	*Fizika Tverdogo Tela
40.	112	*Surface Science
41.	104	Advances in Chemistry Series
42.	104	*Chemical Reviews
43.	100	*Physics Letters
44.	100	Science
45.	96	Annual Review of Physical Chemistry
46.	96	*Theoretica Chimica Acta
47.	92	*Comptes Rendus etc. de l'Academie des Sciences (Paris)
48.	92	Solid State Physics
49.	88	*Berichte der Bunsengesellschaft für Physikalische Chemie
50.	88	Annalen der Physik

Figure 9.14 Journals cited most frequently by *Journal of Chemical Physics*. Asterisks identify journals that also are major sources of references to *Journal of Chemical Physics*.

Relationship Between Chemical Physics and Physical Chemistry (7)

Much has been said about the presumed relationship between the physical chemist and the chemical physicist. To test that relationship, a list was compiled of the journals cited most frequently by the *Journal of Chemical Physics* (Figure 9.14), and then compared to the list previously compiled of the journals most frequently cited by the *Journal of the American Chemical Society* (Figure 9.12). The most striking feature of the *Journal of Chemical Physics* (*JCP*) list is the small number of physical chemistry journals that appear on it, though the *Journal of Physical Chemistry* ranks fourth. The Soviet *Zhurnal Fizicheskoi Khimii.* (ZFK), for example, is conspicuously absent. Its absence, however, may be due to a bias in the source-journal coverage of *SCI* that is a result of the difficulty and cost of covering journals that do not use Roman alphabets. Some of the Soviet journals not covered may cite *ZFK* frequently enough to improve its rank on this list.

A comparison of the *JCP* and *JACS* lists shows that both journals cite *Nature* and *Science,* and at about the same rate. *Nature* ranks twenty-third on the *JACS* list with a frequency of 208 and twentieth on the *JCP* list with a frequency of 248. *Science* ranks forty-second on the *JACS* list with a frequency of 72 and forty-fourth on the *JCP* list with a frequency of 100. Reflecting their historical orientation toward the life sciences, both of them ranked considerably higher among the journals cited by *Biochemistry* (Figure 9.13).

Journal of Experimental Medicine (8)

The *Journal of Experimental Medicine* (*J. Exp. Med.*) was made the subject of a citation analysis because of its high impact factor. The 1969 data showed its average article was cited 8.3 times, which gave it an impact-factor ranking of thirteenth among the journals covered by *JCR*. Generally, high impact factors indicate basic research, but the title of *J. Exp. Med.* describes it as a medical journal.

Lists of the 40 journals it cited most frequently (Figure 9.15) and the 40 journals that cited it most frequently (Figure 9.16) showed that *J. Exp. Med.* is clearly a journal of immunology. Its references are heavily slanted (in terms of volume) to the biochemical and immunology literature, rather than to the clinical literature. On the other hand, it is heavily cited by clinical journals.

An analysis of the *Journal of Immunology* convincingly confirmed this view of *J. Exp. Med.* as being correct. The top 40 journals it cited most frequently (Figure 9.17) and the 40 that cited it most frequently (Figure 9.18) display an amazing similarity to the lists compiled for *J. Exp. Med.* The most significant difference between the two journals is seen in their citation rates and impact factors. *J. Exp. Med.* ranks higher on both counts: 15,536 versus 10,492 in citation rate and 8.3 versus 4.1 in impact factor.

Though the characterization of *J. Exp. Med.* as an immunology journal—and probably the premier one—may not be news to the people who are familiar with it, there is no doubt that there are many medical librarians who subscribe to it on the grounds that it is a medical journal. Conversely, there probably are many departments of biochemistry and immunology that find those same grounds sufficient reason for not subscribing to it.

The Literature of Rheumatology (9)

Peter Thorpe of Geigy Pharmaceuticals in the U.K. did a citation study of the

Rank	Times Cited	Journal Title Abbreviation
1.	1084	J Exp Med
2.	572	J Immunol
3.	236	Nature
4.	168	Immunology
5.	164	Science
6.	156	Proc Soc Exp Biol Med
7.	128	Internat Arch Allergy Appl Immunol
8.	104	Fed Proc
9.	100	J Biol Chem
10.	92	Biochem J
11.	76	Proc Nat Acad Sci USA
12.	76	Transplantation
13.	72	Ann NY Acad Sci
14.	68	Immunochemistry
15.	64	Cold Spr Harb Symp Quant Biol
16.	60	Biochemistry
17.	56	Biochim Biophys Acta
18.	52	J Clin Invest
19.	44	J Cell Biol
20.	40	Progr Allergy
21.	36	Clin Exp Immunol
22.	32	Adv Immunol
23.	32	Austral J Exp Biol Med
24.	32	J Infect Dis
25.	28	J Allergy
26.	28	Lancet
27.	28	Proc Royal Soc B Biol Sci
28.	24	Am J Pathol
29.	24	Ann Inst Pasteur (Paris)
30.	24	Biochem Biophys Res Comm
31.	24	J Nat Cancer Inst
32.	24	Methods Med Res
33.	20	Am Rev Resp Dis
34.	20	Bacteriol Rev
35.	20	Clin Sci
36.	20	Exp Cell Res
37.	20	J Bacteriol
38.	20	J Biophys Biochem Cytol
39.	20	J Histochem Cytochem
40.	20	J Pathol Bacteriol
	1388	All others (220 other journals)
	5296	TOTAL

Figure 9.15 Journals cited most frequently by *Journal of Experimental Medicine*.

Rank	Times Citing	Journal Title Abbreviation
1.	1408	J Immunol
2.	1084	J Exp Med
3.	512	Proc Soc Exp Biol Med
4.	340	Immunology
5.	288	Transplantation
6.	240	J Bacteriol
7.	236	Klin Wschr
8.	224	Proc Nat Acad Sci USA
9.	220	Thromb Diath Haem
10.	196	Ann NY Acad Sci
11.	196	Science
12.	192	Clin Exp Immunol
13.	188	Fed Proc
14.	184	Ann Rev Microbiol
15.	172	J Infect Dis
16.	172	J Nat Cancer Inst
17.	160	Immunochemistry
18.	152	Experientia
19.	152	J Virology
20.	148	Acta Path Scand
21.	148	Nature
22.	144	Lancet
23.	144	Virology
24.	140	New Engl J Med
25.	128	Am J Med
26.	128	Am J Pathol
27.	124	Am J Vet Res
28.	124	Military Med
29.	116	Am J Cardiol
30.	112	Biochemistry
31.	108	Biochem Biophys Acta
32.	104	Ann Inst Pasteur (Paris)
33.	104	Annu Rev Genetics
34.	104	Cancer Research
35.	104	J Gen Virology
36.	100	Lab Invest
37.	96	J Clin Invest
38.	96	Zbl Bakteriol
39.	92	Brit J Exp Pathol
40.	88	J Med Microbiol
	6768	All others (368 other journals)
	15536	TOTAL

Figure 9.16 Major sources of references to *Journal of Experimental Medicine*.

Rank	Times Cited	Journal Title Abbreviation
1.	2176	J Immunol
2.	1404	J Exp Med
3.	588	Proc Soc Exp Biol Med
4.	576	Nature
5.	412	Science
6.	408	Immunology
7.	244	J Biol Chem
8.	240	Fed Proc
9.	196	J Clin Invest
10.	196	Proc Nat Acad Sci USA
11.	188	Internat Arch Allergy Appl Immunol
12.	184	Immunochemistry
13.	168	Biochem J
14.	156	Biochemistry
15.	144	Lancet
16.	140	Ann NY Acad Sci
17.	140	J Infect Dis
18.	120	Biochim Biophys Acta
19.	108	J Bacteriol
20.	100	Adv Immunol
21.	92	Progr Allergy
22.	88	Cancer Res
23.	84	J Nat Cancer Inst
24.	84	Virology
25.	76	J Allergy
26.	68	Acta Pathol Microbiol Scand
27.	68	New Engl J Med
28.	64	J Molec Biol
29.	64	Transplantation
30.	60	Brit J Exp Pathol
31.	60	Cold Spr Harb Symp Quant Biol
32.	56	Clin Exp Immunol
33.	44	Am J Hyg
34.	40	J Lab Clin Med
35.	40	Austral J Exp Biol Med
36.	40	Bacteriol Rev
37.	40	J Amer Chem Soc
38.	40	Lab Invest
39.	36	Ann Inst Pasteur (Paris)
40.	36	Blood
	3112	All others (392 other journals)
	9068	TOTAL

Figure 9.17 Journals cited most frequently by *Journal of Immunology*.

Rank	Times Citing	Journal Title Abbreviation
1.	2176	J Immunol
2.	572	J Exp Med
3.	396	Proc Soc Exp Biol Med
4.	284	Immunology
5.	204	Transplantation
6.	164	Ann Rev Microbiol
7.	152	Clin Exp Immunol
8.	152	Proc Nat Acad Sci USA
9.	148	J Bacteriol
10.	136	Immunochemistry
11.	132	Nature
12.	132	Science
13.	128	J Pediat
14.	120	Prod Probl Pharmaceut
15.	116	Am J Epidemiol
16.	116	Fed Proc
17.	108	J Nat Cancer Inst
18.	104	Am J Trop Med
19.	104	Biochemistry
20.	104	J Virology
21.	100	Ann NY Acad Sci
22.	100	Fol Biol
23.	96	Am J Cardiol
24.	96	Klin Wschr
25.	92	Appl Microbiol
26.	88	Acta Virol
27.	84	Internat Arch Allergy Appl Immunol
28.	84	J Infect Dis
29.	80	Experientia
30.	80	New Engl J Med
31.	76	Lancet
32.	72	Mycopathol Mycol Appl
33.	68	Biochim Biophys Acta
34.	68	Vox Sanguinis
35.	64	Arch Gen Virol
36.	64	Military Med
37.	60	Acta Microbiol Acad Sci Hung
38.	60	Acta Pathol Scand
39.	56	Ann Intern Med
40.	56	Exp Parasitol
	3400	All others (288 other journals)
	10492	TOTAL

Figure 9.18 Major sources of references to *Journal of Immunology*.

rheumatology literature (10) by identifying the 24 journals most frequently cited by each of the two leading journals in that field. The journals whose citing patterns he analyzed were *Annals of the Rheumatic Diseases (Ann. Rheum. Dis.)* and *Arthritis and Rheumatism (Arthr. & Rheum.)*. His two lists are shown in Figure 9.19. Though he based his study on 1970 citations, his lists agreed with similar ones compiled from the *JCR* data for 1969. To extend his study, ISI went one step further and compiled lists of the most frequent sources of citations to the journals he selected. They are shown in Figure 9.20.

The journals cited by *Ann. Rheum. Dis.* and *Arthr. & Rheum.* (Figure 9.19) are essentially the same: 19 journals are common to both lists. Another point about these two lists is that they demonstrate the bibliographic law of concentration. With only four exceptions, all of the 29 journals that are unique to one or the other of the two lists are among the 450 journals that the multidisciplinary and multispecialty *JCR* shows as being the most frequently cited.

The lists of journals that most frequently cite *Ann. Rheum. Dis.* and *Arthr. & Rheum.* (Figure 9.20) also are remarkably similar. Sixteen journals are common to both of these lists.

However, there are obvious differences between the citing and cited lists. Both *Ann. Rheum. Dis.* and *Arthr. & Rheum.* cite literature more heavily and much more widely than they, in turn, are cited. In the case of *Ann. Rheum. Dis.*, it published 1332 references that cited 305 different journals, whereas it was cited 1252 times by only 71 different journals. Comparable figures for *Arthr. & Rheum.* are 3165 references to 387 journals and 1660 citations from only 103 different journals. As is so often the case, the journal that cites most heavily and widely, *Arthr. & Rheum.* is in turn most heavily and widely cited. Another point of difference between the citing and cited lists is that all the journals cited by *Ann. Rheum. Dis.* and *Arthr. & Rheum.* are published in English, but several journals published in French and German appear as major citation sources for them.

Certain journals, namely *Arthr. & Rheum., Ann Rheum. Dis., Acta Med. Scand., Arch. Internal Med., J. Bone Joint Surg.,* and the *Proc. Soc. Exp. Biol. Med.,* appear on all four lists. This strongly suggests, even to someone unfamiliar with the specialty, that these six journals, in addition to the obvious general journals, such as *J. Amer. Med. Assoc., Brit. Med. J., Lancet,* etc., probably are the ones that are the most useful to a rheumatologist.

Relationship Between Pathology and Virology (11)

In an address to a 1971 meeting of the American Phytopathological Association, I used a list of the journals most frequently cited by the journal *Phytopathology* to identify the core literature of the field (Figure 9.21). Everyone in the audience was surprised to find that the second most frequently cited journal, after *Phytopathology* itself, was *Virology*. This unexpected relationship was confirmed by a complementary list of the journals that were the major sources of citations to *Phytopathology* (Figure 9.22). *Virology* ranked a respectable seventh on that list.

	Journals Cited by ANNALS OF RHEUMATIC DISEASES				Journals Cited by ARTHRITIS & RHEUMATISM		
	Title Abbreviation	Times Cited	Cumulated % of Citations		Title Abbreviation	Times Cited	Cumulated % of Citations
*1.	Ann. Rheum. Dis.	211	15.8	*1.	Arthr. & Rheum.	291	9.2
*2.	Arthr. & Rheum.	102	23.5	*2.	Ann. Rheum. Dis.	188	15.1
*3.	Brit. Med. J.	65	28.3	*3.	J. Amer. Med. Assoc.	95	18.1
*4.	Lancet	58	32.7	*4.	New Engl. J. Med.	92	20.0
*5.	J. Bone Joint Surg.	55	36.8	*5.	Ann. Internal Med.	91	23.9
*6.	J. Clin. Invest.	32	39.2	*6.	J. Bone Joint Surg.	90	26.7
*7.	J. Exp. Med.	31	41.3	*7.	J. Exp. Med.	81	29.4
*8.	Nature	28	43.7	*8.	Lancet	81	32.0
*9.	Acta Rheum. Scand.	27	45.7	*9.	Brit. Med. J.	79	34.3
*10.	J. Amer. Med. Assoc.	24	46.6	*10.	Amer. J. Med.	78	36.8
*11.	Ann. Internal Med.	23	49.2	*11.	J. Clin. Invest.	70	39.0
*12.	Amer. J. Med	22	50.9	*12.	Nature	69	41.2
*13.	New Engl. J. Med.	22	52.5	*13.	Proc. Soc. Exp. Biol. Med.	67	43.3
*14.	J. Immunology	22	54.2	*14.	Acta Rheum. Scand.	62	45.3
15.	Proc. Roy. Soc. Med.	20	56.0	15.	Science	56	47.0
*16.	Proc. Soc. Exp. Biol. Med.	18	57.3	*16.	J. Lab. Clin. Med.	47	48.5
*17.	Acta Med. Scand.	16	58.5	17.	J. Immunology	44	49.9
*18.	J. Lab. Clin. Med.	16	59.7	*18.	Clin. Exp. Immunol.	41	51.2
*19.	Clin. Exp. Immunol.	13	60.4	19.	Clin. Orthoped.	40	52.5
*20.	Arch. Internal Med.	12	61.3	*20.	Arch. Internal Med.	39	53.7
21.	J. Chronic Dis.	12	62.2	21.	Canad. Med. Assoc. J.	27	54.6
22.	Q. J. Med.	12	63.1	22.	Fed. Proc.	26	55.4
23.	Immunology	11	64.0	23.	Proc. Nat. Acad. Sci. US	26	56.2
24.	J. Path. Bact.	11	64.9	*24.	Acta Med. Scand.	25	57.0
	All Other (281)	469	100.0		All Other (363)	1360	100.0
	Total	1332			Total	3165	

Figure 9.19 Journals cited most frequently by *Annals of Rheumatic Disease* and *Arthritis & Rheumatism*. Journals common to both lists are marked by asterisks.

Journals That Cited ANNALS OF RHEUMATIC DISEASES

	Title Abbreviation	Times Cited	Cumulated % of Citations
*1.	Ann. Rheum. Dis.	296	23.6
*2.	Arthr. & Rheum.	80	30.0
*3.	Z. Rheumaforsch.	80	36.4
*4.	Acta Med. Scand.	68	41.9
*5.	Mayo Clin. Proc.	64	47.0
*6.	Brit. Med. J.	36	49.8
*7.	Amer. J. Med.	32	52.4
8.	Q. J. Med.	32	55.0
*9.	Schweiz. Med. Wschr.	32	57.5
*10.	Arch. Internal Med.	28	59.7
*11.	J. Bone Joint Surg.	28	62.0
*12.	Lancet	28	64.2
13.	Amer. J. Epidem.	24	66.1
*14.	Deut. Med. Wschr.	24	68.1
15.	Arch. Orthopäd. Unfallchir.	20	69.6
16.	Biochem. Biophys. Acta	20	71.2
17.	Experientia	20	72.8
18.	Clin. Chim. Acta	16	74.1
*19.	Med. Clin. N. Amer.	16	75.4
*20.	Modern Treatment	16	76.7
21.	Amer. J. Clin. Pathol.	12	77.6
*22.	Amer. J. Pathol.	12	78.6
23.	Biochem. Pharmacol.	12	79.6
*24.	Proc. Soc. Exp. Biol. Med	12	80.5
	All Other (47)	244	100.0
	Total	1252	

Journals That Cited ARTHRITIS & RHEUMATISM

	Title Abbreviation	Times Cited	Cumulated % of Citations
*1.	Arthr. & Rheum.	160	9.6
*2.	Mayo Clin. Proc.	136	17.8
*3.	Amer. J. Med.	120	25.1
*4.	Ann. Rheum. Dis.	76	29.6
*5.	Med. Clin. N. Amer.	60	33.3
*6.	Acta Med. Scand.	56	36.6
*7.	Schweiz. Med. Wschr.	52	39.8
*8.	Modern Treatment	48	42.7
*9.	Deut. Med. Wschr.	44	45.3
*10.	Arch. Internal Med.	40	47.7
*11.	Brit. Med. J.	40	50.1
12.	Clin. Exp. Immunol.	40	52.5
13.	Ann. N. Y. Acad. Sci.	36	54.7
14.	J. Amer. Med. Assoc.	36	56.9
*15.	J. Bone Joint Surg.	36	59.0
16.	Rev. Fr. Et. Clin. Biol.	36	61.2
*17.	Amer. J. Path.	32	63.1
18.	Biochem. J.	32	65.1
19.	J. Immunol.	28	66.7
*20.	Proc. Soc. Exp. Biol. Med.	28	68.4
*21.	Zschr. Rheumaforsch.	28	70.1
22.	Tohoku J. Exp. Med.	24	71.6
23.	Amer. J. Clin. Nutr.	16	72.5
*24.	Lancet	16	73.5
	All Other (79)	440	100.0
	Total	1660	

Figure 9.20 Major sources of references to *Annals of Rheumatic Diseases* and *Arthritis & Rheumatism*. Journals common to both lists are marked by asterisks.

Rank	No. of citations	Title
1.	3288	Phytopathology (self-citation)
2.	476	Plant Dis. Reporter
3.	320	Virology
4.	240	Canad. J. Bot.
5.	204	Plant Physiol.
6.	188	Amer. J. Bot.
7.	184	Nature
8.	164	Ann. Appl. Biol.
9.	164	Annu. Rev. Phytopathol.
10.	148	Phytopathol. Zschr.
11.	144	J. Agric. Res.
12.	120	Science
13.	88	J. Bacteriol.
14.	88	J. Biol. Chem.
15.	80	Mycologia
16.	76	Agronomy J.
17.	76	J. Gen. Microbiol.
18.	72	Trans. Brit. Mycol. Soc.
19.	68	Annu. Rev. Plant Physiol.
20.	60	Austr. J. Biol. Sci.
21.	60	J. Econ. Entomol.
22.	60	Soil Sci.
23.	56	Crop Sci.
24.	56	J. Agric. Food Chem.
25.	52	Ann. Phytopathol. Soc.
	4788	All Other (731 other titles)
	11320	Total

Figure 9.21 Journals cited most frequently by *Phytopathology*.

Rank	No. of citations	Title
1.	3288	Phytopathology (self-citation)
2.	1164	Annu. Rev. Phytopathol.
3.	184	Trans. Brit. Mycol. Soc.
4.	168	Canad. J. Bot.
5.	120	Mycologia
6.	112	Mycopathol. Mycol. Appl.
7.	76	Virology
8.	72	Ann. Appl. Biol.
9.	68	Botan. Rev.
10.	60	Canad. J. Microbiol.
11.	56	Canad. J. Plant Sci.
12.	56	Hilgardia
13.	56	Theoret. Appl. Genetics
14.	48	Amer. Potato J.
15.	48	Crop Sci.
16.	48	J. Econ. Entomol.
17.	40	Science
18.	36	J. Bacteriol.
19.	36	J. Gen. Microbiol.
20.	32	J. Stored Prod. Res.
21.	28	C.R. Acad. Sci. D
22.	28	IIRB
23.	28	J. Nematol.
24.	28	Nat. Cancer Inst. Monogr.
25.	28	Radiation Res.
	944	All Other (99 other titles)
	6852	Total

Figure 9.22 Major sources of references to *Phytopathology*.

Later, in an attempt to see whether the relationship between virology and pathology extended to human pathology, I analyzed the citation patterns of *Acta Path. Microb. Scan., Virchows Arch., Pathologie Biologie, J. Pathology,* and *Amer. J. Pathol.* These journals are the top five of the 20 pathology journals covered by *JCR,* when measured by the criteria of the number of references published in 1969. The analysis showed that, with one puzzling exception, they did not cite virology journals at a significant rate. *Virology,* for example, ranked only

Rank	Times Cited	Title
1.	416	Acta path. microb. scand. (self-citation)
2.	240	Nature
3.	148	J. Exp. Med.
4.	116	J. Nat. Cancer Inst.
5.	108	Ann. N.Y. Acad Sci.
6.	104	Arch. Pathol.
7.	104	J. Bacteriol.
8.	96	Amer. J. Pathol.
9.	96	Ann. Human Genetics
10.	96	Proc. Soc. Exp. Biol. Med.
11.	80	Ann. Eugenics
12.	80	J. Histochem. Cytochem.
13.	80	Lancet
14.	76	Biochem. J.
15.	76	J. Biol. Chem.
16.	72	Circulation
17.	72	J. Med. Microbiol.
18.	68	Amer. J. Human Genetics
19.	64	C.R. Acad. Sci.
20.	64	Lab. Invest.
21.	60	Acta genet. med. gemell.
22.	60	J. Immunol.
23.	56	J. Cell Biol.
24.	52	Virology
25.	48	Cancer Res.
	4408	All Other (601 other titles)
	6940	Total

Figure 9.23 Journals cited most frequently by *Acta Pathologica et Microbiologica Scandinavica*.

Rank	Times Cited	Title
1.	172	Nature
2.	132	J. Bacteriol.
3.	124	Virology
4.	120	J. Gen Microbiol.
5.	116	J. Biol. Chem.
6.	116	J. Molec Biol.
7.	92	Cancer Res.
8.	76	Ann. N.Y. Acad. Sci.
9.	72	Biochem. Biophys. Acta
10.	72	Proc. Soc. Exp. Biol. Med.
11.	64	Biochem. Biophys. Res.
12.	60	Ann. Inst. Pasteur
13.	60	Lancet
14.	60	New Engl. J. Med.
15.	60	Science
16.	56	J. Virology
17.	52	Biochem. J.
18.	52	J. Exp. Med.
19.	52	Presse Med.
20.	44	Arch. Biochem. Biophys.
21.	44	Pathol. Biol.
22.	40	Canad. J. Microbiol.
23.	36	Biokhimiya
24.	36	Endocrinology
25.	36	Proc. Nat. Acad. Sci. US
	2464	All Other (400 other titles)
	4308	Total

Figure 9.24 Journals cited most frequently by *Pathologie Biologie*.

twenty-fourth among the journals cited by *Acta Path. Microb. Scand.* (Figure 9.23).

The exception that was so puzzling was *Pathologie Biologie*. As in the case of *Phytopathology, Virology* ranked third among the journals it cited most frequently (Figure 9.24). What made the finding so puzzling was not only that *Pathologie Biologie* was the only one to show such a strong interest in virology, but that it showed little, if any, interest in plant pathology, which would have explained the relationship with virology.

Interestingly enough, a complementary analysis of the major sources of citations to pathology journals uncovered the same situation, but with a somewhat different set of journals. The five most frequently cited pathology journals in JCR are *Amer. J. Pathol., Arch. Pathol., Naunyn-Schmiedebergs Arch. Exp. Pathol. Pharmakol., J. Clin. Pathol.,* and the *Brit. J. Exp. Pathol.* Lists of the major sources of citations to them showed that only one, *Brit. J. Exp. Pathol.,* was cited significantly by virology journals.

This analysis suggested that there may have been a literature gap in the area of applied virology. Certainly the literature on human pathology did not seem to reflect the impact that virology was having on that field, which may be why the report by ter Meulen and Koprowski on the viral factors in multiple sclerosis (12) was published in a general medical journal rather than in one of the specialty virology journals. If there was a literature of applied virology, it probably was scattered throughout the general medical literature. Any publisher looking for a new journal market at that point in time would have been well advised to take a close look at the area of applied virology. This, in fact, happened some time later, when the *Journal of Medical Virology* began publishing.

Journal of Clinical Investigation (13)

Another test of how subtly citation analysis can characterize the editorial orientation of a journal was conducted with the *Journal of Clinical Investigation (J. Clin. Invest).* Like the *Journal of Experimental Medicine,* its title suggests that it would be quite useful in a clinical or hospital library as an interface between basic research and clinical practice. The citation analysis showed that, unlike the *Journal of Experimental Medicine,* it did, in fact, cover that area. The journals it cited most frequently (Figure 9.25) showed it had a close relationship to the basic research fronts. Those that cited it most heavily (Figure 9.26) showed that it also had a significant impact on clinical practice. Its utility among clinicians could be seen plainly by defining as clinical any journal whose title contains the words "clinical," "medical," "medicine," or the name of a medical specialty, but that does not contain the words "laboratory," "experimental," or "research." By that criterion, about 30 of the 50 journals that cited *J. Clin. Invest.* most frequently were clinical, whereas only about 12 of the 50 journals it cited most frequently fell into the same category. And in the cases where *J. Clin. Invest.* did cite clinical journals, it usually did so at a rate much lower than the one at which they cited it.

Another facet of the editorial orientation of *J. Clin. Invest.* was shown by the high ranking of the *Journal of Clinical Endocrinology and Metabolism* on both lists. In keeping with this relationship, *Endocrinology* and *Diabetes* also show up as being heavily cited by *J. Clin. Invest.*

A surprising observation is that the *Journal of the American Medical Association (JAMA)* does not appear on either list, whereas the *New England Journal of Medicine* ranks high on both of them. A similar situation is found with the *British Medical Journal* and *Lancet. Lancet* ranks high on both lists. The *British Medical Journal,* though it does appear on the list of journals that cited *J. Clin. Invest.*

Rank	Times cited	Journal title abbreviation
*1.	1244	J. Clin. Invest. (1244)
*2.	544	J. Biol. Chem. (168)
*3.	368	Amer. J. Physiology (556)
*4.	260	J. Clin. Endocrinol. Metab. (296)
5.	244	Nature
*6.	204	J. Lab. Clin. Med (188)
7.	196	Science
*8.	172	Biochim. Biophys. Acta (356)
*9.	168	Proc. Soc. Exp. Biol. Med. (360)
*10.	164	Biochem. J. (112)
*11.	160	Lancet (272)
12.	152	Endocrinology
*13.	144	Diabetes (188)
*14.	136	New Engl. J. Med (476)
15.	116	J. Lipid Res.
16.	112	Clin. Res.
*17.	100	Ann. New York Acad Sci. (308)
*18.	100	Blood (96)
19.	96	J. Exp. Med.
*20.	92	J. Appl. Physiology (200)
*21.	84	Am. J. Med. (392)
22.	84	Fed. Proc.
*23.	84	J. Physiology (London) (136)
*24.	80	Circulation Res. (100)
25.	76	Analyt. Biochem.
*26.	76	Circulation (284)
*27.	76	Clin. Science (568)
28.	68	J. Pharmacol. Exp. Ther.
29.	64	Acta Physiol. Scand.
30.	64	Cancer Res.
*31.	60	Ann. Internal Med. (212)
*32.	60	Metabolism (188)
33.	56	Arch. Biochem. Biophys.
34.	56	Biochemistry
*35.	56	Gastroenterology (120)
*36.	56	Thromb. Diath. Haemorrh. (116)
37.	52	Rec. Progr. Hormone Res.
38.	48	J. Amer. Chem. Soc.
*39.	48	Proc. Nat. Acad. Sci. USA (100)
*40.	40	Acta Endocrinologica (132)
*41.	40	Clin. Chim. Acta (140)
*42.	40	Klin. Wschr. (248)
*43.	40	Pflugers Arch. (148)
44.	36	Amer. Heart J.
*45.	36	Amer. J. Obst. Gynecol. (168)
46.	36	Biochem. Pharmacol.
47.	36	Physiol. Rev.
*48.	36	Scand. J. Clin. Lab. Invest. (128)
49.	36	Steroids
50.	32	Atherosclerosis
	6428	Total of first 50
	10336	in 512 other publications
	16764	Total

Figure 9.25 Journals cited most frequently by *Journal of Clinical Investigation (J. Clin. Invest.)* Asterisks indicate journals that also are major sources of references to *J. Clin. Invest.* The numbers in parentheses following these journals show the number of times they cited *J. Clin. Invest.*

Rank	Times cited	Journal title abbreviation
*1.	1244	J. Clin. Invest. (1244)
*2.	568	Clin. Science (76)
*3.	556	Amer. J. Physiol. (368)
*4.	476	New Engl. J. Med. (136)
*5.	392	Amer. J. Med. (84)
*6.	360	Proc. Soc. Exp. Biol. Med. (168)
*7.	356	Biochim. Biophys. Acta (172)
*8.	308	Ann. New York Acad. Sci. (100)
*9.	296	J. Clin. Endocrinol. Metab. (260)
*10.	284	Circulation (76)
*11.	272	Lancet (160)
*12.	248	Klin. Wschr. (40)
13.	232	Acta Med. Scand.
14.	232	Arch. Internal. Med.
*15.	212	Ann. Internal Med. (60)
16.	204	Ital. J. Biochem.
*17.	200	J. Appl. Physiology (92)
18.	196	J. Immunology
*19.	188	Diabetes (144)
*20.	188	J. Lab. Clin. Med. (204)
*21.	188	Metabolism (60)
22.	176	Deut. Med. Wschr.
23.	172	Brit. Med. J.
24.	168	Am. J. Digest. Dis.
*25.	168	Amer. J. Obst. Gynecol. (36)
*26.	168	J. Biol. Chem. (544)
27.	160	Amer. J. Clin. Nutrition
*28.	148	Pflugers Arch. (40)
29.	140	Brit. J. Haematol.
*30.	140	Clin. Chim. Acta (40)
31.	136	Amer. J Med. Sci.
*32.	136	J. Physiology (London) (84)
*33.	132	Acta Endocrinologica (40)
34.	128	Gut
35.	128	Israel J. Med. Sci.
*36.	128	Scand. J. Clin. Lab. Invest. (36)
37.	124	J. Pediatrics
38.	124	Pediatrics
*39.	120	Gastroenterology (56)
40.	116	Amer. Rev. Resp. Dis.
*41.	116	Thromb. Diath. Haemorrh. (56)
42.	112	Ann. Surgery
*43.	112	Biochem. J. (164)
44.	112	Respiration Physiol.
*45.	100	Circulation Res. (80)
46.	100	Danish Med. Bull.
*47.	100	Proc. Nat. Acad. Sci. USA (48)
*48.	96	Blood (100)
49.	96	Med. Clin. North Amer.
50.	92	Beitr. Klin. Tuberk.
	10948	Total of first 50
	8168	in 391 other publications
	19116	Total

Figure 9.26 Major sources of references to *Journal of Clinical Investigation (J. Clin. Invest.)* Asterisks indicate journals that also are frequently cited by *J. Clin. Invest.;* the frequency of citation by *J. Clin. Invest.* is shown by the number in parentheses following the journal name.

(Figure 9.26), ranks much lower than *Lancet* and does not make the list of journals cited by *J. Clin. Invest.* (Figure 9.25) at all.

Journal of the American Medical Association Versus *The New England Journal of Medicine (14)*

The absence of the *Journal of the American Medical Association* (*JAMA*) and the prominence of the *New England Journal of Medicine* (*NEJM*) in the citation study of the *Journal of Clinical Investigation* suggested that the latter was more research oriented than the former. A comparative citation analysis of the two journals was conducted to test that hypothesis. The analysis was based, primarily, on the impact-factor ratings of the journals most frequently cited by *JAMA* and *NEJM*, an approach that was chosen because there is a general correlation between the strength of a journal's impact and the degree of its basic-research orientation.

Lists of the titles of the journals cited most frequently by *JAMA* and *NEJM* showed that there was a considerable difference between the two journals. The average impact factors of the two lists showed the nature of the difference. The top 50 journals cited by JAMA (Figure 9.27) had an average impact of 1.562, whereas the average impact of the top 50 cited by *NEJM* (Figure 9.28) was 2.601. Even when the lists were extended to include the top 100 citation targets, the impact superiority of the *NEJM*-cited journals was maintained: 2.377 versus 2.107. The difference of 0.237 is not as trivial as it might seem. Many journals do not achieve an impact factor as high as 0.237.

This evidence of *NEJM*'s greater research orientation may explain not only its close relationship with the *Journal of Clinical Investigation,* but also its striking superiority to *JAMA* in terms of impact. Although *NEJM* and *JAMA* were cited at approximately the same rate (they ranked twenty-fourth and twenty-sixth, respectively, in terms of total citations in 1969), *NEJM* ranked one hundred-sixtieth in impact, with a rating of 2.45, whereas *JAMA* ranked four hundred seventy-fourth, with a rating of 1.027. In fact, when the letters, editorials, and other nonciteable material that tends to lower the impact factors based on 1969 data were removed, the difference between the two became even more marked.

In less abstract terms, the list of journals most frequently cited by *JAMA* contained all the journals needed to provide reasonably complete coverage of the literature relevant to the interests of a practitioner. The practitioner's university colleague, however, may well prefer to choose his journal collection from the list of journals cited most frequently by *NEJM*.

Pediatrics Literature (15)

A study of the journal literature of pediatrics began with identifying all the pediatrics journals on the list of 1000 journals cited most frequently in 1969. There were 13, and they are shown, in alphabetical order, with their citation rate and impact factor, in Figure 9.29. Initially, the core group of pediatric journals included *Child Development* and *Growth,* but they were subsequently dropped from the study. The reason for dropping them was that the analysis showed their citation

Rank	Times Cited	Cited Journal and Its Impact Factor
1.	1212	J. Amer. Med. Assoc. (1.027)
2.	424	N. Engl. J. Med. (2.453)
3.	200	Ann. Internal Med. (1.640)
4.	200	Lancet (1.509)
5.	148	J. Urology (0.950)
6.	140	Amer. J. Med. (4.694)
7.	140	Arch. Internal Med. (1.610)
8.	128	Brit. Med. J. (0.778)
9.	96	Circulation (1.267)
10.	96	J. Clin. Endocr. Metab. (3.829)
11.	88	Science (2.894)
12.	76	Cancer (2.162)
13.	76	HSMHA Health Rep. (0.451)
14.	72	Arch. Dermatol. (0.567)
15.	68	Amer. J. Med. Sci. (0.582)
16.	68	J. Clin. Invest. (3.461)
17.	60	Nature (2.244)
18.	60	Surgery (1.347)
19.	56	Amer. J. Cardiology (2.240)
20.	56	Amer. J. Dis. Children (1.257)
21.	56	Amer. J. Obst. Gynecol. (1.269)
22.	56	Surg. Gynecol. Obst. (1.578)
23.	52	Ann. Surgery (1.665)
24.	52	Arch. Surgery (0.888)
25.	52	Clin. Res. (0.262)
26.	52	J. Lab. Clin. Med. (1.742)
27.	48	Am. J. Epidemiology (1.846)
28.	48	J. Pediatrics (1.459)
29.	48	Neurology (0.868)
30.	48	Radiology (1.533)
31.	44	Proc. Soc. Exp. Biol. Med. (1.964)
32.	40	Amer. J. Roentgenol. (1.257)
33.	40	Anesthesiology (2.040)
34.	40	Southern Med. J. (0.224)
35.	36	Amer. Heart J. (1.980)
36.	36	Amer. J. Clin. Pathol. (0.625)
37.	36	Amer. J. Physiology (3.379)
38.	36	Amer. J. Psychiatry (0.673)
39.	36	Arch. Gen Psychiatry (1.409)
40.	36	Arthritis Rheumatism (0.672)
41.	36	Canad. Med. Assoc. J. (0.350)
42.	36	J. Med. Education (0.393)
43.	36	Medicine (5.217)
44.	36	Obstetrics & Gynecology (0.816)
45.	36	Pediatrics (1.417)
46.	36	Tr. Amer. Soc. Art. Int. Org. (1.367)
47.	32	Arch. Environmental Health (0.632)
48.	32	Arch. Neurol. (1.449)
49.	28	Amer. J. Surgery (0.992)
50.	28	Gastroenterology (1.189)
	4692	Total of first 50
	9360	in 788 others
	14052	Grand Total

Figure 9.27 Journals cited most frequently by *Journal of the American Medical Association*.

Rank	Times Cited	Cited Journal and Its Impact Factor
1.	1172	New Engl. J. Med (2.453)
2.	476	J. Clin. Invest. (3.461)
3.	356	Lancet (1.509)
4.	352	J. Biol. Chem. (6.371)
5.	348	Amer. J. Med (4.694)
6.	308	Ann. Internal Med. (1.640)
7.	300	Circulation (1.267)
8.	288	J. Amer. Med. Assoc. (1.027)
9.	216	Amer. J. Cardiology (2.240)
10.	208	Science (2.894)
11.	196	Brit. Med. J. (0.778)
12.	180	Nature (2.244)
13.	176	J. Clin. Endocrinol. Metab. (3.829)
14.	172	Blood (2.867)
15.	140	Amer. Heart J. (1.980)
16.	140	Arch. Internal Med. (1.610)
17.	140	J. Exp. Med. (9.030)
18.	136	Gastroenterology (1.189)
19.	120	Amer. J. Physiology (3.379)
20.	116	Pediatrics (1.417)
21.	112	Biochem. Biophys. Res. Comm. (4.468)
22.	112	J. Am. Vet. Med. Assoc. (0.448)
23.	112	J. Bacteriol. (3.594)
24.	112	Proc. Nat. Acad. Sci. USA (8.828)
25.	108	Biochim. Biophys. Acta (3.287)
26.	108	Proc. Soc. Exp. Biol. Med. (1.964)
27.	104	Brit. J. Haematol. (2.179)
28.	100	J. Lab. Clin. Med. (1.742)
29.	100	J. Pediatrics (1.459)
30.	88	Ann. New York Acad. Sci. (1.815)
31.	88	Medicine (5.217)
32.	84	J. Heredity (0.600)
33.	80	Clin. Res. (0.262)
34.	80	J. Immunology (4.305)
35.	76	Brit. Heart J. (1.697)
36.	76	Fed. Proc. (0.568)
37.	76	Radiology (1.533)
38.	72	Am. J. Vet. Res. (0.831)
39.	72	Biochem. J. (3.193)
40.	72	Cancer Res. (3.084)
41.	68	Arch. Biochem. Biophys. (3.519)
42.	68	Arch. Pathology (1.509)
43.	68	Biochemistry (5.906)
44.	68	Diabetes (2.039)
45.	60	Amer. J. Dis. Children (1.257)
46.	60	Amer. J. Med. Sci. (0.582)
47.	56	Amer. J. Clin. Pathol. (0.623)
48.	56	Q.J. Med. (4.238)
49.	52	Acta Med. Scand. (1.534)
50.	52	Amer. J. Pathology (1.916)
	7980	in first 50
	17248	in 1019 other publications
	25228	Grand Total

Figure 9.28 Journals cited most frequently by *New England Journal of Medicine*.

links to the other 13, as either the object or source of citations, to be very weak. An examination of the two journals showed that *Child Development* dealt with psychology and education and *Growth* was concerned mainly with biochemistry and physiology.

The next step was a compilation of the 100 journals most frequently cited by the 13 core journals (Figure 9.30). While one would expect that all 13 of the original journals would rank high on such a list (on the strength of self-citation if nothing else), only seven of them appeared among the top 25. When self-citations were excluded from the counts, only nine of the original 13 remained among the top 100 journals they had cited. Of the four that dropped off the list, one was French, one was German, and two dealt with the subspecialty areas of pediatric surgery and neonatal physiology. When all 13 of the original core journals were excluded from the list to examine the tail of the pediatrics literature, it was found that the journals remaining were the same ones that were cited most frequently by the *Journal of the American Medical Association,* the *New England Journal of Medicine,* and the *Journal of Clinical Investigation*—another demonstration of the law of bibliographic concentration.

On the other hand, the list of journals most cited by the 13 included three journals that were not among the 1000 most cited journals of science but, nevertheless, seemed to play an important role in pediatrics: *Clinical Pediatrics, Pediatrie,* and

	Times Cited 1969	Impact Factor	Journal Title
1.	1256	0.678	Acta Paediat. Scand.
2.	4508	1.257	Amer. J. Dis. Children
3.	2376	1.383	Arch. Dis. Childhood
4.	452	0.162	Arch. Franc. Pediat.
5.	372	0.884	Biol. Neonat.
6.	372	0.236	Dev. Med. & Child Neur.
7.	556	1.128	Helv. Paediat. Acta
8.	392	0.539	J. Pediat. Surg.
9.	4916	1.459	J. Pediatrics
10.	524	0.548	Pediat. Clin. N. Amer.
11.	808	0.680	Pediatric Res.
12.	5528	1.417	Pediatrics
13.	492	0.480	Zschr. Kinderheilk

Figure 9.29 Pediatric journals among the 1000 most highly cited journals.

Rank	Times Cited 1969	Journal Title			
1.	2088	**Pediatrics**	52.	100	Amer. Heart J.
2.	1768	**J. Pediatrics**	53.	100	J. Appl. Physiol.
–	1616	*Pediatrics*	54.	100	Med. J. Australia
3.	1412	**Amer. J. Dis. Children**	55.	100	Neurology
4.	1412	Lancet	56.	92	Acta Endocrin.
–	1172	*Amer. J. Dis. Children*	57.	92	Amer. J. Physiol.
5.	1164	New Engl. J. Med.	58.	92	Blood
–	1080	*J. Pediatrics*	59.	92	**Helv. Pediat. Acta**
6.	872	Arch. Dis. Childhood	60.	88	Zschr. Kinderheilk.
7.	776	J. Amer. Med. Assoc.	61.	84	Arch. Neurology
–	716	*Arch. Dis. Childhood*	62.	84	Clin. Pediat.
8.	604	Brit. Med. J.	63.	84	J. Exp. Zoology
9.	428	J. Clin. Invest.	64.	80	Brit. J. Surgery
10.	412	J. Biol. Chem.	65.	80	J. Med. Microbiol.
11.	396	J. Clin. Endocrin. & Metab.	66.	76	Amer. J. Clin. Pathol.
12.	380	**Acta Paediat. Scand.**	67.	76	Cancer
13.	364	J. Urology	68.	76	J. Neuropath. Exp. Neur.
14.	324	Science	–	76	*Pediatic Res.*
15.	304	Surgery	69.	72	Brit. Heart J.
16.	300	Nature	–	72	*Dev. Med. Child Neurol.*
–	272	*Acta Paediat. Scand.*	70.	72	Federation Proc.
17.	260	Amer. J. Med.	71.	72	J. Endocrinology
18.	256	Ann. Surgery	72.	64	Amer. J. Human Genet.
19.	244	Amer. J. Obst. Gyn.	73.	64	Brain
20.	224	**Pediatric Res.**	74.	64	Brit. J. Urology
21.	204	J. Lab. Clin. Med.	75.	64	Pediatrie
22.	200	Proc. Soc. Exp. Biol. Med.	76.	60	Biochim. Biophys. Acta
23.	192	Ann. Internal Med.	–	60	*Helv. Paediat. Acta*
24.	180	Circulation	77.	56	Chest
25.	180	**J. Pediat. Surg.**	78.	56	Lab. Invest.
26.	176	Arch. Surgery	79.	56	Medicine
27.	172	J. Immunology	80.	56	Monatschr. Kinderheilk.
28.	172	Radiology	81.	56	Proc. Roy. Soc. Med.
29.	172	Amer. J. Roentgenol.	82.	52	Amer. J. Mental Defic.
30.	168	J. Thor. Cardiovasc. Surg.	83.	52	Clin. Sci.
31.	164	Surg. Gynecol. Obst.	84.	52	Exp. Cell Res.
32.	164	Biochem. J.	85.	52	Gastroenterology
33.	156	**Pediat. Clin. N. Amer.**	86.	52	J. Clin. Pathology
	156	*Pediat. Clin. N. Amer.*	87.	52	J. Neurosurg.
34.	152	Arch. Pathology	88.	52	Presse Med.
35.	148	Amer. J. Pathology	89.	48	Amer. J. Pub. Health
36.	144	J. Cell Biol.	90.	48	Anat. Record
37.	132	**Biol. Neonat.**	91.	48	Brit. J. Prev. Soc. Med.
38.	132	J. Exp. Med.	92.	48	Electroencephal. Clin. Neurophys.
39.	124	Amer. J. Surgery			
40.	120	Proc. Nat. Acad. Sci. US	93.	48	Endocrinology
41.	120	Arch. Internal Med.	94.	48	Klin. Wschr.
42.	112	Amer. J. Med. Sci.	95.	48	Metabolism
43.	112	Amer. Rev. Resp. Dis.	96.	48	Surg. Clin. N. Amer.
44.	112	**Amer. J. Cardiology**	97.	44	Arch. Gen. Psychiat.
45.	112	**Arch. Franc. Pediat.**	98.	44	Biochemistry
46.	112	Canad. Med. Assoc. J.	99.	44	Birth Defects Origin
47.	108	Ann. New York Acad. Sci.	100.	44	South. Med. J.
48.	108	Deut. Med. Wschr.	–	40	*Arch. Franc. Pediat.*
49.	108	**Dev. Med. Child Neurol.**	–	36	*Biol. Neonat.*
50.	108	J. Physiol. (London)	–	32	*J. Pediat. Surg.*
51.	104	Develop. Biology	–	12	*Zschr. Kinderheilk.*

Figure 9.30 Journals cited most frequently by the highly cited pediatric journals. The journals from which the study data base was compiled appear twice: once in bold type and once in italic. The bold-type entry shows the total citation count. The italic entry shows the total citation count minus self-citations; its position on the list indicates its ranking by this measure.

Monatschrift fur Kinderheilkunde. One-third to half of all the citations received by these three came from four of the core group of pediatric journals.

The high ranking of *Lancet* among the top 100 pediatric journals (Figure 9.30) probably can be attributed, in part, to its heavy interest in human genetics. If that is true, however, it is surprising that the *Amer. J. Human Genet.* ranked only seventy-second on the list, and that the purely genetics journals were completely absent.

Geology and Geophysics (16)

Another way of using *JCR* to define the literature of a particular field was tested with the subject of geology and geophysics. The choice of field was a response to a letter to the editor of *Science,* where the development of *JCR* was first reported, by N. C. Janke of the Department of Geology of the California State University of Sacramento (17). He warned against the use of citation data in journal evaluations and implied that citation data understated the importance of journals in small fields, among which he included his own.

The study began with the assumption that the person doing the analysis would be aware of the existence of the *Journal of Geology.* If so, *JCR* showed that it cited the following journals most frequently:
- *J. Geology* (self-citations).
- *B. Geol. Soc. Amer.*
- *Science*
- *Amer. J. Science*
- *J. Sediment. Petrol.*
- *B. Amer. Assoc. Petrol. Geol.*
- *Nature*
- *J. Geophys. Res.*
- *Geol. Soc. London Quart.*
- *Amer. Mineralogist*

The next stop was to develop a list of the journals most frequently cited by those 10. The result was the list of 132 journals shown in Figure 9.31, where they are ranked by the number of times they were cited by the core group of 10 geology journals.

A separate analysis of the *Amer. J. Science* was conducted to determine whether it was a general-science journal that is important to the field or a hard-core specialty journal of the field. Its title, of course, implies that it is a general-science journal. The title, however, turned out to be deceptive. When the number of times the *Amer. J. Science* was cited by the core group of geology journals was calculated as a percentage of the total number of times it was cited by all journals (936/1940), 48% of its citations were found to come from the former. In contrast, only 4% of the citations to *Science* (1616/39,000) came from the geology journals.

An interesting finding in the list of 132 journals most frequently cited by the core group of geology journals (Figure 9.31) is that the twentieth position is held by "Theses," which are a form of scientific literature that seldom plays a very prominent role in the communications of a field. Sixty-eight of the references to these theses cited ones written at Oregon State University.

Rank	Times Cited 1961-1972	Journal Title	Rank	Times Cited 1961-1972	Journal Title
1.	8032	J. Geophys. Res.	67.	132	J. Appl. Meteorol.
2.	1704	Geochim. Cosmochim. Acta	68.	120	Acta Crystallogr.
3.	1616	Science	69.	116	J. Amer. Chem. Soc.
4.	1608	Astrophysical J.	70.	112	Philosophical Mag.
5.	1452	Nature	71.	112	Zschr. Kristallogr.
6.	1292	B. Geol. Soc. Amer.	72.	100	Geokhimiya
7.	1184	Economic Geology	73.	100	US Geol. Surv.
8.	1164	B. Seismol. Soc. Amer.	74.	96	J. Palaeontology
9.	1164	Planet. Space Sci.	75.	96	Metallurg. J.
10.	1120	J. Atmos. Sci.	76.	92	J. Amer. Ceramic Soc.
11.	1040	J. Sediment. Petrol.	77.	92	Smithsonian Contr. Astrophys.
12.	1004	J. Geology	78.	84	J. Meteor. Soc. Japan
13.	936	Amer. J. Science	79.	80	Comptes Rendus etc.
14.	908	Amer. Mineralogist	80.	76	Agronomy J.
15.	772	J. Atmos. Terr. Phys.	81.	76	Ind. Eng. Chem.
16.	748	Trans. Amer. Geophys. Union	82.	76	J. Physics
17.	584	Soil Sci. Soc. Amer. Proc.	83.	76	Sedimentology
18.	580	Deep-Sea Res.	84.	76	Trans. Roy. Soc. New Zealand
19.	580	Earth Planet. Sci. Lett.	85.	72	J. Geomagn. Geoelect.
20.	552	Theses	86.	72	Meteorologiya Gidrologiya
21.	528	B. Amer. Assoc. Petrol. Geol.	87.	72	New Zealand J. Sci. Techn.
22.	524	Geophys. J. Roy. Astr. Soc.	88.	68	Radiocarbon
23.	508	Izv. Akad. Nauk SSSR FAO	89.	68	Rev. Mod. Phys.
24.	460	Canad. J. Phys.	90.	64	B. Amer. Meteorol. Soc.
25.	432	J. Chem. Phys.	91.	64	Geochem. Int.
26.	428	Proc. Roy. Soc. Lond.	92.	64	J. Geol. Soc. Australia
27.	420	Phys. Rev.	93.	60	Astronomy & Astrophysics
28.	416	Ann. Geophysique	94.	60	Proc. IEEE
29.	416	Icarus	95.	60	Tectonophysics
30.	396	J. Petrology	96.	60	Zschr. Naturforsch.
31.	368	Soil Sci.	97.	56	Agrokhimiya
32.	360	Tellus	98.	56	B. New Zealand Geol. Surv.
33.	336	Space Res.	99.	56	Dev. Sediment. Petrol.
34.	328	Geophysics	100.	56	Limnol. Oceanogr.
35.	324	Quart. J. Roy. Meteorol. Soc.	101.	56	Norsk Geol. Tskr.
36.	320	Astron. Zh.	102.	56	Opt. Spectrosc. USSR
37.	308	J. Fluid Mech.	103.	56	Rep. Ionosph. Space Res.
38.	288	New Zealand J. Geol. Geophys.	104.	56	Soc. Petrol. Eng. J.
39.	280	Canad. J. Earth Sci.	105.	52	Clays Clay Minerals
40.	272	J. Marine Res.	106.	52	Mining Mag.
41.	268	Mineralogical Mag.	107.	48	Z. Petrol. Technol.
42.	268	Rev. Geophys. Space Phys.	108.	48	Trans. Faraday Soc.
43.	244	Hydrocarbon Processing	109.	44	J. Acoust. Soc. Amer.
44.	236	Doklady Akad. Nauk SSSR	110.	44	Philippine Geologist
45.	236	Geomagnetizm Aeronomiya	111.	44	Publ. Astron. Soc. Pacific
46.	220	Astronomical J.	112.	44	Rev. Mod. Phys.
47.	208	Contr. Miner. Petrol.	113.	40	Australian J. Physics
48.	208	Space Sci. Rev.	114.	40	B. Marine Sci.
49.	192	Quart. J. Geol. Soc. London	115.	40	Fuel
50.	188	Appl. Optics	116.	40	Geol. Assoc. Proc.
51.	184	Mon. Not. Roy. Astr. Soc.	117.	40	Mineralium Deposita
52.	184	Radioscience	118.	36	B. Volcanol.
53.	180	J. Appl. Phys.	119.	36	Comm. Lunar Planet.
54.	180	J. Opt. Soc. Amer.	120.	36	Res. Geochem.
55.	176	Marine Geology	121.	32	Chem. Geol.
56.	176	Phil. Trans. Roy. Soc. Lond.	122.	32	J. Quant. Spectrosc.
57.	176	Phys. Fluids	123.	32	Meteor. Z.
58.	172	Sov. Soil Sci.	124.	32	Plant & Soil
59.	172	J. Soil Sci.	125.	28	Australian J. Soil Res.
60.	168	Izv. Akad. Nauk. SSSR	126.	28	B. Can. Petrol. Geol.
61.	164	Mon. Weather Rev.	127.	28	Geol. J.
62.	164	Phys. Rev. Lett.	128.	28	Int. Geol. Rev.
63.	160	J. Phys. Chem.	129.	28	J. Mol. Spectroscopy
64.	148	Carnegie Inst. Yb.	130.	28	Meteor. Monogr.
65.	144	Geol. Mag.	131.	24	Proc. Nat. Acad. Sci. USA
66.	140	B. Earthquake Res. I.T.	132.	24	Publ. Astron. Soc. Japan

Figure 9.31 Highly cited journals in geology and geophysics.

The study demonstrated that citation analysis is as effective a tool for defining the journal literature of a small field as it is for defining the literature of a large one.

Journal of Geophysical Research (18)

A citation analysis of the *Journal of Geophysical Research* (*JGR*), which turned out to be the most frequently cited journal in the geological and geophysical literature, uncovered some interesting cited/citing relationships and demonstrated the role that general-science journals, such as *Science* and *Nature*, play in some specialties. Figure 9.32 shows the 25 journals that cited *JGR* most often. The 25 that it cited the most often are shown in Figure 9.33.

The 25 that cited *JGR* most often accounted for 80% of all the citations it received. In all, *JGR* was cited by 194 source journals, of which it was the most important. Its self-cited rate (percentage of citations received that originated in articles published by itself) was 25%.

The 25 journals that *JGR* cited most often accounted for only 30% of its

	Times Citing	Journal Title
1.	3636	J. Geophys. Res.
2.	1400	Radio Science
3.	604	Space Sci. Rev.
4.	516	Earth Planet. Sci. Lett.
5.	504	Science
6.	496	Planet. Space Sci.
7.	484	Nature
8.	432	Rev. Geophys. Space Phys.
9.	372	Geophys. J. Roy. Astr. Soc.
10.	332	Ann. Geophysique
11.	316	B. Seismol. Soc. Amer.
12.	284	Geol. Soc. Amer. Bull.
13.	220	J. Atmosph. Terr. Phys.
14.	216	Solar Physics
15.	208	Geochim. Cosmochim. Acta
16.	176	J. Atmosph. Sci.
17.	172	Earth Sci. Rev.
18.	144	Rep. Ionosph. Space Res. Japan
19.	140	Aerospace Med.
20.	124	Canad. J. Physics
21.	120	Astrophys. J.
22.	120	Izv. Akad. Nauk SSSR Ser. Fiz.
23.	120	J. Plasma Phys.
24.	116	Canad. J. Earth Sci.
25.	112	Trans. Amer. Geophys. Union
	2920	All Other (169 Journals)
	14284	Total

Figure 9.32 Major sources of references to *Journal of Geophysical Research*.

references to other publications. In all, it cited 323 other publications, though some of them were books, reports, theses, and other nonjournal material. Interestingly enough, the number of references that cited its own material amounted to only 14% of the number it published; so its self-citing rate was considerably lower than its self-cited rate.

The importance of *Science* and *Nature* in the research continuum that stretches from geology to astrogeophysics was demonstrated by the fact that both of them ranked among the top five journals cited by *JGR* and among the top seven sources of citations to *JGR*. The latter point shows the strong geophysical orientation of the two multidisciplinary journals. Undoubtedly, the review quality of many of the articles published in *Science* and *Nature* account, to a significant extent, for the frequency with which *JGR* cited them.

	Times Cited	Journal Title
1.	3636	J. Geophys. Res
2.	380	Science
3.	356	Planet. Space Sci.
4.	284	Trans. Amer. Geophys. Union
5.	276	Nature
6.	268	Bull. Seismol. Soc. Amer.
7.	232	Geochim. Cosmochim. Acta
8.	212	Canad. J. Physics
9.	184	Astrophys. J.
10.	172	Phys. Rev.
11.	168	J. Atmosph. Terr. Phys.
12.	140	Proc. Roy. Soc. London
13.	128	Geol. Soc. Amer. Bull.
14.	124	Phys. Fluids
15.	116	J. Atmosph. Sci.
16.	112	Rev. Geophys. Space Phys.
17.	104	Geophys. J. Roy. Astr. Soc.
18.	104	Tellus
19.	100	J. Chem. Phys.
20.	96	J. Appl. Phys.
21.	92	Ann. Geophysique
22.	76	Quart. J. Roy. Meteorol. Soc.
23.	72	Bull. Earthquake Res. I. T.
24.	72	Deep-Sea Res.
25.	72	Phys. Rev. Lett.
	17468	All Other (298 Journals)
	25044	Total

(continued)

Figure 9.33 Journals cited most frequently by *Journal of Geophysical Research*.

Acta Crystallographica (19)

A letter from Professor Werner Baur, of the University of Illinois at Chicago, led to a study of *Acta Crystallographica* (*Acta Crystallogr.*). The letter pointed out that a

1972 list published by ISI of the 100 most cited chemical papers included 19 on the subject of crystallography, and that 15 of the 19 had been published in (*Acta Crystallogr.*), led to a study of that journal.

The 25 journals most often cited by *Acta Crystallogr.* are shown in Figure 9.34, while the 25 that cited *Acta Crystallogr.* most often are shown in Figure 9.35.

The top 25 journals cited by *Acta Crystallogr.* accounted for about 64% of its references. Significantly, the top six journals, by themselves, accounted for 50% of its references. This narrow citing pattern is dominated by a high degree of self-citation, with *Acta Crystallogr.* showing a self-citing rate of 36%. Overall, *Acta Crystallogr.*'s 7752 references in 1969 cited 440 different publications, mainly journals, but also books, theses, reports, and other nonjournal material.

The list of the 25 journals that cited *Acta Crystallogr.* most often showed that it was cited half again as often as it cited other publications: 11,588 versus 7751. The 11,588 citations came from approximately 280 journals, with the top seven journals accounting for half the total. *Nature* ranks only twenty-second as a source of citations, just below *Sov. Phys. Crystallogr. USSR. Science,* which ranked fourteenth

RANK	Times Cited 1969**	Cumulative Percent of Citations	Journal
1.	2788	36.0	*Acta Crystallogr.
2.	320	40.1	*J. Chem. Soc.
3.	316	44.2	*J. Amer. Chem. Soc.
4.	236	47.2	*J. Chem. Phys.
5.	140	49.0	*Nature
6.	112	50.5	*Z. Kristallogr.
7.	108	51.9	Proc. Roy. Soc. London
8.	96	53.1	*Acta Chem. Scand.
9.	96	54.3	*Inorg. Chem.
10.	96	55.6	Ricerca Scientifica
11.	92	56.8	*J. Molec. Biol.
12.	56	57.5	*Phys. Rev.
13.	56	58.2	Comp. Meth. Phys.
14.	52	58.9	Science
15.	44	59.4	*B. Chem. Soc. Japan
16.	40	60.0	Ark. Kemi
17.	36	60.4	J. Phys. Chem. Solids
18.	36	60.9	J. Phys. Chem.
19.	32	61.3	J. Inorg. Nucl. Chem.
20.	32	61.7	*Phys. Stat. Solidi
21.	32	62.1	*J. Phys. Soc. Japan
22.	32	62.5	Tetrahedron
23.	28	62.9	*J. Appl. Phys.
24.	28	63.3	Angew. Chem.
25.	28	63.5	Physica
	4932	63.6	Total of above 25 journals
	2820	36.4	Citations to 416 other items
	7752	100.0	Total citations

**Figures are an annual extrapolation from a quarterly sample.

Figure 9.34 Journals cited most frequently by *Acta Crystallographica*. Those marked with an asterisk also are major sources of references to *Acta Crystallographica*.

among the journals cited by *Acta Crystallogr.*, did not rank at all among the top 25 sources of citations to *Acta Crystallogr.*, which indicates that its role in the literature of crystallography is minimal.

Fourteen journals are common to the two lists, with the *J. Chem. Soc., Inorg. Chem., Acta Chem. Scand., J. Amer. Chem. Soc., J. Chem. Phys., Z. Kristallogr.*, and *J. Molec. Biol.* being especially noteworthy because of their high rankings on both lists. To anyone unfamiliar with molecular biology, the prominence of *J. Molec. Biol.* in the literature of crystallography would be totally unexpected.

RANK	Times Citing 1969**	Cumulative Percent of Citations	Journal
1.	2788	24.1	*Acta Crystallogr.
2.	756	30.6	*J. Chem. Soc.
3.	596	35.7	*Inorg. Chem.
4.	532	40.3	*Acta Chem. Scand.
5.	388	43.7	*J. Amer. Chem. Soc.
6.	372	46.9	Annu. Rep. Progr. Chem. B
7.	364	50.0	*J. Chem. Phys.
8.	260	52.3	*Z. Kristallogr.
9.	192	53.9	Z. Naturforsch. B.
10.	180	55.5	*J. Molec. Biol.
11.	172	57.0	*J. Appl. Phys.
12.	164	58.4	*Phys. Stat. Solidi
13.	144	59.6	B. Soc. Chim. France
14.	140	60.8	Z. Anorg. Allg. Chem.
15.	120	61.9	Helv. Chim. Acta
16.	120	62.9	*Phys. Rev.
17.	116	63.9	Canad. J. Chem.
18.	112	64.9	J. Less-Common Met.
19.	96	65.7	*J. Phys. Soc. Japan
20.	96	66.5	Proc. Nat. Acad. Sci. USA
21.	96	67.3	Sov. Phys. Crystallogr. USSR
22.	92	68.1	*Nature
23.	84	68.9	*B. Chem. Soc. Japan
24.	76	69.5	J. Appl. Crystallogr.
25.	76	70.2	Rec. Trav. Chim.
	8132	70.2	Total of above 25 journals
	3456	29.8	Citations from 264 other items
	11588	100.0	Total citations

**Figures are an annual extrapolation from a quarterly sample.

Figure 9.35 Major sources of references to *Acta Crystallographica*. Those marked with an asterisk also are among those cited most frequently by *Acta Crystallographica*.

Physics (20)

A study of the physics literature, inspired by Inhaber's ranking of the 24 top physics journals by citation rate, impact factor, and immediacy index (21), showed that the physics journals that are most frequently cited by physicists are considerably different from those most frequently cited by the scientific community at large.

Two types of analysis were used in the study. The first consisted of compiling the

	Journal	'Physical' Citations A	Self- Citations B	Self- Citation Rate (B/A)	Total Citations D	'Physical' Citation Rate (A/D)	Number of Physics Journals Citing	Impact Factor
1.	Phys. Rev.	74224	17808	24.0	82664	89.8	113	3.679
2.	J. Chem. Phys.	27256	14396	52.8	54748	49.8	87	3.180
3.	Phys. Rev. Lett.	23792	2432	10.2	26176	90.9	77	5.114
4.	Nucl. Phys.	15544	6012	38.7	16044	96.8	46	0.858
5.	Sov. Phys. JETP	15196	4564	30.0	16852	90.2	63	3.944
6.	Phys. Lett.	14320	1568	10.9	15740	91.0	57	1.654
7.	J. Appl. Phys.	12828	3364	26.2	21096	60.8	81	1.936
8.	Sov. Phys. Sol. St.	9612	4456	46.4	10420	92.2	38	2.046
9.	Nuovo Cimento	8692	1848	21.3	9768	89.0	42	0.527
10.	P. Roy. Soc. Lond.	7228	412	5.7	19156	37.7	91	2.998
11.	J. Physics	7196	1532	21.2	12724	56.6	68	1.405
12.	Zschr. Physik	5556	760	13.7	7036	79.0	74	1.536
13.	J. Phys. Soc. Japan	5236	1308	25.0	6932	75.5	58	1.045
*14.	J. Amer. Chem. Soc.	5044	—	—	105228	4.8	40	5.859
15.	Acta Cryst.	4748	2788	58.7	11588	41.0	34	2.469
16.	Philosophical Mag.	4616	644	14.0	7696	60.0	63	2.251
17.	Rev. Mod. Phys.	4232	20	0.5	5412	78.2	65	4.508
18.	J. Phys. Chem. Sol.	4092	276	6.7	5676	72.1	47	2.073
19.	Phys. Stat. Sol.	4056	1960	48.3	5252	77.2	39	1.578
20.	Comptes Rendus	3928	1752	44.6	21888	17.9	49	0.780
21.	Phys. Fluids	3556	1224	34.4	5176	68.7	33	1.581
22.	Ann Physics	3368	144	4.3	4384	76.8	56	3.188
23.	Canad. J. Phys.	3312	596	18.0	5292	62.6	54	2.186
*24.	J. Phys. Chem.	3240	—	—	18712	17.3	32	2.429
25.	Opt. Spectr. USSR	3096	1832	59.2	4200	73.7	25	1.331
26.	Appl. Phys. Lett	3092	576	18.6	5272	58.6	34	3.688
27.	J. Math. Phys.	3056	876	28.7	3792	80.5	42	0.492
28.	B. Amer. Phys. Soc.	3016	324	10.7	3532	85.4	34	0.156
29.	Physica	3016	552	18.3	3796	79.5	53	1.755
30.	Prog. Theor. Phys.	2956	1312	44.4	3348	88.3	31	1.513
31.	T. Faraday Soc.	2908	1056	36.3	11644	25.0	30	2.149
32.	Nucl. Instr. Meth.	2752	1468	53.3	3276	84.0	29	1.016
33.	JETP Lett.	2748	920	33.5	3024	90.9	22	2.240
34.	Sov. Phys. Tech. Phys.	2728	1524	55.9	3648	74.8	26	1.322
35.	Sov. J. Nucl. Phys.	2712	1852	68.3	2936	92.4	14	2.054
*36.	J. Chem. Soc.	2516	—	—	55912	4.5	24	3.123
37.	J. Opt. Soc. Amer.	2464	1016	41.2	6316	39.0	35	0.962
*38.	Nature	2452	—	—	61240	4.0	66	2.244
39.	Zschr. Naturforsch.	2452	1228	50.1	8716	28.1	47	1.433
*40.	Astrophys. J.	2260	—	—	17032	13.3	28	4.972
*41.	Dokl. Akad. Nauk USSR	2068	—	—	12404	16.7	42	0.572
*42.	Rev. Sci. Instr.	1928	—	—	4892	39.4	39	0.868
*43.	Acta Metallurg.	1804	—	—	5216	26.9	24	2.278
44.	Nucl. Sci. Eng.	1784	660	37.0	1940	92.0	15	1.290
45.	Sov. Phys. Usp.	1716	412	24.0	2536	67.7	19	4.930
46.	J. Fluid Mech.	1612	972	60.3	3848	41.9	20	2.376
47.	J. Polym. Sci.	1528	1016	66.5	11572	13.2	7	1.039
48.	Sov. Phys. Semicond.	1436	1012	70.5	1548	92.8	13	1.741
49.	Izv. Akad Nauk Fiz.	1404	560	39.9	1800	78.0	17	0.807
50.	J. Inorg. Nucl. Chem.	1380	836	60.6	5540	24.9	17	1.535

Figure 9.36 Fifty journals cited most frequently by 188 physics journals. Those not marked with an asterisk are one of the 188.

50 journals cited most often by the 188 journals listed in the 1969 *SCI* in the categories of *physics* and *nuclear science and technology*. The results are shown in Figure 9.36. Except for the big three of *Physical Review, Journal of Chemical Physics,* and *Physical Review Letters,* the ranking of the journals on this list differed considerably from the lists developed by Inhaber from a data base of multidisciplinary sources. The list also includes eight journals not categorized as physics journals in the *SCI*.

The second analytical approach used was to rank the top 50 physics journals by the percent of total citations accounted for by references from the 188 physics journals used as the source data base. The results of that analysis are shown in Figure 9.37. One of the interesting features of this list was the identification of a number of journals that do not contain the words "physics" or "nuclear" in their title, and that probably would not be classified as physics journals in one or another of the compendiums of scientific journals but that were an important part of the physics literature to the extent that more than 50% of the citations they received came from physics journals.

An interesting feature of both lists is that Soviet physics journals ranked high on them. Another characteristic of both lists demonstrates the danger of treating citation data as an absolute measure of quality. Chen reported (22) that *Physics Today, Science,* and *Nature* ranked among the 13 journals most "important" to physicists. Neither list contained *Physics Today*. *Nature* did appear on the first list (Figure 9.36), but ranked only thirty-eighth, compared with Chen's ranking of thirteenth. It did not appear on the second list (Figure 9.37) at all. *Science* did not show up on either list, though it would have ranked among the second 50 most cited journals if we had extended the first list to the top 100. The words "importance" and "quality" are multifaceted words, and citation data measures only one of their facets.

Cancer Research (23)

A study of 16 cancer journals provided hard data to support the position that applied research in the area of cancer depends heavily on basic, noncancer research. The data came from a citation analysis of a list of core cancer journals suggested by the National Cancer Institute:
- *Bulletin du Cancer*
- *British Journal of Cancer*
- *British Journal of Experimental Pathology*
- *Cancer Chemotherapy Reports*
- *Cancer*
- *Cancer Research*
- *European Journal of Cancer*
- *Gann*
- *International Journal of Cancer*
- *Journal of the National Cancer Institute*
- *National Cancer Institute Monograph*
- *Neoplasma*

	Journal	'Physical' Citations A	Self- Citations B	Self- Citation Rate (B/A)	Total Citations D	'Physical' Citation Rate (A/D)	Number of Physics Journals Citing	Impact Factor
1.	Nucl. Phys (4)	15544	6012	38.7	16044	96.8	46	0.858
2.	Sov. Phys. Semicond. (48)	1436	1012	70.5	1548	92.8	13	1.741
3.	T. Amer. Nucl. Soc. (56)	1168	884	75.7	1260	92.7	9	0.388
4.	Sov. J. Nucl. Phys. (35)	2712	1852	68.3	2936	92.4	14	2.054
5.	Sov. Phys. Sol. St. (8)	9612	4456	46.4	10420	92.2	38	2.046
6.	Nucl. Sci. Eng. (44)	1784	660	37.0	1940	92.0	15	1.290
7.	Phys. Lett. (6)	14320	1568	10.9	15740	91.0	57	1.654
8.	Phys. Rev. Lett. (3)	23792	2432	10.2	26176	90.9	77	5.114
9.	JETP Lett. (33)	2748	920	33.5	3024	90.9	22	2.240
10.	Sov. Phys. JETP (5)	15196	4564	30.0	16852	90.2	63	3.944
11.	Phys. Rev. (1)	74224	17808	24.0	82664	89.8	113	3.679
12.	Nuovo Cimento (9)	8692	1848	21.3	9768	89.0	42	0.527
13.	Prog. Theor. Phys. (30)	2956	1312	44.4	3348	88.3	31	1.513
14.	B. Amer. Phys. Soc. (28)	3016	324	10.7	3532	85.4	34	0.156
15.	Nucl. Instr. Meth. (32)	2752	1468	53.3	3276	84.0	29	1.016
16.	J. Math. Phys. (27)	3056	876	28.7	3792	80.5	42	0.492
17.	Phys. Kondens. Mater. (101)	348	128	36.8	436	79.8	8	2.580
18.	Sol. St. Comm. (55)	1168	264	22.6	1468	79.6	20	1.189
19.	Physica (29)	3016	552	18.3	3796	79.5	53	1.755
20.	Zschr. Physik (12)	5556	760	13.7	7036	79.0	74	1.536
21.	Rev. Mod. Phys. (17)	4232	20	0.5	5412	78.2	65	4.508
22.	Izv. Akad. Nauk. Fiz (49)	1404	560	39.9	1800	78.0	17	0.807
23.	Ann. Rev. Nucl. Sci. (91)	480	116	24.2	616	77.9	12	5.629
24.	Phys. Stat. Sol. (19)	4056	1960	48.3	5252	77.2	39	1.578
25.	Ann. Physics (22)	3368	144	4.3	4384	76.8	56	3.188
26.	Helv. Phys. Acta (65)	932	40	4.3	1216	76.6	31	0.559
27.	J. Phys. Soc. Japan (13)	5236	1308	25.0	6932	75.5	58	1.045
28.	Sov. Phys. Tech. Phys. (34)	2728	1524	55.9	3648	74.8	26	1.322
29.	Opt. Spectr USSR (25)	3096	1832	59.2	4200	73.7	25	1.331
30.	IEEE T. Nucl. Sci. (73)	736	256	34.8	1016	72.4	9	0.722
31.	J. Phys. Chem. Sol. (18)	4092	276	6.7	5676	72.1	47	2.073
32.	Sol. St. Phys. (64)	992	—	—	1388	71.5	24	16.285
33.	Ark. Fiz. (53)	1172	384	32.7	1660	70.6	19	0.993
34.	Surface Sci. (61)	1104	584	52.9	1592	69.3	16	2.982
35.	J. Nucl. Mater. (66)	908	536	59.0	1312	69.2	8	1.398
36.	Phys. Fluids (21)	3556	1224	34.4	5176	68.7	33	1.581
37.	Sov. Phys. USP (45)	1716	412	24.0	2536	67.7	19	4.930
38.	Adv. Phys. (70)	786	0	—	1168	67.3	9	3.857
39.	Phys. Metal. Met. USSR (51)	1236	640	51.8	1912	64.6	13	0.872
40.	Canad. J. Phys. (23)	3312	596	18.0	5292	62.6	54	2.186
41.	J. Appl. Phys. (7)	12828	3364	26.2	21096	60.8	81	1.936
42.	Comm. Math. Phys. (97)	448	344	76.8	744	60.2	10	7.593
43.	Philosophical Mag. (16)	4616	644	14.0	7696	60.0	63	2.251
44.	Sov. Phys. Cryst. (60)	1108	588	53.1	1872	59.2	14	1.339
45.	Appl. Phys. Lett (26)	3092	576	18.6	5272	58.6	34	3.688
46.	J. Physics (11)	7196	1532	21.2	12724	56.6	68	1.405
47.	Zschr. Angew. Phys. (75)	716	256	35.8	1276	56.1	12	0.817
48.	Amer. J. Phys. (96)	452	276	61.1	840	53.8	8	0.298
49.	IEEE J. Quant. Elect. (80)	664	244	36.7	1284	51.7	12	1.303
50.	J. Physique (74)	724	184	25.4	1412	51.3	19	0.391

Figure 9.37 Fifty journals ranked by ratio of citations received from 188 physics journals to citations received from all sources. Numbers in parentheses following the journal titles show ranking in Figure 9.36.

- *Proceedings of the American Association for Cancer Research*
- *Progress in Experimental Tumor Research*
- *Tumori*
- *Zeitschrift fur Krebsforschung*

The analysis consisted of compiling lists of the 50 journals cited most frequently by this core group (Figure 9.38), and the 50 journals that are the major sources of citations to the core group (Figure 9.39). The lists show the following for each journal:

1. Total citations to or from all scientific journals.
2. Citations to or from the core group of cancer journals ("Cancer Citations").
3. Cancer citations as a percent of total citations.
4. Impact factor based on total citations.
5. Impact factor based only on cancer citations ("Cancer Impact").
6. Ratio between total impact and cancer impact.

This last figure is a particularly revealing one because it is a measure of the strength of a journal's cancer orientation. For example, *Neoplasma* in Figure 9.38 was cited only 192 times, which gave it a total impact factor of 0.638. However, 124 of the references that cited it came from the core cancer journals, so its cancer impact was 0.555. The ratio of the two impact figures is 87.0, which is an indication of a very strong cancer orientation. In contrast, the *British Journal of Experimental Pathology* was cited a total of 2420 times, but only 184 times by the cancer journals. While its general impact was 1.476, its cancer impact was only 0.134, and the ratio between the two was only 9.1. When compared with the impact ratios of the other core journals or even some of the journals outside the core (the *Journal of Invertebrate Pathology*, for example, had an impact ratio of 21.1), it is hard to see why it was included on the list of core cancer journals.

The listing of journals that cited the cancer journals (Figure 9.39) shows the core group bunched near the top, indicating a lot of interaction between them. The listing of journals cited by the core group (Figure 9.38), however, shows quite a different story. The core group was cited no more frequently than the basic research journals. As a matter of fact, the citation statistics show they were cited less frequently. Fifty-eight percent of the references in the core group cited basic-research journals.

Another fact underlined by the two lists is that the cancer literature is dominated by three journals: *Cancer, Cancer Research,* and the *Journal of the National Cancer Institute*.

Botany (24)

A study of the botany literature produced the lists shown in Figures 9.40 and 9.41 of the journals that cited and were cited by a core group of botany journals most often. The core group that formed the data base for the analysis was somewhat arbitrary, consisting of the journals categorized as botany journals in the 1969 *SCI*, but not the journals in related subject categories, such as agriculture, agronomy, and ecology.

Figure 9.40 shows the journals that cited the core group most frequently. Of the approximately 14,500 citations received by the core group, 68% came from these 50 journals. *Annual Review of Phytopathology,* and *Botanical Review* ranked second

	Journal	Total Citations (A)	Cancer Citations (B)	(B/A)	Overall Impact (C)	Cancer Impact (D)	Impact Ratio (D/C) x 100
*1.	*Cancer Res.*	9772	3372	34.5	3.084	1.105	35.9
*2.	*J. Nat. Cancer Inst.*	6604	2752	41.7	4.400	2.105	47.8
*3.	*Cancer*	5656	1488	26.3	2.162	0.594	27.4
*4.	Nature	61240	1380	2.3	2.244	0.050	2.2
*5.	P. Soc. Exp. Biol. Med.	20044	868	4.3	1.964	0.118	6.1
*6.	Science	38956	836	2.2	2.894	0.048	1.7
*7.	*Brit. J. Cancer*	1860	804	43.2	1.670	0.722	43.2
*8.	J. Biol. Chem.	68012	796	1.2	6.371	0.054	0.8
*9.	Ann. New York Acad. Sci.	15024	620	4.1	1.815	0.003	0.2
*10.	Lancet	30448	600	2.0	1.509	0.001	0.1
*11.	J. Amer. Med. Assoc.	17952	584	3.3	1.027	0.041	4.0
12.	J. Exp. Med.	15432	528	3.4	9.030	0.227	2.5
13.	P. Nat. Acad. Sci. USA	32824	516	1.6	1.308	0.095	7.2
14.	J. Cell Biol.	19076	480	2.5	3.484	0.076	2.2
*15.	New Engl. J. Med.	18096	456	2.5	2.453	0.069	2.8
*16.	Amer. J. Pathol.	5740	432	7.5	1.916	0.152	7.9
*17.	*Internat. J. Cancer*	1088	428	39.3	2.533	1.062	41.9
18.	Virology	9492	388	4.1	4.720	0.195	4.1
*19.	Surg. Gyn. Obst.	5468	376	6.9	1.578	0.087	5.5
20.	J. Med. Microbiol.	3952	372	9.4	20.000	1.600	8.0
*21.	*Nat. Cancer Inst. Mon.*	576	372	64.6	0.738	1.235	169.2
*22.	Biochim. Biophys. Acta	38000	368	1.0	3.287	0.029	0.9
*23.	Fed. Proc.	13364	364	2.7	0.568	0.135	2.4
*24.	Exp. Cell. Res.	7528	348	4.6	2.273	0.081	3.6
25.	Biochem. J.	30500	292	1.0	3.193	0.030	0.9
*26.	*Gann*	620	292	47.1	0.874	0.318	36.4
27.	Blood	6444	288	4.5	2.867	0.138	4.8
28.	P. Amer. Assoc. Cancer Res.	864	288	33.3	0.421	0.174	41.3
29.	Brit. Med. J.	17156	284	1.7	0.778	0.006	0.7
30.	Lab. Invest.	3668	272	7.4	2.008	0.130	6.5
31.	Ann. Surg.	6504	264	4.1	1.665	0.077	4.6
*32.	*Zschr. Krebsforschung*	664	256	38.6	1.212	0.394	32.5
*33.	Arch. Pathol.	4496	248	5.5	1.509	0.055	3.7
34.	Amer. J. Med.	8752	216	2.5	4.694	0.158	3.4
35.	Comptes Rendus.	21888	196	0.9	0.780	0.007	1.0
*36.	*Brit. J. Exp. Pathol.*	2420	184	7.6	1.476	0.134	9.1
*37.	J. Immunology	10492	180	1.7	4.305	0.109	2.5
38.	Amer. J. Roentgenol.	4976	160	3.2	1.257	0.024	1.9
39.	J. Amer. Vet. Med. Ass.	1924	156	8.1	0.488	0.038	8.5
*40.	*Eur. J. Cancer*	420	148	75.7	2.027	1.609	79.4
*41.	Transplantation	2036	144	7.1	3.164	0.228	7.2
*42.	*Cancer Chemother. Rep.*	796	140	17.6	1.206	0.229	19.0
*43.	Radiology	4700	140	3.0	1.533	0.035	2.3
*44.	Brit. J. Surg.	2356	136	5.8	0.506	0.005	0.9
45.	J. Histochem. Cytochem.	4892	136	2.8	2.442	0.012	0.3
46.	Ann. Internal Med.	7728	132	1.7	1.640	0.021	1.4
47.	Anat. Rec.	5416	124	2.3	0.423	0.002	0.1
*48.	J. Clin. Invest.	19116	124	0.6	3.461	0.004	0.1
49.	J. Invert. Pathol.	924	124	13.4	1.194	0.252	21.1
*50.	*Neoplasma*	192	124	64.5	0.638	0.555	87.0
*86.	*Prog. Exp. Tumor Res.*	192	88	45.8	2.400	1.067	44.4
*87.	*B. Cancer*	228	88	38.5	0.413	0.310	75.1
*113.	*Tumori*	124	44	35.5	0.238	0.119	50.2

Figure 9.38 Journals cited most frequently by 16 cancer journals. Italicized titles identify the 16 cancer journals. Asterisks identify journals that are also major sources of references to the 16 cancer journals.

	Journal	Total Citations (A)	Cancer Citations (B)	(B/A)	Impact Factor	Self-Citing Rate	Self-Cited Rate
*1.	J. Nat. Cancer Inst.	7004	2016	28.8	4.400	37.9	51.8
*2.	Cancer Res.	7056	1884	26.7	3.084	33.5	55.9
*3.	Nat. Cancer Inst. Mon.	10208	1636	16.0	2.673	48.6	17.1
*4.	Cancer	7484	1480	29.8	2.162	57.3	57.6
*5.	Eur. J. Cancer	2804	752	26.8	2.027	75.7	14.9
6.	Sem. Hematol.	1472	732	49.7	3.916		
*7.	Progr. Exp. Tumor Res.	2708	724	26.7	2.400	45.8	2.8
*8.	Proc. Soc. Exp. Biol. Med.	19604	656	3.3	1.964		
*9.	Ann. New York Acad. Sci.	41844	600	10.3	1.815		
*10.	Brit. J. Cancer	1820	520	28.6	1.670	21.4	41.3
*11.	Internat. J. Cancer	1204	416	34.5	2.533	29.0	29.8
*12.	Fed. Proc.	6712	412	6.1	0.568		
*13.	Neoplasma	2248	404	18.0	0.638	100.0	30.7
*14.	Gann	1420	392	27.6	0.874	41.1	30.6
*15.	Exp. Cell Res.	7756	364	4.7	2.273		
16.	Acta Path. Scand.	6940	320	4.6	1.009		
*17.	Lancet	17636	308	1.7	1.509		
18.	Amer. J. Surg.	7496	304	4.1	0.992		
19.	Acta Cytol.	2292	276	12.0	1.046		
20.	Arch. Geschw.	1296	276	21.3	0.500		
21.	Molec. Pharmacol.	2656	264	9.9	4.028		
*22.	J. Immunol.	12084	248	2.1	4.305		
*23.	Zschr. Krebsforschung	1256	248	19.7	1.212	34.3	35.5
*24.	Transplantation	5068	240	4.7	3.164		
*25.	Biochim. Biophys. Acta	41076	232	0.6	3.287		
*26.	Brit. J. Exp. Pathol.	2168	220	10.1	1.476	93.5	78.2
*27.	Nature	27108	204	0.8	2.244		
*28.	New Engl. J. Med.	14064	204	1.5	2.453		
*29.	Science	22796	204	3.5	2.894		
*30.	Arch. Pathol.	3576	180	5.0	1.509		
*31.	Cancer Chemother. Rep.	380	176	46.3	1.206	74.3	59.1
*32.	J. Biol. Chem.	34636	168	0.5	6.371		
33.	Path. Biol.	4308	160	3.7	0.722		
34.	Virch. Arch. B.	2628	156	5.9	1.066		
*35.	Brit. J. Surg.	2692	152	5.6	0.506		
36.	Rev. Fr. Clin.	2132	152	7.1			
37.	J. Pathology	4404	144	3.6	0.037		
38.	Exp. Mol. Path.	2204	140	6.4	1.948		
39.	Acta Med. Oka.	2580	128	5.0	1.400		
40.	J. Neurosurg.	4576	128	2.8	1.320		
41.	Klin. Wschr.	9844	128	1.3	0.723		
*42.	Radiology	8444	120	1.4	1.533		
*43.	J. Amer. Med. Assoc.	8266	116	1.4	1.027		
*44.	Amer. J. Pathol.	3716	112	3.0	1.916		
*45.	Surg. Gyn. Obst.	3680	104	2.8	1.578		
46.	Amer. J. Clin. Path.	3384	100	3.0	0.623		
47.	Deut. Med. Wschr.	16052	100	0.6	0.675		
*48.	J. Clin. Invest.	9160	100	1.1	3.461		
49.	Amer. J. Obst. Gyn.	10948	96	0.9	1.269		
50.	Med. J. Australia	6396	96	1.5	0.501		
*101.	B. Cancer	936	76	8.1	0.413	38.5	
*123.	Tumori	284	32	11.3	0.238	35.5	37.5

Figure 9.39 Major sources of references to 16 cancer journals. Italicized titles identify most of the 16 cancer journals. Asterisks identify journals that are also frequently cited by the 16 cancer journals.

and seventh, respectively, despite very low self-citation rates. The appearance of only one genetics journal—*Theoretical and Applied Genetics, #33*—seemed somewhat surprising.

The journals cited most frequently by the core group are shown in Figure 9.41. Of the approximately 17,700 references published by the core group, 59% of them cited

	Journal	A	B	C	D	E	F	G
1.	Phytopathology	2830	1399	822	49.4	29.1	58.8	1.078
2.	Annu. Rev. Phytopath.	2181	740	30	33.9	1.4	4.1	4.914
3.	Planta	1085	460	123	42.4	11.3	26.7	2.944
4.	Plant Physiology	960	369	200	38.4	20.8	54.2	1.683
5.	Plant Cell Physiol.	820	318	75	38.8	9.2	23.6	1.785
6.	Canad. J. Botany	768	312	62	40.6	8.1	19.9	1.217
7.	Botan. Rev.	772	260	6	33.7	0.8	2.3	3.818
8.	Phytochemistry	1473	258	153	17.5	10.4	59.3	1.907
9.	J. Am. Soc. Hort. Sci.	755	256	175	33.9	23.2	68.4	0.392
10.	Weed Sci.	564	255	171	45.2	30.3	67.1	1.568
11.	Amer. J. Botany	590	226	73	38.3	12.4	32.3	0.956
12.	Comptes Rendus D	3784	220	–	5.8	–	–	0.780
13.	Ecology	991	215	118	21.6	11.9	55.3	1.256
14.	Mycopath. Mycol. Appl.	2831	214	80	7.6	2.8	37.4	0.346
15.	T. Brit. Mycol. Soc.	549	212	73	38.6	13.3	34.4	0.830
16.	New Phytologist	579	210	54	36.3	9.3	25.7	1.382
17.	Agron. J.	1008	196	–	19.4	–	–	0.947
18.	J. Exp. Botany	434	191	63	44.0	14.5	33.0	2.400
19.	Physiol. Plantarum	486	185	52	38.1	10.7	28.1	1.796
20.	Protoplasma	965	184	60	19.1	6.2	32.6	2.183
21.	Plant Soil	820	177	52	21.6	6.3	29.4	0.988
22.	Soil Sci. Soc. Am. P.	608	177	112	29.1	18.4	63.3	0.867
23.	Mycologia	444	163	51	36.7	11.5	31.3	0.901
24.	Weed Res.	467	155	28	33.2	6.0	18.1	0.837
25.	Soil Sci.	405	141	61	34.8	15.1	43.3	0.923
26.	Forest Chron.	485	137	29	28.3	6.0	21.2	–
27.	Indian J. Agr. Sci.	959	129	–	13.5	–	–	0.334
28.	Zeit. Pflanzenphysiol.	414	124	24	30.0	5.8	19.4	1.048
29.	Phyton	364	115	12	31.6	3.3	10.4	0.103
30.	Ann. Amelior. Plant.	323	110	11	34.1	3.4	10.0	0.428
31.	Oesterr. Bot. Zschr.	370	110	55	29.7	14.9	50.0	–
32.	Ann. Botany	242	100	30	41.3	12.4	30.0	1.443
33.	Theor. Appl. Gen.	776	100	–	12.9	–	–	–
34.	Ber. Deut. Bot. Ges.	669	99	20	14.8	2.9	20.2	0.519
35.	Acta Bot. Neerl.	372	98	22	26.3	5.9	22.4	0.535
36.	Austr. J. Botany	266	98	24	36.8	9.0	24.5	0.297
37.	Bull. Torrey Bot. Club	366	98	13	26.8	3.6	13.3	0.623
38.	Dokl. Akad. Nauk SSSR	7647	94	–	1.2	–	–	0.572
39.	Crop Sci.	620	93	–	15.0	–	–	0.712
40.	J. Soil Sci.	302	89	27	29.5	8.9	30.3	0.861
41.	Acta Biol. Crac. Bot.	378	88	27	23.3	7.1	30.7	1.411
42.	Austr. J. Biol. Sci.	1245	88	–	7.1	–	–	1.957
43.	Ann. Appl. Biol.	431	87	67	20.2	15.5	77.0	1.386
44.	Bioch. Bioph. Acta	10269	87	–	0.9	–	–	3.287
45.	Arch. Mikrobiol.	1318	83	–	6.3	–	–	2.120
46.	Naturwissenschaften	1574	82	–	5.2	–	–	0.920
47.	Zschr. Pflanzenzucht.	418	80	21	19.1	5.0	26.3	0.271
48.	Qual. Plant. Mat. Veg.	726	74	25	10.2	3.4	33.8	0.115
49.	Biol. Plant.	299	73	29	24.4	9.7	39.7	0.396
50.	Holz. Roh. Werkst.	244	72	51	29.5	20.9	70.8	0.437

Figure 9.40 Major sources of references to botany journals. A = references to all journals. B = references to botany journals. C = references to self. D = ration of botany references to all references. E = ration of self-citations to all references (self-citing rate). F = ratio of self-citations to botany references. G = overall impact.

196 *Citation Indexing*

material in these 50 journals. Many of the highly cited journals are the same ones that appeared on lists generated in analyses of other fields. *Nature* and *Science* ranked fourth and sixth, respectively. *Virology* ranked twenty-ninth. An unexpected, but interesting, entry was *American Review of Respiratory Diseases*. It owes its place on the list solely to *Mycopathologia et Mycologia Applicata,* which cited it

	Journal	A	B	C	D	E	F	G
1.	Phytopathology	1713	1305	822	76.2	48.0	63.0	1.078
2.	Plant Physiology	1639	961	200	58.6	12.2	20.8	1.683
3.	Amer. J. Botany	1171	647	73	55.3	6.2	11.3	0.956
4.	Nature	15310	578	–	3.9	–	–	2.244
5.	Planta	707	384	123	54.3	17.4	32.0	2.944
6.	Science	9739	319	–	3.3	–	–	2.894
7.	J. Biol. Chem.	17103	315	–	1.8	–	–	6.371
8.	Canad. J. Botany	548	292	62	53.3	11.3	21.2	1.217
9.	Bioch. Bioph. Acta	9500	284	–	3.0	–	–	3.287
10.	Physiol. Plantarum	482	269	52	55.8	10.8	19.3	1.796
11.	J. Am. Soc. Hort. Sci.	357	247	175	69.2	49.0	70.9	0.392
12.	Phytochemistry	588	247	153	42.0	26.0	61.9	1.907
13.	Biochem. J.	7625	231	–	3.0	–	–	3.193
14.	Weed Sci.	311	223	171	71.7	55.0	76.7	1.568
15.	Ann. Botany	424	215	30	50.7	7.1	14.0	1.443
16.	Plant Dis. Rep.	286	205	–	71.7	–	–	0.268
17.	J. Exp. Botany	337	200	63	59.4	18.7	31.5	2.400
18.	Ecology	577	193	118	33.5	20.5	61.1	1.256
19.	Bot Gaz.	312	186	9	59.6	2.9	4.8	0.658
20.	P. Nat. Acad. Sci. USA	8206	164	–	2.0	–	–	8.828
21.	New Phytologist	295	159	54	53.9	18.3	34.0	1.382
22.	Annu. Rev. Pl. Phys.	290	154	0	53.1	0.0	0.0	7.047
23.	Mycologia	302	148	51	49.0	16.9	34.5	0.901
24.	J. Bacteriology	4138	146	–	3.5	–	–	3.594
25.	J. Cell Biol.	4769	145	–	3.0	–	–	3.484
26.	Agron. J.	727	143	–	19.7	–	–	0.947
27.	Soil Sci.	629	136	61	21.6	9.7	44.9	0.923
28.	Arch. Bioch. Bioph.	3647	135	–	3.7	–	–	3.519
29.	Virology	2373	124	–	5.2	–	–	4.720
30.	Austr. J. Biol. Sci.	583	116	–	19.9	–	–	1.957
31.	Ann. Appl. Biol.	453	113	67	24.9	14.8	59.3	1.386
32.	Comptes Rendus	5472	110	–	2.0	–	–	0.780
33.	Plant Cell Physiol.	203	108	75	53.2	37.0	69.4	1.785
34.	J. Agr. Res.	267	101	–	37.8	–	–	–
35.	T. Brit. Mycol. Soc.	263	97	73	36.9	27.8	75.3	0.830
36.	Amer. Rev. Resp. Dis.	874	93	–	10.6	–	–	0.834
37.	Crop. Sci.	353	88	–	24.9	–	–	0.712
38.	J. Chem. Soc.	13978	85	–	0.6	–	–	3.123
39.	Protoplasma	299	85	60	28.4	20.1	70.6	2.183
40.	J. Amer. Chem. Soc.	26307	82	–	0.3	–	–	5.859
41.	Mycopath. Mycol. Appl.	120	80	80	66.7	66.7	100.0	0.346
42.	Ber. Deut. Bot. Ges.	175	76	20	43.4	11.4	26.3	0.519
43.	Annu. Rev. Phytopath.	108	74	30	68.5	27.8	40.5	4.914
44.	Bioch. Biophys. Res.	3404	70	–	2.1	–	–	4.468
45.	Plant Soil	202	68	52	33.7	25.7	76.5	0.988
46.	J. Ecology	156	67	–	43.0	–	–	0.421
47.	J. Forestry	150	66	35	44.0	23.3	53.0	0.197
48.	J. Gen. Microbiol.	1438	65	–	4.5	–	–	2.337
49.	Holz. Roh. Werkst.	123	65	51	53.0	41.5	78.5	0.437
50.	Botan. Rev.	160	64	6	40.0	3.8	9.4	3.818

Figure 9.41 Journals cited most frequently by botany journals. A = citations from all journals. B = citations from botany journals. C = self-citations. D = ratio of botany citations to citations from all journals. E = ratio of self-citations to citations from all journals (self-cited rate). F = ratio of self- citations to botany citations. G = overall impact.

frequently. Despite the availability of an English translation of the botanical section of the *Doklady Akademii Nauk USSR,* that journal was not cited frequently enough to appear on the list. It would have ranked in about one hundred thirtieth on an extended list.

Figure 9.42 shows the journals that are common to both lists. They are ranked by botanical impact, which is the citation rate of the average article when only citations from the core journals are considered. The important journal *Botanical Gazette* did not appear on this list only because it did not cite the core journals frequently enough to be included in Figure 9.40.

	Journal	
1.	Annu. Rev. Phytopath.	251.6
2.	Botan. Rev.	182.0
3.	Planta	182.0
4.	J. Exp. Botany	122.8
5.	Weed Sci.	105.6
6.	Physiol. Plantarum	98.4
7.	Plant Cell Physiol.	97.6
8.	Plant Physiology	96.4
9.	Phytopathology	86.8
10.	New Phytologist	85.2
11.	Canad. J. Botany	72.4
12.	Phytochemistry	70.4
13.	Ann. Botany	63.2
14.	Protoplasma	62.0
15.	Amer. J. Botany	53.6
16.	Ecology	52.8
17.	Mycologia	43.6
18.	Austr. J. Biol. Sci.	40.4
19.	J. Am. Soc. Hort. Sci.	39.2
20.	Ann. Appl. Biol.	31.6
21.	Soil Sci.	28.0
22.	Plant Soil	27.6
23.	T. Brit. Mycol. Soc.	27.2
24.	Holz. Roh. Werkst.	26.0
25.	Agron. J.	24.0
26.	Ber. Deut. Bot. Ges	20.4
27.	Mycopath. Mycol. Appl.	16.8
28.	Crop Sci.	13.2
29.	Bioch. Bioph. Acta	10.8
30.	Comptes Rendus	1.2

Figure 9.42 Journals common to both Figure 9.40 and Figure 9.41, ranked by "botanical impact."

Psychology and Behavioral Science (25)

A study of the literature of psychology and behavioral science produced the results shown in Figures 9.43, 9.44, and 9.45. The data base used for this study consisted of the 77 core journals that are listed in the 1969 *SCI* as belonging to the overlapping subject areas but that did not include in their titles the word "psychiatry" or other clinical terms.

Figure 9.43 shows the top 50 sources of citations to the core journals. These journals accounted for 89% of all the citations received by the core journals. Forty-two of these source journals were members of the core group. The eight that were not, but that cited the core group heavily, are identified by italics. One of them was *Science,* which ranked thirty-seventh. Another was the *Annals of the New York Academy of Sciences,* which ranked seventh. Its appearance probably was an accident of the small data sample used (only a quarter of a year). It frequently devotes an entire issue to a single topic, and the citations from such an issue would loom large enough in a small data sample to exaggerate the relationship between the *Annals* and the subject. Unlike *Science, Nature* did not show up on the top 50, but would have ranked about sixty-fifth on a longer list of major citation sources.

The self-citing rate of the core-group journals in Figure 9.43 is interesting when compared to the botany journals in the earlier study. The average self-citing rate for the botany journals was 34%, whereas the average for the psychology journals was only 11%. However, the situation was reversed when each group of journals was treated in aggregate. When the self-citations of all the psychology journals were added together and divided by the total references published by all of them, the self-citing rate of psychology journals soared to 27%. In contrast, the comparable figure for the botany journals dropped to 11%. The most likely explanation for this turnabout is that the high average self-citing rate of the botany journals reflected the existence of a number of subspecialties served by narrowly focused journals. Either psychology did not have a comparable set of subspecialties or, if it did, they had not yet spawned as many highly specialized journals.

Another interesting feature of Figure 9.43 was the absence of psychiatric journals. The only near exception was the *Archives of General Psychiatry,* whose 41 citations to the core group put it just outside the top 50. No other psychiatric journal cited the core group even that many times; four, in fact, was the highest citation rate. Even journals in audiology and acoustics showed a closer relationship to psychology than that. Though the functional distance between psychology and psychiatry may not be news to those in the field, it is certainly not what people outside the field would expect.

Figure 9.44 shows the journals that were most frequently cited by the core group. Most of them (35 of the 50) appeared on the list of major citation sources as well. Those unique to the highly cited list were either psychology journals or journals concerned with subjects related to psychology. Again, *Science* and *Nature* showed up as important sources of psychology material. The 50 journals in this figure accounted for 77% of all the material cited by the core group during the period studied.

Figure 9.45 shows the 50 journals that had the highest psychology impact ratings, which are based only on citations received from the core group of psychology journals. The interesting thing about this list is that the ranking of the journals was quite close to the way they would be ranked if the total impact factors shown for them in Figures 9.43 and 9.44 had been used. This suggests to me that psychology is characterized by a high degree of parochialism. I would not go so far as to say that psychologists and behavioral scientists are not very open to outside influences, but they do not seem to have much to do with the rest of the research world. If they do,

Journal	A	B	C	D	E	F	G
1. *J. Exp. Psychol.	1482	**1005**	400	67.8	27.0	39.8	1.867
2. *Psychonomic Science	1497	**907**	154	60.6	10.3	17.0	0.616
3. *J. Comp. Phys. Psych.	1208	**616**	298	51.0	24.7	48.4	1.938
4. *Psychol. Reports	1252	**597**	81	46.3	6.5	14.0	0.409
5. *Perc. Motor Skills	1247	**510**	108	40.9	8.7	21.2	0.438
6. *J. Exp. Anal. Behav.	594	**404**	255	68.0	42.9	63.1	2.395
7. Ann. N.Y. Acad. Sci.	10461	**376**	—	3.6	—	—	1.815
8. *J. Pers. Soc. Psych.	701	**370**	163	52.8	23.3	44.1	1.698
9. *Psychol. Bull.	672	**347**	21	51.6	3.1	6.1	3.081
10. *Physiol. Behav.	1032	**305**	48	30.0	4.7	15.7	1.496
11. *J. Cons. Clin. Psych.	718	**273**	61	38.0	8.5	22.3	1.217
12. *Psychol. Rev.	438	**266**	15	60.7	3.4	5.6	4.433
13. Annee Psychologique	573	**241**	11	42.1	1.9	4.6	0.065
14. *J. General Psych.	421	**232**	5	55.1	1.2	2.2	0.259
15. *Psychophysiology	451	**184**	63	40.8	4.0	34.2	0.723
16. *Behav. Res. Ther.	386	**180**	68	46.6	17.6	37.8	1.504
17. *J. Personality	389	**174**	32	44.7	8.2	18.4	0.761
18. *Perc. Psychophys.	333	**168**	41	50.5	12.3	24.4	0.991
19. *J. Verb. Learn. Beh.	265	**166**	45	62.6	17.0	27.1	1.374
20. *J. Abnormal Psych.	423	**165**	28	39.0	6.6	17.0	1.586
21. Acta Psychologica	369	**164**	—	44.4	—	—	1.345
22. Brit. J. S&C Psych.	381	**163**	8	42.8	2.1	14.9	—
23. *J. Soc. Psychol.	376	**151**	25	40.2	6.7	16.6	0.433
24. *J. Couns. Psychol.	328	**125**	57	38.1	17.4	45.6	—
25. *J. Educ. Psychol.	339	**124**	39	36.6	11.5	31.5	1.044
26. J. Clin. Psychol.	294	**117**	40	39.8	13.6	34.2	0.367
27. *J. Genetic Psychol.	373	**115**	15	30.8	4.0	13.0	0.148
28. J. Exp. Child Psych.	237	**106**	13	44.7	5.5	12.3	0.403
29. *Amer. Psychologist	395	**94**	38	40.4	9.6	40.4	0.331
30. *J. Nerv. Ment. Dis.	561	**94**	—	16.8	—	—	0.707
31. *Behaviour	419	**90**	39	21.5	9.3	43.3	1.294
32. *Educ. Psych. Meas.	256	**90**	19	35.2	7.4	21.1	0.279
33. J. Math. Psychol.	219	**90**	17	41.1	7.8	18.9	1.224
34. J. Res. Music. Educ.	411	**88**	—	21.4	—	—	—
35. Amer. J. Ment. Defic.	560	**86**	—	15.4	—	—	0.431
36. *Animal Behavior	395	**84**	41	21.3	10.4	48.8	1.518
37. *Science	5699	**72**	—	1.3	—	—	2.894
38. Pers. Psychophysiol.	189	**68**	18	36.0	9.5	26.5	—
39. *J. Appl. Psychology	149	**63**	28	42.3	18.8	44.4	0.804
40. *Amer. J. Psychology	196	**62**	17	31.6	8.7	27.4	0.464
41. Psychopharmacologia	435	**62**	—	14.3	—	—	2.409
42. Canad. Psychologist	151	**58**	24	38.4	15.9	41.4	0.170
43. *Canad. J. Psychology	100	**55**	4	55.0	4.0	7.3	1.291
44. Jap. Psychol. Res.	98	**55**	—	56.1	—	—	—
45. *J. Exp. Soc. Psych.	127	**52**	6	40.9	4.7	11.5	1.904
46. *Psychometrika	102	**51**	37	50.0	36.3	72.6	0.983
47. *Brit. J. Psychology	159	**50**	8	31.5	5.0	16.0	0.776
48. Int. J. Cl. Exp. Hyp.	236	**49**	—	20.8	—	—	—
49. J. Exp. Educ.	283	**46**	—	16.3	—	—	0.258
50. *J. Psychology	188	**45**	5	23.9	2.7	11.1	0.468

Figure 9.43 Major sources of references to psychology journals. Those marked by asterisks also are frequently cited by psychology journals. A = references to all journals. B = references to psychology journals. C = references to self. D = ratio of psychology references to all references. E = ratio of self-citations to all references (self-citing rate). F = ratio of self-citations to psychology references. G = overall impact.

	Journal	A	B	C	D	E	F	G
1.	*J. Exp. Psychology	1443	1252	400	86.8	27.7	32.0	1.867
2.	*J. Comp. Phys. Psych.	1143	999	298	87.4	26.1	29.8	1.938
3.	*J. Pers. Soc. Psych.	1177	988	163	83.9	13.9	16.5	1.698
4.	*Psychonomic Science	567	482	154	85.0	27.2	32.0	0.616
5.	*J. Exp. Anal. Behav.	504	449	255	89.1	44.6	50.1	2.395
6.	*Psychol. Review	586	447	15	76.3	2.6	3.4	4.433
7.	*Psychol. Bull.	604	434	21	71.9	3.5	4.8	3.081
8.	*Science	9739	423	—	4.3	—	—	2.894
9.	*J. Cons. Clin. Psych.	472	358	61	75.9	12.9	17.0	1.217
10.	*Psychol. Reports	420	334	81	79.5	19.3	24.3	0.409
11.	*J. Verb. Learn. Beh.	344	310	45	90.1	13.1	14.5	1.374
12.	*Amer. J. Psychology	339	238	17	70.2	5.0	7.1	0.464
13.	*Perc. Motor Skills	312	223	108	71.5	34.6	48.4	0.438
14.	*Amer. Psychologist	254	171	38	67.3	15.0	22.2	0.331
15.	J. Clin. Psychol.	217	161	40	74.2	18.4	24.8	0.367
16.	*J. Personality	203	147	32	72.4	15.8	21.8	0.761
17.	*Anim. Behavior	276	127	41	46.0	14.9	32.3	1.518
18.	*J. Appl. Psychol.	175	120	28	68.6	16.0	23.3	0.804
19.	*Canad. J. Psychol.	161	114	4	70.8	2.5	3.5	1.291
20.	*J. Psychology	191	111	5	58.1	2.6	4.5	0.468
21.	*J. Couns. Psychol.	143	110	57	76.9	39.9	51.8	—
22.	*Behav. Res. Ther.	132	108	68	81.8	51.5	63.0	1.504
23.	Psychol. Monogr.	183	108	—	59.0	—	—	—
24.	*Perc. Psychophys.	131	104	41	79.4	31.3	39.4	0.991
25.	*Brit. J. Psychol.	178	101	8	56.7	4.5	7.9	0.776
26.	*Psychometrika	174	98	37	56.3	21.3	37.8	0.983
27.	Q. J. Exp. Psychol.	123	91	—	74.0	—	—	0.389
28.	*Educ. Psych. Meas.	142	87	19	61.3	13.4	21.8	0.279
29.	*J. Abnormal Psych.	151	82	28	54.3	18.5	34.2	1.586
30.	*Psychophysiology	124	82	63	66.1	50.8	76.8	0.723
31.	*Physiol. Behav.	138	80	48	58.0	34.8	60.0	1.496
32.	Child Development	156	76	—	48.7	—	—	0.507
33.	EEG Clin. Neurophys.	719	76	—	10.6	—	—	0.388
34.	*J. Social Psychol.	119	76	25	63.9	21.0	32.9	0.433
35.	Amer. J. Physiology	5417	72	—	1.3	—	—	3.379
36.	Nature	15310	72	—	.5	—	—	2.244
37.	Arch. Gen. Psychiat.	784	68	—	8.7	—	—	1.409
38.	*J. Educ. Psychology	163	68	39	41.7	23.9	57.4	1.044
39.	*Behaviour	135	62	39	45.9	28.9	62.9	1.294
40.	J. Acoust. Soc. Amer.	1203	61	—	5.1	—	—	0.563
41.	Aerospace Medicine	257	58	—	22.6	—	—	0.551
42.	*J. Genetic Psychol.	159	58	15	36.5	9.4	25.9	0.148
43.	*J. Exp. Soc. Psychol.	66	57	6	86.4	7.6	8.8	1.904
44.	*J. General Psychol.	119	56	5	47.1	4.2	8.9	0.259
45.	*J. Nerv. Ment. Dis.	348	54	—	15.5	—	—	0.707
46.	J. Neurophysiology	1015	48	—	4.7	—	—	4.582
47.	Amer. J. Psychiatry	561	45	—	8.0	—	—	0.673
48.	Amer. Sociol. Review	123	45	—	36.6	—	—	—
49.	Endocrinology	2546	45	—	1.8	—	—	2.986
50.	Human Relations	76	43	7	56.6	9.2	16.3	0.347

Figure 9.44 Journals cited most frequently by psychology journals. Those marked by asterisks also are major sources of references to psychology journals. A = citations from all journals. B = citations from psychology journals. C = self-citations. D = ratio of citations from psychology journals to citations from all journals. E = ratio of self-citations to citations from all journals (self-cited rate). F = ratio of self-citations to citations from psychology journals. G = overall impact.

	Journal	PI
1.	Psychol. Review	**351.8**
2.	Psychol. Bull.	**227.3**
3.	J. Exp. Anal. Behav.	**219.2**
4.	J. Exp. Psychology	**174.4**
5.	J. Exp. Soc. Psychol.	**158.7**
6.	J. Pers. Soc. Psych.	**151.8**
7.	J. Comp. Phys. Psych.	**148.5**
8.	J. Verb. Learn. Beh.	**118.4**
9.	Behav. Res. Ther.	**118.4**
10.	Canad. J. Psychol.	**116.7**
11.	J. Abnormal Psych.	**91.3**
12.	J. Cons. Clin. Psych.	**83.0**
13.	Physiol. Behav.	**81.9**
14.	Perc. Psychophys.	**69.8**
15.	J. Educ. Psychology	**68.7**
16.	Anim. Behavior	**67.5**
17.	J. Personality	**66.6**
18.	J. Couns. Psychol.	**64.1**
19.	J. Appl. Psychol.	**59.8**
20.	Psychometrika	**59.0**
21.	Behaviour	**52.9**
22.	Brit. J. Psychol.	**50.5**
23.	Psychonomic Science	**50.0**
24.	Psychophysiology	**42.9**
25.	Psychol. Reports	**34.5**
26.	Perc. Motor Skills	**32.7**
27.	J. Psychology	**32.4**
28.	Child Development	**30.4**
29.	Amer. J. Psychology	**28.7**
30.	J. Social Psychol.	**28.3**
31.	Amer. Psychologist	**27.5**
32.	J. Clin. Psychol.	**25.0**
33.	J. General Psychol.	**18.5**
34.	Educ. Psych. Meas.	**18.2**
35.	Q. J. Exp. Psychol.	**18.2**
36.	*Aerospace Medicine*	**13.8**
37.	*Nature*	**11.8**
38.	*Science*	**11.6**
39.	*J. Nerv. Ment. Dis.*	**11.5**
40.	*Human Relations*	**8.7**
41.	*J. Neurophysiology*	**8.0**
42.	*J. Genetic Psychol.*	**7.4**
43.	*EEG Clin. Neurophys.*	**5.2**
44.	*Endocrinology*	**4.2**
45.	*Amer. J. Physiology*	**3.4**
46.	*J. Acoust. Soc. Amer.*	**2.4**
47.	*Amer. J. Psychiatry*	**1.4**
48.	*Arch. Gen. Psychiat.*	**1.0**
49.	*Psychol. Monogr.*	—
50.	*Amer. Sociol. Review*	—

Figure 9.45 Journals cited most frequently by psychology journals, ranked by "psychology impact."

the literature indicates that they have not found much outside their world that is helpful, or that if they have, they are not admitting it in their references.

Agriculture (26)

One of the things that makes life complicated for librarians and information scientists attempting to define the nature and bounds of a journal collection for a given subject is the difference between the literature of the field and the literature of interest to the researchers working in the field. A study of the journal literature of agriculture demonstrated that the difference can be considerable and that citation analysis can define it.

The data base used for this study was all the journals listed in the 1969 *SCI* for subjects that are obviously agricultural in nature, such as agriculture, food technology, botany, entomology, ecology, fisheries, forestry, horticulture, parasitology, and soil science. From this group, we removed any journals that dealt primarily with genetics or microbiology because we did not want the close relationship of these subjects to other areas of basic reseach to distort the picture of agriculture as a more applied science. We did add to the core group a few journals that we thought appropriate, such as *Pesticides Biochemistry* and the *Journal of the Association of Official Chemists,* but none of the major multidisciplinary journals in which agricultural scientists like to publish. By the time we finished, the core group contained 347 journals.

Figure 9.46 shows the journals most frequently cited by the agricultural core group. Figure 9.47 shows the ones that cited the core group most frequently. The difference between them illustrates the difference between the agricultural literature and the literature that agricultural scientists use.

The list of the major sources of citations to the core group consisted, primarily, of the journals usually thought of as being agricultural—what is considered the literature of the field. In contrast, the list of journals most frequently cited by the core group was dominated by journals that very few people would think of as agricultural, yet they are the journals that agricultural scientists use—the literature of interest to the research scientists working in the field.

A more general view of the difference between the literature of agriculture and the literature of interest to agricultural scientists is shown by the statistics. The core group was shown to have cited 1650 publications, plus innumerable theses. Most of the 1650 publications consisted of journals. The number of journals that cited the core group, however, amounted to only 395.

These results make it obvious that an agricultural library or information service must cover considerably more than the agricultural journals in order to serve its constituency.

Engineering (27)

A citation study of the 240 journals listed by *SCI* in the various categories of engineering (general, chemical, civil, electrical and electronic, mechanical) produced

	Journal	A	B	C	D	E	F	G
1.	Phytopathology	1713	1460	822	85.2	48.0	56.3	1.078
2.	Nature	15310	1128	—	7.4	—	—	2.244
3.	Plant Physiol.	1639	1107	200	67.5	12.2	18.1	1.683
4.	J. Biol. Chem.	17103	791	—	4.6	—	—	6.371
5.	J. Econ. Entomol.	900	778	508	86.4	56.4	65.3	0.782
6.	Amer. J. Bot.	1171	696	73	59.4	6.2	10.5	0.956
7.	Science	9739	638	—	6.6	—	—	2.894
8.	J. Dairy Sci	902	619	382	68.6	42.4	61.9	0.507
9.	Agron. J.	727	529	163	72.8	22.4	30.8	0.947
10.	Biochem. J.	7625	528	—	6.9	—	—	3.193
11.	J. Animal Sci	734	482	247	65.7	33.7	51.0	0.405
12.	Poultry Sci.	697	456	351	65.4	50.4	77.0	0.488
13.	Soil Sci.	629	443	61	70.4	9.7	13.8	0.923
14.	Biochim. Biophys. Acta	9500	438	—	4.6	—	—	3.287
15.	Soil Sci. Soc.	553	400	112	72.3	20.3	28.0	0.867
16.	Planta	707	391	123	55.3	17.4	31.5	2.944
17.	J. Parasitology	708	368	80	52.0	11.3	21.7	1.351
18.	Canad. J. Bot.	548	357	62	65.2	11.3	17.4	1.217
19.	J. Agr. Food Chem.	509	324	98	63.7	19.3	30.3	1.665
20.	J. Bacteriol.	4138	319	—	7.7	—	—	3.594
21.	J. Amer. Soc. Hort. Sci.	357	301	182	84.3	60.0	60.5	0.392
22.	Physiol. Plant.	482	283	52	58.7	10.8	18.4	1.796
23.	J. Ass. Off. An. Chem.	478	277	181	57.9	37.9	65.3	—
24.	Weed Sci.	311	275	171	88.4	55.0	62.2	1.568
25.	Phytochemistry	588	273	153	46.4	26.0	56.0	1.907
26.	J. Agr. Sci.	420	269	106	64.1	25.2	39.4	0.912
27.	Comptes Rendus D	5642	256	—	4.5	—	—	0.780
28.	Ann. Bot.	424	255	30	60.1	7.1	7.1	1.443
29.	Crop Sci.	353	255	104	72.2	29.5	40.8	0.712
30.	Analyt. Chem.	4219	251	—	6.0	—	—	1.661
31.	Ecology	577	251	118	43.5	20.5	74.9	1.256
32.	Arch. Biochem. Biophys.	3647	247	—	6.8	—	—	3.519
33.	Food Technol.	346	242	62	70.0	17.9	25.6	0.787
34.	Exp. Parasitol.	428	240	161	56.1	37.6	67.1	3.000
35.	Plant Dis. Rep.	286	236	—	82.5	—	—	0.268
36.	J. Cell Biol.	4769	234	—	4.9	—	—	3.484
37.	J. Amer. Chem. Soc.	26307	218	—	0.8	—	—	5.859
38.	Austr. J. Agr. Res.	308	212	89	68.8	28.9	42.0	1.051
39.	Ann. Entom. Soc. Am.	329	211	64	64.1	19.5	30.3	0.537
40.	Bot. Gazette	312	210	9	67.3	2.9	4.3	0.658
41.	Ann. Appl. Biol.	453	209	—	46.1	—	—	1.386
42.	J. Exp. Bot.	337	205	63	60.8	18.7	30.7	2.400
43.	J. Sci. Food Agr.	367	202	87	55.0	23.7	43.1	0.881
44.	J. Nutrition	1209	201	—	16.6	—	—	2.087
45.	J. Food Sci.	383	197	41	51.4	10.7	20.8	0.871
46.	P. Nat. Acad. Sci. USA	8206	196	—	2.4	—	—	8.828
47.	J. Protozool.	446	191	104	42.8	54.5	23.3	0.884
48.	Zbl. Bakt. Parasitenk.	407	186	166	45.7	40.8	89.3	0.703
49.	Mycologia	302	185	51	61.3	16.9	27.6	0.901
50.	Austr. J. Biol. Sci.	583	184	—	31.6	—	—	1.957
51.	Canad. Entomol.	225	182	55	80.9	24.4	30.2	0.445
52.	Cereal Chem.	286	182	71	63.6	24.8	39.0	1.210
53.	J. Insect Physiol.	487	180	139	37.0	28.5	77.2	1.932
54.	T. Brit. Mycol. Soc.	263	173	73	65.8	27.8	42.2	0.830
55.	Agr. Biol. Chem.	356	172	143	48.3	40.2	83.1	0.939
56.	New Phytologist	295	172	54	58.3	18.3	31.4	1.362
57.	Virology	2373	171	—	7.2	—	—	4.720
58.	Annu. Rev. Plant Phys.	290	170	—	58.6	—	—	7.047
59.	P. Soc. Exp. Biol. Med.	5011	168	—	3.4	—	—	1.964
60.	J. Agr. Res.	267	167	—	62.6	—	—	—
61.	J. Fish. Res. Bd. Can.	336	164	122	48.8	36.3	74.4	—
62.	Parasitology	297	161	44	54.2	14.8	27.3	0.866
63.	Amer. J. Trop. Med. Hyg.	854	153	—	17.9	—	—	2.078
64.	J. Gen. Microbiol.	1438	145	—	10.1	—	—	2.337
65.	J. Chem. Soc.	13978	142	—	1.0	—	—	3.123
66.	J. Wildl. Managem.	180	128	112	71.1	62.2	87.5	0.501
67.	J. Range Managem.	126	120	60	95.2	47.6	50.0	0.551
68.	Plant Soil	202	116	52	57.4	25.7	44.8	0.988
69.	J. Animal Ecol.	239	115	50	48.1	20.9	43.5	0.795
70.	Plant Cell Physiol.	203	114	75	56.2	37.0	65.8	1.785
71.	Ann. Trop. Med. Paras.	381	113	32	29.7	8.4	28.3	1.398
72.	T. Roy. Soc. Trop. Med.	553	110	—	19.9	—	—	—
73.	Ann. New York Acad. Sci.	3756	107	—	2.9	—	—	1.815
74.	Appl. Microbiol.	583	107	—	18.4	—	—	1.278
75.	Canad. J. Plant Sci.	138	106	32	76.8	23.2	30.2	0.615

Figure 9.46 Journals cited most frequently by agricultural journals. A = citations from all journals. B = citations from agricultural journals. C = self-citations. D = ratio of citations from agricultural journals to citations from all journals. E = ratio of self-citations to citations from all journals (self-cited rate). F = ratio of self-citations to citations from agricultural journals. G = overall impact.

	Journal	A	B	C	D	E	F	G
1.	Phytopathology	2830	1039	822	36.7	31.2	79.1	1.078
2.	J. Econ. Entomol.	1446	660	508	45.6	35.1	77.0	0.782
3.	J. Dairy Sci.	1350	466	382	34.5	28.3	82.0	0.507
4.	Annu. Rev. Phytopath.	2181	453	—	20.8	—	—	4.914
5.	Poultry Sci.	1291	414	351	32.0	27.2	84.8	0.488
6.	Agron. J.	1008	355	163	35.2	16.2	45.9	0.947
7.	J. Animal Sci.	964	349	247	36.2	25.6	70.8	0.405
8.	Plant Physiol.	960	300	200	31.3	20.8	66.7	1.683
9.	Exp. Parasitol.	2219	260	161	11.7	7.3	61.9	3.000
10.	Weed Sci.	564	251	171	44.5	30.3	68.1	1.568
11.	J. Ass. Off. An. Ch.	878	242	181	27.6	20.6	74.8	—
12.	J. Agr. Food Chem.	903	238	98	26.4	10.9	41.2	1.665
13.	J. Am. S. Hort. Sci.	755	235	182	31.1	24.1	77.4	0.392
14.	Planta	1085	213	123	19.6	11.3	57.8	2.944
15.	Phytochemistry	1473	207	153	14.1	10.4	74.0	1.907
16.	Botan. Rev.	772	205	6	26.6	0.8	2.9	3.818
17.	J. Agr. Sci.	653	194	106	29.7	16.2	54.6	0.912
18.	Canad. J. Bot.	768	194	62	25.3	8.1	31.9	1.217
19.	Ecology	991	194	118	19.6	11.9	60.8	1.256
20.	Plant Soil	820	193	52	23.5	6.3	26.9	0.988
21.	Agr. Biol. Chem.	1108	184	143	16.6	12.9	77.7	0.939
22.	Mycop. Mycol. Appl.	2831	177	80	6.3	2.8	45.2	0.346
23.	Soil Sci. Soc.	608	175	112	28.8	18.4	64.0	0.867
24.	J. Insect Physiol.	1129	174	139	15.4	12.3	80.0	1.932
25.	T. Brit. Mycol. S.	549	171	73	31.2	13.3	42.7	0.830
26.	J. Fish. Res. Bd.	1174	166	122	14.4	10.4	73.5	—
27.	Austr. J. Agr. Res.	669	163	89	24.4	13.3	54.6	1.051
28.	Amer. J. Bot.	590	162	73	27.5	12.4	45.1	0.956
29.	Plant Cell Physiol.	820	162	75	19.8	9.2	46.3	1.785
30.	Soil Sci.	405	146	61	36.1	15.1	41.8	0.923
31.	J. Sci. Food Agr.	738	140	87	19.8	11.8	59.6	0.881
32.	Protoplasma	965	143	—	14.8	—	—	2.183
33.	Ind. J. Agr. Sci.	959	135	52	14.1	5.4	38.5	0.334
34.	Weed Res.	467	132	28	28.3	6.0	21.2	—
35.	New Phytologist	579	123	54	21.2	9.3	43.9	1.382
36.	Mycologia	444	120	51	27.0	11.5	42.5	0.901
37.	Physiol. Plant.	486	108	52	22.2	10.6	48.1	1.796
38.	Comptes Rendus D	3784	108	—	2.9	—	—	0.780
39.	Canad. J. Zool.	1663	106	—	6.4	—	—	0.978
40.	J. Austr. I. Agr.	580	102	19	17.6	3.3	18.6	—
41.	J. Brit. Grassl.	346	101	61	29.2	17.6	60.4	0.612
42.	Cereal Chem.	301	99	71	32.9	23.6	71.7	1.210
43.	Ann. Ent. Soc. Am.	673	95	64	14.1	9.5	67.4	0.537
44.	J. Soil Sci.	302	94	27	31.1	8.9	28.7	0.861
45.	J. Chromatogr.	2506	91	—	3.6	—	—	1.378
46.	Z. Pflanzenphys.	414	86	24	20.8	5.8	27.9	1.048
47.	J. Range Managem.	298	81	60	27.2	20.1	74.1	0.551
48.	Ann. NY Acad. Sci.	10461	73	—	0.7	—	—	1.815
49.	Mosquito News	214	72	65	33.7	30.4	90.3	0.428
50.	Bioch. Bioph. Acta	10269	71	—	0.7	—	—	3.287
51.	J. Repr. Fertil.	1203	69	—	5.7	—	—	2.014
52.	Arch. Mikrobiol.	1318	69	—	5.2	—	—	2.120
53.	Zschr. Parasitenk.	434	68	40	15.7	9.2	58.8	2.208
54.	B. Torrey Bot. Club	366	67	13	18.3	3.6	19.4	0.623
55.	Ber. Deut. Bot. Ges.	669	67	20	10.0	3.0	29.9	0.519
56.	J. Animal Ecol.	389	66	50	17.0	12.9	75.8	0.795
57.	Austr. J. Biol. Sci.	1245	66	—	5.3	—	—	1.957
58.	Phyton	364	65	12	17.9	3.3	18.5	—
59.	Amer. Potato J.	182	64	29	35.2	28.6	81.3	0.342
60.	Forest Chron.	485	63	29	13.0	6.0	46.0	—
61.	Theor. Appl. Genet.	776	62	—	8.0	—	—	—
62.	Parasitology	441	61	44	13.8	10.0	72.1	0.866
63.	Oikos	739	60	—	8.1	—	—	1.019
64.	Science	5699	59	—	1.0	—	—	2.894
65.	Bull. Entomol. Res.	238	58	45	24.4	18.9	77.6	0.674
66.	J. Stored Prod. Res.	452	57	18	12.6	4.0	31.6	—
67.	Comp. Biochem.	1945	57	—	2.9	—	—	1.477
68.	Zucker	162	56	56	34.6	34.6	99.9	—
69.	P. NAS India A	658	56	—	8.5	—	—	—
70.	J. Sci. Ind. R. B	976	55	—	5.6	—	—	—
71.	Nature	6777	55	—	0.8	—	—	2.244
72.	T. Amer. Fish. Soc.	386	54	32	14.0	8.3	59.3	0.333
73.	Z. Pflanzenzucht.	418	54	21	12.9	5.0	38.9	—
74.	Appl. Microbiol.	1453	54	—	3.7	—	—	1.278
75.	Phytomorphology	223	52	13	23.3	5.8	25.0	—

Figure 9.47 Major sources of references to agricultural journals. A = references to all journals. B = references to agricultural journals. C = references to self. D = ratio of agricultural references to all references. E = ratio of self-citations to all references (self-citing rate). F = ratio of self-citations to agricultural references. G = overall impact.

the view of the journal literature of engineering that is shown in Figure 9.48 and 9.49. It is important to realize that the role played by the journal literature is not the same in engineering as it is in most of the disciplines of science. The work most heavily cited in the engineering journals tends to be books rather than journal articles. In an unpublished ISI study, we found that books accounted for two-thirds of the items cited nine or more times by engineering journals in 1973. This means that an analysis of the journal literature of engineering leaves undefined a major part of the formal communication system of that particular group of disciplines. Nevertheless, the results of such an analysis still produce some interesting insights.

For example, Figure 9.48 shows that the journal most frequently cited by the core group of engineering journals was the *Proceedings of the Institute of Electrical and Electronic Engineers*. Two aspects of its performance were particularly noteworthy. One was that self-citations contributed very little to its top ranking. Its self-cited rate as a percent of citations originating in references from engineering journals was only 20%, which is unusually low for a high-ranking journal. In contrast, the comparable self-citation rate for *Thermal Engineering USSR* (*Toploenergetika*), which ranked seventeenth, was 93%. The second noteworthy characteristic was that engineering journals accounted for only a little more than 50% of *Proc. IEEE*'s citation rate. The other half of the citations received originated in basic physics journals. This finding says that *Proc. IEEE* was as much a basic physics journal as an engineering journal.

Figure 9.48 also demonstrated the dependence of engineering on basic research. The ubiquitous *Science* and *Nature* were among the 50 journals most frequently cited by the core group, as were *Physical Review, Proceedings of the Royal Society (London), Journal of the American Chemical Society, Journal of Chemical Physics,* and *Journal of Physical Chemistry*. Figure 9.49 shows that the dependence was not mutual. The list of journals that were the major sources of references that cited the core group would have had to be extended to include the top several hundred before *Nature* and *Science* would have been picked up. Only 37 of *Nature*'s references cited the core group, and *Science* did it only 33 times.

The most surprising finding in Figure 9.49 is that *Doklady Akademii Nauk USSR* was the top source of citations to the core group. This reflected the heavy technological orientation of the leading journal of the Soviet Academy of Science, and of Soviet research in general. No fewer than nine Russian journals appeared among the top 50 sources of citations to the core group, whereas only three appeared among the top 50 journals cited by the group.

One more important point made by this study of the journal literature of engineering is worth mentioning, not because it is surprising in any way, but because it provides additional confirming evidence of an important general characteristic of the journal literature. Despite the diversity of engineering subjects, the journal literature that supports all of them exhibited the same bibliographic law of concentration that is seen in the literature of the more tightly focused disciplines and specialties of basic research. The 50 journals in Figure 9.48 accounted for 52% of all the references published by the core group. The 50 journals in Figure 9.49 accounted for 56% of all the citations received by it. And, with just three or four exceptions,

	JOURNAL	A	B	C	D	E	F	G
1. *	Proc. IEEE	1601	870	175	54.3	10.9	20.1	1.372
2.	Indust. & Eng. Chem.	1582	659	101	41.7	6.4	15.3	1.123
3.	Trans. ASME	409	631	0				0.320
4. *	J. Geophys. Res.	3556	520	–	14.6			3.665
5. *	J. Appl. Phys.	5274	493	–	9.4			1.936
6. *	Radiotekhnika i Elektronika	575	475	380	82.6	66.1	80.0	0.756
7. *	IEEE Tr. Power App. & Syst.	460	451	434	98.0	94.4	96.2	0.631
8.	IEEE Tr.	763	396	–	51.9			–
9. *	Bell Syst. Tech. J.	690	395	149	57.3	21.6	37.7	1.990
10.	J. Am. Chem. Soc.	26307	384	–	1.5			5.859
11. *	Tr. Met. Soc. AIME	1348	384	292	28.5	21.7	76.0	4.942
12. *	J. Fluid Mech.	962	370	243	38.5	25.3	65.7	2.376
13. *	AICHE J.	554	362	71	65.4	12.8	19.6	1.559
14.	Phys. Rev.	20666	334	–	1.6			3.679
15. *	Proc. IEE	489	312	130	63.8	26.6	41.7	0.809
16. *	AIAA J.	1247	301	–	24.1			1.228
17. *	Therm. Eng. USSR	336	295	275	87.8	81.9	93.2	0.572
18. *	Chem. Eng. Sci.	425	290	66	68.2	15.5	22.8	1.514
19. *	IEEE Tr. Ant. Propag.	335	287	135	85.7	40.3	47.0	1.568
20.	J. Chem. Phys.	13687	255	–	1.9			3.180
21. *	Radio Science	363	243	194	66.9	53.4	79.8	2.508
22.	Appl. Phys. Lett.	1318	215	–	16.3			3.688
23.	J. Electrochem. Soc.	1371	204	–	14.9			0.797
24. *	IEEE Tr. Microwave Theory & Techn.	273	203	138	74.4	50.6	68.0	1.242
25. *	IEEE Tr. Inform. Theory	263	199	95	75.7	36.1	47.7	0.946
26.	Proc. Roy. Soc. London	4789	192	–	4.0			2.998
27.	J. Phys. Chem.	4678	183	–	3.9			2.429
28.	Nature	15310	181	–	1.2			2.244
29.	J. Chem. Soc.	13978	180	–	1.3			3.123
30. *	IEEE Tr. Autom. Contr.	222	175	112	78.8	50.5	64.0	0.684
31. *	IEEE Tr. Electr. Dev.	298	172	94	57.7	31.5	54.7	0.792
32. *	Nucl. Sci. Eng.	485	172	165	35.5	34.0	95.9	1.290
33.	J. Cryst. Growth	232	171	–	73.7			2.277
34. *	IEEE Tr. Circ. Th.	265	166	91	62.6	34.3	54.8	1.344
35.	Textile Res. J.	446	158	149	35.4	33.4	94.3	0.882
36. *	J. Acoust. Soc. Amer.	1203	152	–	12.6			0.563
37.	J. Atmos. Terr. Phys.	482	152	–	31.5			1.642
38.	Chem. Eng. Progr.	229	145	3	63.3	1.3	2.1	0.162
39.	Solid-State Electr.	348	139	33	39.9	9.5	23.7	1.993
40	Planet. Sp. Sci.	496	138	83	27.8	16.7	60.1	2.753
41.	J. Phys. Chem. Solids	1419	137	–	9.7			2.073
42. *	J. Catalysis	428	131	111	30.6	25.9	84.7	2.448
43.	Phys. Fluids	1294	126	–	9.7			1.581
44. *	Electronics Lett.	311	125	–	40.2			0.810
45. *	J. Spacecraft & Rockets	166	117	113	70.5	68.1	96.6	0.448
46.	Chem. Eng.	251	112	41	44.6	16.3	36.6	–
47.	Phys. Rev. Lett.	6544	110	–	1.7			5.114
48.	Tr. Faraday Soc.	2911	109	–	3.7			2.149
49.	Science	9739	105	–	1.1			2.894
50.	Vest. Mashinostr.	134	105	–	78.4			0.557

Figure 9.48 Journals cited most frequently by engineering journals. Those marked by asterisks also are major sources of references to engineering journals. A = citations from all journals. B = citations from engineering journals. C = self-citations. D = ratio of citations from engineering journals to citations from all journals. E = all ratio of self-citations to citations from all journals (self-cited rate). F = ratio of self-citations to citations from engineering journals. G = overall impact.

	JOURNAL	A	B	C	D	E	F	G
1.	DAN SSSR	7647	958	837	12.5	11.0	87.4	0.572
2.	* Radio Science	2083	689	194	33.1	9.3	28.2	2.508
3.	* AIAA J.	2616	652	502	24.9	19.2	77.0	1.228
4.	* IEEE Tr. Power App. & Syst.	1122	622	434	55.4	38.7	69.8	0.631
5.	Instr. Exp. Techn.	1513	583	469	38.5	31.0	80.5	0.357
6.	Ind. Eng. Chem.	2952	562	101	19.0	3.4	18.0	1.123
7.	* Radiotekhnika i Elektronika	1451	538	380	37.1	26.2	70.6	0.756
8.	* J. Acoust. Soc. Amer.	1440	524	443	36.4	30.8	84.5	0.563
9.	* J. Appl. Phys.	5811	503	–	8.7			1.936
10.	* Proc. IEEE	1702	465	175	27.3	10.3	37.6	1.372
11.	Vysokomol. Soed. A	1750	411	289	23.5	16.5	70.2	0.559
12.	* Electronics Lett.	744	379	108	50.9	14.5	28.5	0.810
13.	* Proc. IEE	891	376	130	42.2	14.6	34.6	0.809
14.	Telecomm. Radioeng. USSR	738	326	48	44.2	6.5	14.7	–
15.	* J. Fluid Mech.	1271	347	243	27.3	19.1	70.0	2.376
16.	J. Appl. Mech	1090	319	103	29.2	9.5	32.3	–
17.	* J. Spacecraft & Rockets	1638	313	113	19.1	6.9	36.1	0.448
18.	* Tr. Met Soc. AIME	1706	312	292	18.3	17.1	93.6	4.942
19.	* IEEE Tr. Electr. Dev.	773	311	94	40.2	12.2	30.2	0.792
20.	* IEEE Tr. Microwave Theory & Techn.	697	306	138	43.9	19.8	45.1	1.242
21.	* Therm. Eng. USSR	770	302	275	39.2	35.7	91.1	0.572
22.	IEEE Tr. Magnetics	1244	299	162	24.0	13.0	54.2	1.340
23.	* IEEE Tr. Ant. Propag.	622	274	135	44.1	21.7	49.3	1.568
24.	Internat. J. Electronics	784	260	43	33.2	5.5	16.5	–
25.	Electr. Comm. Japan	804	247	39	30.7	4.9	15.8	–
26.	* IEEE Tr. Autom. Contr.	649	245	112	37.8	17.3	45.7	0.684
27.	J. Basic Eng.	1010	243	24	24.1	2.4	9.9	–
28.	Chim. Ind. (Milan)	1068	233	44	21.8	4.1	18.9	0.240
29.	Annu. Rev. Fl. Mech.	943	229	–	24.3			
30.	* Bell Syst. Techn. J.	505	215	149	42.6	29.5	69.3	1.990
31.	Tr. Amer. Nucl. Soc.	2019	211	–	10.5			0.388
32.	* Chem. Eng. Sci.	425	200	66	47.1	15.5	33.0	1.514
33.	Meas. Techn. USSR	525	199	186	37.9	35.4	93.5	–
34.	Ind. Eng. Chem. F.	816	187	67	22.9	8.2	35.8	–
35.	* IEEE Tr. Inform. Theory	483	181	95	37.5	19.7	52.5	0.946
36.	IEEE Tr. Computers	489	172	94	35.2	19.2	54.7	0.821
37.	* Nucl. Sci. Eng.	813	168	165	20.7	20.3	98.2	1.290
38.	Phys. Stat. Sol.	4973	166	–	3.3			1.578
39.	Ind. Eng. Chem. Proc. D&D	350	162	–	46.3			–
40.	* J. Geophys. Res.	3671	161	–	4.4			3.665
41.	Tr. Inst. Chem. Eng.	787	158	30	20.1	3.8	19.0	0.583
42.	* IEEE Tr. Circ. Th.	381	153	91	40.2	23.9	59.5	1.344
43.	Autom. Rem. Contr. USSR	437	152	138	34.8	31.6	90.8	0.340
44.	* J. Catalysis	610	148	111	24.3	18.2	75.0	2.448
45.	* AICHE J.	351	137	71	39.0	20.2	51.8	1.559
46.	Eur. Polym. J.	1308	131	–	10.0			–
47.	Nachrichttech. Z.	512	128	–	25.0			–
48.	Russ. J. Phys. Chem. USSR	2527	127	–	5.0			0.838
49.	IEEE Tr. Nucl. Sci.	652	121	64	18.6	9.8	52.9	0.722
50.	Nucl. Instr. Meth.	1656	119	–	7.2			1.016

Figure 9.49 Major sources of references to engineering journals. Those marked by asterisks also are among those journals cited most frequently by engineering journals. A = references to all journals. B = references to engineering journals. C = references to self. D = ratio of engineering references to all references. E = ratio of self-citations to all references (self-citing rate). F = ratio of self-citations to engineering references. G = overall impact.

the journals on both lists that have titles that indicate a high degree of specialization were all found among the 500 journals most frequently cited by the full range of scientific and technical journals. In fact, almost half of the journals on the two lists were among the 152 most cited journals of 1969.

Russian Journal Literature (28)

An analysis of the literature of Russian science was the first of a series of studies aimed at testing the ability of citation analysis to characterize national literatures in some useful ways. The tools of the analysis were the same ones used for the previous studies: a selected group of core journals, a list of the journals most cited by the core group, and a second list of the journals that were the major sources of references that cited the core group. In this particular study, two sets of such lists were produced, one set based on the citation data of 1972 (Figures 9.50 and 9.51) and the other based on the data of 1974 (Figures 9.52 and 9.53). The reason for the two sets was to see if any changes in characteristics could be identified.

The core group on which the study was based consisted of all Russian journals covered as reference sources by *SCI* during 1972 and 1974. Categorized as Russian are the journals published within the Soviet Union, the translation journals published outside of the Soviet Union to make Soviet science more accessible, and a few Slavic journals. In 1972, 83 source journals (accounting for 3.4% of *SCI*'s journal coverage and 7% of its source-item coverage) fit into that category. By 1974, the number had increased to 102 (accounting for 4.2% of *SCI*'s journal coverage and about 6.5% of its source-item coverage). If the core groups appear to be too small to be representative of the Russian literature, it should be noted that all the journals on the two lists of those most cited by the Russian literature (Figures 9.51 and 9.53) are part of *SCI*'s source coverage. In other words, none of the Russian journals not covered by *SCI* were cited frequently enough to rank among the 75 journals cited most frequently by the Russian scientists publishing in the core groups. This indicates that though the core groups used certainly do not cover the entire Russian literature, they do cover the journals that probably are used most by Russian scientists.

There are, however, two important qualifications that must be made about the study. One is that it does not necessarily reflect the total bibliographic impact of all Soviet science and technology. Because the analysis was limited to core groups of Russian journals, the many highly cited articles published by Soviet scientists in "outside" journals were not reflected in the statistics. The other point of qualification is that the citation practices of the translation journals tend to inflate the citation rates of Russian journals through duplicate references. Rather than go into a detailed explanation about how these practices distort the citation picture (28), I will simply say that all possible care was taken to eliminate the effect and to make the counts as accurate as possible.

The main purpose of this study was to measure the amount of cross citation between the Russian literature and other ones, and to determine whether there was any significant change between 1972 and 1974. One such measure was provided by

Journals		A	B	C	D	E	F	G
1.	Dokl Akad Nauk SSSR / Proc Acad Sci USSR	20548	4344	1218	21.14	5.9	28.04	0.372
2.	Zh Fiz Khim / Russ J Phys Chem	7005	2714	1302	38.7	18.6	48.0	0.534
3.	Zh Neorg Khim / J Inorg Chem	7398	2699	1591	36.5	21.5	59.0	0.482
4.	Zh Obshchei Khim / J General Chem USSR	6900	2585	975	37.5	14.1	37.7	0.538
5.	Fiz Tekh Polupr Vodn / Sov Phys Semiconduct	6731	2572	1402	38.2	20.8	54.5	1.530
6.	IAN SSSR Ser Khim / B Acad Sci USSR Chem Sci	6525	2536	1250	38.9	19.2	49.3	0.799
7.	Vysokomolek Soed / High Mol Cpds	7682	2255	1089	29.4	14.2	48.3	0.544
8.	Zh Org Khim / J Org Chem USSR	6580	2183	465	33.2	7.1	21.3	0.807
9.	Zh Eksp Teor Fiz / Sov Phys JETP	4898	2128	1284	43.5	26.2	60.3	2.808
10.	Fiz Tverdogo Tela / Sov Phys Solid State	8187	2120	680	25.9	8.3	32.1	1.591
11.	Zh Prikl Khim / J Appl Chem USSR	6193	1841	494	29.7	8.0	26.8	0.151
12.	Optika Spektroskopiya / Opt Spectrosc USSR	3201	1766	822	55.2	25.7	46.6	0.649
13.	Zh Analit Khim / J Analyt Chem USSR	6976	1660	813	23.8	11.7	49.0	1.008
14.	Yadernaya Fiz / Sov J Nucl Phys	4449	1647	919	37.0	20.7	55.8	0.662
15.	Usp Khim / Adv Chem	12611	1636	144	13.0	1.1	8.8	1.747
16.	Phys Rev B Solid State	28202	1559	—	5.5	—	—	2.814
17.	Zh Eksp Teor Fiz P / JETP Letters	3245	1554	578	47.9	17.8	37.2	1.299
18.	Zh Tekh Fiz / Sov Phys Tech Phys	3514	1405	691	40.0	19.7	49.2	1.170
19.	IAN SSSR Ser Fiz / B #1 Acad Sci USSR Phys Sci	4043	1347	517	33.3	12.8	38.4	0.499
20.	Analytical Chemistry	28806	1346	—	4.6	—	—	5.187
21.	Fiz Met Metaloved / Phys Met Metallogr USSR	3949	1188	508	30.1	12.9	42.8	1.003
22.	IVUZ Fizika / B Inst Higher Educ Phys	4815	1155	390	24.0	8.1	33.8	0.270
23.	Khim Geterotsikl Soed / Chem Het Cpds USSR	3642	1089	447	29.9	12.3	41.1	0.542
24.	Uspekhi Fiz Nauk / Soviet Physics, Uspekhi	6273	1063	70	17.0	1.1	6.6	4.970
25.	Teplofiz Vysok Temp / High Temp USSR	2655	1026	570	38.6	21.5	55.6	0.773
26.	Radiotekh Elektronika / Radio Eng Electr Phys USSR	3124	976	585	31.2	18.7	60.0	0.299
27.	Kristallografiya / Sov Phys Crystallography	2453	953	449	38.9	18.3	47.1	1.061
28.	Ukrainskii Khim Zh / Ukrainian Chem J	3191	953	310	29.9	9.7	32.5	0.287

Figure 9.50 Major sources of references to Russian journals in 1972. A = references to all journals. B = references to Russian journals. C = references to self. D = ratio of Russian references to all references. E = ratio of self-citations to all references (self-citing rate). F = ratio of self-citations to Russian references. G = overall impact.

#	Journal						
29.	Tsitologiya / Cytology	4237	946	473	22.3	11.2	50.0	0.383
30.	Zh Mikrob Epidem Immun / J Microb Epidem Immun USSR	5524	946	649	17.1	11.8	68.6	0.247
31.	Zh Strukt Khim / J Struct Chem USSR	2670	834	414	31.2	15.5	49.6	0.790
32.	Izmertel Tekh / Meas Tech USSR	2236	831	737	37.2	33.0	88.7	0.109
33.	J Chem Phys	42071	829	—	2.0	—	—	3.341
34.	Biull Eksp Biol Med / B Exp Biol USSR	5227	824	313	15.8	6.0	38.0	0.294
35.	Antibiotiki / Antibiotics	3047	820	550	26.9	18.1	67.1	—
36.	Phys Rev A Gen Phys	16036	792	—	4.9	—	—	2.86
37.	Zh Vys Nev Deyatel Pavlov / Pavlov J Higher Nerv Act	2287	785	480	34.3	21.0	61.2	—
38.	Kolloidnyi Zh / Colloid Journal USSR	2009	779	347	38.8	17.3	44.5	0.550
39.	Phys St Sol B	8947	759	—	8.5	—	—	0.962
40.	Avtomat Telemekh / Automat Rem, Contr USSR	2273	755	589	33.2	25.9	78.0	0.004
41.	Phys St Sol A	8373	743	—	8.9	—	—	1.253
42.	Physical Review Letters	15677	705	—	4.5	—	—	4.962
43.	Genetika / Genetics USSR	3798	687	458	18.1	12.1	66.7	0.509
44.	Svar Proiz / Welding Production USSR	1376	662	515	48.1	37.4	77.8	0.069
45.	Biofizika / Biophysics USSR	2651	658	306	24.8	11.5	46.5	0.852
46.	Geokhimiya / Geochemistry International USSR	2503	652	373	26.1	14.9	57.2	0.049
47.	Biokhimiya / Biochemistry USSR	2829	632	308	22.3	10.9	48.7	0.874
48.	Teploenergetika / Therm Eng USSR	1564	630	535	40.3	34.2	84.9	0.507
49.	J Organomet Chem	14458	608	—	4.2	—	—	2.717
50.	Mikrobiologiya / Microbiology USSR	2132	571	293	26.8	13.7	51.3	—
51.	IAN Fiz Atmos Okeana / BAS USSR, Atmos Oceanic Phys	1763	546	314	31.0	17.8	57.5	0.456
52.	Japan Analyst	8828	542	—	6.1	—	—	0.093
53.	Prib Tekh Eksp / Instr Exp Techn USSR	2554	537	167	21.0	6.5	31.1	0.311
54.	Zavod Lab / Industr Lab USSR	3001	524	—	17.5	—	—	0.388
55.	Ukr Biokhim Zh / Ukrainian Biochem J	2409	512	249	21.3	10.3	48.6	—
56.	J Appl Physics	14923	480	—	3.2	—	—	1.645
57.	Nuclear Physics A	23538	480	—	2.0	—	—	2.453
58.	Vestn Mosk Univ Khim	—	475	135	—	—	28.4	0.047
59.	Astronom Zh / Sov Astronomy J	2370	472	336	19.9	14.2	71.2	1.079
60.	Phys Rev D Part Field	17379	458	—	2.6	—	—	2.906
61.	Atomnaya Energiya / Sov Atomic Energy	1732	454	212	26.2	12.2	46.7	0.603
62.	Nuclear Fusion	1760	452	—	25.7	—	—	1.515

Figure 9.50 (continued)

63.	Molekulyarnaya Biol Molecular Biology USSR	2303	440	172	19.1	7.5	39.1	1.070
64.	Khim Prirod Soed Chem Natural Prod USSR	2003	433	274	21.6	13.7	63.3	0.460
65.	Physics Letters A	7733	427	—	5.5	—	—	1.034
66.	Sov Med Soviet Medicine	5656	422	149	7.5	2.6	35.31	0.043
67.	J Electroanalyt Chem	—	400	—	—	—	—	1.349
68.	Radiotekhnika Telecomm Radio Eng USSR 2	2190	400	297	18.3	13.6	74.3	0.129
69.	Bull Soc Chim Fr	17009	395	—	2.3	—	—	1.139
70.	IAN SSSR Ser Biol BAS USSR, Biology	3163	391	—	12.4	—	—	—
71.	Vopr Virusologii Probl Virology	2522	391	256	15.5	10.2	65.5	0.438
72.	Okeanologiya Oceanology USSR	1671	385	195	23.0	11.7	50.7	—
73.	Fiz Goreniya i Vzryva Comb Expl Shock Waves	1207	382	99	31.7	18.2	25.9	—
74.	Phys Rev C Nucl Phys	11481	367	—	3.2	—	—	2.657
75.	Avtomat Svarka Automatic Welding, USSR	976	363	343	37.2	35.1	94.5	0.285

Figure 9.50 (continued)

	Journals	A	B	C	D	E	F	G
1.	Dokl Akad Nauk SSSR Proc Acad Sci USSR	12260	6420	1218	52.4	9.9	19.0	0.372
2.	J Amer Chem Soc	104344	5427	—	5.2	—	—	4.745
3.	Zh Eksp Teor Fiz Sov Phys JETP	13791	5419	1284	39.3	9.3	23.7	2.808
4.	J Chem Phys	9744	3435	—	35.25	—	—	1.591
5.	Zh Fiz Khim Russ J Phys Chem	7039	3421	1302	48.6	18.5	38.1	0.534
6.	Zh Eksp Teor Fiz P JETP Letters	4896	3303	578	67.5	11.8	17.5	1.299
7.	Zh Org Khim J Org Chem USSR	3614	3137	1434	86.8	39.7	45.7	0.807
8.	Fiz Tverdogo Tela Sov Phys Solid State	9744	3028	1426	31.08	14.6	47.1	1.591
9.	J Appl Phys	21168	2502	—	11.8	—	—	1.645
10.	IAN SSSR Ser Khim BAS USSR Chem Sci	3484	2417	1250	69.4	35.9	51.7	0.799
11.	Zh Neorg Khim J Inorg Chem	3701	2343	1591	63.3	43.0	67.9	0.482
12.	Physical Review Letters	27909	2233	—	8.0	—	—	4.962
13.	Nature	64211	2028	—	3.2	—	—	4.228

Figure 9.51 Journals cited most frequently by Russian journals in 1972. A = citations from all journals. B = citations from Russian journals. C = self-citations. D = ratio of citations from Russian journals to citations from all journals. E = ratio of self-citations to citations from all journals (self-cited rate). F = ratio of self-citations to citations from Russian journals. G = overall impact.

14.	Optika Spektroskopiya Opt Spectrosc USSR	3376	1817	822	53.8	24.4	45.2	0.649
15.	J Biol Chem	75415	1700	—	2.3	—	—	5.565
16.	Zh Obshchei Khim J General Chem USSR	3434	1685	975	49.1	28.4	57.9	0.538
17.	Fix Tekh Popl Vodn Sov Phys Semicond	3463	1676	1402	48.4	40.5	83.6	1.530
18.	Fiz Met Metalloved Phys Met Metallogr USSR	3383	1506	516	44.5	15.3	34.3	1.003
19.	Zh Tekh Fiz Sov Phys Tech Phys	3731	1499	691	40.2	18.5	46.1	1.170
20.	IAN SSSR Ser Fiz B Acad Sci USSR Phys Sci	2039	1496	517	73.4	25.4	34.6	0.499
21.	Dokl Akad Nauk Arm SSR P Acad Sci Arm SSR	1442	1415	—	98.1	—	—	0.202
22.	Biochim Biophys Acta	46413	1372	—	3.0	—	—	2.869
23.	J Phys Chem	20479	1344	—	6.6	—	—	2.320
24.	J Org Chem	21202	1276	—	6.0	—	—	1.569
25.	Vysokomol Soed High Mol Cpds	3113	1269	840	40.8	27.0	66.2	0.544
26.	Chem Berichte	13385	1266	—	9.5	—	—	1.652
27.	Zh Analit Khim J Analyt Chem USSR	2405	1134	813	47.2	33.8	71.7	1.008
28.	Yadernaya Fiz Sov J Nucl Phys	1873	1082	919	57.8	49.1	85.0	0.916
29.	Phys Status Solidi	5537	1081	—	19.5	—	—	1.896
30.	Kristallografiya Sov Phys Crystallogr	2318	1053	449	45.4	19.4	42.6	2.320
31.	Biokhimiya Biochemistry USSR	1608	1025	308	63.7	19.2	30.1	0.874
32.	Radiotekh Elektronika Radio Eng Electr Phys USSR	1199	1004	585	83.7	48.8	58.3	0.299
33.	Zh Strukt Khim J Struct Chem USSR	1584	919	414	58.0	26.1	45.0	0.790
34.	Uspekhi Fiz Nauk Sov Phys Uspekhi	2499	904	70	36.2	2.8	7.7	4.970
35.	Uspekhi Khimii Adv Chemistry	1456	892	144	61.3	9.9	16.1	1.747
36.	Astrophys J	17250	890	—	5.2	—	—	3.876
37.	Proc Nat Acad Sci USA	37917	868	—	2.3	—	—	8.288
38.	J Phys Soc Japan	6752	866	—	12.8	—	—	0.945
39.	J Roy Soc London A	12254	851	—	6.9	—	—	1.870
40.	Analyt Chemistry	18471	847	—	4.6	—	—	5.187
41.	Science	43107	845	—	2.0	—	—	4.399
42.	Zh Prikl Khim J Appl Chem USSR	1433	830	494	57.9	34.5	59.5	0.151
43.	Zh Mikrob Epidem Immun J Microb Epidem Immun USSR	942	818	649	86.8	68.9	79.3	0.247
44.	Izmertel Tekh Meas Tech USSR	863	789	737	91.4	85.4	93.4	0.109
45.	Biochemical J	32537	778	—	2.4	—	—	4.386
46.	J Phys Chem Solids	6134	774	—	12.6	—	—	1.646
47.	Ukrain Khim Zh Ukr Chem J	1059	773	310	73.0	29.3	78.4	0.287
48.	Teplofiz Vysok Temp High Temp USSR	922	727	570	78.9	61.8	78.4	0.773

49.	Trans Faraday Soc	11591	719	—	6.2	—	—	2.132
50.	Tsitologiya Cytology	846	719	466	85.0	55.1	64.8	0.383
51.	Zschr Physik	6959	716	—	10.3	—	—	1.309
52.	Acta Crystallogr	9753	713	—	7.3	—	—	2.464
53.	Antibiotiki Antibiotics	—	701	550	—	—	78.5	—
54.	Appl Phys Letters	7164	697	—	9.7	—	—	3.479
55.	J Molec Biol.	21939	693	—	3.2	—	—	7.647
56.	Biofizika Biophysics USSR	1086	692	306	63.7	28.2	44.2	0.852
57.	Kolloidnyi Zh Colloid J USSR	1334	674	347	50.5	26.0	51.5	0.550
58.	Philosophical Mag	7344	663	—	9.0	—	—	2.226
59.	Astronom Zh Sov Astronom J.	1452	641	167	44.2	11.5	26.1	1.079
60.	IVUZ Fizika B Inst Higher Educ Phys	654	622	390	95.1	59.6	62.7	0.270
61.	Teploenergetika Therm Eng USSR	996	613	535	61.6	53.7	87.3	0.507
62.	Bull Soc Chim Fr	9549	599	—	6.3	—	—	1.139
63.	Genetika Genetics USSR	1092	585	458	53.6	41.9	78.3	0.509
64.	Biull Eksp Biol Med B Exp Biol USSR	1379	584	313	42.4	22.7	53.6	0.294
65.	Tetrahedron Letters	16655	581	—	3.5	—	—	2.084
66.	J Bacteriology	16635	578	—	3.4	—	—	2.647
67.	Phys Rev A Gen Phys	7238	551	—	7.6	—	—	2.864
68.	Inorganic Chemistry	12707	547	—	4.3	—	—	2.842
69.	Zschr Anorg Allg Chem	4795	547	—	11.4	—	—	0.986
70.	Acta Metallurgica	5158	541	—	10.5	—	—	2.033
71.	Tetrahedron	9202	539	—	5.9	—	—	1.832
72.	Geokhimiya	—	535	373	—	—	69.7	0.049
73.	Zh Vys Nerv Deyatel Pavlov Pavlov J Higher Nerv Act	—	529	480	—	—	90.7	—
74.	Canad J Chem	9657	524	—	5.4	—	—	1.530
75.	Bull Chem Soc Japan	7906	514	—	6.5	—	—	1.086

Figure 9.51 (continued)

		A	B	C	D	E	F	G
1.	Dokl Akad Nauk Sssr	13013	3317	1424	25.5	10.9	42.9	0.353
2.	Vysokomol Soedin	7115	2836	1809	39.9	25.4	63.8	0.460
3.	Fiz Tverd Tela	7554	2768	1267	36.6	16.8	45.8	0.538
4.	Zh Obshch Khim	6290	2587	1411	41.1	22.4	54.5	0.763
5.	Zh Neorganich Khimii	5827	2554	1671	43.8	28.7	65.4	0.497
6.	Zh Eksp Teor Fiz	6043	2194	1457	36.3	24.1	66.4	1.195
7.	Zh Org Khim	6026	2083	1091	34.6	18.1	52.4	0.649
8.	Zh Fiz Khim	5423	2027	1082	37.4	20.0	53.4	0.333
9.	Sov Phys Semicond	7174	2007	943	28.0	13.1	47.0	0.488
10.	Usp Khim	12319	1831	113	14.9	0.9	6.2	1.079
11.	Opt Spektrosk	4467	1691	923	37.9	20.7	54.6	0.496
12.	Zh Tekhn Fiz	3366	1445	731	42.9	21.7	50.6	0.375
13.	Fiz Metal Metalloved	4026	1421	777	35.3	19.3	54.7	0.454
14.	Jetp Lett-Ussr	2807	1266	509	45.1	18.1	40.2	0.549
15.	Sov J. Nucl Phys	5667	1250	611	22.1	10.8	48.9	0.549
16.	Khim Geterotsikl	3678	1216	613	33.1	16.7	50.4	0.473
17.	Izv An Sssr Khim	2956	1209	551	40.9	18.6	45.6	0.595
18.	Usp Fiz Nauk	5957	1185	148	19.9	2.5	12.5	1.514
19.	J Organomet Chem	26699	1159	--	4.3	--	--	2.392
20.	Izv An Sssr Ser Fiz	4871	1115	517	22.9	10.6	46.4	0.440
21.	Izv Vyss Uch Zav Fiz	2929	1002	292	34.2	10.0	29.1	0.163
22.	Phys Rev. B	27280	928	--	3.4	--	--	2.864
23.	Anal Chem	27658	908	--	3.3	--	--	3.291
24.	Ukr Khim Zh	2288	884	245	38.6	10.7	27.7	0.204
25.	Zh Mikrob Epid Immun	4724	867	683	18.4	14.5	78.8	0.271
26.	Kristallografiya	2311	822	362	35.6	15.7	44.0	0.518
27.	Zavodskaya Laborator	2425	807	412	33.3	17.0	51.1	0.324
28.	Tsitologiya	3955	789	456	19.9	11.5	57.8	0.395
29.	Radiotekh Elektron	2209	784	560	35.5	25.4	71.4	0.244
30.	Antibiotiki	2286	762	590	33.3	25.8	77.4	0.451
31.	Genetika	4834	740	539	15.3	11.2	72.8	0.474
32.	Phys Status Solidi B	9465	725	--	7.7	--	--	1.113
33.	Zh Prikl Khim	1976	725	281	36.7	14.2	38.8	0.106
34.	Prib Techn Eksp	2166	693	448	32.0	20.7	64.7	0.221
35.	Zh Anal Khim	1732	649	330	37.5	19.1	50.9	0.933
36.	Khim Prir Soedin	1722	619	463	35.9	26.9	74.8	0.414
37.	Biofizika	1985	590	335	29.7	16.9	56.8	0.717
38.	J Appl Chem--London	1409	587	--	41.7	--	--	--
39.	Zh Vysh Nerv Deyat	2550	562	486	22.0	19.1	86.5	0.373
40.	Phys Status Solidi A	9410	515	--	5.5	--	--	0.935

Figure 9.52 Major sources of reference to Russian journals in 1974. A = references to all journals. B = references to Russian journals. C = references to self. D = ratio of Russian references to all references. E = ratio of self-citations to all references (self-citing rate). F = ratio of self-citations to Russian references. G = overall impact.

41.	Bunseki Kagaku	12285	462	--	3.8	--	--	0.384
42.	Ukr Biokhim Zh	2224	446	209	20.1	9.4	46.9	0.332
43.	Astron Zh	2142	441	321	20.6	15.0	72.8	0.435
44.	Phys Rev A	13126	427	--	3.3	--	--	2.613
45.	Sov Phys Acoustics	1577	423	245	26.8	15.5	57.9	2.612
46.	Arm Khim Zh	969	399	202	41.2	20.9	50.6	0.309
47.	Farmakol I Toksikol	2684	398	192	14.8	7.2	48.2	0.208
48.	J Chem Phys	33404	397	--	1.2	--	--	2.918
49.	Nucl Phys A	18463	378	--	2.0	--	--	2.423
50.	Phys Rev Lett	11203	354	--	3.2	--	--	5.059
51.	Kolloidnyi Zh	791	339	156	42.9	19.7	46.0	0.254
52.	Vop Virusol	1774	319	244	18.0	13.8	76.5	0.521
53.	Khim Farm Zh	1156	311	155	26.9	13.4	49.8	0.273
54.	Vestn Mosk U Khim	921	310	105	33.7	11.4	33.9	0.228
55.	Phys Rev D	16727	303	--	1.8	--	--	2.723
56.	Vop Med Khim	2196	302	96	13.8	4.4	31.8	0.166
57.	Talanta	3454	283	--	8.2	--	--	1.787
58.	Pure Appl Chem	3151	280	--	8.9	--	--	1.695
59.	Izv An Sssr Biol	2280	278	90	12.2	4.0	32.4	0.300
60.	J Am Chem Soc	46267	252	--	0.5	--	--	4.383
61.	Zh Strukt Khim	1009	248	131	24.6	13.0	52.8	0.687
62.	Dopov Akad Nauk A	1100	247	75	22.5	6.8	30.4	0.056
63.	Zh Obshchei Biologii	1930	235	112	12.2	5.8	47.7	0.277
64.	Mol Biologiya	964	224	88	23.2	9.1	39.3	0.509
65.	Dokl Akad Nauk Bssr	921	211	72	22.9	7.8	34.1	0.070
66.	Phys Rev C	13095	207	--	1.6	--	--	2.299
67.	B Eks Biol Med	1333	199	95	14.9	7.1	47.7	0.183
68.	J. Org Chem	21976	188	--	0.9	--	--	1.495
69.	Phys Fluids	4815	187	--	3.9	--	--	1.181
70.	Biokhimiya	1067	185	101	17.3	9.5	54.6	0.526
71.	P I Elec Elec Eng	5001	184	--	3.7	--	--	2.013
72.	J Chromatogr	11520	182	--	1.6	--	--	2.173
73.	B Soc Chim Fr	11102	177	--	1.6	--	--	1.001
74.	J. Electroanal Ch Inf	6769	176	--	2.6	--	--	1.567
75.	Synthesis	4649	175	--	3.8	--	--	1.342

Figure 9.52 (continued)

		A	B	C	D	E	F	G
1.	Dokl Akad Nauk Sssr	10072	5635	1424	55.9	14.1	25.3	0.353
2.	J Am Chem Soc	98995	4847	--	4.9	--	--	4.383
3.	Zh Eksp Teor Fiz	7753	4670	1457	60.2	18.9	31.2	1.195
4.	Phys Rev	50828	4054	--	8.0	--	--	--
5.	Fiz Tverd Tela	4497	3041	1267	67.6	28.2	41.7	0.538
6.	Zh Obsch Khim	4615	2835	1411	61.4	30.6	49.8	0.763
7.	Zh Neorganich Khimii	3538	2545	1671	71.9	47.2	65.7	0.497
8.	Zh Fiz Khim	3608	2431	1082	67.4	30.0	44.5	0.333
9.	J. Chem Phys	62041	2727	--	4.4	--	--	2.918
10.	Vysokomol Soedin	3047	2203	1809	72.3	59.4	82.1	0.460
11.	Fiz Tekh Poluprovodn	2101	1794	1476	85.4	70.3	82.3	0.731
12.	Phys Rev Lett	29275	1792	--	6.1	--	--	5.059
13.	J Appl Phys	19277	1703	--	8.8	--	--	1.558
14.	Zh Org Khim	2202	1674	1091	76.0	49.5	65.2	0.649
15.	Pisma Zh Eksp Teor	1879	1643	522	87.4	27.8	31.8	1.001
16.	Opt Spektrosk	2396	1627	923	67.9	38.5	56.7	0.496
17.	Izv An Sssr Khim	2825	1572	551	55.6	19.5	35.1	0.595
18.	Nature	59206	1500	--	2.5	--	--	3.636
19.	J Chem Soc	19955	1487	--	7.5	--	--	--
20.	J Biol Chem	81354	1388	--	1.7	--	--	5.843
21.	Zh Tekhn Fiz	1659	1245	731	75.0	44.1	58.7	0.375
22.	Fiz Metal Metalloved	1649	1226	777	74.3	47.1	63.4	0.454
23.	Biochim Biophys Acta	51491	1221	--	2.4	--	--	3.120
24.	Yadernaya Fizika	1807	1181	913	65.4	50.5	77.3	0.818
25.	Izv An Sssr Ser Fiz	1724	1169	517	67.8	30.0	44.2	0.440
26.	J Organ Chem	20539	1142	--	5.6	--	--	1.495
27.	Chem Ber	12629	1140	--	9.0	--	--	1.493
28.	Usp Fiz Nauk	1404	993	148	70.7	10.5	14.9	1.514
29.	J Phys Chem--Us	18086	931	--	5.1	--	--	2.031
30.	Prib Techn Eksp	1056	899	448	85.1	42.4	49.8	0.221
31.	Khim Geterotsikl	1095	894	613	81.6	56.0	68.6	0.473
32.	Phys Rev B	16104	877	--	5.4	--	--	2.864
33.	Zh Anal Khim	2440	864	330	35.4	13.5	38.2	0.933
34.	P Nat Acad Sci Usa	46917	854	--	1.8	--	--	8.989
35.	Usp Khim	1093	829	113	75.8	10.3	13.6	1.079
36.	Kristallografiya	1175	820	362	69.8	30.8	44.1	0.518
37.	Zh Mikrob Epid Immun	939	793	683	84.5	72.7	86.1	0.271
38.	Zavodskaya Laborator	1458	777	412	53.3	28.3	53.0	0.324
39.	Radiotekh Elektron	898	769	560	85.6	62.4	72.8	0.244
40.	Nucl Phys A	12176	714	--	5.9	--	--	2.423

Figure 9.53 Journals cited most frequently by Russian journals in 1974. A = citations from all journals. B = citations from Russian journals. C = self-citations. D = ratio of citations from Russian journals to citations from all journals. E = ratio of self-citations to citations from all journals (self-cited rate). F = ratio of self-citations to citations from Russian journals. G = overall impact.

41.	Biokhimiya	1419	696	101	49.0	7.1	14.5	0.526
42.	J Bacteriol	18375	682	--	3.7	--	--	2.727
43.	Genetika	886	681	539	76.9	60.8	79.1	0.474
44.	Astrophys J	22201	673	--	3.0	--	--	4.063
45.	Phys Status Solidi	4382	665	--	15.2	--	--	--
46.	Antibiotiki	849	661	590	77.9	69.5	89.3	0.451
47.	Science	47505	657	--	1.4	--	--	5.412
48.	Tetrahedron Lett	16509	654	--	4.0	--	--	1.777
49.	Zh Strukt Khim	1377	626	131	45.5	9.5	20.9	0.687
50.	J Phys Soc Japan	7914	626	--	7.9	--	--	1.132
51.	J Mol Biol	24209	623	--	2.6	--	--	7.502
52.	Appl Phys Lett	8625	617	--	7.2	--	--	3.220
53.	Tsitologiya	759	617	456	81.3	60.1	73.9	0.395
54.	Biochem J	31563	610	--	1.9	--	--	3.627
55.	P Roy Soc Lond a Mat	12224	607	--	5.0	--	--	2.215
56.	J Chem Soc--Chem Commun	14454	606	--	4.2	--	--	2.096
57.	Zh Prikl Khim	1361	559	281	41.1	20.6	50.3	0.106
58.	Anal Chem	18190	554	--	3.0	--	--	3.291
59.	Ukr Khim Zh	793	550	245	69.4	30.9	44.5	0.204
60.	Inorg Chem	14310	542	--	3.8	--	--	2.457
61.	Khim Prir Soedin	736	531	463	72.1	62.9	87.2	0.414
62.	Phys Lett B	9958	527	--	5.3	--	--	0.373
63.	Zh Vysh Nerv Deyat	636	525	486	82.5	76.4	92.6	0.373
64.	Biofizika	897	517	335	57.6	37.3	64.8	0.717
65.	J Polymer Sci	4385	516	--	11.8	--	--	--
66.	Kinet Katal	--	514	--	--	--	--	--
67.	Tetrahedron	8903	512	--	5.8	--	--	1.576
68.	J Phys Chem Solids	5766	508	--	8.8	--	--	1.394
69.	Akust Zh	549	501	434	91.3	79.1	86.6	0.605
70.	Z Phys	6662	497	--	7.5	--	--	1.340
71.	T Faraday Soc	8857	492	--	5.6	--	--	--
72.	Can J Chem	9142	490	--	5.4	--	--	1.396
73.	Kolloidnyi Zh	876	489	156	55.8	17.8	31.9	0.254
74.	Ann Chem Just Lieb	6177	481	--	7.8	--	--	1.024
75.	Philosophical Mag	7063	476	--	6.7	--	--	1.836

Figure 9.53 (continued)

Journals	A	B	C	D	E	F	G
1. Dokl Akad Nauk SSSR / Proc Acad Sci USSR	7647	2106	837	27.5	11.0	39.7	0.572
2. Fiz Tverdogo Tela / Sov Phys Solid State	3704	1853	1114	50.0	30.1	60.1	2.046
3. Zh Eksp Teor Fiz / Sov Phys JETP	3170	1769	1141	55.8	36.0	64.5	3.944
4. Zh Fiz Khim / Russ J Phys Chem	2527	1112	796	44.0	31.5	71.6	0.838
5. Yadernaya Fiz / Sov J Nucl Phys	2225	868	463	39.0	20.8	53.3	2.054
6. Usp Fiz Nauk / Sov Phys Uspękhi	2140	802	103	37.5	4.9	12.8	4.930
7. Physical Review	14496	701	—	4.8	—	—	3.679
8. Fiz Tekh Popl Vodn / Sov Phys Semicond	1278	634	253	49.6	19.8	39.9	1.741
9. Vysomolek Soed A / High Mol Cpds A	1750	585	289	33.4	16.5	49.4	0.559
10. Zh Eksp Teor Fiz P / JETP Letters	1070	560	230	52.3	21.5	41.7	2.240
11. Zh Tekh Fiz / Sov Phys Tech Phys	1032	546	381	52.9	36.9	69.8	1.322
12. Radiotekh Elektronika / Radio Eng Electr Phys USSR	1451	518	380	35.7	26.2	73.4	0.756
13. Zavod Lab / Indust Lab USSR	1217	402	301	33.0	24.7	74.9	0.178
14. Phys Status Solidi	4973	382	—	7.7	—	—	1.578
15. Astronom Zh / Sov Astronomy Journal	1106	380	291	34.4	26.3	76.6	1.635
16. IAN USSR Ser Fiz / B Acad Sci USSR Phys Ser	1568	339	140	21.6	8.9	41.3	0.807
17. IVUZ Fizika / B Inst Higher Ed Phys	1285	330	67	25.7	5.2	20.3	—
18. Teploenergetika / Therm Eng USSR	770	326	275	42.3	35.7	84.4	0.572
19. Fiz Met Metaloved / Phys Met Metallogr USSR	764	272	160	35.6	20.9	58.8	0.872
20. Optika Spektroskopiya / Opt Spectrosc USSR	1561	247	—	15.8	—	—	1.331
21. Indust Eng Chem	2952	219	—	7.4	—	—	1.123
22. IAN Fiz Atmos Okeana / BAS USSR, Atmos Oceanic Phys	747	216	117	28.9	15.7	54.2	0.961
23. Svar Proiz / Weld Prod USSR	498	216	209	43.4	42.0	96.8	—
24. Kristallografiya / Sov Phys Crystallogr	490	213	147	43.5	30.0	69.0	1.339
25. Stal / Stal in Engl USSR	502	192	177	38.2	35.3	92.2	0.124
26. Teplofiz Vysok Temp / High Temp USSR	994	189	139	19.0	14.0	73.5	0.423
27. Izmeritel Tekh / Meas Tech USSR	525	189	186	36.0	35.4	98.4	0.163
28. Nuclear Physics A	5011	174	—	3.4	—	—	0.858
29. Atomnaya Energiya / Sov Atomic Energy	1133	171	65	15.1	5.7	38.0	0.479

Figure 9.54 Major sources of references to Russian journals in 1969. A = references to all journals. B = references to Russian journals. C = references to self. D = ratio of Russian references to all references. E = ratio of self-citations to all references (self-citing rate). F = ratio of self-citations to Russian references. G = overall impact.

#	Journal						
30.	Avtomat Telemekh Automat Rem Contr USSR	437	167	138	38.2	31.6	82.6	0.340
31.	J Apllied Physics	5811	174	—	2.9	—	—	1.936
32.	Okeanologiya Oceanology	620	160	92	25.8	14.8	57.5	0.577
33.	Fiz Goreniya Vzryva Comb Expl Shock Waves	345	152	33	44.1	9.6	21.7	—
34.	Organometal Chem Rev B 1961	1961	151	—	7.7	—	—	—
35.	Zh Prikl Mekh J Appl Mech Tech Phys	451	149	119	33.0	26.4	79.9	0.491
36.	Biofizika Biophysics USSR	607	145	72	23.9	11.9	49.7	0.414
37.	Kolloidnyi Zh Colloid Journal USSR	364	144	86	39.6	23.6	59.7	0.574
38.	Prib Tekh Eksp Instr Exp Techn USSR	1513	144	9	9.5	0.6	6.3	0.357
39.	Physical Review Letters	3230	144	—	4.5	—	—	5.114
40.	Akust Zh Sov Phys Acoustics	351	144	123	41.0	35.0	85.4	1.017
41.	Radiotekhnika Telecomm Radio Eng USSR	738	140	48	19.0	6.5	34.3	—
42.	J Chem Phys	10710	137	—	1.3	—	—	3.180
43.	Zh Nauch Prikl Foto J Sci Appl Photogr	418	135	76	32.2	18.2	56.3	0.400
44.	Vestn Mashinostroeniya Russ Eng J	382	131	131	34.3	34.3	100.0	0.557
45.	Eur Polymer J	1308	125	—	9.6	—	—	—
46.	Bull Soc Chim Fr	6283	112	—	1.8	—	—	1.147
47.	Geokhimiya Geochemistry Internat	1356	105	19	7.7	1.4	18.1	—
48.	IAN SSSR Metally Russian Metallurgy (Metally)	446	101	—	22.7	—	—	—
49.	Dokl Soil Sci	502	100	60	19.9	12.0	60.0	0.099
50.	Nauchno-tekhn Inf 1 Sci Techn Inf	418	100	72	23.9	17.2	72.0	
51.	Novo Cimento	3834	100	—	2.6	—	—	0.527
52.	Chemical Reviews	2597	94	—	3.7	—	—	8.680
53.	Ann Rev Nucl Sci	1891	95	—	5.0	—	—	5.629
54.	Physics of Fluids	1512	92	—	6.1	—	—	1.581
55.	J Org Chem	6848	91	—	1.3	—	—	2.407
56.	Koks Khim Coke and Chemistry USSR	328	86	66	26.2	20.12	76.7	0.239
57.	Biull Eksp Biol Med B Exp Biol USSR	430	84	57	19.5	13.2	67.9	0.094
58.	Annu Rep Progr Chem B	5091	83	—	1.6	—	—	—
59.	J Phys Soc Japan	2119	75	—	3.5	—	—	1.045
60.	J Am Chem Soc	10135	70	—	0.7	—	—	5.859
61.	Progr Theoret Phys	1924	70	—	3.6	—	—	1.513
62.	J Phys Chem	4873	68	—	1.4	—	—	2.429
63.	Naturwissenschaften	1574	65	—	4.1	—	—	0.920
64.	Physics Letters	1702	65	—	3.8	—	—	1.654
65.	Annu Rev Fluid Mech	943	64	—	6.8	—	—	—
66.	J Electrochem Soc	1514	61	—	4.0	—	—	0.797
67.	Appl Spectrosc Rev	593	60	—	10.1	—	—	—

Figure 9.54 (continued)

	Journal						
68.	Tekhn Kibernetika	267	60	—	22.4	1.0	7.0	—
69.	Space Sci Rev	1192	60	—	5.0	—	—	2.492
70.	J Inorg Nucl Chem	1839	55	—	3.0	—	—	1.535
71.	J Electroanalyt Chem	1066	54	—	5.1	—	—	1.724
72.	J Polymer Sci Al	1761	52	—	3.0	—	—	1.039
73.	Inorg Chem	3353	51	—	1.5	—	—	3.296
74.	J Chem Soc	3802	49	—	1.3	—	—	3.123
75.	Astrophysical J	3799	48	—	1.3	—	—	4.972

	Journal	A	B	C	D	E	F	G
1.	Zh Eksp Teor Fiz / Sov Phys JETP	4213	2619	1141	62.2	27.1	43.6	3.944
2.	Physical Review	20666	2019	—	9.8	—	—	3.679
3.	Fiz Tverdoga Tela / Sov Phys Solid State	2605	1876	1114	72.0	42.8	59.4	2.046
4.	Dokl Akad Nauk SSSR / Proc Acad Sci USSR	3103	1723	837	55.5	27.0	48.6	0.572
5.	Zh Fiz Khim / Russ J Phys Chem	1385	985	796	71.1	57.5	80.8	0.838
6.	Zh Tekh Fiz / Sov Phys Tech Phys	912	645	381	70.7	41.8	59.1	1.322
7.	Optika Spektroskopiya / Opt Spectrosc USSR	1050	641	458	61.1	43.6	71.5	1.331
8.	Zh Eksp Teor Fiz P / JETP Letters	756	595	230	78.7	30.4	38.7	2.240
9.	Yadernaya Fiz / Sov J Nucl Phys	734	592	463	80.7	63.1	78.2	2.054
10.	Radiotekh Elektronika / Radio Eng Electr Phys USSR	575	535	380	93.0	66.1	71.0	0.756
11.	Prib Tekh Eksp / Instr Exp Techn USSR	559	528	469	94.5	83.9	88.8	0.357
12.	Physical Review Letters	6544	500	—	7.6	—	—	5.114
13.	J Appl Phys	5274	483	—	9.2	—	—	1.936
14.	J Chem Phys	13687	482	—	3.5	—	—	3.180
15.	Usp Fiz Nauk / Sov Phys Uspekhi	634	401	103	63.3	16.3	25.7	4.930
16.	Nuclear Physics	2539	370	—	14.6	—	—	0.858
17.	Vysokomolek Soed / Polymer Sci USSR	565	344	289	60.9	51.2	84.0	0.559
18.	Zavod Lab / Indust Lab USSR	474	336	301	70.9	63.5	89.6	0.178
19	Astronom Zh / Sov Astronomy Journal	541	332	291	61.4	53.8	87.7	1.635
20.	J Amer Chem Soc	26307	327	—	1.2	—	—	5.859
21.	Fiz Tekh Poluprovod / Sov Phys Semiconduct USSR	387	326	253	84.2	65.4	77.6	1.741
22.	IAN SSSR Ser Fiz / B Acad Sci USSR Phys Ser	450	323	140	71.8	31.1	43.3	0.807
23.	Geokhimiya / Geochemistry Internat USSR	342	300	262	87.7	76.6	87.3	—

Figure 9.55 Journals cited most frequently by Russian journals in 1969. A = citations from all journals. B = citations from Russian journals. C = self-citations. D = ratio of citations from Russian journals to citations from all journals. E = ratio of self-citations to citations from all journals (self- cited rate). F = ratio of self-citations to citations from Russian journals. G = overall impact.

24.	Fiz Met Metaloved Phys Met Metallogr USSR	478	294	160	61.5	33.5	54.4	0.872
25.	Teploenergetika Therm Eng USSR	336	281	275	83.6	81.9	97.9	0.572
26.	Physics Letters	3295	280	—	8.5	—	—	1.654
27.	Kristallografiya Sov Phys Crystallogr	468	278	147	59.4	31.4	52.9	1.339
28.	Nature	15310	225	—	1.5	—	—	2.244
29.	J Polymer Sci	2893	198	—	6.8	—	—	1.039
30.	Avtomat Telemekh Automat Rem CONTR USSR	277	193	138	69.7	48.9	71.5	0.340
31.	Izmertel Tekh Meas Tech USSR	207	193	186	93.2	89.9	96.4	0.163
32.	Nuovo Cimento	2442	188	—	7.7	—	—	0.527
33.	J Phys Chem	4678	176	—	3.8	—	—	2.429
34.	Proc Roy Soc London	4693	171	—	3.6	—	—	2.998
35.	IEEE Trans	763	167	—	21.9	—	—	—
36.	J Phys Chem Solids	1419	163	—	11.5	—	—	2.073
37.	Zschr Physik	1759	162	—	9.2	—	—	1.536
38.	Philosophical Magazine	1924	157	—	8.2	—	—	2.251
39.	J Phys Soc Japan	1733	142	—	8.2	—	—	1.045
40.	Teplofiz Vysok Temp High Temp USSR	162	142	135	87.7	83.3	95.1	0.423
41.	Kolloidnyi Zh Colloid Journal USSR	165	140	86	84.9	52.1	61.4	0.574
42.	Phys Status Solidi	1313	139	—	10.6	—	—	1.578
43.	Astrophysical J	4258	136	—	3.2	—	—	4.972
44.	J Physics	3181	136	—	4.3	—	—	1.405
45.	Pro IEEE	1601	136	—	8.5	—	—	1.372
46.	Prikl Mat Mekh PMM J Appl Math Mech	194	126	119	65.0	61.3	94.4	0.491
47.	J Chem Soc	13978	122	—	0.9	—	—	3.123
48.	IAN Fiz Atmos Okeana B Acad Sci USSR Atmos Oceanic Phys.	127	117	117	92.3	92.3	100.0	0.961
49.	Okeanologiya	114	107	89	93.9	78.1	83.2	0.577
50.	Appl Phys Letters	1318	105	—	8.0	—	—	3.688
51.	Avtomat Svarka Automatic Welding USSR	217	105	105	48.4	48.4	100.0	0.315
52.	Vestn Mashinostroeniya Russ Eng J	134	105	105	78.4	78.4	100.0	0.557
53.	Biofizika Biophysics USSR	157	101	72	64.3	45.9	71.3	0.414
54.	IAN USSR Ser Khim. B Acad Sci USSR Chem Ser	362	97	—	26.8	—	—	0.547
55.	IAN USSR B. Acad Sci USSR	70	93	—	33.2	—	—	0.155
56.	Atomnaya Energiya Sov Atomic Energy	249	92	42	37.0	16.9	45.7	0.479
57.	Akust Zh Sov Phys Acoustics	213	90	74	42.3	34.7	82.2	—
58.	Trans Faraday Soc	2911	88	—	3.0	—	—	2.149
59.	Zh Nauch Prikl Fotogr J Sci Appl Photogr Cin	96	85	76	88.5	79.2	89.4	0.400
60.	Rev Modern Physics	1353	81	—	6.0	—	—	4.508
61.	Canad J Physics	1323	77	—	5.8	—	—	2.186

Figure 9.55 (continued)

62.	Rev Sci Instr	1223	77	—	6.3	—	—	0.868
63.	Acta Metallurgica	1304	76	—	5.9	—	—	2.278
64.	Ann Physics	1096	72	—	6.6	—	—	3.188
65.	Analyt Chem	4219	69	—	1.6	—	—	1.661
66.	Biochim Biophys Acta	9500	68	—	0.7	—	—	3.287
67.	Zh Org Chim J Org Chem. USSR	151	68	—	45.0	—	—	0.185
68.	IVUZ Fizika B Inst Higher Ed Phys	92	67	67	72.8	72.8	100.0	—
69.	Science	9739	67	—	0.7	—	—	2.894
70.	Comptes Rendus	5472	66	—	1.2	—	—	0.780
71.	IAN SSSR Metally Russian Metallurgy (Metally)	114	66	—	57.9	—	—	0.429
72.	J Geophys Res	3556	65	—	1.8	—	—	3.665
73.	Biull Eksp Biol Med B Exp Biol USSR	87	64	44	73.6	65.5	89.1	0.094
74.	Electrosvyaz	72	61	41	84.7	56.9	67.2	—
75.	J Opt Soc Amer	1597	60	—	3.8	—	—	0.962

Figure 9.55 (continued)

Figures 9.50 and 9.52, the lists of journals that were the major sources of references that cited the core group during the two years studied. Figure 9.50 shows that 17 of the top 75 sources in 1972 were non-Russian. Figure 9.52 shows that in 1974 the number of major non-Russian sources rose slightly to 21 out of 75. However, if you look at the number of citations received from non-Russian journals (rather than the number of journals) as a percentage of total citations received, you find that the utility of Russian journals by non-Russian scientists held about steady. In 1972, the non-Russian journals accounted for 15% of the source group's citations to the Russian journals. In 1974, the figure was still only 14%, which is a negligible decrease. Looking at it the other way, the Russian core journals also accounted for the same percentage of the total citations originating in the non-Russian journals in the two years studied. In 1972, the non-Russian journals published 265,221 references, of which 4% cited the Russian core journals. In 1974, the total number of references published rose to 323,189, of which 3% cited the Russian core journals.

The analysis of the journals cited most by the core group showed the same story. Figure 9.51 shows that 35 of the 75 journals cited most by the Russian core group in 1972 were non-Russian. Figure 9.53 shows that the figure remained substantially the same, 36, in 1974. The core-group percentage of total citations to the non-Russian journals accounted for 5% of the total citations received by the non-Russian journals; the figure for 1974 was 4%.

Although the analysis of the 1972 and 1974 lists didn't show any significant change in the degree of interaction between the Russian literature and the literature of other countries, an extension of the analysis back to 1969 did suggest that the orientation of the Russian literature has changed. The lists of journals that were the main sources and targets of the core-group citations in 1969 (Figures 9.54 and 9.55) showed a heavy orientation toward physics, chemistry, and their technologies. The lists for 1972 (Figures 9.52 and 9.53), particularly the most frequently cited list (Figure 9.53), showed a moderation of the orientation, manifested by the increasing prominence of biomedical journals. For example, *Nature* improved its ranking on the most frequently cited list from twenty-eighth in 1969 (Figure 9.55) to thirteenth in 1972 (Figure 9.53). The *Journal of Biological Chemistry,* which didn't even rank among the 75 journals cited most often in 1969, showed up in the fifteenth position in 1972. The evidence points in the direction of a definite shift in the emphasis of Soviet research.

French Journal Literature (29)

A similar study of French journals was conducted with the 1974 data from a core group of 129 journals published in France. Again, it should be remembered that the study did not include data on material published by French scientists in "outside" journals, and to that extent it cannot be considered definitive. Nevertheless, the major journals published in France certainly publish a large-enough percentage of the work of French scientists to be roughly representative of French science.

First, some statistics to put the French journal literature into a worldwide perspective. The 129 French journals used as a core group in the study represented about 5.3% of the journals indexed by *SCI* in 1974 and accounted for 3.8% of the source items indexed and 2.6% of the references contained in those items. Although the average source item contained 13 references, the average French source item contained only 8.8.

If the French literature conformed to the international pattern of scientific and technical literature, the list of journals it cited most frequently (Figure 9.56) would have corresponded roughly to the list of journals cited most frequently by all the scientific and technical literatures in 1974. For example, the journal most highly cited by an aggregation of all the literatures in 1974 was the *Journal of the American Chemical Society.* All things being equal, it should also have been the journal most highly cited by the French core group; and, in fact, it did rank first in Figure 9.56. Since the core group contributed 2.6% of the references processed for *SCI* in 1974, it should have accounted for roughly the same percentage of the citations received by *JACS* in that year. And again, it did, accounting for 2.555% of the references that cited *JACS* material.

With the second item on the list, however, the picture changes radically. The journal second most frequently cited by the core group was *Bulletin de la Societe Chemique de France,* which was cited by all the journals covered by *SCI* a total of 6671 times. If the French average of accounting for 2.6% of all references held true, 173 of the citations received by the *Bulletin de la Societe Chemique de France* would have originated in references published by the core group. The analysis showed, however, that the core group accounted for 2471 of the citations, or 37% of the total citation count. Column D in Figure 9.56, which shows the references by the core group as a percentage of the total citation rate of each journal, makes it easy to see where the core group's reference rate varied from its average 2.6% contribution. Obviously, some variation is to be expected, but contributions of 10% or more certainly seem to be a variation of consequence. Interestingly enough, variations of this magnitude occurred in 12 cases, and 11 of them were French journals. Also interesting is the fact that all 11 of these French journals were characterized by a high self-cited rate and a low impact factor.

It would be reasonable to conclude that the 11 journals owed their position on the list to an understandable preference of French scientists for the French language. But if that is so, why are there not more French journals, and why are the impact factors of the journals that are there so low? Even the combination of high self-cited rates and above average reference rates from the core group did not succeed in raising the impact factors to a more respectable level. The language-preference explanation is further weakened by comparing the ranking of the journals on this list with their ranking on an international list. The latter ranking is shown in Figure 9.56 in parenthesis after the journal-title abbreviation. If the language factor is responsible for raising *(Nouvelle) Press Medicale* from three hundred sixty-fifth on the international list to sixth on the French list, why does *Lancet* rank fifth on the French list?

Figure 9.57 shows that most of the references that cited the core group came from French journals and that the self-citing rate of these journals was unusually high. In addition, the list differed significantly from *SCI*'s international list. Only four or five of the major sources of citations to the French journals could be considered physics journals, whereas double that number appeared on the 1974 international list of major reference sources. The same discrepancy showed up on the most cited list.

Overall, the analysis showed the French literature as having relatively little impact on the international community—and even on the French community. The core group cited foreign literature much more than its own, even though its own literature is cited mainly by itself. The mathematics section (A) of the *Comptes Rendus* of the French Academy illustrated both sides of the coin. The entry for it in Figure 9.57 shows that only 30.6% of its references cited journals in the French core group and that most of them (80.6%) were self-citations. Figure 9.56, where it ranks twenty-fifth, shows that 71.3% of the citations it received originated in the core group; and, again, most of them were a function of self-citation.

Although the low impact that the French literature had upon the international community could be attributed to language, the high citation rates enjoyed by older French literature makes it seem unlikely. An additional analysis of core-group material that was cited more than 150 times between 1961 and 1974 turned up 13 items. The most significant characteristic of these itmes is that 11 were published before 1965. And it turned out that several of the articles, though published in French journals, were not written by French scientists.

	JOURNAL	A	B	C	D	E	F	G
1.	J. Amer. Chem. Soc. (1)	98995	2555	–	2.6	–	–	4.38
2.	B. Soc. Chim. France (95)	6671	2471	1700	37.0	25.5	68.8	0.77
3.	C. Rend. Acad. Sci.	8634	2106	626	24.4	7.3	29.7	–
4.	C. Rend. Acad. Sci. D Nat. (206)	3603	1758	1317	48.8	36.6	74.9	0.51
5.	Lancet (9)	37047	1451	–	3.9	–	–	6.67
6.	Nouv. Presse Medicale (365)	2908	1450	323	49.9	11.1	22.3	0.60
7.	Nature (4)	59206	1403	–	2.4	–	–	3.63
8.	J. Biol. Chemistry (2)	81354	1341	–	1.6	–	–	5.84
9.	Biochim. Biophys. Acta (5)	51487	1125	–	2.2	–	–	3.11
10.	New England J. Med. (13)	26726	1125	–	4.2	–	–	8.36
11.	C. Rend. Acad. Sci. C Chim (272)	2857	1082	573	37.9	20.1	53.0	0.51
12.	Circulation (38)	14461	1081	–	7.5	–	–	6.83
13.	J. Chemical Physics (3)	62040	1029	–	1.7	--	–	2.91
14.	J. Clin. Invest. (14)	24768	920	–	3.7	–	–	6.99
15.	Science (8)	46488	887	–	1.9	–	–	5.25
16.	P. Nat. Acad. Sci. USA (7)	46916	836	–	1.8	–	–	8.98
17.	J. Organic Chemistry (21)	20539	799	–	3.9	–	–	1.49
18.	Brit. Med. J. (18)	20700	798	–	3.9	–	–	3.54
19.	J. Amer. Med. Assoc. (30)	17211	748	–	4.3	–	–	3.06
20.	J. Chemical Society (22)	19955	748	–	3.7	–	–	–
21.	C. Rend. Soc. Biol. (283)	2742	698	232	25.5	8.5	33.3	0.30
22.	J. Chim. Physique (306)	2532	657	367	25.9	14.5	55.9	0.88
23.	Amer. J. Medicine (56)	9779	633	–	6.5	–	–	4.41
24.	Physical Review (6)	50842	631	–	1.2	–	–	–
25.	C. Rend. Acad. Sci. A Math (705)	844	602	474	71.3	56.2	78.7	0.20
26.	Tetrahedron Letters (31)	16478	589	–	3.6	–	–	1.77
27.	Biochemical Journal (10)	31563	585	–	1.9	–	–	3.62
28.	Arch. Maladies Coeur (711)	835	569	221	68.1	26.5	38.8	0.64
29.	Amer. J. Cardiology (93)	6811	554	–	8.1	–	–	3.70
30.	J. Urology (135)	5031	542	–	10.8	–	–	0.72
31.	Semaine Hopitaux (645)	974	541	125	55.5	12.8	23.1	0.29
32.	Annals Surgery (84)	7459	512	–	6.9	–	–	2.12
33.	Radiology (99)	6311	492	–	7.8	–	–	1.19
34.	Annals Internal Med. (50)	10231	489	–	4.8	–	–	4.82
35.	Gastroenterology (70)	8693	487	–	5.6	–	–	5.39
36.	P. Soc. Exp. Biol. Med. (28)	18167	477	–	2.6	–	–	1.46
37.	J. Cell Biology (24)	19103	474	–	2.5	–	–	6.77
38.	Amer. J. Roentg. (133)	5038)	469	–	9.3	–	–	1.00
39.	Amer. Heart J. (102)	5994	456	–	7.6	–	–	1.79
40.	C. Rend. Acad. Sci. B Phys. (456)	1522	451	302	29.6	19.8	67.0	0.44
41.	J. Molecular Biology (15)	24209	446	–	1.8	–	–	7.50
42.	J. Physical Chemistry (29)	18086	445	–	2.5	–	–	2.03
43.	Cancer (60)	9498	440	–	4.6	–	–	2.36
44.	Amer. J. Physiology (17)	21519	424	–	2.0	–	–	2.41
45.	Bioch. Bioph. Res. Comm. (16)	23136	422	–	1.8	–	–	3.73
46.	Biochemistry (12)	27080	421	–	1.6	–	–	4.71
47.	Phys. Rev. Letters (11)	29229	401	–	1.4	–	–	5.05
48.	J. Exp. Medicine (19)	20699	400	–	1.9	–	–	11.87
49.	J. Bacteriology (26)	18369	391	–	2.1	–	–	2.72
50.	Amer. J. Obst. Gyn. (66)	8866	389	–	4.4	–	–	2.09

Figure 9.56 Journals cited most frequently by French journals. A = citations from all journals. B = citations from French journals. C = self-citations. D = ratio of citations from French journals to citations from all journals. E = ratio of self-citations to citations from all journals (self-cited rate). F = ratio of self-citations to citations from French journals. G = overall impact. Figures in parentheses following the names of the journals show their ranks on ISI's international list of most highly cited journals.

	JOURNAL	A	B	C	D	E	F	G
1.	C. Rend. Acad. Sci. D Nat.	11129	1952	1317	17.5	11.8	67.5	0.51
2.	B. Soc. Chim. France	11102	1379	869	12.4	7.8	63.0	0.77
3.	C. Rend. Acad. Sci. C Chim.	4762	1151	573	24.2	12.0	49.8	0.51
4.	Semaine Hopitaux	5603	882	125	15.7	2.2	14.2	0.29
5.	Nouv. Presse Medicale	4900	801	323	16.3	6.6	40.3	0.60
6.	J. Organomet. Chem.	22699	655	–	2.9	–	–	2.38
7.	C. Rend. Acad Sci. A Math.	1924	588	474	30.6	24.6	80.6	0.20
8.	J. Chim. Physique	4489	556	367	12.4	8.2	66.0	0.88
9.	C. Rend. Acad. Sci. B Phys.	2243	466	302	20.8	13.5	64.8	0.44
10.	Analytical Chemistry	27658	435	–	1.6	–	–	3.29
11.	Tetrahedron	13059	404	–	3.1	–	–	1.57
12.	Ann. Chirurgie	1916	394	79	20.6	4.1	20.0	0.16
13.	C. Rend. Soc. Biol.	1926	367	232	19.1	12.0	63.2	0.30
14.	Lyon Medical	2771	365	49	13.2	1.8	13.4	0.24
15.	Arch. Maladies Coeur	2466	358	221	14.5	9.0	61.7	0.64
16.	J. Amer. Chem. Soc.	46267	343	–	0.7	–	–	4.38
17.	J. Chem. Soc. Perkin	20327	342	–	1.7	–	–	1.34
18.	J. Organic Chemistry	21976	326	–	1.5	–	–	1.49
19.	Revue Rhumatisme	1543	315	103	20.4	6.7	32.7	0.48
20.	Tetrahedron Letters	11178	269	–	2.4	–	–	1.77
21.	Pathologie Biologie	2866	252	49	8.9	1.7	19.4	0.56
22.	Lille Medicale	1842	249	41	13.5	2.2	16.5	0.13
23.	Canad. J. Chemistry	12685	240	–	1.9	–	–	1.39
24.	Biochimie	4677	236	154	5.0	3.3	65.3	1.63
25.	Neuro-Chirurgie	1363	230	66	16.9	4.8	28.7	0.36
26.	J. Radiol. Electrol.	1264	223	65	17.6	5.1	29.1	0.21
27.	Arch. Fr. Pediatrie	1642	215	72	13.1	4.4	33.5	1.01
28.	J. Chirurgie	1265	215	14	17.0	1.1	6.5	0.15
29.	J. Microscopie (Paris)	1634	212	129	13.0	7.9	60.8	1.60
30.	Eur. J. Med. Chem.	1541	207	112	13.4	7.3	54.1	–
31.	Brain Research	19626	198	–	1.0	–	–	3.10
32.	Ann. Cardiol. Angeiol.	1132	192	13	17.0	1.1	6.8	0.35
33.	Deut. Med. Wschr.	–	187	–	–	–	–	–
34.	Biochim. Biophys. Acta	45366	185	–	0.4	–	–	3.11
35.	Coeur Med. Interne	1308	184	30	14.1	2.3	16.3	0.53
36.	Physical Review B	27280	181	–	0.7	–	–	2.86
37.	Ann. Radiologie	1122	180	24	16.0	2.1	13.3	0.39
38.	J. Urologie Nephrol.	1171	180	107	15.4	9.1	59.4	0.18
39.	Cell Tissue Research	–	177	–	–	–	–	–
40.	J. Physique	1749	177	110	10.1	6.3	62.1	1.84
41.	Arch. Fr. Mal. App. Dig.	1556	172	58	11.1	3.7	33.7	0.72
42.	J. Chemical Physics	33404	172	–	0.5	–	–	2.91
43.	Uspekhi Khimii	12319	172	–	1.4	–	–	1.07
44.	Nouv. Revue Fr. Hemat.	1675	170	98	10.1	5.9	57.6	0.94
45.	Gen. Comp. Endocrinol.	3715	169	–	4.5	–	–	2.03
46.	Humangenetik	3820	165	–	4.3	–	–	1.70
47.	Revue Chir. Orthop.	688	157	70	22.8	10.2	44.6	0.17
48.	Therapie	1352	148	32	10.9	2.4	21.6	0.40
49.	B. Soc. Zool. France	–	147	30	–	–	20.4	–
50.	J. Electroanal. Chem.	6769	147	–	2.2	–	–	1.56

Figure 9.57 Major sources of references to French journals. A = references to all journals. B = references to French journals. C = references to self. D = ratio of French references to all references. E = ratio of self-citations to all references (self-citing rate). F = ratio of self-citations to French references. G = overall impact.

Japanese Journal Literature (30)

A study of the 79 Japanese journals covered by the 1974 *SCI* produced the results shown in Figures 9.58 and 9.59. As in all these studies of selected national literatures, only the journals published in the subject country, and only the work that the country's scientists published in those journals, were included. In this particular case, the coverage of the core group of journals was a bit less than complete in terms in citations. Because of the language problem, citations written in Japanese were not included. What effect this limitation had on the accuracy of the citation counts is unknown. All we know for sure on this subject is that very few of the core-group journals were published in only the Japanese language, and the average number of references per published item in the core-group journals matched the international average just on the strength of the references we did pick up.

The statistics on the relationship of the core group to the international literature are as follows: the group represented 3.2% of the international literature covered by *SCI* in 1974, published 2.7% of the source itmes processed, and produced 2.6% of the references picked up from those source items.

The first finding of the study was that the bibliographic law of concentration applies as much to the Japanese literature as it does to all the others. Though the core group cited 9600 different publications, the 50 cited most frequently (1% of the target group) accounted for 42% of the cited material. Conversely, the 50 major sources of references that cited the core group accounted for 43% of the citations received from 1576 different journals.

Using the core group's proportionate share of the international reference pool as a measure, we found (Figure 9.58) that the group cited the top-ranking *Journal of the American Chemical Society* somewhat more frequently than would be expected in a statistically ideal world: they accounted for 5.2% of its citations compared to their 2.6% share of the reference pool. Figure 9.59 shows that *JACS* did not return the compliment; only 0.8% of its 1974 references cited the 79 Japanese journals. In fact, about the only non-Japanese journal that cited the core group at a rate consistent with the group's 2.7% share of the international pool of source items was *Phytochemistry*.

Probably the most important finding (in terms of characterizing Japanese science) in the analysis of the journals most frequently cited by the core group (Figure 9.58) was the high rankings of the American Chemical Society journals, particularly those dealing with biochemistry. In contrast, *Nature, Science,* and the *Proceedings of the National Academy of Sciences USA* received notably less attention. This suggests a preponderance of chemical research in Japanese science. Another aspect of that characteristic is suggested by *Analytical Chemistry,* which not only ranked twelfth but also owed no less than 8% of its total citation rate to the Japanese core group. This is indicative of an intense interest in analytical methods, which could be considered a reflection of a strong orientation toward industrial development.

An interesting feature of the major sources of references that cite the core group (Figure 9.59) is the strong representation of occidental journals. Although the five major sources are Japanese journals, non-Japanese journals appear in substantial numbers, beginning with the triad of *Biochimica Biophysica Acta, Tetrahedron Letters,* and *Journal of Biological Chemistry,* throughout the remainder of the list.

Journal	A	B	C	D	E	F	G
1. J. Amer. Chem. Soc	98995	5115	— —	5.2	— —	— —	4.38
2. J. Biol. Chem.	81354	3192	— —	3.9	— —	— —	5.84
3. *Bull. Chem. Soc. Japan*	7936	2375	1386	29.9	17.5	58.4	0.93
4. J. Chem. Physics	62040	1764	— —	2.8	— —	— —	2.91
5. Biochim. Biophys. Acta	51487	1720	— —	3.3	— —	— —	3.11
6. Chem. Pharmaceut. Bull.	3477	1617	1076	46.5	30.9	66.5	0.93
7. Analyt. Chemistry	18190	1515	— —	8.3	— —	— —	3.29
8. *J. Phys. Soc. Japan*	7607	1500	1239	19.7	16.3	82.6	1.13
9. *J. Biochemistry Japan*	4765	1361	874	28.6	18.3	64.2	1.71
10. Tetrahedron Letters	16478	1343	— —	8.2	— —	— —	1.77
11. J. Organic Chem.	20539	1308	— —	6.4	— —	— —	1.49
12. *Progr. Theoret. Phys.*	3860	1301	1271	33.7	32.9	97.7	1.41
13. Physical Review	40815	1281	— —	3.1	— —	— —	— —
14. J. Chem. Soc. (London)	14604	1209	— —	8.3	— —	— —	— —
15. *Agric. Biol. Chem.*	2522	1171	796	46.4	31.6	68.0	0.96
16. Nature	59206	1137	— —	1.9	— —	— —	3.63
17. Biochem. J.	31563	1071	— —	3.4	— —	— —	3.62
18. Phys. Rev. Letters	39229	937	— —	3.2	— —	— —	5.05
19. J. Chromatography	7928	930	— —	11.7	— —	— —	2.17
20. J. Appl. Physics	19277	921	— —	4.8	— —	— —	1.55
21. Biochemistry	27080	890	— —	3.3	— —	— —	4.71
22. Biochem. Biophys. Res. Comm.	23136	828	— —	3.6	— —	— —	3.73
23. Proc. Nat. Acad. Sci. USA	46916	779	— —	1.7	— —	— —	8.98
24. J. Phys. Chemistry	18086	749	— —	4.1	— —	— —	2.03
25. J. Bacteriology	18369	729	— —	4.0	— —	— —	2.72
26. Science	46488	679	— —	1.5	— —	— —	5.25
27. Arch. Biochem. Biophys.	15072	672	— —	4.5	— —	— —	2.95
28. Chem. Berichte	9569	577	— —	6.0	— —	— —	1.46
29. Tetrahedron	8903	574	— —	6.4	— —	— —	1.57
30. Surface Science	4600	552	— —	12.0	— —	— —	3.34
31. Chem. Comm.	8457	525	— —	6.2	— —	— —	— —
32. Analyt. Chim. Acta	— —	523	— —	— —	— —	— —	0.10
33. *J. Antibiotics Tokyo*	1161	479	339	41.3	29.2	70.8	2.04
34. *Japan. J. Appl. Phys.*	1847	475	400	25.7	21.7	84.2	0.66
35. Helv. Chim. Acta	7117	472	— —	6.6	— —	— —	1.64
36. J. Pharmacol. Exp. Ther.	13753	468	— —	3.4	— —	— —	3.57
37. Analyt. Biochem.	10206	457	— —	4.5	— —	— —	2.37
38. Phys. Rev. B.	16094	437	— —	2.7	— —	— —	2.86
39. Proc. Roy. Soc. London A	12211	410	— —	3.4	— —	— —	2.20
40. Proc. Soc. Exp. Biol. Med.	18167	390	— —	2.1	— —	— —	1.46
41. *J. Pharmaceut. Soc. Japan*	1301	388	5	29.8	0.4	1.3	0.35
42. J. Molecular Biol.	24209	387	— —	1.6	— —	— —	7.50
43. *Chemistry Letters*	718	385	145	53.6	20.2	37.7	0.86
44. Angew. Chem. Int. Ed.	10579	384	— —	3.6	— —	— —	4.10
45. J. Inorg. Nucl. Chem.	5761	384	— —	6.7	— —	— —	0.96
46. Amer. J. Physiol.	21519	380	— —	1.8	— —	— —	2.41
47. Acta Chem. Scand.	8627	373	— —	4.3	— —	— —	1.03
48. Inorganic Chem.	14310	373	— —	2.6	— —	— —	2.45
49. Liebigs Ann. Chemie	6171	361	— —	5.8	— —	— —	1.02
50. Physics Letters B	9958	359	— —	3.6	— —	— —	3.42

Figure 9.58 Journals cited most frequently by Japanese journals. Those that are Japanese are identified by italicized titles. A = citations from all journals. B = citations from Japanese journals. C = self-citations. D = ratio of citations from Japanese journals to citations from all journals. E = ratio of self-citations to citations from all journals (self-cited rate). F = ratio of self-citations to citations from Japanese journals. G = overall impact.

Journal	A	B	C	D	E	F	G
1. *Bull. Chem. Soc. Japan*	12204	1710	1386	14.0	11.4	81.1	0.93
2. *Chem. Pharmaceut. Bull.*	7163	1682	1076	23.5	15.0	64.0	0.93
3. *J. Biochemistry*	9204	1293	874	14.0	9.5	67.6	1.71
4. *Progr. Theoret. Phys.*	7107	1283	1271	18.1	17.9	99.1	1.41
5. *Agric. Biol. Chem.*	6194	1138	796	18.4	12.9	69.9	0.96
6. Biochim. Biophys. Acta.	53872	596	– –	1.1	– –	– –	3.11
7. *Chemistry Letters*	3502	469	145	13.4	4.1	30.9	0.86
8. *Jap. J. Appl. Phys.*	4816	459	400	9.5	8.3	87.1	0.66
9. *J. Antibiotics Tokyo*	2253	418	339	18.6	15.0	87.1	2.04
10. J. Organic Chem.	23962	395	– –	1.6	– –	– –	1.49
11. J. Amer. Chem. Soc.	51763	394	– –	0.8	– –	– –	4.38
12. Analyt. Chem.	27535	388	– –	1.4	– –	– –	3.29
13. *Japan Analyst*	12695	365	– –	2.9	– –	– –	0.07
14. J. Chem. Soc. Perkin	23011	343	– –	1.5	– –	– –	1.35
15. Tetrahedron Letters	12646	332	– –	2.6	– –	– –	1.77
16. *J. Synth. Org. Chem.*	3900	329	– –	8.4	– –	– –	0.17
17. J. Biol. Chemistry	36942	320	– –	0.9	– –	– –	5.84
18. *J. Ferment. Technol.*	1190	303	154	25.5	12.9	50.8	0.36
19. Physical Review B.	34284	299	– –	0.9	– –	– –	2.86
20. Uspekhi Khimii	14839	281	– –	1.9	– –	– –	1.08
21. J. Chem. Soc. Japan	4194	278	– –	6.6	– –	– –	0.20
22. *Plant and Cell Physiol.*	1852	274	212	14.8	11.4	77.4	1.16
23. *J. Pharmaceut. Soc. Japan*	2449	274	5	11.2	0.2	1.8	0.35
24. Phytochemistry	9347	269	– –	2.9	– –	– –	1.10
25. Tetrahedron	16259	269	– –	1.6	– –	– –	1.57
26. Biochem. Biophys. Res. Comm.	15832	244	– –	1.5	– –	– –	3.73
27. Biochemistry	25071	242	– –	1.0	– –	– –	4.71
28. J. Chem. Physics	43528	218	– –	0.5	– –	– –	2.91
29. J. Pharmaceut. Sci.	9986	217	– –	2.2	– –	– –	1.62
30. *Jap. J. Pharmacology*	2204	217	120	9.8	5.4	55.3	0.66
31. *Gann*	1552	212	136	13.7	8.8	64.2	1.00
32. J. Organometal. Chem.	27075	211	– –	0.8	– –	– –	2.38
33. *J. Phys. Earth*	– –	204	– –	– –	– –	– –	– –
34. *Bull. Jap. Soc. Mech. Eng.*	1623	201	195	12.4	12.0	97.0	0.35
35. *Bull. Jap. Soc. Sci. Fish.*	1456	198	– –	13.6	– –	– –	0.22
36. Physical Review D	18660	197	– –	1.1	– –	– –	2.72
37. FEBS Letters	17840	171	– –	1.0	– –	– –	3.05
38. *Tohoku J. Exp. Med.*	1807	166	124	9.2	6.9	74.7	0.46
39. Eur. J. Biochemistry	18447	163	– –	0.9	– –	– –	3.87
40. *Proc. Japan Acad.*	1530	163	108	10.7	7.1	66.3	0.35
41. *Polymer J. Japan*	1389	159	99	11.4	7.1	62.3	1.30
42. *J. Agr. Chem. Soc. Japan*	982	158	– –	16.1	– –	– –	0.29
43. J. Bacteriology	14219	156	– –	1.1	– –	– –	2.72
44. Arch. Biochem. Biophys.	12573	155	– –	1.2	– –	– –	2.95
45. *Jap. J. Exp. Med.*	1331	155	107	11.6	8.0	69.0	0.78
46. Nuclear Physics A	20623	155	– –	0.8	– –	– –	2.42
47. Inorganic Chem.	16965	152	– –	0.9	– –	– –	2.45
48. Biochem. J.	16318	145	– –	0.9	– –	– –	3.62
49. Cancer Research	14284	144	– –	1.0	– –	– –	3.39
50. J. Inorg. Nucl. Chem.	10465	143	– –	1.4	– –	– –	0.96

Figure 9.59 Major sources of references to Japanese journals. Those that are Japanese journals are identified by italicized titles. A = references to all journals. B = references to Japanese journals. C = references to self. D = ratio of Japanese references to all references. E = ratio of self-citations to all references (self-citing rate). F = ratio of self-citations to Japanese references. G = overall impact.

German Journal Literature (31)

A study of a core group of German journals showed a literature quite different from those of Japan, France, and Russia. The core group consisted of 288 journals, published in East and West Germany, that were covered by *SCI* in 1974. German-language journals of Austria and Switzerland were not included. The core group accounted for almost 10% of the material in the 1974 *SCI*: 9.3% of the journals covered, 8.2% of the source articles processed, and 9.9% of the references compiled.

The list of journals cited most frequently by the core group (Figure 9.60) is interesting in two respects. One is that when the 16 German journals on this list are removed, the composition and ranking of the list roughly matched an international list of the most frequently cited journals.

The other interesting feature of Figure 9.60 is the German share of the total citation rate (column D) of the journals. Since the German share of the international pool of references was 9.9%, the core group should have accounted for roughly the same percentage of the citation rates of the 50 most cited journals. Except for the German journals on the list, the percentage tended to stay within the range of 6.5 to 9, which is quite close to the statistical ideal. It rarely dropped below 6%. In the case of the 16 German journals on the list, the percentage soared far above the share of the international reference pool, as it did with the Japanese and French literature; but, unlike those literatures, only one of the German journals ranked among the top 12.

More than half of the major sources of citations to the core group (Figure 9.61) came from the group itself. With few exceptions—*Nature, Brain Research, Cell Tissue Research*—all the non-German sources were journals of physics and chemistry. Again, as in the case of the French and Japanese literatures, the core group was cited by the German source journals at a rate that exceeded its share of the international pool of source articles processed. Its share of that pool was roughly 8%, while it accounted for two and three times that percentage of the references published by the German source journals. Its shares of the references published by the non-German source journals, however, rarely reached the 8% level. Nevertheless, on a relative basis, the German literature did better in this respect than either the Japanese or French literature.

APPLICATION SCOPE

This series of studies, which is a continuing one (32-37), clearly demonstrates that journal citation data contains much useful information. The nature and quantity of the information, of course, depends, to an important degree, on the types of questions that are posed. But even answers to the most obvious and basic questions are useful, as demonstrated by the fact that they are now being sought by people in policy-making positions (38-40). Knowing the citation rate of a journal, the sources

Journal	A	B	C	D	E	F	G
1. J. Amer. Chem. Soc. (1)	98995	6337	– –	6.4	– –	– –	4.383
2. J. Biol. Chem. (2)	81354	5979	– –	7.3	– –	– –	5.843
3. Nature (4)	59206	4350	– –	7.3	– –	– –	3.636
4. Biochim. Biophys. Acta (5)	51487	3976	– –	7.7	– –	– –	3.170
5. Physical Review (6)	40815	3580	– –	8.8	– –	– –	– –
6. J. Chem. Physics (3)	62040	3578	– –	5.8	– –	– –	2.918
7. *Angew. Chem. (& Int. Ed.)* (136)	10756	3281	1153	30.5	10.7	35.1	4.140
8. P. Nat. Acad. Sci. USA (8)	46916	3213	– –	6.8	– –	– –	8.989
9. Science (7)	46488	2953	– –	6.4	– –	– –	5.412
10. Lancet (9)	37407	2927	– –	7.9	– –	– –	6.677
11. Biochemical J. (10)	31563	2591	– –	8.2	– –	– –	3.627
12. Astrophysical J. (18)	20543	2530	– –	12.3	– –	– –	4.063
13. *Deut. Med. Wschr.* (192)	3878	2480	661	64.0	17.0	26.7	1.017
14. *Chem. Berichte* (44)	9569	2447	1208	25.6	12.6	49.4	1.493
15. J. Molecular Biol. (15)	24209	2120	– –	8.8	– –	– –	7.502
16. *Eur. J. Biochemistry* (49)	11367	2079	1404	18.3	12.4	67.5	3.874
17. J. Clin. Invest. (14)	24768	1930	– –	7.8	– –	– –	6.992
18. New Engl. J. Med. (13)	26726	1854	– –	6.9	– –	– –	8.364
19. *Arzneimittelforschung* (217)	3534	1819	835	51.5	23.6	45.9	0.876
20. Biochemistry (12)	27080	1762	– –	6.5	– –	– –	4.711
21. Amer. J. Physiol. (19)	21519	1735	– –	8.1	– –	– –	2.414
22. Bioch. Biophys. Res. Co. (16)	23136	1689	– –	7.3	– –	– –	3.744
23. J. Physiology (17)	18435	1682	– –	9.1	– –	– –	4.495
24. J. Cell Biology (25)	19103	1615	– –	8.5	– –	– –	6.770
25. J. Organic Chem. (22)	20539	1576	– –	7.7	– –	– –	1.495
26. *Klin. Wschr.* (235)	3301	1570	216	47.6	6.5	13.8	1.033
27. Brit. Med. J. (20)	20700	1560	– –	7.5	– –	– –	3.556
28. J. Chemical Society (23)	14604	1464	– –	10.0	– –	– –	– –
29. Tetrahedron Letters (31)	16478	1464	– –	8.9	– –	– –	1.777
30. J. Amer. Med. Assoc. (30)	17211	1410	– –	8.2	– –	– –	3.068
31. P. Soc. Exp. Biol. Med. (28)	18167	1387	– –	7.6	– –	– –	1.471
32. *Zschr. Anorg. Allg. Chem.* (145)	4698	1371	806	29.2	17.2	58.8	1.019
33. J. Pharmacol. Exp. Ther. (42)	13753	1304	– –	9.5	– –	– –	3.576
34. Physical Review B (57)	16104	1281	– –	8.0	– –	– –	2.864
35. *Zschr. Physik* (98)	6662	1233	653	18.5	9.8	53.0	1.340
36. J. Appl. Physics (24)	19277	1232	– –	6.4	– –	– –	1.558
37. J. Bacteriology (26)	18369	1223	– –	6.7	– –	– –	2.727
38. *Pflugers Arch./ Eur. J. Physiol* (172)	4196	1217	597	29.0	14.2	49.1	1.810
39. *Hoppe-Seyler Zschr. Physiol. Chem.* (150)	3586	1198	504	33.4	14.1	42.1	2.291
40. *Astronomy Astrophysics* (190)	3638	1157	1133	31.8	31.1	97.9	2.267
41. Arch. Biochem. Biophys. (36)	15072	1123	– –	7.5	– –	– –	2.881
42. Physical Rev. Letters (11)	29229	1104	– –	3.8	– –	– –	5.059
43. Circulation (38)	14461	1089	– –	7.5	– –	– –	6.834
44. Annals New York Acad. Sci. (37)	14648	1084	– –	7.4	– –	– –	1.181
45. *Naunyn-Schmiedeberg* (291)	2685	1076	534	40.1	19.9	49.6	2.792
46. *Z. Naturforschung A* (183)	4034	1069	557	26.5	13.8	52.1	1.121
47. *Fschr. Geb. Roentgenf.* (495)	1452	1064	540	73.3	37.2	50.8	0.384
48. FEBS Letters (64)	9094	1059	– –	11.6	– –	– –	3.049
49. J. Exp. Med. (21)	20699	1051	– –	5.1	– –	– –	11.874
50. *Planta* (170)	4308	1049	591	24.4	13.7	56.3	2.589

Figure 9.60 Journals cited most frequently by German journals. Those that are German are identified by italicized titles. A = citations from all journals. B = citations from German journals. C = self-citations. D = ratio of citations from German journals to citations from all journals. E = ratio of self-citations to citations from all journals (self-cited rate). F = ratio of self-citations to citations from German journals. G = overall impact. Figures in parentheses following the names of the journals show their ranks on ISI's international list of most highly cited journals.

Journal	A	B	C	D	E	F	G
1. *Chemische Berichte*	9220	2572	1208	27.9	13.1	47.0	1.493
2. J. Amer. Chem. Soc.	51763	2063	– –	4.0	– –	– –	4.383
3. *Eur. J. Biochemistry*	18447	1934	1404	10.5	7.6	72.6	3.874
4. *Deut. Med. Wschr.*	13507	1813	661	13.4	4.9	36.5	1.017
5. J. Organomet. Chem.	27075	1773	– –	6.5	– –	– –	2.392
6. Bioch. Biophy. Acta	53872	1744	– –	3.2	– –	– –	3.170
7. *Angew. Chem. (& Int. Ed.)*	8157	1713	1153	21.0	14.1	67.3	4.140
8. *Arzneimittelforschung*	9869	1654	835	16.8	8.5	50.5	0.876
9. Cell Tissue Res.	8759	1550	– –	17.7	– –	– –	– –
10. *Zschr. Anorg. Allg. Chem.*	4975	1411	806	28.4	16.2	57.1	1.014
11. J. Organic Chem.	23962	1269	– –	5.3	– –	– –	1.495
12. *Astronomy Astrophysics*	8907	1157	1133	13.0	12.7	97.9	2.267
13. Brain Res.	23135	1149	– –	5.0	– –	– –	3.104
14. *Phys. Stat. Sol. A*	10851	1014	589	9.3	5.4	58.1	0.935
15. J. Chem. Physics	43528	1005	– –	2.3	– –	– –	2.918
16. *Phys. Stat. Sol. B*	11896	999	610	8.4	5.1	61.1	1.113
17. Analytical Chemistry	27535	985	– –	3.6	– –	– –	3.291
18. *Zschr. Naturforschung A*	6408	974	– –	15.2	8.7	57.2	1.121
19. FEBS Letters	17840	973	– –	5.5	– –	– –	3.049
20. J. Biol. Chemistry	36942	954	– –	2.6	– –	– –	5.843
21. Tetrahedron Letters	12646	953	– –	7.5	– –	– –	1.777
22. *Hoppe-Seyler Zschr. Physiol. Chem.*	5469	938	504	17.2	9.2	53.7	2.291
23. Astrophysical J.	21445	923	– –	4.3	– –	– –	4.063
24. *Naunyn-Schmiedeberg*	4635	890	534	19.2	11.5	60.0	2.792
25. Biochemistry	25071	829	– –	3.3	– –	– –	4.711
26. *Makromolek. Chemie*	5507	837	628	15.2	11.4	75.0	1.088
27. Tetrahedron	16259	831	– –	5.1	– –	– –	1.576
28. *Psychopharmacologia*	5430	823	673	15.2	12.4	81.8	2.347
29. *J. Liebigs Ann. Chemie*	3616	815	– –	22.5	– –	– –	1.024
30. *Fschr. Geb. Roentgenf.*	3840	800	450	20.8	11.7	56.3	0.384
31. *Pharmazie*	5841	800	285	13.7	4.9	35.6	0.675
32. J. Chem. Soc. Perkin	23011	782	– –	3.4	– –	– –	1.348
33. *Klin. Mbl. Augenheilk.*	3686	780	669	21.2	18.1	85.8	0.631
34. *Zschr. Chemie*	3905	772	264	19.8	6.8	34.2	0.178
35. *Zschr. Physik*	7150	769	653	10.8	9.1	84.9	1.340
36. *Planta*	4326	768	591	17.8	13.7	77.0	2.588
37. Physical Review B	34284	766	– –	2.2	– –	– –	2.864
38. *Pflugers Arch./Eur. J. Physiol.*	5365	755	597	14.1	11.1	79.1	1.810
39. *Chromosoma*	3426	739	642	21.6	18.7	86.9	3.875
40. *Acta Biol. Med. Germ.*	3862	731	301	18.9	7.8	41.2	0.678
41. Uspekhi Khimii	14839	721	– –	4.9	– –	– –	1.079
42. Nature	30125	718	– –	2.4	– –	– –	3.636
43. *Klin. Wschr.*	6179	697	216	11.3	3.5	31.0	1.033
44. Proc. Nat. Acad. Sci. US	28352	697	– –	2.4	– –	– –	8.989
45. *Ber. Bunsenges. Phys. Chem.*	5425	695	318	12.8	5.9	45.8	1.382
46. *Zschr. Naturforschung B*	4618	676	171	14.6	3.7	25.3	1.032
47. Biochemical J.	16318	665	– –	4.1	– –	– –	3.627
48. Bioch. Bioph. Res. Comm.	15832	659	– –	4.2	– –	– –	3.744
49. *Molec. General Genetics*	5156	650	516	12.6	10.0	79.4	2.699
50. *Humangenetik*	4313	618	373	14.3	8.6	60.4	1.703

Figure 9.61 Major sources of references to German journals. Those that are German journals are identified by italicized titles. A = references to all journals. B = references to German journals. C = references to self. D = ratio of German references to all references. E = ratio of self-citations to all references (self-citing rate). F = ratio of self-citations to German references. G = overall impact.

of the references that cite it, and the journals it cites makes it possible to measure its utility as a source of research information, characterize its editorial orientation with a high degree of subtlety, and, depending upon the journal, define the core literature of a specialty or discipline. When these same questions are asked about a core literature, the answers provide insights into the research performance, orientation, and relationships of the discipline, specialty, or nation represented by the literature. And all these characteristics can be quantified well enough to make valid comparisons: time periods can be compared to detect significant changes, journals can be compared to determine relative merits, and core literatures can be compared to define in more detail the nature of the relationships between different research communities.

There is, however, even more useful information to be extracted from journal citation data. The extraction will require a more sophisticated set of questions from those who are concerned with the history, sociology, evaluation, and planning of science. These questions are just starting to be formulated, but I think that they will soon come flying thick and fast. By making the answers to the simpler questions more accessible, *JCR* should stimulate the formulation of the more sophisticated ones. The selected bibliography at the end of this chapter provides some idea of how far we had come in this application of journal citation data by the time the first formal edition of *JCR* was published in 1975. I think the studies it identifies represent only the beginning of what will be done with journal citation data to increase both our understanding of how science works and our ability to make it work better.

REFERENCES

1. **Garfield, E.** "Journal Citation Studies 17. Journal Self-Citation Rates—There's a Difference." *Essays of an Information Scientist,* Vol. 2 (Philadelphia: ISI Press, 1977). Pp. 192-194.
2. **Garfield, E.** "Introducing *Journal Citation Reports.*" *Essays of an Information Scientist,* Vol. 2 (Philadelphia: ISI Press, 1977). Pp. 556-571.
3. **Garfield, E.** "Citation Analysis as a Tool in Journal Evaluation." *Science,* **178**:471-479, 1972.
4. **Garfield, E.** "The Mystery of the Transposed Journal Lists—Wherein Bradford's Law of Scattering is Generalized According to Garfield's Law of Concentration." *Essays of an Information Scientist,* Vol. 1 (Philadelphia: ISI Press, 1977). Pp. 222-223.
5. **Garfield, E.** "The Significant Journals of Science." *Nature,* **264**:609-615, 1976.
6. **Garfield, E.** "What is the Core Literature of Biochemistry as Compared to the Core of Chemistry?" *Essays of an Information Scientist,* Vol. 1 (Philadelphia: ISI Press, 1977). Pp. 262-265.
7. **Garfield, E.** "What is the Core Literature of Chemical Physics?" *Essays of an Information Scientist,* Vol. 1 (Philadelphia: ISI Press, 1977). Pp. 274-277.
8. **Garfield, E.** "Journal Citation Studies 3. *Journal of Experimental Medicine* Compared With *Journal of Immunology*; or, How Much of a Clinician is the Immunologist?" *Essays of an Information Scientist,* Vol. 1 (Philadelphia: ISI Press, 1977). Pp. 326-329.
9. **Garfield, E.** "Journal Citation Studies 4. The Literature Cited in Rheumatology is not Much Different From That of Other Specialties." *Essays of an Information Scientist,* Vol. 1 (Philadelphia: ISI Press, 1977). Pp. 338-341.
10. **Thorpe, P.** "An Evaluation of the Rheumatology Periodical Literature Used in Britain and the USA." *Methods of Information in Medicine,* **11**:119-121, 1972.
11. **Garfield, E.** "Citation Analysis of Pathology Journals Reveals Need for a Journal of Applied Virology." *Essays of an Information Scientist,* Vol. 1 (Philadelphia: ISI Press, 1977). Pp. 400-403.
12. **Garfield, E.** "Most Frequently Cited Phytopathology Journals." *Phytopathology News,* 6:4, 1972.
13. **Garfield, E.** "Journal Citation Studies 6. *Journal of Clinical Investigation.* How Much 'Clinical' and How Much 'Investigation'?" *Essays of an Information Scientist,* Vol. 2 (Philadelphia: ISI Press, 1977). Pp. 13-16.

14. **Garfield, E.** "Journal Citation Studies 7. *Journal of American Medical Association* vs. *New England Journal of Medicine.*" *Essays of an Information Scientist,* Vol. 2 (Philadelphia: ISI Press, 1977). Pp. 17-20.
15. **Garfield, E.** "Journal Citation Studies 9. Highly Cited Pediatric Journals and Articles." *Essays of an Information Scientist,* Vol. 2 (Philadelphia: ISI Press, 1977). Pp. 97-101.
16. **Garfield, E.** "Journal Citation Studies 10. Geology and Geophysics." *Essays of an Information Scientist,* Vol. 2 (Philadelphia: ISI Press, 1977). Pp. 102-106.
17. **Janke, N.C.** "Journal Evaluation." *Science,* **189**:1197-1198, 1973.
18. **Garfield, E.** "Journal Citation Studies 11. *Journal of Geophysical Research.*" *Essays of an Information Scientist,* Vol. 2 (Philadelphia: ISI Press, 1977). Pp. 114-117.
19. **Garfield, E.** "Journal Citation Studies 13. *Acta Crystallographica.*" *Essays of an Information Scientist,* Vol. 2 (Philadelphia: ISI Press, 1977). Pp. 128-133.
20. **Garfield, E.** "Journal Citation Studies 14. Wherein We Observe That Physicists Cite Different Physics Journals Than Other People." *Essays of an Information Scientist,* Vol. 2 (Philadelphia: ISI Press, 1977). Pp. 154-157.
21. **Inhaber, H.** "Is There a Pecking Order in Physics Journals?" *Physics Today,* **27**:39-43, 1974.
22. **Chen, C.C.** "How Do Scientists Meet Their Information Needs?" *Special Libraries,* **65**:272-280, 1974.
23. **Garfield, E.** "Journal Citation Studies 15. Cancer Journals and Articles." *Essays of an Information Scientist,* Vol. 2 (Philadelphia: ISI Press, 1977). Pp. 160-167.
24. **Garfield, E,** "Journal Citation Studies 18. Highly Cited Botany Journals." *"Essays of an Information Scientist,* Vol. 2 (Philadelphia: ISI Press, 1977). Pp. 205-209.
25. **Garfield, E.** "Journal Citation Studies 19. Psychology and Behavior Journals." *Essays of an Information Scientist,* Vol. 2 (Philadelphia: ISI Press, 1977). Pp. 231-235.
26. **Garfield, E.** "Journal Citation Studies 20. Agriculture Journals and the Agricultural Literature." *Essays of an Information Scientist,* Vol. 2 (Philadelphia: ISI Press, 1977), Pp. 272-278.
27. **Garfield, E.** "Journal Citation Studies 21. Engineering Journals." *Essays of an Information Scientist,* Vol. 2 (Philadelphia: ISI Press, 1977). Pp. 304-309.
28. **Garfield, E.** "Journal Citation Studies 22. Russian Journal References and Citations in the *Science Citation Index* Data Bank." Paper presented at the US/USSR Symposium on Forecasting Information Requirements and Services. (New Haven, Conn.: Yale University, October 20-23, 1975).
29. **Garfield, E.** "Journal Citation Studies 23. French Journals—What They Cite and What Cites Them." *Essays of an Information Scientist,* Vol. 2 (Philadelphia: ISI Press, 1977). Pp. 409-414.
30. **Garfield, E.** "Journal Citation Studies 24. Japanese Journals—What They Cite and What Cites Them." *Essays of an Information Scientist,* Vol. 2 (Philadelphia: ISI Press, 1977). Pp. 430-435.
31. **Garfield, E.** "Journal Citation Studies 25. German Journals—What They Cite and Vice Versa." *Essays of an Information Scientist,* Vol. 2 (Philadelphia: ISI Press, 1977). Pp. 467-473.
32. **Garfield, E.** "Journal Citation Studies 26. Latin-American Journals." *Essays of an Information Scientist,* Vol. 2 (Philadelphia: ISI Press, 1977). Pp. 577-583.
33. **Garfield, E.** "Journal Citation Studies 27. Australian and New Zealand Citers and Citees." *Essays of an Information Scientist,* Vol. 2 (Philadelphia: ISI Press, 1977). Pp. 584-589.
34. **Garfield, E.** "Journal Citation Studies 28. Scandinavian Journals." *Essays of an Information Scientist,* Vol. 2 (Philadelphia: ISI Press, 1977). Pp. 599-605.
35. **Garfield, E.** "Journal Citation Studies 29. East European Journals." *Essays of an Information Scientist,* Vol. 2 (Philadelphia: ISI Press, 1977). Pp. 623-630.
36. **Garfield, E.** "Journal Citation Studies 30. Italian Journals." *Current Contents,* No. 4, 5-9, January 24, 1977.
37. **Garfield, E.** "**La science francais est-elle trop provinciale?**),*La Recherche,*7:757-760, 1976.
38. **Bishop, C.T.** "Canadian Science Journals are Better Than Some Think." *Science Forum,* **10**(3):20-2, 1977.
39. **Inhaber, H.** "Canadian Scientific Journals: Part 1, Coverage." *Journal of the American Society for Information Science,* **26**:253-257, 1975.
40. **Inhaber, H.** "Canadian Scientific Journals: Part II, Interaction." *Journal of the American Society for Information Science,* **26**:291-293, 1975.

Selected Bibliography
on
Journal Citation Analysis and Its Applications

This bibliography is by no means exhaustive. The author has endeavored, however, to include what he believes to be valuable background and useful examples of the application of citation analysis to the study of the sociology of science. Many of the items listed are the author's own work. Their number reflects no exclusive scope or merit of activity, but rather the author's interest and his access to ISI®'s unique data bank.

Allen E S. Periodicals for mathematicians. *Science* **70**:592-94, 1929.

American Institute of Biological Sciences. "Citation of Russian literature in 25 selected U.S. biological sciences journals for the years 1959, 1960, and 1961." Biological Sciences Communication Project Communique 5-62. American Institute of Biological Sciences, Washington, July 1962.

Atanasiu D P. Citatele ca instrument de evaluare a publicatillor primare (Citation as a tool for the evaluation of primary publications). *Studii si Cercetari de Documentare* (4):443-56, 1968.

Barnard C C. The selection of periodicals for medical and scientific libraries. *Library Association Record, Series 4* **5**:549-57, 1938.

Barrett R L & Barrett M A. Journals most cited by chemists and chemical engineers. *J. Chem. Education* **34**:35-38, 1957.

Bath University Library. "Clustering of journal titles according to citation data; report on preparatory work, design, data collection, and preliminary analyses." Working Paper Number 11, April 1973.

Bourne C P & Gregor D. Planning serials cancellations and cooperative collection development in the health sciences; methodology and background information. *Bull. Med. Library Assoc.* **64**:366-77, Oct. 1975.

Brodman E. Choosing physiology journals. *Bull. Med. Library Assoc.* **32**:479-83, 1944.

Burton R E. Citations in American engineering journals. 1. Chemical engineering. *Amer. Documentation* **10**:70-3, 1959.

————— Citations in American engineering journals. 2. Mechanical engineering. *Amer. Documentation* **10**:135-37, 1959.

Burton R E. Citations in American engineering journals. 3. Metallurgical engineering. *Amer. Documentation* **10**:209-13, 1959.

Bush W C, Hamelman P W & Staaf R J. A quality index for economic journals. *Rev. Economics Statistics* **56**:123-25, 1974.

Carpenter M P & Narin F. Clustering of scientific journals. *J. Amer. Soc. Inform. Sci.* **24**:425-36, 1973.

Casey A E. Influence of individual North American and British journals on medical progress in the United States and Britain. *Bull. Med. Library Assoc.* **30**:464-66, 1942.

Chambers G R & Healey J S. Journal citations in masters theses; one measurement of a journal collection. *J. Amer. Soc. Inform. Sci.* **24**:397-401, 1973.

Coats A W. The role of scholarly journals in the history of economics; an essay. *J. Econ. Lit.* **13**:29-44, 1971.

Computer Horizons, Inc. "Analysis of research journals and related research structure in special education". Final Report for the U.S. Department of Health, Education and Welfare, Office of Education, Contract No. OEC 5-70-0047 (509), 1965.

————— "The Collection and analysis of health services research journal literature 1965-1969." Final Report for the National Center for Health Services R&D. Contract No. HSM 110-70-290, April, 1971.

————— "Exploration of the possibility of generating importance and utilization measures by citation indexing of approximately 250 journals in the physical sciences." First Annual Report, Contract No. NSF-C 627, August 1971.

Computer Horizons, Inc. "Development of U.S. and international indicators of the quantity and quality of scientific literature." Phase I Report Amendment No. 2, Contract No. NSF-C 627, December 1971.

────── "Annotated bibliography of international publication and citation comparisons." Supplement to Second Annual Report, Contract No. NSF-C 627, August, 1972.

────── "Evaluation of research in the physical sciences based on publications and citations." Third Annual Report, Contract No. NSF-C 627, November, 1973.

────── "Exploration of the possibility of generating importance and utilization measures by citation indexing of approximately 500 journals in the physical sciences." Second Annual Report, Contract No. NSF-C 627, Second Printing, December, 1973.

────── "Subject classification and influence weights for 2,300 journals." Final Task Report, Contract No. NSF-C 627, June 30, 1975.

Dalziel C F. Evaluation of periodicals for electrical engineers. *Library Quarterly* 7(3):354-372, 1937.

────── Journals for electrical engineers. *Electrical Engineering* 57(3):110-13, 1938.

Dierks H. Ueber die Zitierhäufigkeit von Zeitschriften auf dem Gebiete der Physik; eine Untersuchung (A study of citation frequency of physics periodicals). *Arbeiten aus dem Bibliotekar-Lehrinstitut des Landes Hordheim-Westfalen.* Vol. 41 (Cologne: Greven Verlag, 1972), 115 pp.

Durand D E. Citation count analysis of behavioral science journals in influential management literature. *Acad. Management J.* 17:579-83, 1974.

Eagly R V. Economic journals as a communications network. *J. Econ. Lit.* 13:878-88, 1975.

Finison L J & Whittemore C L. Linguistic isolation of American social psychology; a comparative study of journal citations. *Amer. Psychologist* 30:513-16, 1975.

Friis T. The use of citation analysis as a research technique and its implications for libraries. *Suid Afrikaanse Biblioteke* 23:12-15, 1955.

Garfield E. What is a journal? *Current Contents*® (*CC*®) No. 36, 8 September 1964, p. 3-4.

────── What is a significant journal? *CC* No. 18, 6 May 1970, p. 4-5.

────── Is publication in "minor" journals tantamount to burial? *CC* No. 37, 16 September 1970, p. 4-5.

────── A basic journal collection--ISI lists the fifty most-cited scientific and technical journals. *CC* No. 2, 12 January 1972, p. 3-5.

────── Citation analysis as a tool in journal evaluation. *Science* 178:471-79, 1972.

────── Journal citation studies. 1. What is the "core" literature of biochemistry as compared to the "core" of chemistry? *CC* No. 5, 2 February 1972, p. 6-9.

────── Citation statistics may help scientists choose journals in which to publish. *CC* No. 7, 16 February 1972, p. 5-6.

────── Citations-to divided by items-published gives journal impact factor; ISI lists the top fifty high-impact journals of science. *CC* No. 8, 23 February 1972, p. 6-9.

────── Most frequently cited phytopathology journal. *Phytopathology News* 6:4, March 1972.

────── Journal citation studies. 2. What is the "core" literature of chemical physics: *CC* No. 9, 1 March 1972, p. 5-8.

────── Is citation frequency a valid criterion for selecting journals? *CC* No. 14, 5 April 1972, p. 5-6.

────── ISI's *Journal Citation Index* data base-a multi-media tool. *CC* No. 16, 19, April 1972, p. 5-8.

────── Journal citation studies. 3. *Journal of Experimental Medicine* compared with *Journal of Immunology;* or, how much of a clinician is the immunologist? *CC* No. 23, 7 June 1972, p. M1-4.

────── Journal citation studies. 4. The literature cited in *Rheumatology* is not much different from that of other specialties. *CC* No. 31, 2 August 1972, p. 5-8.

────── What scientific journals can tell us about scientific journals. *IEEE Transactions Professional Communication* **PC16**:200-02, 1973.

Garfield E. Citation analysis of pathology journals reveals need for a journal of applied virology! *CC* No. 3, 17, January 1973, p. 5-8.

──────Citation frequency and citation impact--and the role they play in journal selection for *Current Contents* and other ISI services. *CC* No. 6, 7 February 1973, p. 5-6.

──────Journal citation studies. 5. Is paleontology a life or a physical science? *JCI* reveals gap in coverage of paleontology and need for better small journal statistics. *CC* No. 13, 28 March 1973, p. 5-6.

──────Citation impact depends upon the paper, not the journal; don't count on 'citation by association'! *CC* No. 22, 30 May 1973, p. 5-6.

──────The new *ISI Journal Citation Reports* should significantly affect the future course of scientific publication. *CC* No. 33, 15 August 1973, p. 7-8.

──────Which journals attract the most frequently cited articles? Here's a list of the top fifteen. *CC* No. 39, 26 September 1973, p. 5-6.

──────Journal citation studies. 6. *Journal of Clinical Investigation.* How much 'clinical' and how much 'investigation'? *CC* No. 4, 23 January 1974, p. 5-8.

──────Journal citation studies. 7. *Journal of American Medical Association* vs *New England Journal of Medicine. CC* No. 5, 30 January 1974, p. 5-8.

──────Journal citation studies. 8. Some highly cited articles from highly cited general medical and clinical journals. *CC* No. 27, 3 July 1974, p. 5-12.

──────Journal citation studies. 9. Highly cited pediatric journals and articles. *CC* No. 29, 17 July 1974, p. 5-9.

──────Journal citation studies. 10. Geology and geophysics. *CC* No. 30, 24 July 1974, p. 5-9.

──────Journal citation studies. 11. *Journal of Geophysical Research. CC* No. 33, 14 August 1974, p. 5-8.

──────Journal citation studies. 12. *Astrophysical Journal* and its supplements. *CC* No. 35, 28 August 1974, p. 5-7.

──────Journal citation studies. 13. *Acta Crystallographica. CC* No. 37, 11 September 1974, p. 5-10.

Garfield E. Journal citation studies. 14. Wherein we observe that physicists cite different physics journals than other people. *CC* No. 40, 2 October 1974, p. 5-8.

──────Journal citation studies. 15. Cancer journals and articles. *CC* No. 42, 16 October 1974, p. 5-12.

──────Journal citation studies. 16. *Clinical Chemistry* and *Clinical Chimica Acta. CC* No. 48, 27 November 1974, p. 5-9.

──────Journal citation studies. 17. Journal self-citation rates--there's a difference. *CC* No. 52, 25 December 1974, p. 5-7.

──────Journal citation studies. 18. Highly cited botany journals. *CC* No. 2, 13 January 1975, p. 5-9.

──────Journal citation studies. 19. Psychology and behavior journals. *CC* No. 9, 3 March 1975, p. 5-9.

──────Is there a future for the scientific journal? *Sci-Tech News* **29**:42-4, April 1975.

──────Journal citation studies. 20. Agriculture journals and the agricultural literature. *Current Contents* No. 20, 19 May 1975, p. 5-10.

──────No growth libraries and citation analysis: or pulling weeds with *ISI's Journal Citation Reports. CC* No. 26, 30 June 1975, p. 5-8.

──────Journal citation studies. 21. Engineering journals. *CC* No. 27, 7 July 1975, p. 5-10.

──────''Journal citation studies. 22. Russian journal references and citations in the *Science Citation Index* data bank.'' Paper presented at the US/USSR Symposium on Forecasting Information Requirements and Services, Yale University, New Haven, Conn., 20-23 October 1975.

──────What is a name? If it's a journal's name, sometimes there's too much! *CC* No. 46, 17 November 1975, p. 5-8.

──────Journal citation studies. 23. French journals--what they cite and what cites them. *CC* No. 4, 26 January 1976, p. 5-10.

Ghosh J S & Neufeld M L. Uncitedness of articles in the *Journal of the American Chemical Society, Inform. Storage Retrieval* **10:**365-69, 1974.

Gregory J. An evaluation of medical periodicals. *Bull. Med. Library Assoc.* **25**:172-88, 1937.

——— The evaluation of medical periodicals. *Bull. Med. Library Assoc.* **27**:242-44, 1939.

Gross P L K & Gross E M. College libraries and chemical education. *Science* **66**:385-89, 1927.

Gross P L K & Woodford A O. Serial literature used by American geologists. *Science* **73**:550-64, 1931.

Hackh I. The periodicals useful in the dental library. *Bull. Med. Library Assoc.* **25**:109-112, 1936.

Hamelman P W & Mazze E M. Toward a cost/utility model for social science periodicals. *Socio-Economic Planning Sciences* **6**:465-75, 1972.

——————————— Measuring the research impact of business journals; the CASPER model. *J. Economics and Business* **25**:164-67, 1973.

——————————— Cross referencing between AMA journals and other publications. *J. Marketing Research* **10**:215-19, 1973.

——————————— A program for selecting journals and other publications. *J. Marketing Research* **11**:444-45, 1974.

——————————— How business journals cite one another. *J. Advertising Research* **14**(3):23-25, 1974.

——————————— Citation patterns in finance journals. *Journal of Finance* **29**:1295-1301, 1974.

Hockings E F. Selection of scientific periodicals in an industrial research library. *J. Amer. Soc. Inform. Sci.* **25**:131-32, 1974.

Hooker R H. A study of scientific periodicals. *Rev. Sci. Instruments* **6**:333-38, 1935.

Inhaber H. Is there a pecking order in physics journals? *Physics Today* **27**:39-43, 1974.

——— Canadian scientific journals. 1. Coverage. *J. Amer. Soc. Inform. Sci.* **26**:253-58, 1975.

——— Canadian scientific journals. 2. Interaction. *J. Amer. Soc. Inform. Sci.* **26**:290-93, 1975.

Institute for Scientific Information. *1969 Journal Citation Reports (JCR®)*, 1973.

Jakobovits L A & Osgood C E. Connotations of twenty psychological journals to their professional readers. *Amer. Psychologist* **22**:792-800, 1967.

Jenkins R L. Periodicals for medical libraries. *J. Amer. Med. Assoc.* **97**:608-10, 1931.

——— Periodicals for child-guidance clinics. *Mental Hygiene* **16**:624-30, 1932.

Leith J D. Biomedical literature, analysis of journal articles collected by a radiation and cell biologist. *Amer. Documentation* **20**:143-48, 1969.

Louttit C M & Lockridge L L. Psychological journals. *Amer. J. Psychology* **46**:147-48, 1934.

McDonough C C. The relative quality of economics journals revisited. *Quarterly Rev. Economics Business* **15**:91-7, 1975.

McNeely J K & Crosno C D. Periodicals for electrical engineers. *Science* **72**:81-4, 1930.

Malin M V & Weinstock M. Finding the core journals of science through citation feedback. *Biosciences Communications* **1**:237-250, 1975.

Martyn J & Gilchrist A. An evaluation of British scientific journals. Aslib Occasional Publication Number 1, Aslib, London, 1968.

Munn R F. The division of the collection between the medical and the general university library. *Bull. Med. Library Assoc.* **44**:99-109, 1956.

Narin F & Garside D. Journal relationships in special education. *Exceptional Children* **38**:695-703, 1972.

Narin F, Carpenter M P & Berlt N C. Interrelationships of scientific journals. *J. Amer. Soc. Inform. Sci.* **23**:323-31, 1972.

Narin F & Carpenter M P. National publication and citation comparisons. *J. Amer. Soc. Inform. Sci.* **26**:80-93, 1975.

Orient J M. Statistical study of the citation of papers on analytical chemistry. *Zavodskaya Laboratoriya* **33**:1383-86, 1973.

Patterson A M. Journal citations in the *Recueil* 1937-1939. *Rec Trav. Chim. Pays-Bas* **59**:538-44, 1940.

Peraza R P. Journal self citation patterns in representative American, British and Canadian chemistry and physics journals. Drexel Institute of Technology, Masters thesis, June 1971.

Raisig L M. Mathematical evaluation of the scientific serial. *Science* **131**:1417-19, 1960.

Raisig L M. World biomedical journals, 1951-60; a study of the relative significance of 1388 titles indexed in *Current List of Medical Literature. Bull. Med. Library Assoc.* **54**:108-25, 1966.

Sandison A. Densities of use and absence of obsolescence in physics journals at MIT. *J. Amer. Soc. Inform. Sci.* **25**:172-82, 1974.

Sengupta I N. The ranking of biomedical periodicals from the Indian scientist's point of view; analysis of data for 1959-1968. *Unesco Bulletin for Libraries* **24**(3):143-52, 1970.

———— Factors determining changes in ranking of scientific periodicals; a study in relation to biomedical journals during the postwar period. *Internat. Library Rev.* **3**:271-85, 1975.

———— Impact of scientific serials on the advancement of medical knowledge; an objective method of analysis. *Internat. Library Rev.* **4**:169-95, 1972.

———— Growth of the biochemical literature. *Nature* **244**:75-6, 1973.

———— Choosing physiology periodicals; a recent study of the growth of its literature. *Ann. Library Sci. Documentation* **20**:39-57, 1973.

———— Recent growth of the literature of biochemistry and changes in ranking of periodicals. *J. Documentation* **29**:192-211, 1973.

———— Choosing pharmacology periodicals; study of the growth of literature in the field. *Ann. Library Sci. Documentation* **21**:1-21, 1974.

———— Choosing microbiology periodicals; study of the growth of literature in the field. *Ann. Library Sci. Documentation* **21**(3):95-111, 1974.

Sengupta I N. Physiology periodicals. *Internat. Library Rev.* **6**:147-65, 1974.

———— The literature of microbiology. *Internat. Library Rev.* **6**:353-69, 1974.

Sherwood K K. Relative value of medical magazines. *Northwest Medicine* **31**:273-76, 1932.

Singh R S. Ranking of periodicals in chemistry from the point of view of Indian scientists. *Ann. Library Sci. Documentation* **21**:55-67, 1974.

Smith M H. The selection of chemical engineering periodicals in college libraries. *College Res. Libraries* **5**:217-27, 1944.

Stevens R E. The study of the research use of libraries. *Library Quarterly* **26**:41-51, 1956.

Subramanyam K. Criteria for journal selection. *Special Libraries* **66**:367-71, 1975.

Van Styvendaele J H. Discovering the most consulted scientific serials in the Antwerp State University Centre library. *J. Librarianship* **6**:241-54, 1974.

Voigt M J. Scientific periodicals as a basic requirement for engineering and agricultural research. *College Res. Libraries* **8**:354-59, 375, 1947.

Williams J F & Pings V M. A study of the access to the scholarly record from a hospital health science core collection. *Bull. Med. Library Assoc.* **61**:408-15, 1973.

Windsor D A. Rational selection of primary journals for a biomedical research library; the use of secondary journal citations. *Special Libraries* **64**:446-51, 1973.

Chapter Ten

Perspective on Citation Analysis of Scientists

The use of citation analysis to produce measures, or indicators, of scientific performance has generated a considerable amount of discussion (1-10). Not surprisingly, the discussion grows particularly intense when the subject is the use of these measures to evaluate people, either as individuals or in small formal groups, such as departmental faculties in academic institutions. Published descriptions of how citation analysis is being used to define the history of scientific development, or to measure the activity and interaction of scientific specialties, generate relatively little comment from the scientific community at large. And what is generated tends to be calm and reasoned. In contrast, any mention of using citation analysis to measure the performance of specific individuals or groups produces an automatic, and often heatedly emotional, response from the same people who otherwise remain silent. A case in point is a 1975 review in *Science* (11) of the way citation analysis is being used, on an exploratory basis, by science administrators. The article included a discussion of the use of citation measures to define and monitor changes in the specialty structure of science. This application could have a major impact on the development of science policies. But the spate of letters to the editor that commented on the article dealt only with the use of citation data to help measure individuals and academic departments in cases of tenure, promotion, and grant awards.

It is not surprising that the published comments these applications elicit from the general-science community are almost always critical. After all, scientists are no less sensitive to performance measures than other people. And when you consider that some 25% of the scientific papers published are never cited even once (12) and that the average annual citation count for papers that are cited is only 1.7 (13) it is not hard to understand why citation counts might seem a particularly threatening measure to some. Another reason for the defensive attitude might be the relative newness of citation data as a measure of performance. It will be interesting to compare the reactions of humanities scholars to the one of scientists when the *Arts &*

Humanities Citation Index (14) becomes better known. Being cited is already considered an important mark of scholarship in the humanities, so there is reason to believe that scholars in that area will find formal citation measurements more acceptable.

Interestingly enough, the comments from the science historians and sociologists, who specialize in the difficult task of figuring out how science works and how it can be measured usefully, show much more balance. Their general attitude about citation measures consists of approximately equal parts of healthy skepticism (they know how difficult it is to quantify the quality of scientific performance) and the scientific objectivity needed to accept the positive findings of properly conducted studies. In fact, the criticism coming from some quarters of the scientific community is in the face of a long list of studies (15–21) that show citation counts correlate very highly with peer judgments, which are widely accepted as a valid way of ranking scientific performance.

The large body of evidence supporting the use of citation measures to help evaluate scientists, individually and in groups, is no reason, however, to ignore the criticism of the practice. Discussion and controversy have the capacity for increasing our understanding of a subject, and there is much need to do just that where citation measures are concerned. Though the primary criticisms have been answered in detail many times, the answers are scattered through the literature of hundreds of papers, study reports, and letters to editors. Pulling all the salient points together in a single document, as I intend to do here, may well serve the ultimate goal of increasing and broadening the understanding of a method of measurement that is potentially very important to the way science is practiced.

Another important reason for continuing and intensifying the discussion is that none of the criticisms are unfounded. Most of them are based on facets of citation analysis that pose either theoretical or real problems in using the technique to evaluate people. Citation data is subtle stuff. Those using it to evaluate research performance at any level, but particularly at the level of individuals, must understand both its subtleties and its limitations. The position of those who advocate the use of citation data to evaluate people is not that it is simple and foolproof, but that the problems associated with it can be solved satisfactorily with a reasonable amount of methodological and interpretive effort. In other words, none of the grounds for criticism are insurmountable obstacles in the way of using citation data to develop fair, objective, and useful measures of individual or group performance, which is something I now will attempt to demonstrate.

CAN CITATION COUNTS BE ACCURATE?

The opposition to the use of citation counts to evaluate people is based on two sets of perceived weaknesses: one has to do with the mechanics of compiling the data; the other, with the intrinsic characteristics of the data. The mechanical weaknesses stem from characteristics of the *Science Citation Index* (*SCI*) and the *Social Sciences Citation Index* (*SSCI*), the most frequently used sources of citation data, that can affect the accuracy of the citation rate compiled for an individual.

One such characteristic is that the *Citation Index* of *SCI* and *SSCI* lists cited items only by the first author. If you search the *Citation Index* for the cited work of a given scientist, you will find only those publications in which the scientist was listed as first author. Thus, the citation data compiled for that scientist will not reflect work on which he or she was a secondary author. Obviously, this characteristic can affect the accuracy of someone's citation rate.

How greatly this inaccuracy distorts relative citation measurements is a matter of considerable debate (22). One study by Cole and Cole showed that the omission of citations to secondary-author publications "does not affect substantive conclusions." (23). However, that study dealt only with physicists.

Lindsey and Brown take the opposite position. They theorize that limiting citation counts to primary-author papers does introduce a measurement error if the primary-author papers are a unique subset of an author's publication record; that would be the case if coauthor sequence were based on importance of contribution (24). The size of the error would depend on the extent to which the primary-author papers are not a random, representative sample of all the papers.

Work done by Roy (25) suggests that the problem might not exist if the comparisons are being made within and between small, homogeneous groups, such as faculty departments. Reasoning that the citation counts for primary- and secondary-authorship papers are either roughly the same, or that any deviation that does exist is constant within the homogeneous universe, he has worked out the following formula for computing total citation counts:

$$CT = CF \times \frac{TP}{FP}$$

where CT = total citations
　　　 CF = citations to primary-author papers
　　　 TP = total papers
　　　 FP = primary-author papers

If his hypothesis is correct, it may not always be necessary to go to the trouble of compiling the citation data on secondary-author papers to arrive at a total citation count. Using a bibliography to obtain the total number of papers published, it would be possible to calculate the total citation count from primary-author data alone. To test the formula, Roy used it to calculate the total citation counts for two faculty departments from a compilation of primary-author data and then compared the counts with compilations of both primary- and secondary-author data. The correlation between the calculated and compiled counts was .98 for a materials-science department and .94 for one in physics. Much more data are needed, however, to verify the accuracy of the formula.

Another element of uncertainty is introduced by the uneven incidence of multiauthor papers from field to field. Although the trend toward collaborative science and multiauthored papers is a strong one (26), the Lindsey and Brown study shows that multiauthor papers accounted for only 17–25% of samples of published papers in the fields of economics, social work, and sociology, but 47–81% of samples of published papers in gerontology, psychiatry, psychology, and biochemistry.

Preliminary stratification studies at ISI have shown that failure to include secondary-author papers in citation counts introduces a substantial error at the very highest stratum of cited scientists. A list of the 250 most cited scientists, taken from a compilation of only primary-author counts, had only 28% of its names in common with a similar one taken from a compilation of all-author counts (22). Further studies are being conducted to determine the degree of error throughout the entire range of cited scientists.

As long as this uncertainty persists, the only fair way of developing relative citation counts is to compile the performance of all the published material that is listed on a comprehensive bibliography. At ISI, where these studies are conducted on a scale that requires computer compilation, this is standard practice, and in 1978 the same procedure was put into effect for all stratification studies.

Obviously, the same thing can be done in small-scale studies, where the data is compiled by researchers. If a bibliography is not available, the *SCI/SSCI Source Index,* which shows for each author listed all the items published in the journals covered by the index during the given time period, can be used to compile one. Since the source coverage of *SCI/SSCI* is not exhaustive, this approach does entail some risk of incompleteness. On the other hand, *SCI/SSCI* covers all the highly cited journals, so if what is missed is a journal item, the probability of it being cited a significant number of times is relatively low. Nevertheless, because it is always possible that a highly cited paper will be published in a journal that has a low citation rate, the most thorough way of compiling someone's citation rate is by working from a bibliography known to be complete.

Citation analyses for comparative purposes should also take into consideration the impact that coauthorship has on writing productivity. Price and Beaver (27) found that in one sample of scientists four papers in five years was the high for authors working alone or with only one coauthor. In contrast, those working with more than 12 collaborators produced a minimum of 14 papers during the same time period. Obviously collaboration increases productivity, which can affect total citation count. This potential distortion can be handled in a number of different ways, depending upon the situation. In some cases, it may be enough to calculate the average citation count per paper and make that the basis for comparison. Lindsey and Brown suggest the procedure of allocating equally the citation count of a given paper among all its authors (24). If the authors and their work are well known by the person doing the evaluation, it may be possible to allocate citation credits among the coauthors of a given paper on the basis of a subjective judgment of their relative contributions.

The second characteristic of *SCI/SSCI* that can affect the accuracy of an individual's citation count is the homograph problem of distinguishing between two or more people with the same last name. An example of the problem is the name R. A. Fisher, which identifies both the well known theoretical statistician and a lesser known physicist. The chances are that any annual edition of *SCI* during the past 10 years will list under that name cited works for both the statistician and physicist.

There are two solutions to the problem, depending upon the size of the evaluation study being done. If the study involves few enough people to make it practical to compile their citation counts from the printed index, the distinction between people with the same name frequently can be made by examining the titles of the journals in which the cited work and the citing work were published. For example, the *Citation Index* of the 1974 *SCI* lists 137 cited works under the single name of J. Cohen, but an examination of the titles of the cited and source journals involved clearly identifies eight different people: a psychologist, surgeon, physicist, chemist, ophthalmologist, gynecologist and obstetrician, mathematician, and a biostatistician.

The second solution to the name-homograph problem is the same simple one that eliminates the error potential of counts based only on primary-author credits: a complete bibliography of the person being evaluated. This should always be used in any evaluation study large enough to justify a computer analysis of the *SCI/SSCI* data base. And, of course, there is no reason why it cannot be used by researchers on smaller analyses to avoid whatever trouble may be involved in matching journal titles against fields of study and to eliminate the small possibility of mistakes or ambiguities in such an operation.

WHAT DO CITATION COUNTS MEASURE?

All the rest of the grounds for criticism are concerned with intrinsic characteristics of citation counts that are said to invalidate them. Some of these characteristics have to do with what citation counts measure, others with what they do not measure.

Those who claim that citation counts measure too much to be valid talk about negative citations, self-citations, and methodological papers. The first two points represent problems that appear to be more theoretical than real. For example, while it is theoretically possible that a high citation count could be produced by publishing low-quality work that attracted a lot of criticism, the apparent reluctance of scientists to go to the trouble of refuting inferior work makes such a situation very unlikely. Two sociologists of science have commented on this trait. G. M. Carter [21] wrote, "Citations of articles for negative reasons are extremely rare and unlikely to distort the use of frequency counts of citations as measures of research output." A. J. Meadows was even more explicit about the trait [28]: "Surprisingly enough, despite its acceptance of the need for organized skepticism, the scientific community does not normally go out of its way to refute incorrect results. If incorrect results stand in the way of the further development of a subject, or if they contradict work in which someone else has a vested interest, then it may become necessary to launch a frontal attack. Otherwise, it generally takes less time and energy to bypass erroneous material, and simply allow it to fade into obscurity."

These observations add a dimension of subtlety to the negative-citation question. If scientists tend to ignore inferior work that is of little importance, then the work that they do go to the trouble of formally criticizing must be of some substance. Why, then, should negative citations be considered a sign of discredit? Criticism, as well as communication, is one of the fundamental functions of the process of scientific publication. Many new theories and findings of importance are criticized initially. It seems presumptuous to assume that the critics are always right. They are just as likely to be wrong. A significant number of the early papers of Nobel Prize winners were rejected for publication by the leading journals of their fields. And even when the paper being criticized is wrong, does the mistake diminish to zero the contribution of the scientific work being described? Do not mistakes important enough to be formally refuted serve the constructive purpose of clarifying, focusing, and stimulating?

The question of whether negative citations invalidate citation counts as a measure of individual performance evokes the more fundamental question of what facet of scientific performance do citation counts measure. If citation statistics were purported to be a precise measure of the number of times an individual was right, negative citations certainly would be an unacceptable aberration. But citation counts are not that kind of measure. What they are is a very general measure of the level of contribution an individual makes to the practice of science. Since scientists tend to ignore the trivial, negative citations seem to say as much about that rather abstract facet of scientific performance as positive ones.

The question of the validity of self-citations is a simpler one. Theoretically, self-citations are a way of manipulating citation rates. On the other hand, the practice of citing oneself is also both common and reasonable. Studies show that at least 10% of all citations are self-citations, when self-citations are defined as a scientist citing work on which he or she appeared as primary author. If the definition were expanded to include references to work on which the scientist was the secondary author, or to the work of a collaborator (team self-citation), the percentage undoubtedly would be much greater. Since scientists tend to build on their own work, and the work of collaborators, a high self-citation count, more often than not, indicates nothing more ominous than a narrow specialty.

The reason why this is almost always the case is that it is quite difficult to use self-citation to inflate a citation count without being rather obvious about it. A person attempting to do this would have to publish very frequently to make any difference. Given the refereeing system that controls the quality of the scientific literature in the better known journals, the high publication count could be achieved only if the person had a lot to say that was at least marginally significant. Otherwise, the person would be forced into publishing in obscure journals. The combination of a long bibliography of papers published in obscure journals and an abnormally high self-citation count would make the intent so obvious that the technique would be self-defeating.

The third point of criticism, which is the high citation counts of some methodological papers, deserves more attention. Many scientists feel that methodological advances are less important than theoretical ones. Some of them who feel that way conclude that citation counts cannot be a valid measure because they favor those who develop research methods over those who theorize about research findings.

Such a conclusion overlooks several important points. The most obvious one is the questionable validity of the judgment that methods are inherently less important than theories. It may be that they are, but no one can deny that some methods, and instruments too, have opened up major new areas of research. Whether such methods are less important than theories that have had the same impact is a classic subject for debate, rather than a scientific truth. Some indication of the interaction between methodology and theory can be found in *Citation Classics,* a weekly series of statements by authors of highly cited papers that is published in *Current Con-*

tents. The authors of methods papers discuss, among other things, the impact their work has had on theory and practice.

Another, less contentious, point that is overlooked is that methods papers do not inevitably draw a large number of references. Thousands of them are never cited. If you look at the 100 most cited works in the chemical literature as compiled from *SCI* data for any given time period, for example, you will find that roughly 73% do not deal primarily with experimental methodology (29). So, while some methods papers are highly cited, certainly most are not. It varies according to the orientation of the field. In fields highly oriented to methodology, such as analytical chemistry, methods papers do tend to be highly cited. But in those that do not have a particularly strong methodological orientation, high citation counts are as much the exception, rather than the rule, for methods papers as they are for theoretical papers.

The most subtle point that is overlooked concerns the question raised earlier about the quality that citation counts measure. People talk about citation counts being a measure of the "importance," "significance," or "impact" of scientific work, but those who are knowledgeable about the subject use these words in a very pragmatic sense: what they really are talking about is utility. A highly cited work is one that has been found to be useful by a relatively large number of people, or in a relatively large number of experiments. That is the reason why certain methods papers tend to be heavily cited. They describe methods that are frequently and widely used. O. H. Lowry's 1951 paper on protein measurement is a classic example. It was cited 50,000 times between 1961 and 1975, a count that is more than five times as high as the second most highly cited work. The only thing the count indicates about this particular piece of Lowry's work was best said by him: "It just happened to be a trifle better or easier or more sensitive than other methods, and of course nearly everyone measures protein these days." (30).

Conversely, the citation count of a particular piece of scientific work does not necessarily say anything about its elegance or its relative importance to the advancement of science or society. The fact that Lowry's paper on protein determination is more highly cited than Einstein's paper on his unified field theory certainly does not indicate that Lowry's contribution is more significant than Einstein's. All it says is that more scientists are concerned with protein determination than are studying unified field theory. In that sense it is a measure of scientific activity.

The only responsible claim made for citation counts as an aid in evaluating individuals is that they provide a measure of the utility or impact of scientific work. They say nothing about the nature of the work, nothing about the reason for its utility or impact. Those factors can be dealt with only by content analysis of the cited material and the exercise of knowledgeable peer judgment. Citation analysis is not meant to replace such judgment, but to make it more objective and astute.

WHAT CITATION COUNTS DO NOT MEASURE

While one school of critics is concerned with what citation counts do measure, another is equally concerned about what they do not measure. The inability of citation counts to identify premature discoveries—work that is highly significant but so far ahead of the field that it goes unnoticed—is one reason this school gives for questioning their validity. This criticism could appropriately be called the "Mendel syndrome," since those who voice it invariably refer to the long-dormant work of Gregor Mendel.

It is true, of course, that citation counts will not identify significance that is unrecognized by the scientific community. They are, after all, nothing more, nor less, than a reflection of that community's work and interests. To go beyond that is to begin questioning the validity of the community's perception of things, which is another area that calls for peer judgments.

The fact is, other forms of citation analysis can be helpful in going beyond the scientific community's general perception of things (31). There are techniques that might be useful in identifying not only premature work, but the more prevalent phenomenon of immature fields, which are characterized by being small, young, and potentially much more important than their level of activity or citation rate would indicate. But this is another subject.

As far as evaluating individuals is concerned, the inability of citation counts to go beyond the general perceptions of the scientific community seems to be irrelevant to the question of how accurately they reflect those perceptions.

Another issue that is relevant is caused by the phenomenon of obliteration, which takes place when a scientist's work becomes so generic to the field, so integrated into its body of knowledge that people frequently neglect to cite it explicitly (32). This happens, of course, to all high quality work eventually, but in some cases it happens within a relatively short time period. For example, most of Lederberg's work on the sexual reproduction of bacteria was published in the early 1950s (33) but became so much a part of the field of genetics so quickly that the rate at which it is now cited is much lower than its importance would lead one to expect. When this happens, the long-term citation count of the scientist responsible for the work may fail to reflect the full magnitude of his contribution. That is why I suggested in 1963 that a PERT-type measure be used to establish the current impact of old work (34).

There is, however, not much chance of obliteration causing inequities. It happens only to work that makes a very fundamental and important contribution to the field; and before the obliteration takes place, both the citation count and reputation of the scientist responsible for the work usually reach a level that makes additional citation credits superfluous. Of course, obliteration might lead to bad judgments by people unfamiliar with the field, but this possibility is just another reason why evaluations should always be made by, or in consultation with, people knowledgeable in the fields of the scientists involved.

Some people are also concerned because raw citation counts do not take into account the standing, or prestige, of the journal in which the cited work was published. This is true, although the *Journal Citation Reports* section of *SCI/SSCI* provides rankings of journals, based on several different citation measures, that can be used for this purpose. Theoretically, it is possible, as Narin has shown (35), to weight the citation counts to reflect this factor, but it is not very clear how the weights should be used. Should citations to a paper published in *Science* count for more, to reflect the accomplishment of publishing in *Science,* or less, to reflect the possible increase in citation potential that may be attributed to the high visibility of *Science* material. And, what about the journals that published the citing articles? Is not the prestige of the journal that published the citing work just as important as the one that published the cited work?

Though it is easy to speculate on the effect that journal prestige may have upon citation counts, it does not seem to be a very important factor. Since abstracting and indexing services generate visibility for the material published in most journals, it is doubtful whether publication in any particular journal increases the probability of being cited enough to justify a negative weight. Even in a journal as well known and regarded as the *Physical Review,* 47% of all the articles published in 1963 had a 1966 citation rate of 0 or 1 (36). Another reason for discounting the prestige of the journal is that most papers cited highly enough to make any difference are published in a small group of journals that all enjoy a high level of prestige and visibility.

Another, more relevant, concern of the "can't-do" school of critics is that citation counts cannot be used to compare scientists in different fields. This is partially true, depending on the methodology used to make the comparison. It certainly is improper to make comparisons between citation counts generated in different fields.

What makes it improper is that citation potential can vary significantly from one field to another. For example, papers in the biochemistry literature now average 30 references, whereas those in the mathematical literature average fewer than 15. The potential for being cited in the biochemistry literature, then, is two times that of the mathematical literature. Work by Koshy (12) shows that the variations in citation rates and patterns that exist from one discipline to another extend to such citation characteristics as how quickly a paper will be cited, how long the citation rate will take to peak, and how long the paper will continue being cited.

In fact, there is reason to believe that the disciplinary distinctions made between fields may not always be fine enough to avoid unfair comparisons. Work on co-citation analysis (31) suggests quite strongly that the literature varies considerably from one specialty to another in characteristics that affect the potential of being cited. The characteristics identified are the size, degree of integration, and age of the literature. Interestingly enough, the size of the field is measured by the size of its core literature, rather than by the number of researchers. Probably the most common misconception held about citation counts is that they vary according to the number of researchers in the field (7). This is simply not true. Citation potential is an expression of something considerably more complex than the number of people who are theoretically available to cite a paper—though that number does affect the probability of generating extremely high citation rates. It also has much to do with the ratio of publishing authors to total research population, the distribution of published papers over the population, and the distribution of references over the existing literature. While we do not know very much about these variables, it is quite likely that they vary from field to field according to social factors, degree of specialization, and the rate of research progress. In the absence of any detailed knowledge of either the variables or the factors that influence them, the most accurate measure of citation potential is the average number of references per paper published in a given field, and that number does not necessarily correlate with field population.

Reasons aside, citation potential does vary among fields, and the boundaries of fields may be drawn much more finely and narrowly than one might expect. In a controversy over the use of cats in research on the physiology of sexual behavior (37, 38), Dr. Lester R. Aronson claimed that people using rats for that kind of research read and cite only studies on that particular species.

Evaluation studies using citation data must be very sensitive to all divisions, both subtle and gross, between areas of research; and when they are found, the study must properly compensate for disparaties in citation potential. This can be done very simply. Instead of directly comparing the citation count of, say, a mathematician against that of a biochemist, both should be ranked with their peers, and the comparison should be made between rankings. Using this method, a mathematician who ranked in the 70 percentile group of mathematicians would have an edge over a biochemist who ranked in the 40 percentile group of biochemists, even if the biochemist's citation count was higher.

It can be said that this type of analysis is an involved one, and there is no doubt that it is. But making comparisons across disciplines or specialties is a complicated matter. Presumably, the resasons for doing so are significant enough to justify a reasonable amount of effort to make the evaluation fair.

Still another school of criticism discounts citation measures on the grounds that they are too ambiguous to be trusted. One ambiguity that bothers them is that although all Nobel Prize winners and most members of the U.S. National Academy of Sciences have high citation rates (39), there are other people with equally high rates who have not won this type of peer recognition. And they point out the ambiguities that are inherent in a measure that makes no distinction between a scientist who was cited 15 times a year for two years and one who was cited six times a year for five years. Crosbie and Heckel (7) make the additional point that citation measures of departmental performance are extremely sensitive to the time period covered by the analysis and can easily produce ambiguous results, which need careful interpretation, from multiple time periods.

All of these points are perfectly valid ones. There are ambiguities associated with the use of citation counts as a measure of individual performance that prevent them from being completely definitive. They very definitely are an interpretive tool that calls for thoughtful and subtle judgments on the part of those who employ them.

PROS AND CONS

Any fair appraisal of citation analysis as an aid in evaluating scientists must acknowledge that there is much about the meaning of citation rates that we do not know. We are still imprecise about the quality of scientific performance they measure. We still know very little about how sociological factors affect citation rates. There is still much uncertainty about all the possible reasons for low citation rates. And there is still much to learn about the variations in citation patterns from field to field.

On the other hand, we know that citation rates say something about the contribution made by an individual's work, at least in terms of the utility and interest the rest of the scientific community finds in it. We know that high citation rates correlate with peer judgments about scientific excellence and the importance of contributions. And we know enough about overall citation patterns and the variables that affect them to devise a useful statistical model to predict a scientist's lifetime citation rate in terms of the average number of citations per paper.

Such a model has been developed and tested by Geller, de Cani, and Davies (40). It is based on our knowledge of gross citation patterns and the annual growth of the scientific literature. The input to the model is a citation history, covering at least four years, of all of an individual's existing papers. From this, the model projects the total citation count of each paper for a 40-year time period, which is considered the lifetime of a paper. The average lifetime citation count per paper is calculated from the aggregate 40-year total. A validation technique is included to identify papers whose history indicates a citation pattern that differs enough from the norm to require special attention.

The development of such a model is an important step forward in systematizing the use of citation data and reducing the incidence of methodological errors. But there is still a need to be careful (41). There is still a need to understand the limitations of citation data as a measure of relative scientific performance (42). As with any methodology, citation analysis produces results whose validity is highly sensitive to the skill with which it is applied. The apparent simplicity of counting citations masks numerous subtleties associated with comparing citation counts. Superficial citation studies that ignore this dimension of subtlety can be very misleading. Valid citation studies call for a thorough understanding of the intricacies of making comparisons (38), particularly when dealing with citation counts that are not extraordinarily high.

When all there is to say, pro and con, about citation rates as an evaluation tool has been said, two facts stand out as being fundamental to the debate. One is that as the scientific establishment grows bigger, and its role in society more critical, it becomes more difficult, more expensive, and more necessary to make the evaluations that identify those people and groups who are making the greatest contribution. The second fact is that citation measures have been demonstrated to be a valid form of peer judgment that introduces a useful element of objectivity into the evaluation process and involves only a small fraction of the cost of surveying techniques. While citation analysis may sometimes require significantly more time and effort than judgments made on nothing but intuition, professional evaluations certainly are important enough to justify such an investment.

REFERENCES

1. **Johnson, A.A. and Davis, R.B.** "The Research Productivity of Academic Materials Scientists." *Journal of Metals,* **27**(6):28–29, June 1975.
2. **Shapley, D.** "NSF: A 'Populist' Pattern in Metallurgy, Materials Research?" *Science,* **189**(4203):622–624, August 22, 1975.

3. Wert, C.A. "The Citation Index Revisited." *Journal of Metals,* 27(12):20–22, December 1975.
4. Gustafson, T. "The Controversy Over Peer Review." *Science,* 190(4219):1060–1066, December 12, 1975.
5. Shapley, D. "Materials Research: Scientists Show Scant Taste for Breaking Ranks." *Science,* 191(4222):53, January 9, 1976.
6. Roy, R. "Comments on Citation Study of Materials Science Departments." *Journal of Metals,* 28(6): 29–30, June 1976.
7. Crosbie, G.C. and Heckel, R.W. "Citation Criteria for Ranking Academic Departments." *Journal of Metals,* 28(9):27–28, September 1976.
8. Arbiter, N. "Letter to the Editor." *Journal of Metals,* 28(12):33, December 1976.
9. Agarwal, J.C., et al. "Letter to the Editor." *Journal of Metals,* 28(12):33, December 1976.
10. Altstetter, C.J. "Letter to the Editor." *Journal of Metals,* 28(12):33–35, December 1976.
11. Wade, N. "Citation Analysis: A New Tool for Science Administrators," *Science,* 188(4187): 429–432, 1975.
12. Koshy, G.P. "The Citeability of a Scientific Paper." *Proceedings of Northeast Regional Conference of American Institute for Decision Sciences* (Philadelphia, Pa., April/May 1976). Pp. 224–227.
13. Garfield, E. "Is the Ratio Between Number of Citations and Publications Cited a True Contant?" *Essays of an Information Scientist,* Vol. 2 (Philadelphia: ISI Press, 1977). Pp. 419–421.
14. Garfield, E. "Will ISI's *Arts & Humanities Citation Index* Revolutionize Scholarship?" *Current Contents,* No. 32: 5–9 August 8, 1977.
15. Sher, I.H., and Garfield, E. "New Tools for Improving and Evaluating the Effectiveness of Research." In Yovits, M.C., Gilford, D.M., Wilcox, R.H., Stavely, E., and Lerner, H.D. (eds.). *Research Program Effectiveness* (New York: Gordon and Breach, 1966). Pp. 135–146.
16. Martino, J.P. "Citation Indexing for Research and Development Management." *IEEE Transactions on Engineering Management,* EM-18(4):146-151, 1971.
17. Bayer, A.E. and Folger, J. "Some Correlates of a Citation Measure of Productivity in Science." *Sociology of Education,* 39:381-390, 1966.
18. Virgo, J.A. "A Statistical Procedure for Evaluating the Importance of Scientific Papers." *The Library Quarterly* 47:415–430, 1977.
19. Garfield, E. "Citation Indexing for Studying Science." *Nature,* 227(5259):669–671, 1970.
20. Bernier, C.L., Gill, W.N., and Hunt, R.G. "Measures of Excellence of Engineering and Science Departments: A Chemical Engineering Example." *Chemical Engineering Education,* 9:94–97, 1975.
21. Carter, G.M. "Peer Review, Citations, and Biomedical Research Policy: NIH Grants to Medical School Faculty." *Rand Report,* R-1583-HEW (Santa Monica, California: Rand Corporation, 1974). 90 pp.
22. Garfield, E. "The 250 Most-Cited Primary Authors, 1961–1975. Part III. Each Author's Most Cited Publication." *Current Contents,* No. 51: 5–20, December 19, 1977.
23. Cole, J.R. and Cole, S. *Social Stratification in Science.* (Chicago: University of Chicago Press, 1973). 283 pp.
24a. Lindsey, D. and Brown, G.W. "Problems of Measurement in the Sociology of Science: Taking Account of Collaboration." (unpublished) 1977.
24b. Zuckerman, H. "Patterns of Name-Ordering Among Authors of Scientific Papers." *American Journal of Sociology,* 74:276–291, 1968.
25. Roy, R. "Approximating Total Citation Counts From First-Author Counts and Total Papers." Working Paper, April, 1977.
26. Price, D.J.D. *Little Science, Big Science.* (New York: Columbia University Press, 1963). 118 pp.
27. Price, D.J.D. and Beaver, D.B. "Collaboration in an Invisible College." *American Psychologist,* 21:1011–1018, 1966.
28. Meadows, A.J. *Communication in Science* (London: Butterworths, 1974). p. 45.
29. Small, H.G. *Characteristics of Frequently Cited Papers in Chemistry,* Final Report on NSF Contract #C795 (1974). See also Garfield, E. "A List of 100 Most Cited 'Chemical' Articles." *Current Contents,* No. 10:5–12, March 9, 1977.

30. **Lowry, O.H.** Personal communication to D.J. Price, November 11, 1969.
31a. **Small, H.G. and Griffith, B.C.** "The Structure of Scientific Literatures, I: Identifying and Graphing Specialties." *Science Studies,* 4:17-40, 1974.
31b. **Griffith, B., Small, H.G., Stonehill, J.A., and Dey, S.** "The Structure of Scientific Literature, II: Towards a Macro- and Micro-Structure for Science." *Science Studies,* 4:339-365, 1974.
32. **Merton, R.K.** *Social Theory and Social Structure* (New York: The Free Press, 1968). Pp. 26-28, 35-38;**Merton, R.K.** *On the Shoulders of Giants: a Shandean Postscript* (New York: Harcourt Brace & Jovanovich, 1965). pp218-219.
33. **Lederberg, J.** "A View of Genetics." *Science,* 131:269-276, 1960.
34. **Garfield, E. and Sher, I.H.** "Citation Indexes in Sociological and Historical Research." *American Documentation,* 14:289-291, 1963.
35. **Narin, F.** *Evaluative Bibliometrics: The Use of Publication and Citation Analysis in the Evaluation of Scientific Activity.* (Cherry Hill, N.J.: Computer Horizons, Inc., 1976). 500 pp. NTIS-PB252339/AS.
36. **Cole, J.R. and Cole, S.** "The Ortega Hypothesis." *Science,* 178:368-375, 1975.
37. **Garfield, E.** "Citation Analysis and the Anti-Vivisection Controversy." *Current Contents,* No. 17: 5-10, April 25, 1977,
38. **Garfield, E.** "Citation Analysis and the AntiVivisection Controversy. Part II. An Assessment of Lester R. Aronson's Citation Record." *Current Contents,* No. 48: 5-14, November 28, 1977.
39. **Garfield, E.** "The 250 Most-Cited Primary Authors, 1961-1975. Part II. The Correlation Between Citedness, Nobel Prizes, and Academy Memberships." *Current Contents,* No. 50: 5-15, December 12, 1977.
40. **Geller, N.L., deCani, J.S., and Davies, R.E.** "Lifetime Citation Rates as a Basis for Comparisons Within a Scientific Field." In Goldfield, E.D. (ed.) *American Statistical Association Proceedings of the Social Statistics Section.* (Washington, D.C.: American Statistical Association, 1975. Pp. 429-433.
41. **Garfield, E,** "Caution Urged in the Use of Citation Analysis." *Trends in Biochemical Sciences,* 2(4):N84, April 1977.
42. **Lindsey, D. and Brown, G.W.** "The Measurement of Quality in Social Studies of Science: Critical Reflections on the Use of Citation Counts." (unpublished) 1977.

Epilogue: The Future of Citation Indexing

The primary focus of this book is the past and present of citation indexing. But what about the future?

Citation indexing promises to be at least as robust in the future as it is in the present. The popularity of citation indexes as a tool for conducting retrospective searches of the scientific literature will continue to increase, and probably at an accelerated rate.

The acceleration will powered by several factors. The increasing availability of on-line searching facilities throughout the world will place the *SCISEARCH®* *system at the fingertips of most working scientists and scholars. Improvements in on-line software will increase the use of *SCISEARCH* by those already familiar with it.

The increased awareness that citation indexes are used as part of the research evaluation process will induce more scientists to learn how to use *SCI*. Hopefully, good refereeing will prevent those who would from compromising legitimate reference practices.

Access to the *SCI/SSCI* data bases will become more convenient. Microstorage techniques or minicomputers could eventually make it economically practical for individual scientists and departmental groups to have their own copies of the data bases. Alternatively, the increase in accessibility will come from continuing reductions in the cost of providing on-line, remote links to data bases stored in central computers.

In addition, ISI is thoroughly examining the idea of producing disciplinary citation indexes whose source coverage would be based on the journal literature of a single discipline. However, the cited and citing material would reflect the full scope and diversity of interests in the field. This would include all the references by the publishing authors of the discipline, as well as all citations to the field by authors outside the discipline.

The critical problem that must be solved to do this remains the one faced in the design of the *Genetics Citation Index* (Chapter Two): how to define the literature in a way that minimizes irrelevant material without interfering with the ability of a citation index to reflect the disciplines's interaction with other disciplines. One way, tested in the *Genetics Citation Index* project, is to define a subset of cited authors in the combined multidisciplinary *SCI/SSCI* data base that meets some disciplinary criteria and then from that to work back to the source material (Chapter Two). Another way, suggested by the journal citation studies done in recent years (Chapter Nine), is to use the *Journal Citation Reports* to identify the source journals of the discipline first and then use straightforward methods to compile a citation index to the material they publish. Either way, the sharper focus of disciplinary citation in-

---

*A registered trademark of the Institute for Scientific Information.

dexes will produce search tools priced and sized to the requirements of departmental and personal libraries.

Such disciplinary indexes would be cumulated for long periods. For example, a geosciences citation index for 20 years is now under evaluation. Although some fields have a greater dependence on the older literature than others, a large-scale multiyear cumulation provides any field with an important historical perspective that is otherwise difficult to obtain. That is why I have set an ISI goal of extending the *SCI* back through the first 60 years of the twentieth century.

Not only will the use of citation indexes for literature searching accelerate within the scientific community, but it also will spread to the arts and humanities community. That has already begun to happen as the scholars in that community begin to respond to the *Arts & Humanities Citation Index.*(1)

The use of citation data to measure performance and for historical and sociological studies will also accelerate and spread (2). Despite the controversy that presently surrounds some of the applications of citation data (Chapter Ten), it has become a standard tool for exploring the social systems of science. At the present time, the literature on citation studies is growing quite rapidly. At least 100 papers per year are published—most independent of the various ISI studies published in *Current Contents* and elsewhere.

When Cole, Rubin, and Cole studied the peer review procedures on which the National Science Foundation bases its grant awards, citation counts were one of the variables that were examined to determine whether grant proposals were being prejudged (3). The fact that they were included suggests that they are increasingly accepted as a legitimate indicator of research significance. The fact that the citation counts were found to have an insignificant correlation with actual grant awards demonstrates that a potential for abuse is not equivalent to actual abuse. I hope this will not change in the future.

ISI is working to make citation data as precise as possible. The recent publication of the first comprehensive comparison between primary-author and all-author data (4) was an important step in this direction. This data not only showed how careful one must be in compiling citation data, but it also demonstrated some of the subtleties of interpreting the data. Consider the matter of high rates of coauthorship. In the case of a science administrator who coauthors numerous papers with members of the research staff, a very high coauthorship rate raises questions about the ethics of the authorships. In the case of a teacher who coauthors papers with numerous graduate students, a very high coauthorship rate suggests a measure of the teacher's impact. Both types of cases were found in the data.

Several key developments presage a substantial expansion of the use made of citation data for sociological studies. One is an NSF grant to ISI to compile a citation index of the 1920s journal literature of physics. The data base will be used to determine whether citation analyses can provide some new and sociologically useful insights into a decade of activity that has come to be called the "golden age of modern physics." Plans call for the eventual development of citation networks (5-8) and maps of co-cited clusters (9) from the data base that historians and sociologists can study.

Of even greater importance to the scholarly community is the recent agreement signed by ISI and NSF. This agreement gives any NSF-supported scholar access to the complete *SCI* data base for program planning, science policy studies, and so on. I am also hopeful that a similar agreement will be made with most foreign nations. The Japanese Ministry of Education has already leased ISI files and I expect the U.S.S.R. will do so in the near future. The National Research Council of Italy has been using *SCI* files for a variety of information purposes for several years.

Another development important to the expanded use of citation analysis is the *Arts & Humanities Citation Index* (1). The concept of producing a citation index to the arts and humanities literature dates back to at least 1955. In November of that year, I presented a paper at the American Documentation Institute Annual Meeting in which I outlined the concept of a citation index to the Bible that would be useful in studying the interaction between science and the humanities (10). The *Arts & Humanities Citation Index* should facilitate and stimulate new studies of that critical but little understood relationship.

A fourth development that can be expected to increase the sociological impact of citation analyses is Price's general theory of cumulative advantage processes (11). Cumulative advantage processes are ones that operate in situations where success breeds success. Merton (12) and then Cole and Cole (13) have described such processes at work in the social systems of science. Price's general theory for these processes proposes a statistical model that predicts the distributions they produce. What makes this highly significant is that the distributions predicted by the model fit those derived from such empirical laws as the Lotka distribution for scientific productivity, the Bradford law for journal use, the Pareto law of income distribution, and the Zipf law for literary word frequencies. What Price calls the "cumulative advantage distribution" also fits the empirical results of citation-frequency analysis. The theory, then, appears to provide a unifying conceptual framework for all of the empirical laws and citation data that make up the study of bibliometrics.

This promises to have a major impact on both the field of bibliometrics and on the use of citation data within the field. For one thing it appears to represent an important step forward in the attempt to determine what it is that citation data and other bibliometric measures define. It also should provide the type of conceptual foundation needed to increase the rate at which useful empirical generalizations and underlying theories are derived from the rich lode of citation data that exists. Although it is not possible to predict the outcome of such advances, it is reasonable to speculate that they could have a very significant impact on the practice of science.

As long as scientists and scholars continue to use the instrument we call "papers" as a primary communications medium, citation indexing and analysis will play an increasingly significant role in the management of mankind's knowledge and the processes by which that knowledge is produced. The future of the scholarly paper has often seemed in jeopardy. Whether the technological changes available to the next generation of scholars will undermine the role of the paper in the process of scholarship remains to be seen. My innate optimism gives me hope that it will not, and that citation indexing will have an increasingly strong, positive influence on scholarship.

References

1. **Garfield, E.** "Will ISI's *Arts & Humanities Citation Index* Revolutionize Scholarship?" *Current Contents* No. 32:5-9 August 8, 1977.
2. **Garfield, E. Malin, M.V. and Small, H.** "Citation Data as Science Indicators." In Elkana, Y., Lederberg, J., Thackeray, A. Merton, R.K., and Zuckerman, H. (eds.). *Toward a Metric of Science.* (New York: John Wiley & Sons, Inc., 1978). Pp. 179-207.
3. **Cole, S. Rubin, L. and Cole, J.R.** "Peer Review and the Support of Science." *Scientific American,* 237(4):34-41, 1977.
4. **Garfield, E.** "At Last: The 300 Most Cited Authors, 1961-1976, Including Co-Authors." *Current Contents,* No. 28:5-17, July 10, 1978.
5. **Garfield, E.** "Citation Indexes in Sociological and Historical Research." *American Documentation,* 14:289-291, 1963.
6. **Garfield, E. Sher, I. H. and Torpie, R.J.** *The Use of Citation Data for Writing the History of Science.* (Philadelphia: Institute for Scientific Information, 1964). 86 pp.
7. **Garfield, E.** "When Citation Analysis Strikes Ball Lightning." *Essays of an Information Scientist,* Vol. 2 (Philadelphia: ISI Press, 1977). Pp. 279-490.
8. **Cawkell, A. E.** "Search Strategy, Construction, and Use of Citation Networks With a Socio- Scientific Example: Amorphous Semiconductors and S.R. Ovshinsky." *Journal of the American Society for Information Science.* 25:123-130, 1974.
9. **Small, H. and Griffith, B.C.** "The Structure of Scientific Literatures. I: Graphing Specialities." *Science Studies,* 4:17-40, 1974.
10. **Garfield, E.** "Citation Indexes—New Dimension in Documentation (Citation Index to tne Old Testament)." Paper presented at American Documentation Institute Annual Meeting, Philadelphia, November 1955.
11. **Merton, R.K.** "The Matthew Effect in Science." In Storer, N.W. (ed.). *The Sociology of Science* (Chicago: University of Chicago Press, 1973). pp. 439-459.
12. **Cole, S.** "Professional Standing and the Reception of Scientific Discoveries." *American Sociological Review,* 76:286-306, 1970.
13. **Zuckerman, H.** "Stratification in American Science." *Sociological Inquiry,* 40:235-257, 1970.
14. **Zuckerman, H. and Merton, R.K.** "Age, Aging, and Age Structure in Science." In Riley, M.W. et al. (eds.) *A Sociology of Age Stratification* (New York: Russell Sage Foundation, 1972). pp. 292-256.
15. **Cole, J.R. and Cole, S.** *Social Stratification in Science* (Chicago: University of Chicago Press, 1973).
16. **Allison, P.D. and Stewart, J.A.** "Productivity Differences Among Scientists: Evidence for Accumulative Advantage." *American Sociological Review,* 39:596-606, 1974
17. **Zuckerman, H. and Cole, J.R.** "Women in American Science." *Minerva,* 13:82-102, 1975.
18. **Zuckerman, H.** *Scientific Elite: Nobel Laureates in the United States* (New York: Free Press, 1977). Chapters 3 and 8.
19. **Price, D.J.D.** "A General Theory of Bibliometric and Other Cumulative Advantage Processes" *Journal of the American Society for Information Science,* 27:292-306, 1976.

Cited Author Index

This index lists the names of all authors cited in the references of this book. It is designed to enable the reader to locate the chapters of this book in which the work of specific authors is discussed. Not included as entries are names of authors from lists of highly-cited articles and the like, which several of the chapters contain. Citations of E. Garfield have also been omitted. Entries refer the reader to a page number and a reference number. Thus, the entry *Hart, H. C., 40r2,* means reference number 2 on page 40 is to H. C. Hart.

Aaronson, S., 79r1
Ackermans, E., 146r22
Agarwal, J. C., 251r9
Allison, P. D., 256r16
Alstetter, C. J., 251r10
Arbiter, N., 251r8
Asimov, I., 80r16, 97r16

Bath University Library, 146r28
Batzig, J. H., 36r3
Bayer, A. E., 80r7, 251r17
Beaver, D. B., 251r27
Berlt, N. C., 145r7
Bernal, J. D., 97r9, 97r12
Bernier, C. L., 251r20
Bichteler, J., 61r7, 61r8
Bishop, C. T., 234r38
Bradford, S. C., 36r1
Brown, G. W., 251r24a, 252r42

Cani, J. S. de, 80r13, 252r40
Carpenter, M., 145r7
Carter, G. M., 251r21
Cawkell, A. E., 61r1, 61r2, 61r3, 256r8
Chen, C. C., 234r22
Chomsky, N., 18r4
Chubin, D. E., xir2
Clark, K. E., 80r6, 146r24
Cole, J. R., xir2, xir5, 146r27, 251r23,
    252r36, 256r3, 256r15, 256r17
Cole, S., xir2, xir5, 146r26, 251r23, 252r36,
    256r3, 256r12, 256r15

Crane, D., 145r4
Crawford, S., 145r2
Crosbie, G. C., 251r7

Davies, R. E., 80r13, 252r40
Davis, R. B., 250r1
Dey, S., 96r6, 146r12, 252r31b
Dietrich, L., xir5

Eaton, E. A., 61r8
Elkana, Y., xir5

Field, H. G., 18r1
Folger, J., 80r7, 251r17

Gaston, J., xvr4
Geller, N. L., 80r13, 252r40
Gill, W. N., 251r20
Goffman, W., 145r8, 146r18
Griffith, B. C., 96r5, 96r6, 145r3, 146r11,
    146r12, 146r20, 252r31a, 252r31b, 256r9
Gustafson, T., 251r4

Harris, Z. S., 18r3
Hart, H. C., 40r2
Heckel, R. W., 251r7
Himwich, W. A., 18r1
Hunt, R. G., 251r20

Inhaber, H., 234r21, 234r39, 234r40

Jahn, M., 146r9

Janke, N. C., 234r17
Jaspars, J. M. F., 146r22
Johnson, A. A., 250r1

Kaplan, N., xir1
Kassab, J. L., 80r8
Kessler, M. M., 146r15
Koshy, G. P., 251r12
Kuhn, T. S., 146r21

Larkey, S. V., 18r1
Leake, C. D., 97r14
Lederberg, J., xir4, xir5, 252r33
Lin, N., 146r23
Lindsey, D., 251r24a, 252r42
Lowry, O. H., 252r30

Magyar, G., 146r19
Malin, M. V., xir5, 80r17, 256r2
Marshakova, I. V., 146r17
Martino, J. P., 79r2, 251r16
Meadows, A. J., 80r11, 251r28
Merton, R. K., xir3, xir5, xvr3, xvr4, 252r32, 256r11, 256r14
Messeri, P., xir3
Moitra, S. D., xir2
Moravcsik, M. J., xir2
Mullins, N. C., 145r3
Murugesan, P., xir2
Myers, C. R., 146r25

Narin, F., 145r7, 252r35

Orr, R. H., 80r8

Parsons, R. G., 61r7
Ping, V. M., 61r5
Popper, K., 146r32
Price, D. J. D., 80r10, 80r14, 96r1, 96r2, 96r3, 96r4, 97r13, 145r5, 145r6, 146r29, 146r30, 251r26, 251r27, 256r19

Resnick, A., 18r2
Revesz, G. S., 36r3
Roy, R., 251r6, 251r25
Rubin, L., 256r3

Sadgopal, A., 97r19
Sager, N., 18r5
Schiminovich, S., 61r6
Seidel, A. H., 40r1
Shapley, D., 250r2, 251r5
Sher, I. H., 18r10, 61r4, 79r3, 80r15, 97r8, 97r17, 145r1, 251r15, 252r34, 256r6
Shryock, R., 97r15
Small, H., xir5, 80r17, 96r5, 96r6, 146r10, 146r11, 146r12, 146r13, 146r14, 146r16, 251r29, 252r31a, 252r31b, 256r2, 256r9
Stewart, J. A., 256r16
Stonehill, J. A., 96r6, 146r12, 252r31b

Thackray, A., xir5
Thorpe, P., 233r10
Torpie, R. J., 80r15, 97r8, 145r1, 256r6
Toulmin, S., 147r33

Virgo, J. A., 80r9, 251r18

Wade, N., 80r12, 251r11
Weinstock, M., 18r12
Wert, C. A., 251r3
Whittock, J. M., 18r1
Williams, J. F., 61r5
Wood, J. L., 36r4

Yermish, I., 97r18, 147r34

Zuckerman, H., xir5, 146r27, 251r24b, 256r13, 256r14, 256r17, 256r18

Subject Index

Note: Mention or discussion of individuals in the *text* is required for a personal name to appear as an entry in this index. However, since not every person whose work is cited is actually mentioned in the text, readers should also consult the *Cited Author Index* when using personal names as search terms.

A&HCI, see *Arts & Humanities Citation Index*
Abraham, G. E., search, 42
Abstracting and indexing services, 21, 248
 see also Citation indexes and indexing; Indexes and indexing
Abstracts, citation indexing, 7
Academie des Sciences, citation analysis, 224
Academies of science, membership of highly cited authors, 64
Acoustics journals, citation analysis, 198
Acta Anaesthesiologica Scandinavica, citation analysis, 150
Acta Chemica Scandinavica, citation analysis, 188
Acta Crystallographica, citation analysis, 186
Acta Medica Scandinavica, citation analysis, 170
Acta Pathologica et Microbiologica Scandinavica, citation analysis, 173
Adair, William C., history of citation indexing, 7
Agriculture literature, citation analysis, 202
Air Force Office of Scientific Research
 citation analysis, 70
 DNA research, 72
 network diagrams, 81
Allen, Gordon, network diagrams, 81
Allosteric systems literature, co-citation clusters, 118
American Chemical Society, citation analysis, 227
American Documentation Institute, citation indexes, 255
American Journal of Human Genetics
 citation analysis, 183
 citation indexing, 14
American Journal of Pathology, citation analysis, 173
American Journal of Physics, citation analysis, 154
American Journal of Science, citation analysis, 183
American Mineralogist, citation analysis, 183
American Phytopathological Association, citation analysis, 170
American Review of Respiratory Diseases, citation analysis, 196
American Society of Human Genetics, development of *Genetics Citation Index*, 13
American Sociological Review, citation analysis, 72
Analytical Chemistry, citation analysis, 227
Annalen der Physik, citation indexing, 4
Annals of Mathematical Statistics, citation indexes, 11
Annals of Rheumatic Diseases, citation analysis, 170
Annals of the New York Academy of Sciences, citation analysis, 198
Annual Review of Phytopathology, citation analysis, 192
Archives of General Psychiatry, citation analysis, 198

Subject Index

Archives of Internal Medicine, citation analysis, 170
Archives of Pathology, citation analysis, 175
Armed Forces Medical Library, history of citation indexing, 6
Aronson, Lester R., citation analysis, 249
Arthritis and Rheumatism, citation analysis, 170
Arts & Humanities Citation Index
  Citation Index, 33
  first publication, 16
  future, 254
  inclusion of reference citations from source items, 33
  origin, 255
  potential for citation analysis, 240
  production process, 27
  Source Index, 33
  see also Citation indexes and indexing; *Science Citation Index,* and *Social Sciences Citation Index*
ASCA (Automatic Subject Citation Alert)
  basis of *Journal of Histochemistry and Cytochemistry* citation index, 16
  profiles, 60
  weekly search service, 60
Asimov, Isaac, DNA research, 72, 83
Astrogeophysics literature, citation analysis, 186
Atlas of Science, mapping the structure of science, 142
Audiology journals, citation analysis, 198
Authors, citation analysis, 240, 254
Awards and memberships, highly cited authors, 64, 249, 254
  See also Nobel Prize

Bardeen, J. M., search, 50
Barland method for isolating surface membranes, search, 46
Bath University, mapping structure of science, 135
Baur, Werner, citation analysis, 186
Behavioral sciences literature, citation analysis, 197
Bell's palsy, search, 46
Bible, citation index, 255
Bibliographic coupling, co-citation analysis, 99
Bibliographic-verification searches, 42
  see also Searches
Bibliography of Non-Parametric Statistics, citation indexes, 11

Bibliography on journal citation analysis, 235
Bibliometrics
  emergence, x
  impact of cumulative advantage processes, 255
Biochemistry, citation analysis, 163
Biochemistry, core literature, citation analysis, 163
Biochemistry doctorates, citation analysis, 64
Biochimica et Biophysica Acta, citation analysis, 227
Biological membranes literature, co-citation clusters, 122
Biomedical literature
  citation analysis, 64
  co-citation clusters, 76, 78, 104, 113, 115, 122
Black holes, search, 50
Botanical Gazette, citation analysis, 197
Botanical Review, citation analysis, 192
Botany literature, citation analysis, 192
Bradford's law, 21, 160, 255
Brain Research, citation analysis, 230
Breast cancer literature, co-citation clusters, 118
British Journal of Cancer, citation analysis, 190
British Journal of Experimental Pathology, citation analysis, 175, 190
British Medical Journal, citation analysis, 170, 175
Bulletin de la Societe Chimique de France, citation analysis, 223
Bulletin du Cancer, citation analysis, 190
Bulletin of the American Association of Petroleum Geologists, citation analysis, 183
Bulletin of the Geological Society of America, citation analysis, 183

CAC/IC
  see Current Abstracts of Chemistry & Index Chemicus
California State University, citation analysis, 183
Cancer, citation analysis, 190
Cancer Chemotherapy Reports, citation analysis, 190
Cancer journals, citation analysis, 190
Cancer Research, citation analysis, 190

Subject Index

Cancer research literature, co-citation clusters, 116, 118
Capital, plagiarism, viii
Carlson, P. S., search, 54
Carter, G. M., negative citations, 244
Cats, work of Lester R. Aronson, 249
CC
  see Current Contents
Cell Tissue Research, citation analysis, 230
Chemical Abstracts
  coverage, 21
  cross references, 7
  DNA research, 86
  indexing methods, 7
  patents, 12, 38
Chemical physicists, citation analysis, 166
Chemische Technik, history of citation indexing, 9
Chemistry literature
  citation analysis, 71, 246
  co-citation clusters, 104, 113, 115, 122
  core literature, 163
  highly cited papers, 246
  methodological papers, 246
Child Development, citation analysis, 181
Chromosome literature, co-citation clusters, 122
Citation analysis
  see also Citation indexes and indexing, Citations, Co-citation analysis and clusters
  individuals and institutions
    Academie des Sciences, 224
    accuracy of citation counts, 241
    Air Force Office of Scientific Research, 70
    American Chemical Society, 227
    American Phytopathological Association, 170
    Aronson, Lester R., 249
    authors, 240, 254
    Baur, Werner, 186
    biochemistry doctorates, 64
    California State University, 183
    Carter, G. M., 244
    chemical physicists, 166
    Clark, K. E., 64
    Cole, J. R., viii
    Cole, Stephen, viii
    comparison of scientists in different fields, 248
    Consiglio Nationale della Richerche (CNR), 71

correlation between citation counts and awards and memberships, 64, 249, 254
correlation between citation counts and journal referees, 64
correlation between citation counts and peer judgments, 63, 69, 131, 241, 246, 250
criticism, 63, 240
Davies, Robert E., 71, 250
Cani, John S. de, 72, 250
departmental performance at universities, 64, 240, 249
Einstein, Albert, 4, 246
evaluating individual scientists, ix, 62, 240
evaluating research, 62, 240, 246, 250, 253
first author problem, 242
French Academy of Sciences, 224
Geigy Pharmaceuticals, 167
Geller, Nancy L., 71, 250
government agencies, 70
highly cited scientists, 62, 240
homographs, 243
immature fields, 247
Inhaber, H., 188
Italian government, 71
Janke, N. C., 183
Jensen, J. H. D., 64
Kaplan, Norman, viii
Landau, L. D., 64
Lederberg, Joshua, 247
lifetime citation rates, 71, 250
litigation, 72
Lowry, O. H., 246
Meadows, A. J., 244
measure of scholarship in the humanities, 241
measure of scientific performance, 64, 240, 249
Mendel syndrome, 247
multi-authored papers, 63, 242, 254
National Academy of Sciences USA, 249
National Cancer Institute, 71, 190
National Institute of Mental Health, 71
National Research Council of Italy, 71
National Science Foundation, 71, 254
Nobel Prize winners, ix, 63, 91, 249
obliteration phenomenon, viii, 247
Oregon State University, 183
perspective on, 240

physical chemists, 166
premature discoveries, 246
Price, D. J. D., 71, 81, 99, 142, 243
protein measurement, work of O. H. Lowry, 246
psychologists, 64, 135
quality in psychological research, 64
radiology authors, 69
reward system of science, viii
science administrators, 240
scientists, ix, 62, 71, 91, 149, 240, 249, 254
secondary authors, 242
self-citation, 63, 72, 149, 245
sexual reproduction of bacteria, obliteration phenomenon, 247
shortcomings, 99, 246
significance, 244
Soviet Academy of Science, 205
surgery authors, 69
tenure decisions, 71, 240
Thorpe, Peter, 167
unanswered questions, 249
university departments, 64, 240, 249, 253
University of Illinois at Chicago, 186

journals and fields
  acoustics journals, 198
  Acta Anaesthesiologica Scandinavica, 150
  Acta Chemica Scandinavica, 188
  Acta Crystallographica, 186
  Acta Medica Scandinavica, 170
  Acta Pathologica et Microbiologica Scandinavica, 173
  agriculture literature, 202
  American Journal of Human Genetics, 183
  American Journal of Pathology, 173
  American Journal of Physics, 154
  American Journal of Science, 183
  American Mineralogist, 183
  American Review of Respiratory Diseases, 196
  American Sociological Review, 72
  Analytical Chemistry, 227
  Annals of Rheumatic Diseases, 170
  Annals of the New York Academy of Sciences, 198
  Annual Review of Phytopathology, 192
  Archives of General Psychiatry, 198
  Archives of Internal Medicine, 170
  Archives of Pathology, 175
  Arthritis and Rheumatism, 170
  astrogeophysics literature, 186
  audiology journals, 198
  behavioral sciences literature, 197
  bibliography, 235
  Biochemistry, 163
  biochemistry, core literature, 163
  Biochemica et Biophysica Acta, 227
  biomedical literature, 64
  Botanical Gazette, 197
  Botanical Review, 192
  botany literature, 192
  Brain Research, 230
  British Journal of Cancer, 190
  British Journal of Experimental Pathology, 175, 190
  British Medical Journal, 170, 175
  Bulletin de la Societe Chimique de France, 223
  Bulletin du Cancer, 190
  Bulletin of the American Association of Petroleum Geologists, 183
  Bulletin of the Geological Society of America, 183
  Cancer, 190
  Cancer Chemotherapy Reports, 190
  cancer journals, 190
  Cancer Research, 190
  Cell Tissue Research, 230
  chemistry, core literature, 163
  chemistry literature, 71, 246
  Child Development, 181
  Clinical Pediatrics, 181
  Comptes Rendus, 224
  correlation between citation counts and expert opinions, 131
  Current Contents, 254
  defining core literature, 79, 253
  Diabetes, 175
  DNA research, 72, 83
  Doklady Akademii Nauk USSR, 197, 205
  Endocrinology, 175
  engineering literature, 21, 202
  European Journal of Cancer, 190
  French journals, 223
  Gann, 190
  genetics literature, 72, 83
  Geological Society of London Quarterly, 183
  geology literature, 183
  geophysics literature, 183
  German journals, 230

Subject Index

Growth, 181
immediacy index, 150
impact factor, 24, 78, 149
Inorganic Chemistry, 188
International Journal of Cancer, 190
Japanese journals, 227
Journal Citation Reports, 78, 150, 247
journal evaluation, 78, 148
Journal of Biological Chemistry, 223, 227
Journal of Bone and Joint Surgery, 170
Journal of Chemical Physics, 166, 188, 190, 205
Journal of Clinical Endocrinology and Metabolism, 175
Journal of Clinical Investigation, 175, 178, 181
Journal of Clinical Pathology, 175
Journal of Experimental Medicine, 167, 175
Journal of Geology, 183
Journal of Geophysical Research, 183, 185
Journal of Immunology, 167
Journal of Invertebrate Pathology, 192
Journal of Medical Virology, 175
Journal of Molecular Biology, 188
Journal of Pathology, 173
Journal of Physical Chemistry, 167, 205
Journal of Sedimentary Petrology, 183
Journal of the American Chemical Society, 163, 167, 188, 205, 223, 227
Journal of the American Medical Association, 175, 178, 181
Journal of the Association of Official Analytical Chemists, 202
Journal of the Chemical Society, 188
Journal of the National Cancer Institute, 190
journals in a scientific specialty, 25
Lancet, 170, 175, 224
mathematics literature, 248
Mathematische Annalen, 154
Mathematische Zeitschrift, 154
methodological papers, 71, 115, 244, 246
Monatschrift fur Kinderheilkunde, 183
Mycopathologia et Mycologia Applicata, 196
National Cancer Institute Monograph, 190
Nature, 167, 183, 185, 187, 190, 196, 198, 205, 223, 227, 230

Naunyn-Schmiedebergs Archiv fur Pharmakologie, 175
Neoplasma, 190
network of DNA research, 72, 83
New England Journal of Medicine, 175, 178, 181
Nouvelle Presse Medicale, 224
Pathologie Biologie, 173
pathology literature, 170
pediatrics literature, 178
Pediatrie, 181
Pesticides Biochemistry, 202
Physical Review, 190, 205, 248
Physical Review Letters, 190
physics literature, 188
Phytochemistry, 227
Phytopathology, 170
Presse Medicale, 224
Proceedings of the American Association for Cancer Research, 192
Proceedings of the Institute of Electrical and Electronics Engineers, 205
Proceedings of the National Academy of Sciences USA, 227
Proceedings of the Royal Society (London), 205
Proceedings of the Society for Experimental Biology and Medicine, 170
Progress in Experimental Tumor Research, 192
psychiatry literature, 198
psychology literature, 197
pulsars research literature, 71
rheumatology literature, 167
Science, 158, 167, 183, 185, 187, 190, 196, 198, 205, 227, 247
Solid State Communications, 158
Soviet journals, 167, 205, 208
Soviet Physics-Crystallography, 187
Teploenergetica, 24, 205
Tetrahedron Letters, 227
Theoretical and Applied Genetics, 195
Thermal Engineering USSR, 24, 205
theses, 183
Tumori, 192
Virchows Archiv, 173
Virology, 196
virology literature, 170, 175
Zeitschrift fur Krebsforschung, 192
Zeitschrift fur Kristallographie, 188
Zhurnal Fizicheskoi Khimii, 167

Subject Index

structure of science
  areas of sudden activity, 71, 144
  DNA research, 72, 83
  Genetic Code, 72, 83
  historical research into science, 62, 72, 81
  historiograms, 86
  historiographs, 73, 86
  history of scientific developments, 72, 81, 98
  identifying social relationships in science, viii, 144, 255
  immature fields, 247
  immediacy index, 72, 78
  literary model of science, 81, 99, 143, 255
  mapping scientific specialties, 75, 111
  mapping the structure of science, 72, 81, 98
  on-line system, 93
  physics, 99
  Science Citation Index, ix, 4, 23, 62, 90, 100, 150, 241
  sociological studies of science, xi, 72, 254
Citation Classics, Current Contents, 245
Citation Index for Statistics and Probability, 16
Citation Index of *Science Citation Index, Social Sciences Citation Index*, and *Arts & Humanities Citation Index*
  homographs, 243
  listing of first authors, 242
  production process, 33
Citation indexes and indexing
  see also Citations, *Science Citation Index, Social Sciences Citation Index, Arts & Humanities Citation Index, Genetics Citation Index, Journal Citation Reports, Shepard's Citations*
  abstracts, 7
  Adair, William C., 7
  American Documentation Institute, 255
  American Journal of Human Genetics, 14
  Annalen der Physik, 4
  Annals of Mathematical Statistics, 11
  Armed Forces Medical Library, 6
  ASCA, 16
  Bible, 255
  Bibliography of Non-Parametric Statistics, 11
  Chemical Abstracts, 7
  Chemische Technik, 9
  Citation Index for Statistics and Probability, 16
  computer technology, 31
  conceptual basis, 1
  cross-disciplinary nature, 4
  cumulations, 254
  Current Contents data base, 13, 25
  Current List of Medical Literature, 7, 86
  design and production, 19
  Dobzhansky, T., 14
  early production model, 10
  economic considerations, 20
  Einstein, Albert, 4
  Essays of an Information Scientist, xiii
  Eugene Garfield Associates, 11
  future, 77, 142, 253
  Garfield, Eugene, vii, xiii
  Gates, R. R., 14
  genetics, 12
  Genetics Society of America, 13
  history, xiv, 6
  Index Medicus, 3, 7, 11, 86
  Johns Hopkins University, 6
  Journal of Biochemistry and Cytochemistry, 16
  Journal of Clinical Endocrinology, 11
  Journal of Histochemistry and Cytochemistry, 16
  Journal of Molecular Biology, 12
  Journal of the American Statistical Association, 11
  Leake, Chauncey D., 7
  linguistics, 8
  McKusick, V. A., 14
  Microbial Genetics Bulletin, 14
  minicomputers, 253
  National Institutes of Health, 12
  National Library of Medicine, 6
  Nature New Biology, 3
  new concept in information retrieval, xiii
  patents, 12, 34, 37
  physics, 254
  pilot tests, 11
  practicality for scientific literature, 10
  Ranganathan, S. R., 11
  R&D Press, 16
  results of early trials, 15
  searching scientific literature, vii, 41
  Selye, Hans, 11
  Shepard's Citations, 7, 10, 15, 18
  Shepard's Law Review Citations, 18
  sociology of science, vii

specific disciplines, 253
structural linguistics, 8
title word, 1
titles, 7
Tukey, J. W., 16
U.S. Patent Office, 32, 39
Welch Medical Library, 6
Williams and Ping study, 45
Citation potential of scientific fields, 248
Citations
   see also Citation analysis
   accuracy of counts, 241
   among journals, 149
   first author problem, 242
   indexing terms, 3, 9, 41
   linkages between papers, 1
   methodological papers, 71, 115, 244
   negative citations, 244
   old vs. new papers, 91
   self-citations, 63, 72, 149, 245
   semantic stability, 9, 41
Cited Journal Package of *Journal Citation Reports*, 154
Citing Journal Package of *Journal Citation Reports*, 153
Clark, K. E., citation analysis, 64
Clinical Pediatrics, citation analysis, 181
Co-authorship of scientific papers, 243
   see also scientists
Co-citation analysis and clusters
   see also Citation analysis
   allosteric systems literature, 118
   bibliographic coupling, 99
   biological membranes literature, 122
   biomedical literature, 76, 78, 104, 113, 115, 122
   breast cancer literature, 118
   cancer research literature, 116, 118
   chemistry literature, 104, 113, 115, 122
   chromosome literature, 122
   Cole, J. R., 135
   Cole, Stephen, 135
   collagen literature, 124
   computer sciences literature, 114
   counseling literature, 137
   crystal structure of enzymes literature, 115
   crystallography literature, 122
   cyclic AMP literature, 122
   DNA polymerase literature, 118
   DNA/RNA hybridization literature, 118
   earth sciences literature, 114
   economics literature, 137
   free recall literature, 140
   gel electrophoresis of RNA literature, 118
   Griffith, Belver, 99, 111, 115
   immunoglobulins literature, 116
   immunology literature, 116, 122
   invisible college, 144
   Lowry, O. H., 115
   management science literature, 137
   mathematics literature, 115
   measuring size of scientific field, 248
   memory and learning literature, 137
   methodological papers, 135
   microtubule protein literature, 122
   multidimensional scaling literature, 114, 137
   muscle, myosin and cytochalasin-B literature, 122
   natural sciences literature, 102
   normalization of co-citation strength, 135
   nuclear physics literature, 105
   nuclear reaction theory literature, 115
   numerical taxonomy literature, 114
   on-line system, 145
   organizational structure literature, 137
   particle physics literature, 105
   peer validation of studies, 131
   physics literature, 105
   plate tectonics literature, 114
   political science literature, 137
   polyadenylic acid literature, 118
   protein kinase literature, 122
   protein structure literature, 118
   psychiatry literature, 137
   psychoanalysis literature, 137
   psychology, structure, 135
   reverse transcription literature, 110, 116
   RNA viruses literature, 118
   Small, Henry, 99, 122, 133
   social psychology literature, 137
   social psychology, structure, 135
   social sciences literature, 134
   sociology, structure, 135
   stability index, 131, 144
   Structure of Scientific Revolutions, 145
   unanswered questions, 144
   validation studies, 118
   viral genetics literature, 122
   Zuckerman, H., 135
   see also Citation analysis
Cole, J. R.
   citation analysis, viii
   co-citation analysis, 135
Cole, Stephen
   citation analysis, viii

266 Subject Index

co-citation analysis, 135
    Matthew Effect, 255
Collagen, history of research, 99, 123
Collagen literature, bibliography, 128
    co-citation clusters, 124
Comprehensive bibliography searches, 58
    See also Searches
Comptes Rendus, citation analysis, 224
Computer sciences literature, co-citation clusters, 114
Computer searches, 60
    see also Searches
Computer technology, citation indexing, 31
Concept searches, 50
    see also Searches
Consiglio Nationale delle Richerche (CNR), citation analysis, 71
Corporate Index of *Science Citation Index*, 34
Counseling literature, co-citation clusters, 137
Crick, Francis, DNA research, 12, 86
Criticism of citation analysis, 63, 240
Cryogenic storage, search, 52
Crystal structure of enzymes literature, co-citation clusters, 115
Crystallography literature, co-citation clusters, 115
Cumulative advantage processes, impact on bibliometrics, 255
Current Abstracts of Chemistry & Index Chemicus, 21
Current awareness services, 60
Current Contents
    citation analysis, 254
    Citation Classics, 245
    citation indexing, 13, 25
Current List of Medical Literature, citation indexing, 7, 86
Cyclic AMP literature, co-citation clusters, 122
Cycling, searches, 60

Davies, Robert E., lifetime citation rates, 71, 250
de Cani, John S., lifetime citation rates, 72, 250
Deverdier, C. H., search, 58
Diabetes, citation analysis, 175
Dilling, W. L., search, 47
Dissertations
    see Theses

DNA polymerase literature, co-citation clusters, 118
DNA research
    Air Force Office of Scientific Research, 72
    Asimov, Isaac, 72, 83
    Chemical Abstracts, 86
    citation analysis, 72, 83
    Crick, Francis, 12, 86
    historiographs, 86
    Index Medicus, 86
    Nature, 86
    network diagrams, 72, 83
    Proceedings of the National Academy of Sciences USA, 86
    Watson, James D., 12, 86
DNA sequences, search, 51
DNA/RNA hybridization literature, co-citation clusters, 118
Dobzhansky, T., citation indexing, 14
Doklady Akademii Nauk USSR, citation analysis, 197, 205
Donnan equilibrium theory, search, 46

Earth sciences literature, co-citation clusters, 114
Economics literature, co-citation clusters, 137
Editing and coding of journals for *Science Citation Index*, 25
Einstein, Albert
    citation analysis, 4, 246
    concept of citation indexing, 4
Endocrinology, citation analysis, 175
Engineering literature, Bradford's law, 21
    citation analysis, 21, 202
    Garfield's law of concentration, 205
Eponymic searches, 46
    see also Searches
Essays of an Information Scientist, history of citation indexing, xiii
Eugene Garfield Associates, history of citation indexing, 11
Euphenics, search, 4
European Journal of Cancer, citation analysis, 190

First author listing in *Science Citation Index*, 242
First author problem, 242
Follow-up searches, 47
    see also Searches
Free recall literature, co-citation clusters, 140

French Academy of Sciences, citation analysis, 224
French journals, citation analysis, 223
French language in science, 224

Gann, citation analysis, 190
Garfield, Eugene, history of citation indexing, vii, xiii
Garfield's constant, 23
Garfield's law of concentration
   1969 study, 160
   basic concept, 23
   engineering literature, 205
   Japanese journals, 227
   pediatrics literature, 181
   rheumatology literature, 170
Gates, R. R., citation indexing, 14
Geigy Pharmaceuticals, citation analysis, 167
Gel electrophoresis of RNA literature, co-citation clusters, 118
Geller, Nancy L., lifetime citation rates, 71, 250
Genetic Code, citation analysis, 72, 83
Genetics literature
   citation analysis, 72, 83
   citation indexing, 12
Genetics research history
   impact of molecular biology, 12
   Nature, 12
   network diagrams, 72, 83
Genetics Citation Index, 13, 15
Genetics Society of America, citation indexing, 13
Geological Society of London Quarterly, citation analysis, 183
Geology literature, citation analysis, 183
Geophysics literature, citation analysis, 183
German journals, citation analysis, 230
Government agencies, citation analysis, 70
Griffith, Belver, co-citation analysis, 99, 111, 115
Growth, citation analysis, 181

Hart, Harry C., patent citation indexing, 37
Hemoglobin binding, search, 57
Highly cited scientists, 62, 240
Historiograms, 86
Historiographs, 73, 86
History of science, 72, 81
   see also Science
Hodgkins disease, search, 46
Homographs, 243

Immediacy index, 72, 78, 150
Immunoglobulins literature, co-citation clusters, 116
Immunology literature, co-citation clusters, 116, 122
Impact factor, 24, 78, 149
Index Medicus
   citation analysis of DNA research, 86
   comparison to early citation index, 11
   indexing methods, 7
   usage, 3
Indexes and indexing
   see also Citation indexes and indexing
   cross-disciplinary vocabulary, 9
   depth, 2
   intellectual judgments, 8
   journal coverage, 20
   linguistic analysis, 8
   machine-produced, 6, 7
   search effectiveness, 2
   selectivity, 7
   semantic problems, 2, 7
   title word, 1
   titles and abstracts, 7
   traditional, 1, 11
Information science, vii, xii
INFROSS, mapping structure of science, 135
Inhaber, H., citation analysis, 188
Inorganic Chemistry, citation analysis, 188
Institute for Scientific Information
   access to data base by Japanese Ministry of Education, 255
   access to data base by National Research Council of Italy, 255
   access to data base by National Science Foundation grantees, 255
   establishment, 12
   first publication of citation indexes, xiv
   National Science Foundation grant to study 1920's physics literature, 254
   research center for citation analysis, x
International Journal of Cancer, citation analysis, 190
Invisible college, co-citation analysis, 144
ISI
   see Institute for Scientific Information
Italy
   Consiglio Nazionale della Richerche (CNR), 71
   government's use of citation analysis, 71
   National Research Council, 71, 255

Subject Index

Janke, N. C., citation analysis, 183
Japanese journals
  citation analysis, 227
  Garfield's law of concentration, 227
Japanese Ministry of Education, access to Science Citation Index data base, 255
JCR
  see Journal Citation Reports
Jensen, J. H. D., citation analysis, 64
Johns Hopkins University, history of citation indexing, 6
Journal Citation Reports
  see also Citation analysis
  Cited Journal Package, 154
  Citing Journal Package, 153
  identifying core journals of a scientific discipline, 253
  journal analysis, 247
  Journal Ranking Package, 150
  part of Science Citation Index, 24
  practical applications, 78
  studying journal citation behavior, 150
Journal of Biochemistry and Cytochemistry, citation indexing, 16
Journal of Biological Chemistry, citation analysis, 223, 227
Journal of Bone and Joint Surgery, citation analysis, 170
Journal of Chemical Physics, citation analysis, 166, 188, 190, 205
Journal of Clinical Endocrinology
  citation indexes, 11
  search, 42
Journal of Clinical Endocrinology and Metabolism, citation analysis, 175
Journal of Clinical Investigation, citation analysis, 175, 178, 181
Journal of Clinical Pathology
  citation analysis, 175
  search, 58
Journal of Experimental Medicine, citation analysis, 167, 175
Journal of Geology, citation analysis, 183
Journal of Geophysical Research, citation analysis, 183, 185
Journal of Histochemistry and Cytochemistry, citation indexes, 16
Journal of Immunology, citation analysis, 167
Journal of Invertebrate Pathology, citation analysis, 192
Journal of Medical Virology, citation analysis, 175
Journal of Molecular Biology
  citation analysis, 188
  citation indexes, 12
Journal of Pathology, citation analysis, 173
Journal of Physical Chemistry, citation analysis, 167, 205
Journal of Sedimentary Petrology, citation analysis, 183
Journal of the American Chemical Society, citation analysis, 163, 167, 188, 205, 223, 227
Journal of the American Medical Association, citation analysis, 175, 178, 181
Journal of the American Statistical Association, citation indexes, 11
Journal of the Association of Official Analytical Chemists, citation analysis, 202
Journal of the Chemical Society, citation analysis, 188
Journal of the National Cancer Institute, citation analysis, 190
Journal of the Patent Office Society, patent citation indexing, 37
Journal Ranking Package of Journal Citation Reports, 150
Journals
  see also Scientific publication
  bibliographic formats, 26
  citation analysis, 78, 148
  citation rates, 149
  citation records, 23
  immediacy index, 72, 78, 150
  impact factor, 24, 78, 149
  Journal Citation Reports, 78, 150, 247
  nature and frequency, 20
  overlapping coverage, 21
  refereeing system, 64, 245, 253
  self-citation rates, 149

Kaplan, Norman, history of citation analysis, viii
Kerr geometry, search, 50
Keysave system, production of citation indexes, 31

Lancet, citation analysis, 170, 175, 224
Landau, L. D., citation analysis, 64
Leake, Chauncey D., history of citation indexing, 7

Lederberg, Joshua
   author of Foreword to book by
      E. Garfield, ix
   citation analysis, 247
   search, 4
Linguistics, history of citation indexing, 8
Lipschitz, D. A., search, 58
Literary model of science, 81, 99, 143, 255
Literature searches
   see Searches
Litigation, citation analysis, 72
Lotka distribution, 255
Lowry, O. H., citation analysis, 246
   co-citation clusters, 115
   protein measurement, 246

Management science literature, co-citation clusters, 137
Mapping the structure of science
   see also Co-citation analysis and clusters; Citation analysis
   Atlas of Science, 142
   Bath University, 135
   citation analysis, 72, 81, 98
   collagen research, 99
   INFROSS, 135
   scientific specialties, 75, 111
Marx, Karl, plagiarism, vii
Mathematical Physics, search, 3
Mathematics literature
   citation analysis, 248
   co-citation clusters, 115
Mathematische Annalen, citation analysis, 154
Mathematische Zeitschrift, citation analysis, 154
Matthew Effect, 255
McKusick, V. A., citation indexing, 14
Meadows, A. J., negative citations, 244
Mechanical translation, 8
Memory and learning literature, co-citation clusters, 137
Mendel syndrome, citation analysis, 247
Merton, Robert K.
   cumulative advantage processes, 255
   foreword, vii
   history of *Science Citation Index*, xiv
Meryman, H. T., search, 53
Methodological papers
   co-citation analysis, 135
   high citation rate, 71, 244
   highly cited chemical papers, 246
   impact on co-citation analysis, 115

Methodology searches, 46
   see also Searches
Microbial Genetics Bulletin, citation indexing, 14
Microtubule protein literature, co-citation clusters, 122
Minicomputers, future citation indexing, 253
Molecular biology, impact on genetics, 12
Monatschrift fur Kinderheilkunde, citation analysis, 183
Multi-authored papers
   effect on citation analysis, 63, 242, 254
   indication of a scientist's writing productivity, 243
Multidimensional scaling literature, co-citation clusters, 114, 137
Multidisciplinary searches, 52
Muscle, myosin and cytochalasin-B literature, co-citation clusters, 122
Mycopathologia et Mycologia Applicata, citation analysis, 196

National Academy of Sciences USA, membership of highly cited authors, 249
National Cancer Institute, citation analysis, 71, 190
National Cancer Institute Monograph, citation analysis, 190
National Institute of Mental Health, citation analysis, 71
National Institutes of Health, citation indexes, 12
National Library of Medicine, history of citation indexing, 6
National Research Council of Italy
   access to *Science Citation Index* data base, 255
   citation analysis, 71
National Science Foundation
   citation analysis, 71
   citation data in evaluating grant proposals, 254
   grant to ISI to study 1920's physics literature, 254
   grantees' access to *Science Citation Index* data base, 255
   support of research in citation analysis, 145
Natural sciences literature, co-citation analysis, 145

Subject Index

Nature
   citation analysis, 167, 183, 185, 187, 190, 196, 198, 205, 223, 227, 230
   DNA research, 86
   euphenics, 4
   genetics research, 12
   work of J. M. Bardeen, 50
   work of Watson and Crick, 86
Nature New Biology, citation indexes, 3
Naunyn-Schmiedebergs Archiv fur Pharmakologie, citation analysis, 175
Negative citations, 244
Neoplasma, citation analysis, 190
Network diagrams
   Air Force Office of Scientific Research, 81
   Allen, Gordon, 81
   DNA research, 72, 83
   genetics, 72, 83
   Pasteur's discoveries, 81
   scientific papers, 85
   staining of nucleic acids literature, 81
New England Journal of Medicine, citation analysis, 175, 178, 181
Nobel Prize
   1950-75 winners, 64
   1962-63 winners, 63, 91
   correlation with citation counts, ix, 249
   rejection of winners' publications by journals, 244
Normalization of co-citation strength, 135
Nouvelle Presse Medicale, citation analysis, 224
Nuclear physics literature, co-citation clusters, 105
Nuclear reaction theory literature, co-citation clusters, 115
Numerical taxonomy literature, co-citation clusters, 114

Obliteration phenomenon, viii, 247
Official Gazette, U.S. Patent Office, patent citation indexing, 38
On-line system
   citation analysis, 93
   co-citation analysis, 145
   Science Citation Index, 253
   Social Sciences Citation Index, 253
Oregon State University, citation analysis, 183
Organizational names and addresses (Keysave), 32

Pareto law of income distribution, 255
Particle physics literature, co-citation clusters, 105
Pasteur's discoveries, network diagrams, 81
Patent Citation Index of *Science Citation Index*, 34, 37
Patents
   Chemical Abstracts, 12, 38
   citation indexing, 12, 34, 37
   Hart, Harry C., 37
   Journal of the Patent Office Society, 37
   Official Gazette, U.S. Patent Office, 38
   Seidel, Arthur H., 37
   Shepard's Citations, 27
Pathologie Biologie, citation analysis, 173
Pathology literature, citation analysis, 170
Pediatrics literature
   citation analysis, 178
   Garfield's law of concentration, 181
Pediatrie, citation analysis, 181
Peer judgments, x, 63, 69, 131, 241, 246, 250
Peer recognition in science, vii
Peer validation of citation studies, 131
Permuterm Subject Index of *Science Citation Index* and *Social Sciences Citation Index*
   starting point for citation search, 34
   title word index, 30, 34
Perspective on citation analysis of scientists, 240
Pesticides Biochemistry, citation analysis, 202
Physical chemists, 166
Physical Review, citation analysis, 190, 205, 248
Physical Review Letters, citation analysis, 190
Physics literature
   citation analysis, 188
   citation index, 254
   co-citation clusters, 105
Physics, structure, citation analysis, 99
Phytochemistry, citation analysis, 227
Phytopathology, citation analysis, 170
Plagiarism, viii
Plant hybridization, search, 54
Plate tectonics literature, co-citation clusters, 114
Political science literature, co-citation clusters, 137
Polyadenylic acid literature, co-citation clusters, 118
Pre-1961 *Science Citation Index*, 254

Subject Index

Pre-editing of journals, 25
Premature discoveries in science, 246
Presse Medicale, citation analysis, 224
Price, D. J. D.
   citation analysis, 71, 243
   cumulative advantage processes, 255
   literary model of scientific process, 255
   structure of physics, 99
   structure of science, 81, 142
Proceedings of the American Association for Cancer Research, citation analysis, 192
Proceedings of the Institute of Electrical and Electronics Engineers, citation analysis, 205
Proceedings of the National Academy of Sciences USA
   citation analysis, 227
   DNA research, 86
Proceedings of the Royal Society (London), citation analysis, 205
Proceedings of the Society for Experimental Biology and Medicine, citation analysis, 170
Procollagen, history of research, 123
Profiles for *ASCA* system, 60
Progress in Experimental Tumor Research, citation analysis, 192
Property
   intellectual, vii
   private, viii
Protein kinase literature, co-citation clusters, 122
Protein measurement, work of O. H. Lowry, citation analysis, 246
Protein structure literature, co-citation clusters, 118
PSI
   see Permuterm Subject Index
Psychiatry literature
   citation analysis, 198
   co-citation clusters, 137
Psychoanalysis literature, co-citation clusters, 137
Psychologists, citation analysis, 64, 135
Psychology literature, citation analysis, 197
Psychology, structure, co-citation analysis, 135
Pulsars research literature, citation analysis, 71

R&D Press, citation indexes, 16

Radiology authors, correlation between citation counts and peer judgments, 69
Rae's theory on DNA sequences, search, 51
Ranganathan, S. R., history of citation indexing, 11
Rats, work of Lester R. Aronson, 249
Refereeing system of scientific journals, 64, 245, 253
   see also Scientific publication, journals
References
   see Citations
Reissman, K. R., search, 58
Research
   see Science
Reverse transcription literature, co-citation clusters, 110, 116
Review articles, 2, 7
Reward system of science, viii
Rheumatology literature
   citation analysis, 167
   Garfield's law of concentration, 170
RNA viruses literature, co-citation clusters, 118

SCI
   see Science Citation Index
Science
   citation analysis, 158, 167, 183, 185, 187, 190, 196, 198, 227, 247
   coverage in *Current Contents*, 13
Science
   history, 72, 81, 98
   immature fields, 247
   literary model, 81, 99, 143, 255
   mapping specialties, 75, 111
   mapping structure, 98
   methodological superstructure, 115
   obliteration phenomenon, viii, 247
   peer recognition, vii
   premature discoveries, 246
   reward system, vii
   sociology of, vii, x, xiv, 72, 254
   structural models, 144
Science administrators, citation analysis, 240
Science Citation Index
   see also *Social Sciences Citation Index*, *Arts & Humanities Citation Index*, Citation indexes and indexing
   access to data base by Japanese Ministry of Education, 255

Subject Index

access to data base by National Research Council of Italy, 255
access to data base by National Science Foundation grantees, 255
accuracy, 241
advanced computer technology, 31
bibliographic-verification searches, 42
citation analysis, ix, 4, 23, 62, 90, 100, 150, 241
Citation Index, 33, 242
compiling author's bibliography, 243
comprehensive bibliography searches, 58
comprehensiveness, 44
computer searches, 60
concept searches, 50
Corporate Index, 34
coverage, 19
cycling, 60
data base for *Journal Citation Reports*, 150
design and production, 19
editing and coding of journals, 25
Einstein, Albert, 4
eponymic searches, 46
first author listing, 242
first publication, xiii, xiv, 16
follow-up searches, 47
for entire 20th century, 254
growth, 17
inevitability, xiv
influence of *Shepard's Citations*, 18
influence on *Shepard's Law Review Citations*, 18
Journal Citation Reports, 24
Keysave system, 31
Merton, Robert K., xiv
methodology searches, 46
minicomputers, 253
multidisciplinary searches, 52
on-line system, 253
Patent Citation Index, 34, 37
Permuterm Subject Index, 30, 34
photocomposition, 30
post-editing, 27
pre-1961, 254
pre-editing of journals, 25
production process, 25
sample searches, 41
Source Index, 33, 42, 243
specific question searches, 51
standardization of names and addresses, 32
state-of-the-art searches, 57

Science management, 62
Science policy, 98, 144, 240
Scientific papers
  comparison of citations of old versus new papers, 91
  methodological papers, 71, 115, 135, 244, 246
  network diagrams, 85
  primary communications medium, 255
  review articles, 2, 7
Scientific publication
  see also Journals
  annual rate of growth, 250
  primary communications medium, 255
  refereeing system, 64, 245, 253
  review articles, 2, 7
Scientists
  citation analysis, ix, 62, 71, 91, 149, 240, 249, 254
  co-authorship, 243
  comparison of citation counts in different fields, 248
  highly cited, 62, 240
  lifetime citation rates, 71, 250
  publications as intellectual property, vii
SCISEARCH, 253
Search Check, 40
Searches
  Abraham, G. E., 42
  ASCA, 60
  Bardeen, J. M., 50
  Barland method for isolating surface membranes, 46
  Bell's palsy, 46
  bibliographic-verification, 42
  black holes, 50
  Carlson, P. S., 54
  comprehensive bibliography, 58
  computer, 60
  concept, 50
  cryogenic storage, 52
  cycling, 60
  Deverdier, C. H., 58
  Dilling, W. L., 47
  DNA sequences, 51
  Donnan equilibrium theory, 46
  effectiveness with citation indexes, 2
  eponymic, 46
  euphenics, 4
  follow-up, 47
  hemoglobin binding, 57
  Hodgkins disease, 46
  Journal of Clinical Endocrinology, 42

Journal of Clinical Pathology, 58
Kerr geometry, 50
Lederberg, Joshua, 4
Lipschitz, D. A., 58
Mathematical Physics, 3
Meryman, H. T., 53
methodology, 46
multidisciplinary, 52
plant hybridization, 54
Rae's theory on DNA sequences, 51
Reissman, K. R., 58
Science Citation Index, 41
serum iron, 58
specific question, 51
state-of-the-art, 57
trimethoprim, 47
Young, D. S., 58
Secondary authors, 242
Seidel, Arthur H., patent citation indexing, 37
Selective-dissemination-of-information (SDI), 60
  see also ASCA
Self-citations, 63, 72, 149, 245
  see also Citations; Citation analysis
Selye, Hans, citation indexes, 11
Semantic stability of citations, 9, 41
Serum iron, search, 58
Sexual reproduction of bacteria, obliteration phenomenon, 247
Shepard's Citations
  earliest major citation index, 7
  influence on *Science Citation Index*, 18
  manual coding process, 15
  model for later citation indexes, 10
  patents, 27
Shepard's Law Review Citations, influence of *Science Citation Index*, 18
Shortcomings of citation analysis, 99, 246
Small, Henry, co-citation analysis, 99, 122, 133
Social psychology literature, co-citation analysis, 137
Social psychology, structure, co-citation analysis, 135
Social sciences literature, co-citation analysis, 134
Social Sciences Citation Index
  see also *Science Citation Index*, *Arts & Humanities Citation Index*, Citation indexes and indexing
  accuracy, 241
  Citation Index, 33, 242

compiling an author's bibliography, 243
  first publication, 16
  inclusion of reference citations from source items, 33
  on-line system, 253
  Permuterm Subject Index, 30, 34
  production process, 25
  Source Index, 33, 42, 243
Sociology, structure, co-citation analysis, 135
Sociology of science, vii, x, xiv, 72, 254
Solid State Communications, citation analysis, 158
Source Index of *Science Citation Index*, *Social Sciences Citation Index*, and *Arts & Humanities Citation Index*
  bibliographic verification tool, 42
  comprehensive bibliography, 243
  production process, 33
Soviet Academy of Science, citation analysis, 205
Soviet journals, citation analysis, 167, 205, 208
Soviet Physics-Crystallography, citation analysis, 187
Specific question searches, 51
  see also Searches
SSCI
  see *Social Sciences Citation Index*
Stability index, co-citation analysis, 131, 144
Staining of nucleic acids literature, network diagrams, 81
State-of-the-art searches, 57
  see also Searches
Statistics, methodological importance in social sciences, 141
Structural linguistics, history of citation indexing, 8
Structure of science
  see Co-citation analysis and clusters; Citation analysis; and Mapping the structure of science
Structure of Scientific Revolutions, future of co-citation analysis, 145
Subject indexes
  see Indexes and indexing
Sudden activity in science, identification by citation analysis, 71, 144
Surgery authors, correlation between citation counts and peer judgments, 69

Tenure decisions, citation analysis, 71, 240

Teploenergetica, citation analysis, 24, 205
Tetrahedron Letters, citation analysis, 227
Theoretical and Applied Genetics, citation analysis, 195
Thermal Engineering USSR, citation analysis, 24, 205
Theses, citation analysis, 183
Thorpe, Peter, citation analysis, 167
Title, citation indexing, 7
Title word indexing, 1
Translation
 see Mechanical translation
Trimethoprim, search, 47
Tukey, J. W., history of citation indexing, 16
Tumori, citation analysis, 192

University departments, citation measures of performance, 64, 240, 249, 253
University of Illinois at Chicago, citation analysis, 186
U.S. Patent Office, history of citation indexing, 32, 39

Viral genetics literature, co-citation clusters, 122

Virchows Archiv, citation analysis, 173
Virology, citation analysis, 196
Virology literature, citation analysis, 170, 175

Watson, James D., DNA research, 12, 86
Welch Medical Library indexing project, 6
Who is Publishing in Science, 135
Williams and Ping study, citation indexing, 45
WIPIS
 see Who is Publishing in Science

Young, D. S., search, 58

Zeitschrift fur Krebsforschung, citation analysis, 192
Zeitschrift fur Kristallographie, citation analysis, 188
Zhurnal Fizicheskoi Khimii, citation analysis, 167
Zipf's law, 255
Zuckerman, H.
 co-citation analysis, 135
 social stratification in American science, 255

SOUTHEASTERN MASSACHUSETTS UNIVERSITY
Z697.S5 G37
Citation indexing – its theory and appli

3 2922 00091 397 7

WITHDR

DUE